P9-CFJ-192

DISCARD

WEST GEORGIA REGIONAL LIBRARY
HEADQUARTERS

THE
PETER
FREUCHEN
READER

THE
PETER
FREUCHEN
READER

A Selection by
DAGMAR FREUCHEN

JULIAN MESSNER
New York

Published by Julian Messner
Division of Pocket Books, Inc.
8 West 40 Street, New York, N.Y. 10018

© Copyright 1965 by Dagmar Freuchen

Printed in the United States of America

Library of Congress Catalog Card No. 65-23224

Contents

1-136616

PREFACE

Preface

Peter Freuchen was a great Arctic adventurer and explorer, but I began really to know him in the tropics. We had decided to write a book together, and one evening while we were hard at it, comfortably settled on a hotel veranda in Haiti overlooking a lush garden and Port-au-Prince's moonlit harbor, we were interrupted by a soft knock and the entrance of our host's nine-year-old son.

"Captain Freuchen," he said, "my friends and I wonder if you will tell us some stories about the Arctic while you are here."

"Why the Arctic?" Peter demanded.

"Well, you see, my friends and I have never been there. I have never seen snow."

There could be no better reason for curiosity, Peter admitted, so an appointment was made for next morning. Work on our book stopped short despite my protests because Peter said he had to figure out how to explain the Arctic to little boys who never had seen snow.

When I saw him again he was stretched out, all six feet four inches of him, on a big wicker chaise, water dripping down his beard after a plunge in the pool, while three sun-browned children crouched at his feet as bewitched by word, smile and gesture as the young of Hamelin had been when they listened to the Pied Piper.

Peter was telling them how he and his great friend, Knud Rasmussen, another Danish explorer, crossed the Greenland ice cap in 1912—a trip no one ever had made before—with a couple of Eskimos and four dog teams. For most of the distance they struggled through soft snow, dry and thin "just like flour blown about in clouds by the endless winds which never stop on this high plateau," Peter explained. After many days they neared the coast where the glacier was clean of snow and sloped down so steeply that the dogs slipped and slid.

"We had to go on because it was too slippery for the dogs to go back, and then suddenly we came to the edge of the glacier. It was a cliff of ice dropping straight down fifty feet or more to the coast and stretching along in each direction as far as we could see. Our only chance was to lower ourselves and our dogs and our sleds, but all we had to do it with were some sealskin harpoon lines. We did not know if they were strong enough to hold us, so because I was the heaviest I went first. If the lines would hold me the others would be safe."

Peter was halfway down the cliff of ice when he let out a yell of pain. They had not been able to remove one of the harpoons, and it bit deep into his thigh. The line was too slippery for him to raise himself a little to ease the pressure and work the point loose. For some minutes he hung helplessly, then gritted his teeth and with one vigorous kick tore the harpoon from his flesh.

"I was lucky," he reassured his wide-eyed listeners. "It missed bone, nerves and big arteries. So we were able to go on all right."

"How did it feel to hang there like that?" one of the boys asked.

Peter chuckled. "Ever since, I have known what it is like to be a fish," he said. "It taught me to be careful. Sometimes though one forgets to be careful, and that is when you get into trouble."

From this experience and dozens of others marked by privation and danger it might have been supposed that he would become indifferent to the orderly rules of civilization and to the feelings of others, as he was to pain in his own body. But his adventures had just the opposite effect. Anyone who rode in his automobile soon noticed his care for the sensibilities of his fellow man.

He drove in the manner of a helmsman holding a difficult course in heavy weather, sitting up very straight and watchful, his big hands gripping the wheel firmly. There was no hint of the recklessness he displayed in the frozen wastes of the North where he was far from help. On paved roads he would never exceed a posted speed limit, pass a red light or ignore a warning to slow down.

Nor would he pass a hitchhiker without stopping, even if he had no more room in the car or was just about to turn off the highway. Then he would pull over to the side anyway to explain why he couldn't give the stranger a lift. I suggested once that this seemed an exaggerated courtesy.

"You never know when one of them might not have bus fare," he replied. "It makes them feel better if someone stops and shows he cares about them."

To anyone he knew who was confined to bed by illness Peter wrote a letter every day. "When you are weak you need to know you have friends," he explained.

For children he had a special concern, and in his much cluttered study he kept a box of pictures clipped from newspapers and magazines. Whenever he wrote to a child, his letter was profusely illustrated with carefully pasted up samples from this store. Children, of course, adored him because he told them wonderful stories and treated them seriously as well as courteously. For several blocks around his New York apartment and in Noank on Long Island Sound where he spent weekends and holidays, every urchin would greet him happily with "Hi, Peter!" or sometimes even "Hey, Santa Claus!" In Danish towns and Eskimo villages the childish greetings were as warm, if more respectful.

He himself said he learned from the Eskimos to be considerate of people. More than any other explorer or trader, he had studied and known them before they adopted European ways. His home in Greenland had been further north than any white man then lived. His first wife, Navarana, was an Eskimo, and she commanded his lifelong devotion, although she died of a fever ten years after their marriage, while their two children were quite small.

Among her people, he used to say, there was an innocent enjoyment of life combined with mutual tolerance and helpfulness such as he never had seen in Europe or the United States. He pointed out that they shared their food, scanty or plentiful, with strangers, never regarding it as a gift but as one of the rights which all human beings possessed. He delighted in their sense of humor, even when it took a somewhat grisly turn.

"I learned from the Eskimos to laugh at misfortune," he said. "It really is funny when fate plays tricks on you."

His first lesson of this kind occurred during a long Arctic trip when he and two Eskimo companions, after many days of marching on short rations, arrived at a cache of meat left to tide them over the last stage of the journey. Every morsel had been eaten; a bear had found it first.

"Those two Eskimos, hungry as they were, simply roared with laughter," Peter recalled. "Their only thought was that this was going to be a good joke to tell our friends. As for me, I was wondering if we ever would see our friends again to tell them anything."

He found less humor in the incident at the time because it brought about his introduction to dog meat. The three men had to kill some of their sled dogs to feed the rest and themselves, and although this was to happen to Peter over and over again on his Arctic travels, it was one feature of the life which he never accepted gracefully.

"It is not that I had any compunction about eating dogs more than any other meat," he would say defensively. "A pot of hot food when one is starving cannot be unwelcome. But it must be admitted that dogs do not taste good."

He defended vigorously points of view that he was not prepared to accept completely. That an Eskimo mother who killed her baby rather than watch the child starve to death was honored, not blamed, always seemed strange to him. He did not get used to husbands lending their wives to lonesome friends as quite normal hospitality (although he was the willing recipient of such courtesies in his time). But if someone suggested that these were the acts of unfeeling savages, Peter would get angry.

"These may not be our ways," he would declare, "but they are worthy of respect. They come from the Eskimo's sense of human dignity."

Peter was sure that the primitive Arctic peoples of his youth were happier than the more civilized Eskimos of today. But he admitted that there might be some advantages in material progress. He used to describe with great feeling his sensations during his first visit to Greenland when he escorted an Eskimo beauty to a dance. She had dressed her hair specially for him by shampooing it in a pail of urine. That night he was grateful that his height lifted his nose high above his partner's elegant coiffure, but for once he decided he was not quite tall enough. Therefore his very last letter, written from Alaska the day he died, chronicled with satisfaction one big change in Eskimo customs.

"Some of the women fly to Fairbanks from Point Barrow once a month to visit the hairdresser," he wrote. "The trip costs $36 and they have the money now."

Peter was born to a life of adventure in the little port of Nykøbing Falster, Denmark, in 1886. He used to say that his grandfather had been the last Danish pirate, but actually the old gentleman never did anything more lawless than a bit of filibustering and gunrunning in South America. Peter himself served before the mast on sailing ships while still a boy and then went to Copenhagen to study medicine. He left the university at nineteen for a job as stoker on a rusty old steamship which carried the then famous Danish explorer Mylius-Erichsen to Greenland, and he fell in love with the people, the life and the scenery.

By the time he was twenty-three Peter was an experienced Arctic traveler, capable of taking astronomical observations, mapping strange territory, building an igloo, shooting and butchering seal or walrus, controling a team of hungry sled dogs. He even had become adept at the odd barter tactics of the Eskimos, which consist of deprecating one's own wares as worthless while praising the other fellow's to the skies.

That was the year 1909, when Dr. Frederick Cook turned up in Greenland with a claim of having discovered the North Pole, and the resulting controversy turned Peter into a newspaperman. He happened to be in Copenhagen on a visit, and the leading Danish paper, *Politiken,* asked him to write a piece about Arctic travel, especially the sort of obstacles Cook must have overcome.

"I have been on the payroll ever since," Peter used to say with satisfaction.

Later, when Cook arrived in Denmark to be feted and decorated, his stories to the assembled news correspondents struck Peter as suspicious. The only other doubter was Philip Gibbs, best-known English reporter of his day, and the two men prepared a series of articles for Gibbs's paper which exposed discrepancies in Cook's claims—impossible mileage for a day's sledding, mistakes in geography, unlikely astronomical data and so on. Peter himself wrote an article in Danish declaring Cook was a fraud, but *Politiken* would not print it because the paper was arranging a dinner in the Doctor's honor. Peter never forgot that he was able to get his work published in only one of the smallest Danish journals—nor that he received no more than three dollars for it. He was vindicated, though, when

Robert E. Peary reached the farthest north telegraph line—on
the very day of *Politiken*'s dinner for Cook—with his account
of discovering the Pole.

Peter's reputation as an expert on the Far North was made,
and he went back to Greenland to establish a trading post—later
a great American base—which he called Thule from the clas-
sical "Ultima Thule," or uttermost northern limits. He mapped
part of the island and explored more; the northwestern corner
was named Freuchenland. He circumnavigated the globe,
mostly within the Arctic Circle, before any airplane ever landed
on Arctic ice. He obviously was pleased when people told him
he must be very brave, but he insisted quite seriously that he
was not sure what bravery really is.

"A man who never had seen an automobile before would
marvel at the courage of a fellow crossing Times Square," he
said once. "Anyway, in the Arctic, and I suppose in Times
Square too, experience and good sense are more valuable than
being without fear."

His own experiences brought him the friendship of all the
notable explorers of more than half a century. He knew Peary
and Bob Bartlett, Roald Amundsen and Lincoln Ellsworth, the
Norwegian Sverdrup, the Italian Nobile, the Australian Wilkins. But of them all he reserved his highest admiration for
Fridtjof Nansen of Norway. It was not so much that Nansen
had even more powerful muscles than Peter, nor that he had
advanced northern exploration many years by his scientific
studies of Arctic Ocean currents, nor that, according to his admirer, he introduced to the world the hitherto exclusively
Norwegian sport of skiing. Peter appreciated these achievements
to the full, but what elevated Nansen to the highest pedestal in
his private pantheon was the work that attached the Norwegian's name to two Nobel Peace Prizes—relief of the starving
in Russia and the Near East after World War I and the later
aid to stateless victims of war and aggression whose most prized
document was known as "a Nansen passport."

Of all the men he had met, only one other reached as high in Peter's esteem and for much the same reason. Herbert Hoover's relief work was an incomparable service to humanity, he thought.

"Maybe this will be known as the Age of Frightfulness, as much for what happened between the wars as during them," Peter said. "Those two men did more than anyone else to help the refugees from frightfulness."

Because a man's heroes often reveal a lot about him, I was curious as we worked on *Peter Freuchen's Book of the Seven Seas* to learn just which of the innumerable stalwarts whose exploits he chronicled with immense gusto had become his favorites. He had decided opinions. He read a great deal about scientists, as well as adventurers, and had a fabulous memory for what he read. So he could back his selections with a wealth of reasons.

His pet pirate was William Dampier, a contemporary of Captain Kidd and the man whose ship rescued Alexander Selkirk, the original of Robinson Crusoe, from the Island of Juan Fernandez. Dampier had Peter's scientific curiosity. When not collecting loot on the Spanish Main he spent his time in nature studies instead of getting drunk and roistering with his shipmates. Dampier won the friendship of London intellectuals of his day by publishing some very advanced observations on plants and animals, winds and currents.

Peter's other "firsts" were as revealing of his attitude toward people and life. Some of them were:

Greatest navigator: the Englishman James Cook, who explored more waters and mapped more new territory than anyone else. "He was the first to explore really scientifically, but more than that he was the first European to treat primitive peoples like human beings."

Greatest sea captain: Nat Palmer of Stonington, Connecticut, boy discoverer of the Antarctic Continent, skipper of opium clippers and Atlantic packets in the great days of sail. "He handled his sailors like men and not animals. They never had to eat rotten meat on his ships."

Greatest marine scientist: Otto Pettersson, Swedish oceanographer who worked out some original theories on the tides and their influence upon mankind. "He made his great discoveries without ever in all his ninety-three years leaving his home in Bohuslan on the Baltic, but just watching and measuring the tides in this one fjord."

Peter himself had the instincts and habits of a tourist. Wherever he went, he insisted on seeing the recommended sights and asking people endless questions about how they lived and worked. We spent one blazing hot afternoon tramping along the waterfront of a Caribbean port because Peter had to find out why there were so many fish in the sea and so few in the market. He interviewed fishermen, market stall keepers, barefoot women shoppers, port officials, members of the United Nations technical mission. Finally he established to his own satisfaction that the problem was lack of ice. In that climate fish spoil in four hours without refrigeration. Ice put the price out of the people's reach, and it was impossible to get the catch from the fishing grounds to the consumer in four hours.

"I never knew before how lucky the Eskimos are," Peter commented. "After all, they have been quick-freezing meat for hundreds of years, and these poor people cannot even keep a fish overnight."

His habits of reading and asking questions stored up in his mind a remarkable fund of information and brought him his greatest popular triumph. He was invited to appear on a television show, "The $64,000 Question," and proved himself in that and a companion program, "The $64,000 Challenge," a showman of parts. Years earlier he had been in Hollywood as a writer and technical expert on Arctic matters, but the part of his film career he enjoyed most was playing the role of a bearded villain in a movie called *Eskimo*, based on one of his stories. So he appeared before the television cameras with the aplomb of a veteran.

He chose the Seven Seas as his topic, and caught the popular fancy promptly. His bearded face could be very expressive, and his slow, accented speech emphasized the picturesque phrases with which he answered questions about some part of a ship's rigging—he would interpolate a bit about why sailors hated it— or the force of winds. When he was asked which was saltier, the Suez Canal or the Panama Canal, he replied scornfully:

"That's a damn silly question!"

The studio audience laughed for nearly a minute while the master of ceremonies apologized for the stupidity but added that he had to have an answer. Then Peter explained that the water in the Panama Canal is fresh, not salty at all. Later when I asked him why this was sillier than any of the other questions, he chuckled happily.

"It wasn't," he said, "but offhand I didn't have the answer. I knew that complaining about the question would kill a little time and give me a minute to think. If I had answered right off, the way they expect you to, I would just have guessed and probably been wrong."

The quick wit which saved his life in the Arctic also won him friends in the centers of civilization. Once Peter was auctioneer for the Explorers' Club, to sell a live lion someone had presented to the organization. The members had high hopes of raising a lot of money and turned out in considerable numbers for the sale. But it seems that even among explorers the demand for live lions is small. In spite of his best efforts, Peter had to accept a disappointingly low bid from a rather wealthy gentleman. Then, as the disconsolate clubmen were turning away, he called out:

"Wait! We have auctioned the lion. Now I'm going to auction the cage. What am I bid for the cage?"

His audience entered into the spirit of the thing and made the purchaser of the lion pay handsomely.

Peter had his share of vanity, perhaps a little more. He took pains to make his appearance thoroughly distinctive, which his size and beard and leather stump insured anyway, and dressed his part carefully. His nautical cap, sailor's pea jacket and flannel shirt were in the seafaring tradition. I noticed that the coat, which superficially resembled something out of a ship's slop chest, hung most gracefully and fit remarkably well across the shoulders. I commented that he was lucky to be able to wear such casual garments with so much distinction.

"Well, you see, I have them made for me by the King's tailor in Denmark," he confessed, smiling sheepishly.

He was given to bragging about his strength and endurance, which had made him an outstanding figure in the Arctic. He told with obvious pride of coming to an ice-filled raging torrent which had to be crossed, and he was the only one in the party powerful enough to stand up in the current and walk across. He did it four times, carrying a man on his back each time. But whenever he recounted one of these tales, he would follow it up with an anecdote about someone even stronger than himself.

One of his favorites concerned a Russian girl to whom he was strongly attracted on board a ship called the *Molotov* which took him through the Arctic Ocean to Korf Bay off Kamchatka. She was the chief engineer and looked like an amiable Valkyrie, a combination that so intrigued Peter that he determined to find an opportunity to talk with her. His chance came when volunteers were called for to work a hand pump supplying fresh water to the boilers. Peter followed the girl and grasped the handle opposite to hers.

"But that was a terrible strong young woman," he would say wryly. "She set such a pace that I had to save all my breath for pumping. Just as everything was going black before my eyes we finished, fortunately, but she was not even breathing hard! The only word I spoke to her at all was a gasp that I would sit a while to enjoy the view, and she left me. For the first time in my life I felt I was growing old."

Perhaps part of his chagrin was due to the fact that he was used to the admiration of women all his life, and he liked it. American girls especially were impressed when he bowed over their hands in courtly fashion, blending an old-fashioned Danish courtesy with Eskimo dignity. In his later years his apartment frequently was full of the most lovely models in New York because his wife, Dagmar, whom he married in 1945, is a fashion illustrator. Although he was a favorite with all of them, he never could tell them apart. One day a gorgeous creature rushed up to him on Madison Avenue and cried:

"Oh, Mr. Freuchen, I'm so glad I saw you. Please tell your wife I've lost those three pounds! Now maybe she will want me to pose for her."

Her dazzling smile as she walked away did not console him for failing to remember who she was. He was genuinely distressed because he was afraid his forgetfulness had cost her a job, and he gave Dagmar what he thought was a perfect description. It was no help in identifying the girl; Dagmar said it fitted every model in town, and she added that for today's styles any of them could well lose three pounds.

Peter grew accustomed to having people run up to him on the street or in restaurants to ask for his autograph, especially after he became a "TV personality," and he grumbled about it convincingly. At least I was convinced until one day while lunching at the United Nations where Peter was a correspondent for *Politiken;* the headwaiter informed a group of young people who had surrounded us that asking for autographs was forbidden. Peter, who had been muttering that a man could no longer eat in peace (but he had uncapped his pen immediately), tried to intervene.

"Ah, just this once," he urged. "What can it matter?"

The headwaiter insisted that rules had to be obeyed, and whisked the youngsters away, but not before Peter managed to scrawl his name for one of them.

He was so proud of his appearance that even when he joined the Danish underground during the Nazi occupation he refused

for a long time to shave his beard and wear an artificial foot
instead of the distinctive stump. He started his subversive career
by picking up and hiding British parachutists. Then he undertook to store and distribute arms and ammunition and serve as
a courier under the guise of making lecture tours. Finally he
edited and helped to print anti-Nazi newspapers. He was arrested at last, and consented to a measure of disguise only after
he had been rescued with other underground workers by a band
of Danes who dynamited one of the prison walls.

"It was hard to sacrifice my beard," he mourned later, "especially as a manufacturer had offered me five thousand kroner
for a picture of me shaving it off with one of his razors, and I
think I could have got him up to ten thousand if I had had time
to bargain. As it was, I got nothing and even had to pay the
barber."

He was arrested again and recognized in spite of his disguise.
This time the Germans beat him, deprived him of his artificial
foot for weeks and confined him in a camp which soon was
crowded with Danish prisoners. Once more Peter's escape was
arranged, partly by bribery no doubt, since he simply climbed
the camp fence and walked away when no one was looking.

Eventually he was smuggled out of Denmark to Sweden with
six other underground workers, including his daughter, Pipaluk,
who was as distinctive in appearance among the blonde Danish
girls as he among the men because she looks very much like her
mother, Navarana. Each fugitive was nailed up in a packing
case in the hold of a ship and warned to make no sound lest a
Nazi inspector hear them. Peter's crate was too small for him,
neither enough space nor enough air.

"I was very sorry for myself until, when we were brought
out after the ship got safely into Swedish waters I learned that
a little old lady next to me had been badly cut by the nails that
held her box together but never let out a whimper."

With all his vanity, Peter was ready enough to accuse himself
of mistakes or faults, but he was slow to judge others.

"No, no," he would protest if talk around a table drifted

into denunciation of some man's cowardice or meanness under pressure. "It is too easy to sit here comfortably and say what other fellows ought to do when they are in great danger."

He had known the truth of this, he told me once, ever since an incident in Greenland in 1917. He was sitting comfortably in his trading post at Thule while his friend Rasmussen took two Danish scientists on an expedition to the inland ice. One was Lauge Koch, a student who became a well-known archaeologist. The other was a botanist, Dr. Torild Wulff. Three Eskimos accompanied them. On the way back they encountered unusually severe storms and could find hardly any game. One of the Eskimos was torn to pieces by wolves. The survivors were so weak from hunger by the time they finally neared the coast that only Rasmussen, Peter's equal in endurance and fortitude, could travel more than a few miles a day. He undertook to push on ahead to organize a rescue party while the others followed as fast as they could.

Wulff, apparently sick as well as starving, repeatedly sprawled on the snow and insisted that he could not rise. The others were too feeble to carry him; they could only wait and urge him on until he staggered to his feet to stumble forward another few hundred feet. At last he cried that he would rather die than struggle further. The two Eskimos took him at his word and walked slowly away but Koch remained. He could not persuade the botanist to make another effort. Wulff used his last bit of strength to write a letter to his family and gave it to his companion, saying he himself was beyond help now. Only then did Koch leave him.

Back in Denmark there was angry criticism of the student, Koch. It got no support from Peter nor from Rasmussen.

"Later on people used to ask me if I would have left Wulff to die, and I had to tell them I did not know," Peter said.

Yet he had been in similar circumstances and with the same man. The previous winter he had taken Wulff on a sled trip across the glacier. The ice proved impassable, so they turned back and soon exhausted their supplies. But Wulff refused to travel more than four hours a day.

"For the first and last time in my life, I threatened a colleague with a beating," Peter said. "I cracked my long dog whip so close to his legs that he was scared, and he got up and came along."

"Well, if he hadn't been able to move, would you have left him?" I asked.

"That's what I don't know," Peter replied, his heavy-lidded eyes giving him a brooding expression. "If I had not been able to carry him, I hope I would have had as much sense as Koch, because what would be the use if both of us died? But I do know that no one has the right to judge another man in such a case."

He was a fanatic about tolerance in lesser matters. When he heard someone making fun of a foreigner's speech, he would exaggerate his own Danish accent or switch the conversation to the foreigner's own language. If the talk veered toward anti-Semitism, he would tell the gathering that he himself was a Jew. He looked so much like one of Michelangelo's Old Testament prophets that many people believed him, although it was not true, but he said it so often that the fiction crept into several of his published obituaries.

"I do it because it stops people from talking vicious nonsense," he explained.

He neither drank nor smoked. The last alcohol to pass his lips, he told me, was some champagne handed to him by the King of Denmark in person during a great celebration in Greenland. But he was abstemious from no moral scruples; he just didn't like the taste and he certainly didn't need the stimulus. Sometimes he would say that man was the only animal who used either alcohol or tobacco, and he couldn't make up his mind whether that accounted for man's cleverness or his stupidity.

For all his impenitence in the matter of eating sled dogs in a time of desperate need, he was as fond of animals as he was of men. He used to buy presents for his friends' pets, and even for his wife's cat, which he pretended to dislike but for which he would cook up special tidbits when no one was looking. The first portion of the $64,000 he won on the TV quiz show went for a grand new cage for his birds, which twittered around him in his study in a noisy disharmony that he enjoyed. But then his own singing voice was such, he boasted, that it scared off Arctic wolves and had saved his life more than once. His voice was off key certainly, although not as bad as he indicated, but Peter always liked to be picturesque.

We were nearing the end of our book when he announced in a self-consciously casual tone: "I've got to go to the North Pole for a couple of days." He laughed delightedly at my exclamation of surprise, then told me such a trip is nothing in these days. He would be with three of his old comrades—Bernt Balchen, Donald MacMillan and Sir Hubert Wilkins, almost the last survivors of their generation of Arctic explorers—in an expedition designed to re-enact some of the adventures of their prime. Not that he didn't feel in his prime still, strong as a bull and twice as healthy even if he was seventy-one. Certainly he was as eager as a boy and as gay, working with unusual concentration so we could finish in time. Within a matter of hours after we had agreed on how the last chapter should be rewritten, he was off for the airport, shouting jovially that he would be back in two weeks.

Three days later I was sitting in our publisher's office with the final typescript, promising that Peter would be on hand to help correct proofs. The telephone rang. It was a friend calling to inform us a radio broadcast had just announced that Peter had died the day before. He dropped dead after running up a long flight of steps at an Alaskan air base with luggage in his hands, laughing at younger men who wanted to carry his bags, as if they thought they were stronger than he. They said not even death erased his smile.

David Loth

August, 1965

IN THE ARCTIC

Remembrance

Sixty years ago a nineteen-year-old Danish medical student named Peter Freuchen caught his first glimpse of Greenland, and while Denmark lost a physician the Far North gained its most colorful, accurate and sympathetic chronicler. No other explorer or trader who had anything approaching the intimate knowledge of the Arctic and its people which he acquired has ever been so gifted a storyteller. He was one of those rare souls who can come back from strange and distant places to tell about them in terms both intelligible and fascinating to stay-at-homes.

His descriptions of the Eskimos, their life and beliefs, traditions and characteristics are vivid because he joined them as a friend and companion, not as an intruder with a superior attitude observing some lesser breed. He lived as they did, and sought to learn what they could teach.

The young man already had decided that a medical career was not for him when he went to see Ludvig Mylius-Erichsen in Copenhagen to ask for a place in the Greenland expedition which Mylius-Erichsen was then fitting out. He had read accounts of other Arctic explorations and was fired with an ambition to emulate them. He was so eager that he accepted Mylius-Erichsen's offer of a job as stoker, working his way to the land of his dreams in that arduous capacity.

In the next year he became a full-fledged member of the last Mylius-Erichsen expedition, during which the leader and two companions lost their lives, while Peter, stationed with one of the other scientists, learned a great deal about taking observations of the sun and stars. It was this talent that was to take him a few years later

19

to Mylius-Erichsen's last desolate camp in Northern Greenland where a few heartbreaking traces remained, as Peter tells in "The First Thule Expedition."

On his return to Copenhagen in 1908, Freuchen met the man who, he always said, meant more to him than any other he ever knew, Knud Rasmussen, whose name appears often in the selections in this book. Rasmussen had also been a member of one of Mylius-Erichsen's expeditions, had then explored and travelled and hunted on his own.

"He was at heart an Eskimo," Peter once wrote of Knud, which was high praise indeed, and the two became close friends at once.

In the aftermath of the discovery of the North Pole in 1909, Rasmussen suggested that a trading post in Northern Greenland, where there had never been a permanent white settlement, could profitably exchange for valuable furs the tools and weapons which Peary had introduced to the Eskimos. He invited Freuchen to be his partner in such a venture, and the place they selected for their headquarters will become familiar to the reader of these pages. Peter gave it the name of Thule, which it bears still and which, he explained, is "from the expression Ultima Thule, which means, of course, north of everywhere and everybody."

Long before anyone flew planes into the Arctic, Thule was the base of Freuchen's life and adventures. It was from there that he would set out on his exploring or hunting trips—the Fifth Thule Expedition mentioned here was typical of them—across the then unknown glaciers and along the badly mapped coast. It was to Thule that he returned happily at intervals all the rest of his life. One of his last visits inspired the account with which we begin these selections from his extensive writings about the people and the places he knew and loved so well.

The Eskimos are moving away from Thule these days. They are deserting their ancient settlement. I read in the papers that two spokesmen for the Thule Eskimos have gone to Copenhagen to ask the Danish government to move their village to the north, away from the deafening noise of the American airplanes. They can no longer remain in the place where their ancestors lived in isolation for centuries, because modern civilization has moved in and Thule in northern Greenland, not far from the North Pole, has been turned into one of the world's major airports.

My friends laugh at the Eskimos. "Do they have such sensitive nerves?" they ask me. "Does the sound of the engines hurt their delicate ears?" my friends inquire. "Perhaps the Eskimos will become used to it like the rest of us."

How little they understand. I was in Thule not long ago and I met all my old friends again. They had always lived a proud and carefree life, but when I saw them they were badly off. They had no meat left. I talked to my old friend Odark, the last of the North Pole Eskimos. He upholds the traditions in Thule, he defends the old customs of his tribe.

"Things are not like they used to be, Pita," he told me. "When we were young and strong we chased the bear, the seal and the walrus ourselves. We got meat where we wanted it. Today," he snorted, "today the meat is sold for money! I have money enough. The king gives me more than I need, but I shall never stoop to buying my meat. I shall never pay my friends to feed my dogs.

"Do you remember when you first came to Thule, Pita? I fed your dogs and I fed them well. Today meat is put on the scales and every morsel is weighed. No longer does a man know how to chase a bear or catch a fish. He waits for the fish to come by itself and swallow a lazy hook. I have never caught any fish but the salmon I stabbed with my spear.

"Things are not like they used to be when you were young. Do you remember the house you built in Thule, Pita? The first house ever built here. Today there is a city of white men, and the noise they make has chased away all living things. No longer does the ice bear cross to Melville Bay, seals and walrus have left for happier hunting grounds, and the wild geese are gone. Life seems a heavier burden than death to me today, Pita. And death cannot be far away when our land is like it is today and when my friends take money for meat!"

Odark was my friend. When I first met him forty years ago he had just killed Uvisakavsik and married his wife. Odark had gone to the North Pole with Peary; he was respected and renowned. Denmark pays him twice the normal pension, and through the Explorers' Club he receives an annual sum from the United States. He is not without money, but he has no meat. Never has he paid for his meat and he will not do so in his old age. "Let my dogs fend for themselves," says Odark. He does not need them. There are no more animals to hunt. His legs are not themselves any more, he says—the legs that once walked to the Navel of the Earth because the white man wanted to see how it was made.

We bridged the years and talked of our youth. "Can you remember when we had to eat our dogs to fill our stomachs? And when we were stranded in the middle of Melville Bay, when the ice would not freeze and we had no food for five days and nights? But when we returned to Thule every man was our host, and there was always too much to eat."

We were always on the move in those days when I spent years of my life in Thule with Navarana, my Eskimo wife. When there were no sinews left for sewing, the whole family moved north where the narwhales snorted and played close to the shore. When the men wore fur pants so old they put the family to shame, they were soon ready to go south to Melville Bay, where they could not fail to meet polar bears—soon ready but not quite ready to go. Only when the women had worn out the long soft hair from the bear's mane which they used to decorate their kamiks, only then were they ready to leave. "Women have no power," said Odark, "but they decide everything. We travel according to their desires, but never according to their orders!"

My last trip to Thule taught me more than all my other visits to this Arctic outpost to which I gave the name so many years ago, and I saw in true perspective the old Eskimo custom of moving from place to place. An Eskimo never takes root until he dies. When he is taken to his grave, to his final resting place, he settles down at last. During his lifetime he has no place of his own, no home where he truly belongs.

Nomads are always on the move—not because restlessness is their nature, but because living conditions drive them from place to place. The Arctic Eskimo must catch seals for meat and kamik skins and other things he needs. He must get walrus tusks in order to have flensing knives and harpoon points. He finds foxes at the mountains where the birds are too numerous to count. He goes north and he goes south. Thus it has been for so long that he no longer knows why he is moving.

Before the white man came to the Arctic Eskimos, they got bows and arrows from the Eskimos who moved in from Baffin Land in 1864. From the same people they got the kayak back. In ancient days there had been kayaks in northern Greenland, but when there was no wood left the small craft disappeared. When the Baffin Eskimos brought them kayaks their hardships were eased. Now they could chase the walrus and the seal at sea, and the hunting season was longer. Now they could get across the islands and gather birds' eggs when they wanted.

In the old days they had to go to the islands while the ice could carry them and had to stay for months. My friends told me of their visits to the islands when they were still children. They were kept inside the tents for days while the birds were laying eggs. The women went out once a night to collect them, and the birds must not know there were people on the islands or they would move away and lay their eggs elsewhere. With the kayaks the Eskimos could row across and get their eggs whenever they wanted.

As the years went by, ships from the south came to the Arctic, and the white man brought tools which made life easier for the Eskimos. Admiral Peary's many visits were a blessing. The Eskimos got knives and axes of steel and a new era began. Their old knives—most of them crudely fashioned from the iron found in meteorites—were thrown away.

All that seemed to belong to an ancient past. When I last

returned to Thule most of my friends were still there, and they tried to explain to me what had happened to them. During the war Denmark agreed to let the United States establish military bases on Greenland, and at that time all supplies came from the United States in generous amounts. Denmark made only one condition: The American forces were to be withdrawn at the end of the war. This promise was never fulfilled.

When I was last in Greenland there were seven thousand American soldiers in Thule—or rather in Pitufik across the bay at the mouth of the wide valley stretching all the way to the ice cap. Hundreds of times we had gone up this valley, driven across the glacier and down to Cape York or Parker Snow Bay. And Pitufik used to be the place where the polar bear came ashore in fall. They are crafty animals, the bears. They knew the short-cut across the peninsula to the south. They went up the valley, across the glacier and down to Puisortok in the fjord behind Cape York where they would be sure of finding seals.

Sometimes they fell asleep on the way. Only half of the bears hibernate. If they are not fat enough they cannot remain idle for many months, but when they are well fed they can afford the luxury of sleeping all through the winter. Behind Pitufik they settled down by the glacier's edge. They knew their geography, the old bears. They picked a spot where the snow would cover them until the sun woke them up in spring.

There are no bears by Pitufik any more. There are seven thousand soldiers.

There was beauty and peace in springtime by Pitufik. Swarms of the majestic Canadian snow geese came to hatch their eggs by the quiet lakes behind Pitufik. Soft, green grass covered the valley floor, the view was wide and the geese could protect their young ones against all enemies. In the Arctic spring we used to go hunting by the lakes. But the birds come to Pitufik no longer.

Odark does not worry about the birds, nor does Inukitsork or Qaviarsuaq. They are concerned with the larger animals, the seals and the walrus which stay too far away from Thule. The land is there, beautiful as ever, but the hunting grounds are too distant these days.

We sailed across the bay from Thule. On the way we came across dead birds floating in the water. Perhaps they had drowned, perhaps they had choked to death. I do not know. Their feathers were covered with thick, black oil. I shot a few birds who were already black. They could no longer fly and would die, even if I had not shot them.

The bird mountains outside Thule were always like a larder in the old days. We used to move out to the islands in spring. We loved them like no other place, and the food supply was inexhaustible. I spent weeks there with Navarana, my wife.

The Eskimos spent happy days on the islands at a time when trading or stealing wives happened more frequently and easily than now. The birds might have stayed there even if the people left. For thousands of years they have lived there and fed the people. They have survived shooting and hunting with nets, they have ignored the Eskimos stealing their eggs. There were always too many to be counted.

But American warships come in large flotillas to Thule today. They have powerful engines and go faster than a whale can swim. They cut through ice that could not be broken before. The engines must be fed, they must have oil and grease, the oil must be changed. When it is useless the oil goes over the side into the sea. The American ships must move ahead. The oil makes spots on the sea, they increase, they cover many miles. From the air they look beautiful to a bird. In stormy weather they look like calm, restful places where a bird can settle down and rest, dip in the water and dream. Swarms of birds swoop down, but they never come up again. The feathers get black with oil, their wings cannot carry them, they are paralyzed with fear and they all die. Not a few birds, not just a few hundred birds but thousands and thousands. In a few years the mountains that used to be teeming with birds will be deserted.

The same thing has happened in other parts of the world.

Something as useless as birds on a mountain in Greenland cannot change world politics, I suppose. I only know what I saw in Greenland. The walrus does not enter the fjord any more. No animal is as sensitive to smells as a walrus. If a house is heated with coal the smoke is enough to keep the walrus far away. The white whales go out to sea now; the narwhales have not been heard snorting in Ugdli for many years. The Eskimos have to go away; they must follow the animals.

No one is to be blamed. No one can say that one thing is more important than the other. Sentimental thoughts must be forgotten, for they lead nowhere. But where he has dreamed the dreams of his youth, there a man wants to return.

My friends received me with open arms when I came back to this new Thule. To the young men who only knew me through the tales of their parents, through the stories of happiness and danger in the old days, that way of life may seem remote and strange. But their soul is the same as the soul of their fathers. In them the soul of the Eskimo lives on. And for that very reason there is no bitterness in their hearts. They are used to giving in to fate, to accept the ways of nature. Their task is to find a way to become reconciled to powers beyond their control —and they are masters at this task.

I was asked to go across the bay to the military camp and lecture to the American soldiers, young, happy men—one cannot help loving them. They are strong and exuberant. They are far from home, and they like to hear about the land and the people they only glimpse in the distance. They are not allowed to mingle with the Eskimos. The American rules have built a wall between them—in the long run an intolerable rule, a violation of the human dignity of the Eskimos—but a rule that is necessary for practical reasons.

The young soldiers are lonely, and there are no girls in Pitufik. They look across the bay where they can see the Eskimo girls, and they are full of longings and desires. Some days before I got to Thule three boys had made their way around the bay and turned up in the settlement. They met some lovely girls and tried to take them by force. In the end a messenger was sent across to the American authorities; an expedition was dispatched to Thule to capture the three men, but the lovesick Yankees had managed to escape inland. The Eskimos felt sorry for them and sent their pursuers on a wild goose chase in the wrong direction. The men returned to camp without being caught, but their escapade led directly to the erection of a control tower which is manned day and night to make sure that no soldier crosses the bay to the forbidden side.

The American authorities have done everything in their power not to ruin life for the Eskimos. The soldiers are not allowed outside a certain area which has been determined by agreement with the Danish government. The principle is good enough, but the Eskimos ask with good reason what right the Danes have to make any such decision. It is their land, but they are used to being ignored.

The Americans have brought large supplies of goods and machinery to Thule. A harbor, the like of which has never been seen in Greenland, had to be built for the large freighters coming up north. A pier was built, extending all the way out to deep water. Day and night trucks carried stone and gravel from the mountains to the water. Every third minute a truckload of thirty tons was emptied into the water; bulldozers and excavators did their job until a modern harbor was made ready. This is no place for seal and walrus.

When I first came to Thule, in 1910, a piece of wood the length of a man's arm was priceless. A man might kill for such a treasure. Today the freighters bring crates so large an Eskimo can build his whole house inside them. Eskimos were allowed to cross the bay once a week to pick up the wood free of charge. The old values disappeared. The kindhearted Americans began filling the crates with food and clothing for the Eskimos, which resulted in a barter that had to be stopped, for an Eskimo always feels an obligation when he accepts a gift. He insists on returning a *qujanasat,* which means "a thing of gratitude," entirely different from regular payment. The Americans could not understand this old tradition and the barter was stopped. No more wood was given away, but there was no longer any need for it. The bay is full of driftwood—crates and logs and sheets of plywood. When Odark and I were young, good runners under our dog sleighs were invaluable. Today such runners can be picked up anywhere on the beach.

Old and new customs are in conflict. One hunter may be able to buy a motorboat and pay for it by the fox furs he can get in two seasons. When he sets out in his boat in spring to go far away and bring home the meat which can no longer be found near Thule, his friends turn up to join him. They have no boats of their own and they ask to go along. They fill the boat with their catch; the owner gets less but he has the same expenses.

"They don't remember that a boat does not go by itself, Pita," Qaviarsuaq told me. "A boat needs gasoline which has to be bought for cash. And the owner has to take care of the expense."

I suggested a more equitable system. They might share the cost; they might buy the boat together and divide the catch evenly. My friend listened to me in silence.

"I have heard your words before," Qaviarsuaq replied. "You forget that different people have different customs. I would be ashamed to ask money of a friend who went with me in my boat. He has none of his own. His need for meat is as great as mine. Let him go with me and get his share, according to the custom of our fathers."

Only one way out is open to the Eskimos. They can move. They can go farther north and settle down once more. The cost of a move is nothing to the United States which built the enormous air base. And a move is no symbol of defeat to the Eskimos. They are used to it; for centuries they have followed the animals. Here in the extreme north they have been successful in their fight against the hardest climate in the world. They have proved their invincible strength by surviving centuries of isolation and by absorbing and digesting modern civilization in the shortest span of time that has ever elapsed between the stone age and the air age. The meeting of the two ages was like an explosion. The Eskimos had to learn in a single generation what has taken other parts of the world hundreds of years to learn.

In the process the Eskimos have not lost their exuberance, their love of life. Men who have lived through famines know how to appreciate food. Men who have faced death time and again know how to enjoy life. And men who have known for years the monotony of a life without any unexpected events are quick to exploit every single piece of news, and they are eager to meet people. For these reasons the Eskimos are a happy race.

I was fortunate enough to experience their first awakening from the ancient ways of the stone age to the tempo of modern days. I learned their language, I married an Eskimo, and I lived for years with them in Thule. I heard the wise men tell their tales of days gone by. They gave me a happiness which was the foundation of my future life. Wherever I went in the world— Siberia or South America, Alaska, Hollywood or New York—I never forgot my first wife, Navarana, and her family and friends. Her influence and the life I lived for years in Thule stamped me forever.

My return to the place of my youth brought it all back. I saw again the house where my children were born. I wondered whether only years had gone by, and I marveled at the change.

My faithful old friends asked me to talk to the Americans. Qaviarsuaq and Odark and Inuarssuk suggested moving north.

"We have to go farther and farther away," said Odark. "We don't blame your American friends, Peterssuaq. But there are things they must do for us. They must help us get settled again. We would like you to explain things to your American friends."

It was a hard thing they asked of me, I told them. They were just a small part of a larger picture. There was not much I could do.

"Oh, Pita, my friend!" sighed Inuarssuk. "There was a time

when your voice was strong in the land, and all men listened to your words."

"That was long ago," I told him. "Now we are all old and weak!"

We laughed together, my friends and I, but there was sadness in our laughter and a nostalgia in our eyes.

The Eskimo Way of Life

The nostalgia which Peter felt was all the keener because no one knew better than he that the wonders of modern civilization had replaced most of the genuinely aboriginal Eskimo way of life. No matter how much they may have wanted to learn what that was, later visitors could never find out because it had vanished. But he had entered into it with an enthusiasm which was rare, and without any reservations, for he never regarded Eskimo culture as inferior to that of Europe, only different.

He learned the language so well that it became a second tongue to him, and permitted him to become one of the people. He used his command of it to learn rather than to expound the virtues of Europe as so many white men were prone to do. Because he was so clearly sincere Eskimo his friends took him to their hearts. More to the point, they revealed themselves to him as to few other foreigners.

The result was that Freuchen, writing about Eskimo customs or traditions, habits or beliefs, work or play, was able to speak of them with fluent authority.

To many of his contemporaries and most of his predecessors, Eskimo sex relations or table manners or methods of rearing children or techniques for hunting and fishing were fantastic at best and usually wicked. Peter looked upon them as the special features of an admirable people, no more unnatural—perhaps less so—than the courting practices of Danish youth or the hair styles of French women or the business practices of American men.

He was the most accurate as well as, I think, the most interesting of all the chroniclers of the Arctic peoples. The point should be

31

emphasized because he was criticized sometimes for what was sup-
posed to be sacrificing truth to a good story. Yet no one was able
ever to prove an instance of exaggeration, much less inaccuracy.
He was as meticulous as he was colorful.

Everything about the Polar Eskimos, the way they look, the way
they live and even the way they think and feel, is largely determined by the extreme arctic conditions under which they
live. In their isolated existence north of everywhere they love
to receive visitors, and when they come running toward you to
welcome you, all excited, they may, especially because of their
heavy fur clothes, seem thickset and somewhat ferocious. The
way to alleviate this impression is to smile. Deceit they have
never known; they take a smile for what it is and return it. They
smile often and willingly, and you soon learn to know them as
warm and friendly, with a great capacity for humor and compas-
sion.

But Eskimos are strong. There can be no weaklings among the
people whose neighbor is the North Pole, and since, as they
themselves say, "there is strength in beauty," they are also
handsome, free and graceful.

The first impression one gets of the women is that they are
far from primitive. They wear their hair in a low bun on the
back of the head, kept in place with a bit of string or ribbon.
It is long, straight and blue-black, loose strands framing a broad
oval face whose eyes seem to brim with savage, unashamed passion. Yet their manners are modest and docile. When they are
seen wrapped in several thousand dollars worth of furs, with
their strong white teeth gleaming in a perpetual smile that
spreads to the black eyes, one cannot wonder that white men
have been taken with them. They seem to have more natural
grace, more zest for life, than their white sisters. When one sees
them inside their houses, one notices their small and well-
shaped hands and feet. They have broad cheeks and small

noses, but otherwise the Mongolian features are not very dominant in the Polar Eskimos.

The men usually have pretty well defined features, sometimes with classic aquiline noses. Not until they are well up in
their twenties do they grow a little beard on the upper lip and
on the chin, lending them what would be a certain sardonic
elegance if it weren't for their always blubber-smeared faces
and hands. They wear their black hair long and falling loosely
to the shoulders, somewhat greasy and unkempt, but perhaps
held a little in control by a narrow band around the head. Even
so, it falls down in their faces all the time, forcing them to make
many oblique movements that—together with their broad
smiles—give them a certain coquettish grace. This becomes so
much more surprising when you realize with what ferocious
heroism they procure the daily sustenance for themselves and
their families.

Both men and women wear boots of sealskin, called *kamiks*.
They are roomy, and inside there are stockings made of hare
skins. For further protection of the feet, always the most exposed part of the body, they put a layer of dried grass in between the two pairs of soles, and this is changed every day. The
men's kamiks reach the kneecap, where they meet a pair of
shining white bearskin trousers. These are worn below the
waist, somewhat loosely around the hips. A coat of fox fur
covers the rest of the man—this has a hood which can be turned
up to protect the head completely. The mittens are of seal or
caribou skin.

The Eskimos have discovered that for maximum protection
against the cold the hair of the fur must be outside. Under the
coat they wear birdskin shirts with the feathers inside. These
are the only tight-fitting garments. Otherwise, the skin clothes
are loose and do not overlap too much, so as to allow for ventilation. It is important that they be kept as dry as possible. If they
should get too wet from perspiration and then be taken off, it

could be difficult or even impossible to put them on again, as they would be frozen stiff.

In summer, the fox fur coat is replaced by a seal fur coat which is less warm. And in particularly clement weather, the birdskin shirt is often worn alone. When new it has a handsome dark yellow color.

The coat has a snip both in front and behind, and the hood and the sleeves are brimmed with foxtails. Sometimes the men will wear two foxtails sewn together around each leg, just above the kamik, to take the bite off the cold air coming in.

The women's costume is essentially the same as the men's, but their kamiks are much longer. They reach the crotch, and instead of trousers they wear short panties made of foxskin. The kamiks are brimmed on top with the mane hairs of the male bear, the longer the more elegant. The coat hoods are made of sealskin, pointed, and edged with foxtails.

The children, darling little creatures with shining eyes, vastly spoiled by their parents, are dressed like the grownups according to their sex. Only the babies, carried in their mothers' *amauts,* differ from this pattern. With the Polar Eskimos, such an amaut is really an expansion of the back of the mother's coat, made so that the baby sits in comfort in the nude against the mother's nude back. While there is a hood to protect the baby, the mother has a loose hood for her own use. This mode is necessary since it might sometimes be necessary to feed the baby under rough weather conditions, and the mother can then just shift it over to her breast under the protection of the coat. It is true that a healthy, normal baby will do all kinds of things on the mother's back! But that has to be tolerated.

The women are cleaner than the men. They wash themselves a little, or rub themselves down with a little blubber oil, after each menstruation. As for the men, they might go for years without being washed. However, the hygiene is not in an altogether bad state because both men and women take most of their clothes off, getting their bodies "aerated," when they are inside the house.

The familiar igloo is used by the Polar Eskimos only as a temporary shelter during travels. Most of the winter they live in permanent winter houses made of stones and peat. Permanent, that is, for the winter, for each spring they are left by the inhabitants and automatically become public property the next fall.

You enter the winter house through an entrance tunnel, usually about fifteen feet long so as to provide both ventilation and protection against the outside cold. Since the house usually faces the sea, it is on a hill which the horizontal tunnel cuts into. The floor of the tunnel is laid with flat stones, the walls are piled-up stones, and the ceiling is made of flat stones covered with peat or turf. It is low, so that you have to crawl in on your hands and knees.

In the tunnel, you will find a strange little instrument, a little saber of wood or bone, called a *tilugtut*. When snow is falling or drifting outside, thousands of snow crystals will be lodged in the long hair of your skin clothes. If you enter the warm house like that, they will melt and make your clothes wet and heavy. Moreover, if you soon have to go out again, they will freeze. The tilugtut is used to beat the clothes free of snow while still in the entrance tunnel. During this procedure, it is a good idea to call out a few remarks, like: "Somebody comes visiting, as it happens!" so that the people inside are prepared to see you. It is true that an eskimo home is open to visitors at almost any time of day or night, but there are strained relationships everywhere in the world, and it is neither wise—nor polite—to show up in the house without a word of warning!

The entrance tunnel ends up just inside the front wall of the house itself, and you find yourself a couple of feet below the level of the floor, which you then step onto. Now you are in a room, rarely more than fifteen feet in diameter and roughly circular, inasmuch as the wide front wall, the converging side walls, and the narrower back wall of the house are curved evenly into each other. It is about nine feet high from floor to ceiling, but the roof slants toward the back wall. Besides, the whole back half of the room is filled from wall to wall by a big platform about three feet high. Since the house is sunk a little into the earth to give it extra protection against the gales, the platform usually represents the level of the ground outside. It is laid with flat stones which are extended along the front edge so as to create an overhang, under which there is storage space. On the sides, they extend into two side platforms that rest on stone supports, but also have storage space under them. What is left of the floor, which is also laid with flat stones, is then only a space about seven feet square in the front center part of the house. It serves well when game or frozen meat has to be brought in for the family meal.

The walls of the house are double, two layers of stones with peat or earth filled in between them. The roof is made of flat stones, deftly built up and overlapping each other, at last reaching so far toward the center that a main stone slab can rest on them, their outer ends being weighed down with boulders for stability. The size of a house largely depends upon how many large flat stone slabs can be found for this purpose. Only when an extra large house is wanted will the Eskimos solve the problem by building pillars up from the platform to support the ceiling.

Lumber in sizes sufficient to support a roof was rare before the white man came to Thule. Sometimes the Eskimos could barter a few little pieces of wood from the whalers, precious objects that they guarded with their lives. Also, they would find a little driftwood on their shores, and some of them believed that it came from forests that covered the bottom of the ocean like those in the white man's country. Actually, the driftwood was supplied by the rivers of Siberia and had drifted across the Polar Basin. After several years in salt water, it had chipped and was hard and difficult to work with. But its presence caused the Eskimos never completely to forget the use of wood.

The platform in the house is the family's sleeping bunk. Here they sleep in a neat row with their feet toward the back wall. Against the back wall are usually piled extra clothes and skins so that it isn't too cold. The bunk is covered with a thick layer of dried grass, upon which skins of musk ox and caribou are spread. The family and its prospective guests sleep under blankets made of fox, hare, caribou and eider duck skins. The natural colors of these animals' feathers and fur are used to make beautiful patterns.

Only when it is overcrowded are the side bunks used for sleeping, but they are less desirable because they are colder. Otherwise, the blubber lamps are placed on the side bunks. One of them may be used to place a piece of meat or game on for everybody to nibble on. Then there is a bucket or sealskin basin for ice to thaw in for drinking water. Whenever possible, the lady of the house gets this ice from one of the icebergs floating in the fjord by the beach. That water tastes fresh and sweet. A dipper is placed in the basin or bucket for everybody to use when drinking, and this dipper is usually passed around after each meal.

On the other side bunk, there would then be knives, trays and other household gear. The storage space under the bunks is used for skins and other property. On the walls may be pegs of caribou ribs or antler for hanging things on. Under the ceiling is suspended a framework of wood or bones. As it is for drying clothes on, it is directly above one of the blubber lamps. It is very important, especially for the kamiks and stockings. Every evening, when the master of the house comes home from the day's hunting, his wife takes his kamiks and stockings and hangs them up to dry overnight. In the morning she chews them carefully till they are pliable and soft enough for his feet, and she puts new dried grass in between the soles. The women go every fall up to the rocks to cut the grass off, dry it in the sun and carry it home. The best harvest is naturally around the bird cliffs, and they have to get a whole year's supply for their families before winter.

Both men and women are usually undressed around the house. The wife is only in her scant foxskin panties, and she sits placidly on the main bunk most of the time. Her cooking pots are suspended from the ceiling over the blubber lamp; everything is within her easy reach, and no bustling around is necessary. Since she has to cut and sew the skin garments of the entire family, that is what busies her most. Like a Turkish tailor, she sits with her legs stretched out at right angles to the body, her favorite position, with her work between her toes. Her most important tool is the *ulo,* a curved knife with a handle in the middle of the blade. From intuition, she cuts her skins in the proper pieces and sews them together, rarely measuring anything. The furs of the blue and the white fox are woven together in intricate patterns, and her work puts the finest Paris furrier to shame. With small, hardly visible stitches she weaves her narwhale sinew thread in and out until the skin pieces look as if they had grown together.

No wonder the needle is one of the most important Eskimo tools. It can be fatal, during a trip, if a torn garment cannot be repaired to protect against the cold, or new garments cannot be sewn. It is perfectly truthful to say that the lack of needles has caused the death of many travelers in the Arctic. For this reason, the woman's ability to sew well is one of her chief attractions.

The husband also undresses in the house. He may keep his bearskin trousers on, or he may be in the nude. When his clothes have dried, he ties them together in a bundle with a thong and hangs them up under the ceiling by a hook. That is in order to get as few lice in them as possible.

The house has one window, which is in the front wall above the entrance. The windowpane is made out of the intestines of the big bearded seal, which are split and dried and sewn together, then framed with sealskin, and the whole thing is put in the wall opening and fastened to the sides. One cannot see through such a window, but it lets quite a good light through. At one side there is a little peephole to look out of. More important, the ventilation of the house is provided through another and larger opening in the upper corner of the windowpane. Fresh air comes in through the entrance tunnel and is often regulated by a skin covering the entrance hole. This skin, when weighed down with a couple of stones, will also keep the dogs out of the house when the family is asleep. The dogs are rarely allowed in the house, anyway, but in very rough weather they may be resting in the entrance tunnel.

The flow of air through the hole in the windowpane is regulated by a whisk of hay stuck in it. It is easy to see when the air is getting close because the flame in the blubber lamp starts to burn low. And although no draft is ever felt, the house is always well ventilated.

Although the blood and blubber from the killed game smeared over floor and side bunks often give the new observer the impression of an animal cave, he will soon realize that the stone house is ingeniously suited to the arctic conditions. And it is well heated and lighted by the blubber lamps.

The Eskimo lamp is cut out of soapstone. It has a deep depression in the middle, at one side of which a whisk of long-burning moss is placed. Lumps of blubber are put in the lamp, and as the moss burns, the blubber melts and is sucked up in the moss to be consumed. By placing the lamp on three stones or on a tripod, and slanting it at the right angle, one can regulate the flow of blubber to the side where the moss-wick is. A stick serves to open or close the wick, making it narrow or wide according to whether a large or a small flame is wanted. This demands great practice, and only Eskimo women know this art to perfection. The lamp is kept burning at all times; when the house goes to sleep the flame is made very narrow, and the lamp is filled with fresh blubber. If it is properly regulated it burns easily through the period of sleep.

There are two types of lamps. One is oval, with a slanting bottom to help the regular flow of the blubber; the other is kind of shell-shaped, with a row of little knobs along the long curved side. This latter is a prototype of the Thule culture and is the one used by the Polar Eskimos.

This is rather significant, for there are few household possessions that play as big a part in Eskimo domestic life as the lamp. The wife has to tend the lamp, and it belongs under her jurisdiction. The more lamps she can take care of the cleverer she is, and many lamps are a sign of wealth and prestige. Since there rarely is any permanent place called home, the lamps become the symbol of the home.

In a Polar Eskimo house, though, there are rarely more than two lamps, one on each side bunk. It is the younger woman who runs the household and has all the power. The widowed mother-in-law is a dethroned ruler. She loses her say over the lamps when her son brings home a wife, although the young bride may have a kind disposition and leave her one lamp to take care of. In these situations there are no false sentiments. There was once an Eskimo girl who married a white man and was going with him to his country. Her happiness made her feel so generous that she told her husband she would let his mother have one lamp to take care of so that the old lady wouldn't feel neglected. But poor little Aqradaq soon learned differently, for in the home of her husband there were no lamps to tend. At first alone, later with her baby and an Eskimo nursemaid, she remained in an upstairs room and was not permitted to come down when there was company. She was like a prisoner, and she cried and pleaded with her husband to send her back, or she would die. It was not the isolation she minded, but the humiliation of seeing her mother-in-law run the household.

A constant concern of the Eskimo household is the lice, even though Eskimos get rather used to them. The wife delouses the husband, particularly his long hair, when the plague becomes too bad. And the husband, I have seen, often delouses the children and eats their lice with great relish, only once in a while handing one to the tot so that he also can have a little pleasure from them.

In their cold climate, cleanliness (the little they could have of it) was not the answer. Lice don't die from a little exposure to water. I have made scientific experiments along this line. Once I soaked a T-shirt filled with lice in water overnight. When I dried it and put it on without picking it clean, the little animals were right there.

And once I took some specimens of these unpopular creatures and put them in a test tube. I put it out in the cold of winter for four days, at a temperature of forty below or more. But when I took it inside the warm house again, and poured them out in my hand, it wasn't long before they started wiggling again.

The house is not the scene of all social life in wintertime. There are usually five or six houses in a settlement, and at a central point the men have built the meat rack. That is a high scaffold of stones on which all the hunters lay their catch so that it is out of reach of the dogs. Around it there are one or several cooking places, that is, fireplaces built up of a couple of stones and sheltered with walls of snow. When the weather permits, the whole settlement congregate around a pot of boiling meat at a cooking place and have their evening meal together. Men, women and children sit and stand around with their portions of steaming meat and eat while they gossip. The whole ceremony is a good expression of the fact that the fight to obtain sufficient food is so difficult, so important in these barren regions, that every meal is a festive occasion.

For the Eskimos, placid living in the winter house is only a temporary thing. Most of their time is spent hunting or traveling around to get the various materials needed for the household. It is not out of any desire for nomadism that the Eskimos are on the go all the time. It is simply that the goods of life are so thinly spread over their vast hunting grounds that they must constantly travel to get them. Take the Eskimos of the Thule district, for instance, who were scattered along a long coast and few in numbers. At only three places in the district could they get soapstone for their lamps and pots. Before Peary came, all their knives were provided from the famous meteorite stones on Salve Island in the northern part of Melville Bay (the stones are now in the American Museum of Natural History). But before they could go there to chisel parts of them off and beat them into shape with their crude tools, they had to go way up north to Humboldt's Glacier, there to find a certain kind of agate that was suited to use on the soft ironstone.

Seals were essential for kayak skins, boots and summer coats, and when they had procured these, it might suddenly be necessary to go to another place to get bearskins for men's trousers. Foxes were to be found around the bird cliffs, so it was necessary to spend some time there. And so on. It may easily be seen that the Eskimos had to develop superior traveling methods, which in turn enabled them to perform their long-distance migrations.

The dogsled is the principal means of transportation in the Arctic and, until modern times, the only means used for long-distance traveling. The firm sea ice is the best road for dogsleds, so these are seldom used when the ice has broken up in summer. Around Thule that was only one month out of the year.

The type of dogsled used in Greenland has two runners about seven feet long and shod with steel. It is more than four feet wide and has about ten thwarts sitting closely together. On the back are attached two stanchions with a crossbeam on top. They serve to support the load, and the driver can help push the sled by means of them. The dogs are hitched to the sled in fan shape. Each dog has a little harness to which is attached a single trace of sealskin line. All the dogs' traces are the same length and meet in a little ring, which is attached to the sled by means of two strong lines. The ends of the runners are upturned. Pulled by about ten dogs, such a sled can transport eight hundred pounds or more under good conditions.

The sleds used by the Polar Eskimos are almost similar, the differences being that the stanchions are only about three feet high, and the sled itself is longer and narrower. In the old days, when wood was scarce, such a sled would often be made out of whalebone and caribou antlers lashed together with sinew; this was a formidable task.

A Polar Eskimo's dog team is his pride and glory. He tends to have no less than eight and preferably twelve good dogs, and it is his pleasure in life to see them well fed and to hear himself praised and envied on account of them. In all matters, the sign of manhood is the ownership of dogs, especially as he trains them to help him hunt bears, the big animals that provide him with skins for his trousers.

This is the reason why dogs in the Thule district are tied by the houses, while those in southern Greenland and Canada are allowed to roam around, freely foraging for themselves. The Polar Eskimo's dogs are so trained to hate bear that a bear happening by could cause them to run away from the settlement and thus lose their way, and perhaps never return to their owners. They are therefore tied with sealskin lines, and already as puppies they have their teeth dulled with a file so that they cannot chew their lines or traces to pieces.

For this reason it is always a problem to have suitable dog feed. They cannot chew, and the walrus hide—which is what they are most often fed—must be cut into pieces for them to swallow. If it is frozen, it must be thawed. On the other hand, the meat stays a long time in their stomachs when it has been swallowed like that, and during travel the dogs should not be fed more than every second day. Even so, you don't get their best performance out of them on the day they have been fed. It is on the day that their stomachs are empty that they are the fastest and most lively.

Knud Rasmussen and I were well supplied with powerful dogs at all times because Knud's uncle, Carl Fleischer, the colony manager at Tassiussak, was one of the finest dog breeders in Greenland. Even if he had had to give Knud his last dog, he would not for the honor of the family tolerate his nephew's use of an inferior team.

Every year that I lived at Thule, the mail journey was an important annual event. I had to leave Thule on about January 15 so as to make connection with those mail sleds that transported letters and packages down south to Holsteinsborg, where the steamer from Denmark arrived on April 20.

Often I made several trips a year down across Melville Bay, and I know its mountains and its ice so well that no place there is strange to me, and I could find my way there even in the middle of the dark months. Navigation can be a problem in the High Arctic. At Thule our compasses pointed southwest, toward the North Magnetic Pole, and the misdirection was constantly varying. In the dark months, therefore, trips were usually made with the beginning moon. Another direction finder was the so-called *sastrugi,* snow crystals on the ice which the wind has arranged in stripes pointing in its direction. Since the southwest is by far the dominant wind in all of western Greenland, it was no problem finding one's direction when sastrugi were present. Only on new ice, and with the moon hiding, did we have to rely completely upon our knowledge of landmarks silhouetted against the sky.

Melville Bay is something special. No other place in the Arctic has been the scene of so much adventure. It was the road of migration when the Eskimos came from the north and took over Greenland, and it was the background for the whalers' heroism in the years when whale oil was one of the necessities of civilization, when sailing ships were dominant and large ships' crews every year made their way through the notorious pack ice of the bay. Here we crossed during the dark months every year.

There was adventure in the journey every time, and spirits were high. The first night we always spent in a cave on Saunders Island—a cave about which the Eskimos who accompanied me could tell many mysterious stories of ghosts and spirits.

The next day we reached the settlement of Cape York. It is placed on a rocky precipice so that the houses look glued between the boulders. We were usually the first guests of the winter at the place, so they were happy to see us and fed both us and our dogs to capacity.

After Cape York, the secret of the trip was to pull out to the new ice away from the coast. There wasn't as much snow, so traveling was lighter, provided the ice had not packed itself together. But sometimes the ice could be like a mighty ocean stiffened in a surge of fury, and we had to turn left and right to find the best passage. In the darkness we often ran straight into mountains of ice and broke up the sleds. No trip over that stretch was commonplace.

If there was snow, we would usually see bear tracks in it, for every fall the bears migrated in great numbers across the ice and up the promontory at this place. The dogs were trained to smell whether the tracks were old or fresh and promising, and if it didn't carry us too far off course, we let them run in the tracks so that they could have the pleasure of looking at the pawmarks of their archenemy.

It takes some training to go bear hunting in the dark. When the dogs smell bear, they are taken with fury, they jump forward as if the sled had no weight, and the one who falls off can't catch up with them again. Nobody can worry about him! The only thing to do is to follow one's sled and hope that it gets stuck in some pack ice. If you stay on the sled, you must sit in the darkness and mind the balance and lean now to the left, now to the right, and hope that the sled doesn't turn over.

Then you cut loose your best dog, the leader of the team; he disappears in a wink. If then, from the darkness out ahead, you hear a howl as he is hit by a paw, you know that there is a bear, and you let the rest of the team go. They dart up to the bear to surround it, they jump wildly around it under its constant attacks. The bear is adroit like a cat, it tries to beat the dogs back and flee, but they are all over it. It is difficult to get in to shoot, and in the darkness it is necessary to walk all the way up to the bear.

When you see the bear like this, in its awesome height and wrath, you understand why the Eskimo with his spears considers the bear his most distinguished quarry and talks about "the great lonely roamer" with the greatest respect. It is out of this same respect that many of those hunters who had guns nevertheless preferred to attack the great animal with their spears, particularly if there were two or three together.

"A bear is so constructed that it does not like to have spears in it," say the Eskimos. As if to prove what they say, the bear— as they run right up to the beast with their incredible courage and hurl their puny weapons at it—takes the spears that have lodged deeply in its flesh and breaks them as if they were matchsticks.

When the bear finally is felled, the dogs calm down with a strange suddenness. They lie down on the ice and watch without excitement as their fallen enemy is being skinned. According to Eskimo custom, all the hunters present are to get parts of the quarry, in this case of both meat and skin. There are three pairs of trousers in a bearskin. If there are more than three hunters present, the ones who threw their spears last will usually be generous enough to leave their parts of the skin to the others. The hunter who fixed his spear first in the bear gets the upper part. That is the finest part, for it includes the forelegs with the long mane hairs that are so much desired to border women's kamiks. The headskin doesn't really count, for it is only good for a seat on the sled or to put under a wetting baby in the amaut. So the hunter measures with his whip handle from the neck down, and marks the length of his own thighs on the skin and cuts off at that mark. The next hunter does likewise with the next piece, and the third one gets the rest.

Since the white men like to have a whole bearskin with head and claws on it, a rule was made in the Thule district that if the hunter who had "first harpoon" needed the skin to sell in the shop, he had only to say: "I skin with claws." Then he had to give his mates parts in the meat only, not in the skin. Often it is the intention of a young man to get himself income easily and quickly, just by saying these four little words. But they are difficult to pronounce, for they show that he isn't able to catch foxes enough to trade with; in addition, they make his friends trouserless. Often a remark is heard about "the good sense in keeping the skin whole!" and "This is a nice skin. Here is a man who uses his good luck when it comes along!" Such sarcasms do not fail to hit home. But then the young man breaks out in a Homerian laughter: "Naw, now I must laugh. At last, there is something amusing to tell others! Game mates think that the bear was to be skinned with snout and claws so as to rob them of the much desired trouser skins. Of course, it was a joke. The skin belongs to everybody!" With that, he feels relieved and can—since he shot the bear—go up to the next two in line and measure the length of their thighs with his whip handle to transfer it to the bearskin. There is much satisfaction in this gesture.

Bear meat tastes good when you don't get it too often. But with the new ice in September, lots of bears always came to Thule. They went ashore at Pitufik, where the American air base is now. Bears are wise, they know their geography. They crossed the glacier and came directly down behind Cape York to Melville Bay. This way is shorter, and they passed onto one of the richest seal places in the district.

But some of them didn't get so far. They lay down to sleep by the edge of the glacier. They thought it peaceful there, and they let themselves be snowed down. Not all bears hibernate, but if they are fat enough they like to do it. From the warmth of their breath a cave formed over them, and they slept until the light returned. Then they came out, miserably lean, and for some days they had to practice walking on the ice, for they had been sucking their paws, which thus became sore.

Almost daily we saw bears go ashore over there, and we killed so many that we got bored with the taste of their meat, which is best raw and frozen, anyway. Our pot was hung up on a tripod formed of three harpoons, and we continued boiling meat till nobody could get another bite down. And the dogs got their well-deserved part.

Our fire was usually made on blubber and lit with moss, which we all brought along. These campfires lent the trips across Melville Bay a certain romantic mood. Knud and I always lived like Eskimos and traveled like Eskimos. We didn't carry a tent with us, and in good weather we would just simply sleep in the shelter of some pack ice. I will always remember the festive hours when the flames from the blubber fire welled up. I used to go away from the others for a little while and take in the scenery: the huge blubber fire against the background of the contour of the mighty mountains, the little skin-clad figures darting back and forth, unloading sleds, cutting up dog feed and doing all the hundred things that are necessary in a camp on the ice.

When the meat in the pot was done, the fire attendant called out, and we all crowded around the pot with our knives in hand. We had to take our mittens off to eat, of course, so it was nice to be near the heat, and it was always amusing to see the savage faces, framed by the fur hoods and with the long black hair sticking out, in the shifting glare from the fire. During the long winter darkness, we rarely saw each other's features sharply, but here by the cooking fire we "discovered people again," said the Eskimos. Joy, joy!

When the meat was eaten, the pot was passed around, and we drank as much of the soup as we could. Soup from bear meat

is fat; it tastes strong and spicy as it goes down. Of course, a
pot that has been over a blubber fire is very sooty, so we were
not exactly handsome to look at when the meal was over.

When nobody wanted more soup, the owner of the pot always
had a dog that needed something extra for the road, so the dog
was invited to come up and lick the pot clean.

If the fury of the gale was over Melville Bay, we had to build
ourselves an igloo to camp in until it had abated. To build an
igloo, the Thule Eskimos use a snow knife, which is really more
like a broad-bladed saw.

A typical igloo is about twelve feet in diameter and nine feet
high, and inside it has—just like the house—a platform about
three feet high, serving as sleeping place. If a family is out
traveling, building the igloo is the man's job. A woman could
do it, as she may sometimes have to in order to save her life,
but she would never admit to it; it is decidedly a man's job.
Carefully, but with the speed of years of practice, he cuts out
the large wedge-shaped blocks. The base circle consists of about
fifteen large blocks. As the walls get higher, and the rings narrower, he cuts the blocks smaller, and he has to step inside to
put them up, while somebody may help him by handing the
blocks to him from the outside. The last circle has five blocks
in it, and he closes the top hole with a block in which he bores
a hole for warm air to escape. A well-constructed igloo will
never collapse, only sag in the middle, but the rising heat from
the people and the blubber lamp would eventually melt it completely if it were not for the little air hole in the top, which,
incidentally, is regulated with a whisk of hay just like the air
hole in the house.

When the igloo is completed, the man cuts a low arch for an
entrance hole, and he crawls outside and builds an entrance
tunnel which not only serves to keep the direct impact of the
cold away from the igloo when somebody enters or leaves, but

also becomes storage space for hunting gear and other things they do not want to leave on their sled.

In the meantime, the wife and the children have been tightening the cracks between the snow blocks with snow, and they throw snow over the whole construction. As soon as the igloo is finished, the wife takes her skins and cooking gear and goes inside to arrange the bunk and make the igloo livable.

The construction of an igloo takes perhaps an hour for an experienced hand, and it is usually used only overnight, but sometimes it is lived in for several days while a storm exhausts its fury. It is because of the ingenious invention of the igloo that arctic travelers can take the gale in their stride, and actually even welcome this change in the routine of daily travel.

The dogs take care of themselves. They huddle together at a place where there is a little shelter from the wind, and they curl up with their snouts under their bushy tails. They fight and yammer a little while they all try to get the place in the middle where it is warmest, but finally they quiet down, and they let themselves get covered completely by the drifting snow. In this snow cover they can keep themselves alive and warm for many days if necessary.

If it is anticipated that an igloo will have to be used for a longer period, it can be secured in the following manner: The man lights a fire inside it. He closes the hole in the ceiling, leaves the igloo and walls up the entrance. As the heat builds up inside, the walls melt, and the water from them is absorbed by the porous snow. Then the igloo is opened again, the fire is put out, and the full cold of the outside is let in. The watery walls freeze to almost solid ice than can withstand any gale. But so as to keep them cold from the inside and also protect the inhabitants against moisture and seepage, the woman lines the walls with a drapery of skins inside. Usually, this is simply the skin for the summer tent that now is hung up inside the igloo by means of lines going through small holes in walls and ceiling.

When they leave the igloo to continue their voyage, the last

H-136616

thing the travelers do is to relieve themselves, using it as a comfort station.

This is due to one peculiarity about the Eskimo dogs: they love human excrement more than anything else in this world. Out in the open, distressing situations can therefore arise. The process has to be done quickly, because of the cold, but the dogs crowding around can make it even more difficult. If there are other people in the party, somebody will take position in front of the suffering one and keep the dogs at bay with a whip.

But while the igloo is available, everybody takes advantage of it. Afterward, of course, the always hungry dogs are let in so that they can do away with the garbage and other things they can find.

This was an added factor in the problem of hygiene at our Thule station. Water closets were out of the question because of the low temperatures and the lack of running water. I had built a three-walled shelter where a certain amount of privacy and protection could be obtained. But loose-running puppies and single dogs came rushing up in a horde when they saw somebody "with bowed head," as the expression went, come walking toward this shelter, and they flocked around ready to jump in. Only one could get the warm mouthful, of course, but to obtain this honor they would willingly let themselves be bitten bloody, and the violent fight wouldn't subside until a long time after.

I hired a special boy to accompany guests out to the difficult spot. Qupagnuk (whose name means "the snow starling") was not very old, but from the time he could walk he had handled a dog whip, and his ability at hitting home was phenomenal. Proudly, he took position in front of the shelter and defended the occupant's peace.

This Qupagnuk I had taken into our house because he led a miserable existence. His real name was Ungarpaluk ("the little harpoon"). But because his father had died, and his widowed mother did piecework around the various households to earn

WEST GEORGIA REGIONAL LIBRARY
HEADQUARTERS

her keep, there was no real home, and the boy was reduced to foraging for himself. Somebody would throw a pair of old kamiks to him, or they would let him have other dilapidated garments. He was so full of lice that nobody liked to have him sleeping in their house, and he usually slept in the tunnel of an abandoned house. He was happy, though. He played with the other children, and he looked well fed. But he was always hungry, so when the hunters were feeding their dogs he came running to get his share of the walrus hide or meat. He jumped in among the voracious, battling dogs, who often bit him in the face and on the hands, and he saved himself a morsel or two. This got him the name of "Snow Starling," because the Eskimos said that just like that little bird he had to pick up a little to eat where it was found. And he responded willingly to the name of Qupagnuk. When I first saw him at Cape York, I pitied him, and I announced that I thought it was shoddy of the great hunters there that they couldn't bring home enough food to give a poor orphan suitable clothes and nourishment. I referred to their own children, whom they watched over and stuffed with all the delicacies the house had to offer.

They listened to me a little—patiently, as they always did. But then one of them said: "Pita, you speak both wisely and at the same time like the newborn man you are in this country! An orphan who has a hard time should never be pitied, for he is merely being hardened to a better life. Look, and you will see that the greatest chief hunters living here have all been orphans. Myself, I can remember how Qisunguaq was left behind by starving foster parents and still made out by seeking out the winter depots of the foxes and at the same time training himself more in hunger than people thought possible. Today, it is impossible for Qisunguaq to feel cold. Look at Angutidlu-arssuak, who always manages to cross the treks of the game animals, and who endures all hardships and can live without sleep more than anybody else. His childhood was spent in constant starvation, and for several winters his only food was stolen

from the hunters' meat graves. Look at little Iggianguaq here.
Here see a man who may be slight to look at, but who outdoes
everybody in bear hunting because he never gets tired of long-
time sled driving."

I thus understood that the Eskimos had their own method
of caring for orphans, and perhaps not such an inhuman one.
But I nevertheless took Ungarpaluk with me to the station.

To return to the igloos, around Hudson Bay it was a lot faster
to build them than in Greenland. People dug down in the
snow at the same time as they built up, and their snow knives,
broad-bladed curved knives, formerly made of bone or antler
but now sold by the trading stations, were a lot more efficient
in cutting the snow rather than sawing through it. It must be
said that there is often much more snow around those regions
than you ever find in Greenland, and in order to build his igloo
the Hudson Bay Eskimo must first find out if the snow is deep
enough. For this purpose he has a special snow gauge, a thin
stick of bone or tusk, about three feet long, which he holds
gingerly with two fingers and sticks down into the snow. The
feel tells him how deep the snow is and of what consistency,
and he is able to start his igloo at the most desirable spot without wasting any more time. In half an hour he puts up a sizable
one.

As a whole, since so many of the Canadian Eskimos do not
use permanent winter houses, they are more ingenious at snow
building than the Greenlanders. Among the Musk Ox People
I once saw an igloo that was built specially for drum dances,
and which could house more than sixty people with room to
spare in the center for the performance. The other igloos were
grouped around it and had corridors leading into it, so that the
whole complex was like a sheltered village.

When the Hudson Bay Eskimos got in trouble, it was usually
because of lack of game and not because of failure of transporta-

tion, for their sleds and their sled driving have many advantages over those of the Polar Eskimos. Even when they have wood, they do not have to be concerned about making the sleds light, for most of their land is flat and barren. Since they usually stick to land when out in a sled, they do not have to worry about rough ice. The land is almost entirely covered with snow. They can, therefore, make their sleds much larger, and a Hudson Bay sled of the type that I used during the Fifth Thule Expedition, though it is only two and a half feet wide, is up to eighteen feet long and furnished with a lot of thwarts sitting rather far apart. The dogs, usually ten or twelve of them, are hitched to the sled in a double row, not in fan shape formation as in Greenland. There are no stanchions on the sled, but I put some on mine, because I was used to them.

Since there is so much soft snow, the Hudson Bay Eskimo does not use steel shoes for his sled; he covers the runners with a thick layer of mud. This mud he procures in the summertime and stores for the winter, when it is to be used. When he prepares his sled, he brings several balls of mud into the house to be thawed. Then he puts it on the sled runners in layers several inches thick. When it is frozen stiff, he planes it down with a knife until it is even and smooth. Finally, a thin layer of ice is applied to the mud; for this he obtains a pot of lukewarm water and brushes it on with a foxtail or piece of skin.

The sled runs on this thin ice crust, and very smoothly at that. During a day's journey it might get worn off; then the driver will very often use his own urine to renew it, since it has just the right temperature. Moreover, it gives a tougher ice. But it is a matter of great concern not to get the ice crust chipped. The driver has a thong which is attached to the fore end of the sled. If he sees a stone sticking up through the snow, he hurries to throw the sled out to the side by pulling in the thong. If the ice crust gets chipped away, it has to be repaired immediately, since it can reduce his speed considerably. This is most quickly done with a piece of meat which is chewed free of all fat and then applied to the crack in the runner.

I had no real trouble finding my way about in the foreign country, for by that time I was well versed in the Eskimo language, and I could always get rather exact topographic descriptions from the Eskimos who had taken the same route. They have a very practical custom of always giving descriptive names to landmarks. *Pingo* everywhere means a round-topped mountain; *Kuksuaq* is the big river; *Tassersuaq* is the big lake, etc.

The sled being the man's property and pride, it has a certain significance as a symbol. One of the first days I was in Canada I met a party of Eskimos whose dogs were in bad condition. The women were running by the sleds instead of sitting on them. My Greenland Eskimos and I invited them to sit up on our sleds. They smiled hesitatingly, then they asked for permission from their husbands. This was granted, and happily they mounted our conveyances and settled down. This with the exception of a young wife whom I invited to sit on my sled. She turned her hood down and pointed to her head. I didn't understand her meaning, and urged her to climb up so that we could continue our trip.

Only later did I learn that they had all understood that we had taken these women on our sleds because we wanted them for company the following night. But this woman had her hair hanging down loose, which was a sign that she was having her menstrual period. So it was in order not to cheat me that the honest girl had shown what state she was in. When I invited her anyway, they all laughed a lot, for they thought I was saying that it didn't bother me in the least.

Old women who have lost their sexual attraction are exempted here, of course, and everywhere among the Eskimos you will find these unattached old females whose only pleasure it is to travel from place to place, meet their relatives and gossip. If they get a yen to go where you are going, they just settle down on your sled with their little bundles. To chase such a woman away would be a dog owner's eternal shame! She will surely say with a toothless grin: "Perhaps your dogs cannot pull my weight!" And she will spread the story wherever she goes.

There is one place in the Eskimo world where dogsleds are not known at all. That is in the southern tip of Greenland, where the sea doesn't freeze over at all. Here, the *umiak* is used for transportation. The umiak is a large, deep boat made of one or two layers of sealskin tightened over a framework of wood or whalebone. It is rowed with regular oars, and the Danes call it the "women's boat," because it is rowed only by women.

The umiak has always been thought by outsiders to be a regular feature of the Eskimo world, yet it is not really common except in the two extremes of Eskimo country, namely Alaska, where it is used for whaling, and south Greenland.

The performance of these large skin boats is a delight. They float like giant birds on the waves and take no water except for a little spray from the waves. Even this could add up considerably if it were not for the escort of the kayaks. On a trip, the umiak is surrounded by kayaks, like a battleship surrounded by destroyers, and they take the impact of the waves.

On my first umiak trip I sat in the stern of the boat watching the kayakmen. But at length I couldn't sit idle while the women were working, so I insisted upon taking an oar, much to the amusement of both the men and the girls. A couple of hours of the pace set by the girls left me exhausted, and I had to hand the oar back to the embarrassed young woman who had been trying to coach me.

The stamina of those girls was astonishing. When we reached our destination they had been rowing for thirteen hours, yet they attended the common merrymaking in the evening and danced for five hours.

The Greenland *kayak* is also a skin boat, about fifteen feet long, very slender, and round on the bottom. The kayakman wears a watertight garment of sealskin, and the manhole is covered with skin in which there is a wooden ring that closes tightly around the hunter's waist. The hunter's hood and sleeves are tight-fitting also, and neither man nor boat takes a drop of water.

During a storm the kayakman must be able at will to turn his craft bottom side up and then make it turn up again. For if he sits upright and lets a breaker hit him, his spine may be broken. No, he throws his boat over and takes it at the bottom. Many kayakmen who are well practiced in this sport prefer to hunt the seal in stormy weather with big waves, because they can get much nearer to the seal under cover of the waves.

The kayak is principally a hunting tool and the most important one in Greenland. The hunter has his harpoon lying on the deck of the kayak. The Eskimo harpoon is a six-foot-long shaft with a detachable point of walrus ivory. Through the point goes a line. When a seal is harpooned, the shaft falls off and floats around to be picked up later. The point stays in the seal which—if it is still alive—dives to the bottom of the fjord, and drags the line with it. The other end is attached to a seal-skin filled with air that works like a drift anchor and also tells the hunter where the seal is. Sooner or later it has to come up again, and then he can kill it with one of his pikes.

This form of sealing was used all over Greenland both summer and most of the winter (except among the Polar Eskimos), and it was the basis of the old Greenland culture. But it was a very dangerous form of hunting, what with the rough and capricious weather around the cliffs and reefs of the fjords, and it was considered a natural death for a man to be lost while out in his kayak. Every evening, the women went up on the hills around the settlement and gazed out over the sea, each one waiting for her husband. That picture of the worried wives and mothers standing up there waiting evening after evening will for me always be the symbol of old Greenland.

But the danger was not lurking in stormy weather alone. The Greenland fjords are peculiar for the spells of completely quiet weather, when there is not enough wind to blow out a match and the water is like a sheet of glass. The kayak hunter must sit in his boat without stirring a finger so as not to scare the shy seals away. Actually, he can only move his eyes, as even the slightest move otherwise might mean game lost. The sun, low in the sky, sends a glare into his eyes, and the landscape around moves into the realm of the unreal. The reflex from the mirror-like water hypnotizes him, he seems to be unable to move, and all of a sudden it is as if he were floating in a bottomless void, sinking, sinking, and sinking. . . . Horror-stricken, he tries to stir, to cry out, but he cannot, he is completely paralyzed, he just falls and falls.

This trance may last until perhaps a slight ripple of wind on the surface of the water brings reality back to him. It is the notorious kayak illness, a nervous sickness, but none the less real. It has claimed quite a toll of otherwise able-bodied hunters who were not capable of pursuing the only profession they knew of, because every time they would go out in a kayak, they would be stricken with panic. It has meant poverty and ruin for many a Greenland family.

The Polar Eskimos cannot use their kayaks for more than a couple of months out of the year, so with them sealing on the ice is much more important. This is also almost the only form of hunting they can continue during the dark months, since the moon gives them sufficient light to go out on the ice and watch the blowholes.

At this time, Smith Sound is completely covered with thick ice, and the hunters take advantage of the seals' need to come to their blowholes to breathe. The hunter takes up his position by such a breathing hole and waits patiently. It is cold, of course, but he doesn't dare to move his foot the slightest bit. If he does, the snow and ice crystals on the ice might crack and betray his presence. The seals are sensitive and suspicious animals. If there is no snow on the ice, as is the case when it is new, the hunter puts bearskin soles under his kamiks so that the hard soles won't sound against the ice. The slightest sound is clearly heard by the seal in the water, it flees immediately, and the long wait starts all over again.

Every seal uses many blowholes, and each blowhole is used by many seals. How they find them in the dark is a riddle that no naturalist has been able to answer to my satisfaction. The blowhole is quite small at the surface of the ice, and it expands dome-shaped down to the water, for since the ice is often three feet thick, the seal must be able to get its entire body into the opening and yet only show its snout to the outside world. When the hunter hears the seal come up in the hole, he must take care to wield a powerful thrust with his harpoon just as the seal is under the little opening in the surface of the ice. He cannot see the seal, yet he must hit it directly in the head, and often he kills it with the first thrust. Seals are quite nervous and faint easily from just a light blow on the head. But it might happen, if it is a big seal, that the hunter has to fight with it for quite some time to hold it there. Once the seal is dead, the hunter chops a wider hole in the ice to get it out.

Apart from the seals caught at the blowholes, the Polar Eskimo family, during the months that the darkness lasts, lives mostly on the provisions collected the previous summer. This is therefore also the time to go visiting, both to the neighbors and on longer trips, so as to taste each other's good things.

But the hunter's wife has one important task to perform, that of setting and tending the fox traps. The fur of the arctic fox, which has been poor all summer, is beautiful again now with the beginning of the dark period. While her husband is at the blowholes, the wife borrows the dogsled and goes out to set and tend her traps.

These are permanent constructions built of stone. The flat stones are used to form a kind of cage which is hidden under peat and snow. The bait is at the bottom of the cage, and the fox can enter at its front. When the fox takes the bait, he releases a string which has been holding the stone which closes the cage, and there he sits. Of course, these traps become more effective as the winter goes along and the foxes become hungrier and hungrier. Sometimes, also, snares are used, and when we arrived at Thule we introduced steel traps, since we were interested in getting in trade as many skins as possible. Until that time, fox trapping was considered the woman's work, the reasoning being that they didn't fight or run away, the cowardly animals, and therefore they were not worthy of a man's attention. Now, with our arrival, the possession of many foxes meant wealth in the white man's goods, and soon the men began to realize what a cunning animal the fox really was, well worth busying oneself with.

But the women still trapped for their own use and that of their families. And the care of the furs was their responsibility, at any rate. They chewed each skin carefully for hours until there wasn't a speck of fat left on it, then they tanned it in hot water and dried it. That was all that was necessary in the clean germless air. And the foxes from the Thule district have always been considered among the finest in the world.

Melville Bay
and The Whalers

One of the Eskimo traits which became part of Peter Freuchen's nature was the trick of boasting in reverse. The Eskimos called attention to their greatest achievements and most prized possessions by deprecating them outrageously. So when Freuchen wrote of his adventures, he was apt to understate his own role, as in this account of an Arctic rescue.

The hilltop where he began the story was the best vantage point for seeing the ship which brought him his fastest contacts with home and the goods he and Rasmussen traded for furs. Thule looks out across Melville Bay on the west coast of Greenland, a part of the much larger Baffin Bay. It was almost a highway for the partners, so often did they cross it or part of it on their expeditions and hunting trips.

At the time of this incident, Peter had not been married long—he tells in more detail in the next selection the story of his wedding. He did not usually waste much time on this sort of sentinel duty because most years the Thule harbor was open for less than a month, usually from about August 1 to 25. So his eagerness to catch a glimpse of the ship after nearly a year was understandable.

What he and his wife finally saw from their vantage ground and what followed is an excellent example of the Freuchen technique of weaving the customs and folklore of the Eskimos into a tale of high adventure. The asides and explanations, couched in the inimitable style of the great Danish teller of tales, fall neatly into place in a pattern in which men's struggles against ice and gales and

61

all the manifold perils of the North stand out against a background of the Eskimos' day-by-day routine.

I was sitting on my hilltop again, staring out across the sea and ice for a ship, when Navarana joined me. I heard her footsteps approaching me, nearly inaudible in her kamiks, the soft fur boots she wore. I did not have to turn around. I knew her foot-steps, light and steady.

She sat down next to me with a shy smile. She thought that I was still hurt, and she had come to comfort me. In a small, em-barrassed voice she explained to me that as soon as the ship arrived my wealth would put Arnawrik to shame, and then the old woman would have to forget about the narwhale her hus-band had been lucky enough to hit with his harpoon. The husband, Asayuk, had never been known as a good hunter, she assured me, and thus it was necessary for his talkative wife to boast when he finally managed to make a good catch. But why, Navarana wondered, had Asayuk given away his narwhale? Why had he not given a party himself?

"Do not think about it, Pita," my wife told me. "When the food is good, people eat and eat. Their stomachs do not ask where the food comes from. It is all forgotten, Pita."

I had already forgotten the episode, but her words showed me that she was still hurt. Now she was doing her best to make me feel better, to make me forget her own humiliation and mine.

When I did not answer, Navarana pointed to the binoculars I held in my hand.

"Just look at your glasses," she said. "They are enough to prove your superiority. Who could ever make such a wonderful thing here in Greenland? Black pipes with little glasses that make you see great distances."

I looked through the binoculars once more. I did not want to admit that I was looking for a ship, and had to pretend searching for something else. The bright summer day was without a breath of wind, and every sound carried a long way. It would not be beneath my dignity, I thought, to look for the source of some of the sounds I heard, to see if a walrus had come up for air. Navarana could not notice that I took a quick glance around the wide horizon, across the vast expanse of ice, to see if there was still no trace of a ship. There was nothing in sight, however, and with a sigh I dropped the binoculars.

Suddenly Navarana jumped up and stared intently across the ice in the direction of Saunders Island and further north.

"What do you see?" I asked her.

"Can a woman see anything when her husband sits next to her?" she returned modestly, but she did not move her eyes. She kept on staring.

I did not want to say any more and risk being further humiliated, but without saying a word I held out the binoculars to her.

"One is born with eyes," she said quietly and sat down again next to me. Surreptitiously she pointed her finger, however, and once more I held the binoculars to my eyes. There was nothing to be seen. Ice, ice—nothing but ice. Some large floes had turned upside down and looked like weird figures, a few icebergs loomed large on the horizon; otherwise there was only the flat pack ice. I stared until my eyes started watering.

People who have not spent a whole summer in the Arctic looking for a ship never understand how one can mistake an iceberg or anything else for a real vessel, but it happens again and again. Week after week I had waited, and I do not know how many times I had seen a ship—only to have it turn out to be an iceberg or a small cloud, or even a walrus moving on the ice far, far out.

Our harbor at Thule had open water that summer, but outside, the pack ice closed all approaches both from Smith Sound to the north and from Baffin Bay to the south. When we went hunting we had to go deeper into the fjord from Thule. In the late spring we had settled down at Ugdli, where there were many narwhales and where we lived happily in our tents.

Navarana was very proud of ours. There is an old custom among the Polar Eskimos that while the men, naturally, build the stone houses, the women make the tents that they use in the summer, and they alone decide the size of the summer home. Sometimes a husband may force his wife to limit the size of the tent, but only if he is an unlucky hunter and unable to provide enough skins for the tent. Such a thing never happened in our fjord where the seals were abundant. If one of our tents was small, it was only because the woman was lazy, or perhaps had too many children to look after and did not have time to sew a large one.

Enlarging a small tent involves a great deal of work—as well as a number of skins—since the skins have to be added to the bottom of the tent where the circumference is largest. If a woman has any pride she will always do this work, provided she has the necessary poles to support a large tent. All the poles, particularly the central rafters, have to be very long. They are the pride of a Polar Eskimo, and they stay in the family for generations, always being handed down from mother to daughter, never from father to son. Navarana had provided me with very long poles and we had a large tent.

During the early part of summer the narwhales came in close to the glacier where they helped themselves to the Arctic flounders that could always be found there. The narwhale is a strange animal, shaped like a white whale but nowhere near as fast. Like walrus, seals and the larger whales, they do what the Eskimos call *putinerpokk*—meaning that they remain quiet on the surface for quite a while, breathing rapidly several times. The white whales come up, fill their lungs with fresh air and dive again in a flash, never resting on the surface.

With their heavy kayaks the Polar Eskimos can never catch a white whale unless it happens to surface right next to the kayak, inviting a harpoon. Pursuing a white whale is out of the question. Further south the Eskimos in Disko Bay can do it. They have small fast kayaks and harpoons which they can throw quite a distance. In northern Greenland my friends had to be right next to the animal before they could use their harpoons. A Polar Eskimo has only his arm, no wood with which he can lengthen it.

The narwhales were easy prey, and we got a large number of them. Their skin—or *mattak,* as the Eskimos call it—is a great delicacy. It is cut out in large pieces, shiny and clean. The fat that sticks to the skin tastes like a rich, fresh juice while the outer skin has a delicious nutty flavor. The coarser inner skin is always swallowed without chewing and is supposed to give great strength. I have since learned that this mattak is rich in vitamins and provides effective protection against scurvy. It tastes like fresh vegetables and cool milk—all of Greenland concentrated in this tasty food. No man has ever been heard complaining or quarreling when the Eskimos gather around a fresh narwhale, tasting a piece of the delicate mattak before the flensing begins.

When we cut up the whales we caught at Ugdli, we found that their stomachs were always filled with small Arctic flounders. We salvaged the fish and boiled it just as it came out of the narwhale. It tasted as if it had been prepared in a fine sharp sauce, and such a meal was so rare that we hardly dared to speak while we enjoyed it. Fish is, after all, practically nonexistent in Thule. Once or twice during the summer some old woman might catch a few, but no hunter with any self-respect would dream of fishing for something that volunteered to be caught and attached itself to a hook.

We had a wonderful summer in Thule and Ugdli that year—long ago, in 1911. We were waiting for a ship, but we knew that there was no hope as long as we could see the solid pack ice outside Cape Athol. The water was open in the fjord because the glacier had broken up the ice and because many small rivers ran down to the fjord and melted the ice along the shore.

I believe this was the happiest summer in Navarana's life. She was accepted in Greenland as my wife. She had complete control over all my possessions which, to the Eskimos, seemed overwhelming. As soon as the ship arrived there would be still more riches, and all the Eskimos realized that it was to their advantage to be in her good graces. To Navarana, there was only one drawback: her husband was, of course, not so good a hunter as most of the men in our settlement. I had never been lucky enough to catch a narwhale from my kayak, and thus I had never been able to serve our guests the much desired tail piece —the most festive food that is reserved for guests of honor. I knew that Navarana was unhappy about it. She had the ambition to serve a meal like her friends and be able to tell them that she was ashamed to serve such unworthy food.

"We have nothing fit to offer our guests!" So went the standard ritual when this best of all possible foods was served. "My husband does not know how to catch a good animal. Pure chance brought him close to a narwhale, and he has saved this miserable tail piece. It has spoiled, of course, it is not prepared right. I know you cannot like such food, and I am only happy to know that there are other houses here where you can satisfy your hunger as soon as you leave us!"

It satisfies the vanity of the Eskimo woman to be able to use such words with false modesty when serving a rare treat. The protests of the guests and their enormous appetite add to the honor of her husband, and such a meal will be remembered in the family for a long time. There is no place in the world where the appetite of the guests and their appreciation of the food are commented upon as eagerly as in Greenland.

This was an experience Navarana waited for. She could always offer tea and sugar, or even pass around a large tobacco pouch—all precious and rare in Greenland. Such treats added to her prestige, but they could never take the place of a tail piece from a narwhale caught by her husband. A few times we had served a fabulous meal, offering all the things I had brought along from Denmark, delicacies our friends had never even seen before. They were grateful, they admired the taste and quantity of the food, they ate enough to satisfy three times their number in any other part of the world. But the end was always the same: they asked politely for permission to boil some meat in order to appease their hunger and feel that they had something substantial in their stomachs.

The day Navarana joined me on the hilltop to comfort me I had taken pity on her and managed to serve a tail piece of a narwhale. Navarana's mother was visiting Thule, and my wife wanted to honor her with a great party. I got hold of a narwhale which had decomposed to exactly the right shade of green and yellow, indicating that the blubber would have a superb taste. My friend Asayuk had caught the whale, and I had bought it from him for a stiff price in tobacco. I had looked forward to Navarana's triumph, but my efforts proved a complete failure.

When the guests were assembled and Navarana, according to the ritual, asked me if I had anything edible to offer, I went outside to get the tail piece. I tried to keep the solemn expression on my face which the occasion called for, and walked out slowly and indifferently while my guests watched in silence. When I began pulling in the enormous piece of meat some of the younger men came to my assistance, groaning under the weight in order to demonstrate my wealth and hospitality to the other guests.

Asayuk was one of the guests, and he stuck to his bargain, never revealing the source of my meat. Unfortunately he had brought his wife, Arnawrik, and she could not control herself. When she saw the delicious tail piece she announced in a loud voice:

"I am proud to see, Pita, that you have found some use for the whale my husband caught. It gives great pleasure to be able to provide a festive meal for your party!"

The whole event was ruined for Navarana. All of the guests had, of course, known that I had not caught the narwhale myself, but there are no people in the world more tactful than the Eskimos. They had all been prepared to keep a straight face and not humiliate me by showing that they knew the shameful thing I had done: offering my guests another man's food. Only Arna-wrik had not been able to keep it up. She was too proud and, perhaps, too jealous of Navarana. There was no longer any happy pride in the voice of my wife as she begged the guests to eat more. To make matters worse we had no more tea or coffee left. We had run out of supplies while waiting for the ship. For the hostess, the party was a miserable failure.

When the guests had left, I went outside. It was a lovely evening. Low on the horizon the sun was shining as it would all night. The air was soft and mild without a breath of wind—an Arctic summer night in all its unbelievable beauty. I could not sleep. I decided I would rather go hunting, or pretend to hunt, as I walked up the mountain. I took my binoculars and set out.

Navarana had followed me, and there we sat together, staring out across the sea. Ice, nothing but ice, and no chance of a ship coming through until a strong north wind set the ice pack moving south. The summer was well advanced, however, and there ought to have been more movement in the ice. The walrus had arrived early at Saunders Island that summer. When the ice is solid they swim north in the open channel which is always there from Cape Holm in the south to Cape York at the northwestern end of Melville Bay—"the Mouth of the Sea," as my friends called the channel. It is easy enough for the walrus to follow this route across the enormously long mouth of Melville Bay, but here they find no mollusks which are their main diet. It may be because the bay is too deep or perhaps because it is not deep enough and the icebergs scrape the bottom, driving the mollusks away.

Nobody knows why, but it is a fact that a walrus always has seal meat in its stomach when it comes up to our part of Greenland. There is nothing else to eat during the long trip north. For that reason the walrus always prefer to stay around Saunders

Island for quite some time, filling up on the large mollusks to be found there. In the late spring and summer we could always find large numbers of them.

They are easy to catch because they are as regular as a clock. They stay underwater for seven minutes before they come up for air. They remain on the surface long enough to breathe deeply five times before they submerge again. In seven minutes they reappear, and it is relatively easy to have the kayak in the right spot when they do.

Sometimes the walrus go to shallow water where one can study their feeding habits. I have watched them and found the explanation for the extraordinary fact that the shells of the mollusks they eat are never to be found in their stomachs. I have known explorers and scientists to give various reasons for this. It has been claimed that the walrus has a particularly agile tongue and is able to chew the shells to pieces and spit them out again. This beautiful theory is completely untenable. I have cut out the tongues of hundreds of walrus, and I have yet to find out how they might use their short, clumsy tongues to get rid of the shells.

As a matter of fact, the mollusks are already shelled before they enter the mouth of the walrus. The shelling is done in a very simple and clever way which has never been told in any description of the life of the walrus that I have seen. I found it out by studying the animals in the shallow, clear water off Thule. The walrus dives down to the bottom, and with his long tusks he plows up the soft mud and sand. The tusks tell the story very clearly. They are never worn on the inside or underside. The tusks slant in such a way that only the outside of the ivory is used. With his enormous hard foreflippers the walrus grabs an armful of mud and swims upward. A short distance from the bottom he starts rubbing his foreflippers against each other. There is great strength in these flippers which the animal uses for walking on the ice, and the walrus breaks the hardest shell into tiny pieces.

When the job is done, the walrus lets go of the whole mess while he stands straight up in the water. Sand, pebble and broken shells are heavy and sink quickly to the bottom, but the soft flesh of the mollusks, not much heavier than the salt water, remains afloat. At his leisure the walrus can gobble up the clean morsels of shelled mollusk.

We always tried to be on Saunders Island when the walrus arrived—a wonderful island with its steep mountains. The fulmars built their nests high up near the top of the mountains, where I ventured only once in my life. I was surprised by a snowstorm and had to spend a night and a day on a small ledge where I could hardly move. I made a promise to myself—one of the few I have kept—that if I should survive, I would never again return to the top of the mountains on Saunders Island.

More accessible are the auks and the numerous other birds that are always good to eat. We caught a great many of them, and used them not only for food but for clothing as well. In those days there was no store in Thule, and the Eskimos could not buy material that was easy to wash and to mend. They used bird skins for shirts as they had done for generations. The old women had to chew the skins to get rid of all the fat; they were the only ones who would not ruin the soft skins because they had no sharp teeth left.

As soon as the eiders arrived we forgot all about the other birds. The eiders taste better than any bird in the Arctic, and their oily meat has a delicious, sharp flavor. The eiders taste like the very spring in Greenland—and with the eiders come the walrus. No wonder we considered Saunders Island a paradise in summer.

And now we sat on the mountains behind Thule looking over the ice toward Saunders Island. Again and again I had climbed high up to get a good view, hoping to see a ship. I was perfectly happy where I was. Navarana was a wonderful wife, the people around us were perfect neighbors. I was young, strong and healthy, and I led a life few other people in the world could ever hope for. I lived north of everything and everybody—a circumstance which somehow added to my pleasure. And yet . . .

The ship was always there, a great expectation, a symbol of something that was never quite clear to me. I had more or less decided to spend the rest of my days where I was. Why shouldn't I? The place was ideal, I had no wishes that could not be satisfied. And yet . . .

Perhaps I was so happy in my little corner of the world—the extreme north of Greenland—because I was there of my own free will. I always knew that I could break up and go home whenever I wanted to—and that was just why I did not do it. That is the way we are all made. If I had been exiled to Greenland, if I had been forced to remain in Thule, everything would have been different. All other circumstances being equal it still would have been a living hell because I could not have left.

It is the same as with food. If we ate our last European food supplies we suffered agonies and felt like martyrs because we were compelled to live exclusively on the Eskimo diet. But leave a little—just a bit of tea or flour, save only half a pound of sugar —and everything is different. Then one can live happily like the natives because one knows that there is always something in reserve. If one knows that something is there in case it is desperately wanted, one does not touch it. It has happened time and again that people have died of starvation although they still possessed one last bit of food. But they died before they had the heart to touch that final reserve.

I had no longing to go away, but I did long for a ship. The arrival of a vessel from the south is—or rather, was, since things are quite different today—an event which is hard to describe, a peculiar pleasure one cannot put into words. The best part of it was, perversely, the departure of the ship. We had had a few hectic days, the place had been turned upside down, nothing had been normal. And it was always a wonderful feeling to see the ship disappear again behind Cape Athol and to sigh with relief because now we would have peace for another year. We had

Greenland to ourselves again, we would not be bothered by strangers upsetting our routine, asking questions and wearing us out.

That feeling is entirely forgotten, however, when summer is back, when a year has passed and one is once more waiting for a ship.

The icebergs appeared on the horizon and disappeared again. They all had strange shapes, they all seemed to look like a ship. I knew it was not, it could not be a ship, and yet . . . Whenever I was ready to go down to our tent, there was always another strange shape that looked somewhat like a sail in the distance. Up went my binoculars. Yes, wasn't it . . .? Was it? No, it never was!

And that particular day, Navarana joined me in my watch. I had already forgotten the dinner that had been such a source of humiliation to her. I was still Danish enough to consider it perfectly natural to serve meat I had bought just as well as the things I caught myself, but my wife felt differently. It had been a blow to her, and she was consequently convinced that I had gone up to the mountains to be alone with my shame—the way unfortunate hunters might do when their lack of luck is mentioned publicly.

In Greenland there is no such thing as a poor, or a bad, hunter. There are only good hunters. Some are great hunters, or large-handed men, as they are called. Those who are unable to bring home a good catch are simply unfortunate hunters, they are out of luck. Their family and friends complain of their lack of luck, never of their lack of ability. Among the Thule Eskimos there were only two or three exceptions, a few men who did not mind being laughed at. They had been accepted as permanently lazy and unfit for hunting. They did just as well as their friends and neighbors, however, living on the abundance of the other Eskimos. Any man has the right to take part in the flensing of the animals. As long as a man has a pair of dogs he is a member of the tribe. Should his family suffer merely because the provider is inadequate and unable to stand on his own feet? His women and children always get enough to eat, but never the choice parts. If he wants to offer heart or tongue or liver to his guests, he has to serve another man's meat and humiliate his women.

Navarana knew that I was important in other ways, even if I disappointed her as a hunter. She alone in the tribe realized that it might be part of the work of a grown man to write on paper or read a book. The others did not always see it that way; they knew only what they had been told by their fathers.

Nobody could be sweeter than Navarana, or more jealous of her husband's reputation. She was unhappy because I had lost face, because the words of an old woman had hurt me. And now that we were alone, with no Eskimo to listen, she wanted to tell me that she was sorry for me.

"But you are such a great man," she told me. "You should not go away by yourself to the mountain and thus show the whole tribe that you are ashamed and wounded by the words of a mere woman."

We sat there for a long time without talking, two young people in love. Love cuts across all barriers of language and race, and yet it is impossible fully to understand some of the deep emotions in a person of another race. One can only realize that there is a feeling which is common to the whole race, and accept it as such. Navarana was convinced that I was in misery because I was an inferior hunter. It would only hurt her still more if I were to tell her that I was utterly indifferent to the scornful words of an old woman, to the insult wrapped in poisonous pleasantry. Such indifference would have run counter to all her conceptions of right and wrong, her sense of values. To Navarana the most important thing now was that the man she loved should be honored by her tribe and should prove himself worthy of the respect and admiration of all our friends.

It was impossible for me to explain to her that I was simply looking for a ship, with no other thought in my mind. She would have regarded it as evidence that I was dissatisfied with my life in Thule and with her, that my thoughts were going back to my own country, away from her. We were far apart that summer night on the mountain as we searched for the right words, each trying to comfort the other.

There was always this insurmountable difference between us. Navarana knew her own worth. In spite of her youth she was a master in the art of sewing and preparing skins and furs. During the winter she had caught many more foxes than she could use. Her father and grandfather were honored men in the tribe; their words were law among the Thule Eskimos. For my part, I knew that even if the main task in Greenland was the ceaseless struggle for food, there were other and more important things to strive for in life than hitting a narwhale with a harpoon. There was nothing I could do or say to make her understand.

When I talked to Navarana about my own country, which she was eager to visit, I was always told she was happy for my sake that I had escaped from this flat, dull land without seals or walrus, a land where one could get food only by paying for it in a store. A land where a woman worked in the same house winter and summer! No excitement, no hard and dangerous journeys, no change from stone houses in winter to tents in summer, no opportunity to prove one's ability and courage! What did a man know about his woman if she never had a chance to show how she could survive in a blizzard? When she did not even sew her husband's clothes or carry her children in a leather pouch, her amaut, on her back?

Navarana could never understand why some women preferred living in Denmark. She realized that there was food growing in the fields, she knew that the king was the head of the people and the most honored man. But what would happen, she would ask, if the king proved himself a poor provider? Would he still be the man to think for all the people in Denmark? And on what experience did he base his thoughts and decisions if he had never proved himself in difficult and dangerous situations?

There was ignorance on both sides, a difference in outlook and emotions which could never be reconciled. But we forgot it that night on the mountain as the midnight sun smiled on us and we were waiting for a ship.

"Pita, you are good to a woman who worries when you are sad," Navarana told me with a shy smile. "You are a wise man, and you bring new thoughts into the head of an ignorant woman."

We fell silent again. I toyed with my binoculars as I watched my wife. Her eyes did not move from whatever she thought she saw far, far out on the ice. She was staring beyond Saunders Island toward the Carey Islands, invisible beyond the horizon. She still had not said anything about her imagined discovery. Looking into the distance, she snuggled down in the moss and sighed contentedly.

"How wonderful our country is in the summer," she murmured happily. "Every week we have days like this, so mild and quiet, with the sun shining all night long. The only trouble is that people get lazy in such weather and forget to use their eyes," she added, closing first one eye and then the other in an effort to see better—whatever she saw.

I was a little annoyed as I put the binoculars to my eyes again. I searched the entire horizon, I concentrated on Saunders Island and the empty ice beyond it. There just wasn't anything to be seen, and again I tried to give Navarana my binoculars.

"One is born with eyes," she repeated.

My eyes had become tired from the strain of watching day after day. And I knew that the moment a ship did appear, it would be impossible not to see it, that it was stupid to wear myself out looking for something I knew was not there, could not be there. Navarana seemed unable to wear out her eyes and she had no need for the binoculars. She was born with keen senses that she put to good use. She had certainly seen something, but she did not want to claim the discovery for herself.

Her husband had just suffered a defeat, this was his chance to rehabilitate himself, to regain the admiration of his friends. Even to me she would not say a thing or admit that she had seen something before I did.

I admired her self-control as I used the binoculars again. She did not help me, she did not explain. She wanted me desperately to be the first to see it.

"There is nothing there, Navarana," I sighed at last. "What on earth are you staring at?"

"A little to the left of that dirty iceberg," she whispered. "A trifle beyond it."

Now she was tense with excitement. I looked again. I was prepared to discover at least a herd of walrus on the ice, or perhaps a flock of birds—but there was simply nothing. I readjusted the glasses, I polished the lenses—all in vain.

Finally it was too much for Navarana. She could not control herself any longer.

"*Inuit*—people!" she exclaimed. "People from the north are coming to visit us. They are moving. Several people! Perhaps it might be useful to call down to our friends that visitors are coming. Most of them are asleep after their great meal."

My good Navarana had worked it so that it would help restore my reputation if I proved myself alert when others slept, the one man to discover the arrival of many people from the north. It would, of course, never dawn on anyone that she, a mere woman, had the better eyes and had made the discovery first.

And still I did not see it. Navarana had to explain it to me in detail.

"See the iceberg there, the dirty one beyond Saunders Island? To the left of it you can see some bright, shiny snow on an ice floe. Next to it there are two small ice peaks, little fingers pointing to the sky. All right? A little below them and a trifle to the right . . . you see, it is moving. And the color is different, it is not like dirty snow, it is much darker. It is moving all the time.

People . . . many people visiting us. Soon they will disappear behind Umivik."

At last! I could see something like tiny ants against the snow. They were obviously not seals or birds, they moved in a different way. When Navarana said she saw people, I was quite sure of it, but I would never have seen it myself. She had seen them with her naked eye long before I could discover them with my binoculars. But once I had finally seen them, she agreed to look through the glasses. She stared for a long time and at last she announced:

"It is possible that the travelers are white men."

I was getting impatient with her. "How do you know?" I asked her. "They are much too far away. You cannot possibly see what kind of people they are. Let me have a look."

They were still only dark spots on the ice. If they had not moved it would have been almost impossible to distinguish them.

"There are movements different from ours," Navarana answered calmly. "But what does a woman know! Use your good glasses and see for yourself. You'll see it more clearly than any woman can."

I did not follow her advice. I did not want to prove my ignorance. And I was never able to discover what she had seen to convince her that the black spots on the ice were white men.

On the way back to the tent I wondered about our visitors. Had our good ship *Cape York* been in trouble? No, that was out of the question. The man in charge, "Cape York Pete," was the best ice navigator in the world. He never got caught in the ice. Perhaps they were Eskimos from the north. They might have been in contact with my ship. *Cape York* might be icebound some place, and the Eskimos might be coming with mail and messages from "Cape York Pete."

All the Eskimos came running up the mountainside when they heard our news. And Navarana, of course, let me take all the credit. "One has seen people," she announced calmly while

I was shouting in my excitement. She explained to our friends just where her clever husband had discovered the visitors. They were easily seen with the naked eye now, but they were heading straight for Umivik and would soon be out of sight. They were clearly making for Saunders Island and our spring camp which faced the open sea. They would find all the food they needed in the depots we had left behind—meat and eider eggs and other delicacies.

We discussed the great news for a while. It was as good as the arrival of a ship, perhaps even better, the Eskimos felt. There might be news from the north, from friends and relatives. And they were all eager to meet the travelers.

"One might like to taste some eggs again," one of the young Eskimos remarked casually. "The sight of strangers brings to mind the eggs that are stored on Agpat [Saunders Island]."

"Agpat is a bad place to leave meat too long," said another. "How often one has left good supplies there, only to please the bears. Perhaps one left too much there in the spring."

"The travelers out there may have forgotten that kayaks may get ruined in the ice," Aviangernak mused. "Such travelers often forget to take along supplies for sewing and mending their kayaks. One might bring them what they need."

All the Eskimos were eager to make the trip to Saunders Island, but they knew that they had to wait for my decision. I had the only available wooden boat which could be pulled across the ice without being damaged when there was no open water. The kayaks might easily be cut to pieces by the ice and were of little use for such a trip. If I did not go to Saunders Island myself or refused to lend them my boat, some of them would probably go in their kayaks anyhow—a risky and strenuous expedition. In any case, many days would go by before they returned, and if the ship arrived in the meantime every hand would be needed for the unloading. On the other hand, if I went myself, "Cape York Pete" might turn up in my absence.

In the end my curiosity got the upper hand. I was reasonably sure that any ship coming into the fjord would be visible from Saunders Island and that I would be able to be back in time to meet it. I was perhaps even more curious than the Eskimos, for if Navarana was right the visitors were white men, and I would have to take care of them.

Finally I announced that we would use my boat for the trip but that we would take along one or two kayaks for the hunting on the way to the island. I uttered the decisive words with the proper indifference, and the Eskimos listened with an equal lack of apparent interest.

"It might be necessary to go along with Pita in order to bring back some walrus teeth left on the island," one of them said calmly.

"A leather bag was forgotten this spring when we left the island," said Uvdluriaq, my father-in-law. "It might be picked up again if there is an opportunity."

They all made similar casual statements, since none of them wanted to ask for permission to come along. If the request was refused, it would mean humiliation and ridicule. The more eager the Eskimos are, the more indifferent they appear.

I did not commit myself. I simply stated that it might be good to get some sleep. I knew, of course, that nobody would sleep, but I wanted to be left in peace for the trip back across the mountain, down the valley and finally over the swampy lowland. The trip could be made in a little more than half a day if one hurried. Once I had expressed my desire for sleep I would not have to be ashamed if it took me longer, if I walked slowly and rested on the way.

Our crossing from Thule did not call for any elaborate preparations, although it would not be an easy expedition. None of the women was allowed to come along. There were eight of us going, and the boat was not particularly suitable for the trip. It was a clumsy, heavy whaleboat with four pairs of oars. It would be no easy task to pull it any distance across the pack ice, but among the eight of us I thought we would manage. Three of the Eskimos brought their kayaks, and at first we did not see much of them. They paddled ahead of us searching for seals, or they served as scouts looking for open passages when the ice seemed to close in on us. Whenever it proved impossible to row the boat and we had to pull it up on the ice, the three of them were out of sight.

Old Mequsaq, my wife's grandfather, sat stolidly at the tiller and saw more with his one eye than the other four pairs of eyes together. He was a wise and honored man. We trusted him and knew that he would find the safest and quickest way through the ice. Sometimes he would keep us rowing when there did not seem to be any way out of the ice, sometimes he would stop us for a moment to confer with the men in the kayaks. Once in a while he had to admit that there was no alternative—we had to get up on the ice and pull the boat across until we found the next open channel.

We were only a few hours away from Thule when we caught the first seal, and the Eskimos, of course, wanted to eat it at once. If I had tried to protest I would only have spoiled their happy mood, and they would have lectured me on the advisability of eating the seal while it was still warm. The Eskimos are convinced that the sooner the animal is eaten after the killing, the more strength and energy it will give. After a solid meal of raw, warm meat one can go hungry for a long time and "the stomach will not get bored," as they express it. Anyhow it was a small seal; we could finish it up in one meal and would not have to carry a still heavier load.

The meal was quite a treat, since during the spring and summer, we had nothing but narwhale. It may be stored for any length of time and it is delicious as *niko,* or dried meat, but when it was fresh we always ate it raw.

The good meal made us lazy, but why should we hurry? The strangers might already have reached the island, but we would find them whenever we got there. The time of the ice breaking was near, however, and deep below us there was a hard, relentless pressure against the ice, although we could not see any movement. But suddenly, while we still dawdled over our meal, the ice floe on which we were resting broke in two. It happened so fast that old Mequsaq did not have time to get away. The rest of us jumped to our feet and ran over to the boat before the water separated us, but Mequsaq moved more slowly, and all at once he realized that there was no support for his left foot. Before he managed to step back there was none for his right foot either, and the old man was thrashing around in the icy water.

He did not utter a sound, but I could see a silent appeal in his eyes. I threw myself down by the edge of the water and grabbed him—but not before he had ducked once or twice. I pulled him safely back on the ice, and everybody laughed at the episode, including Mequsaq, who was dripping wet. It was out of the question to express any sympathy or to suggest that he should put on dry clothes. The summer day was reasonably warm, and in a day or two his clothes would be dry.

At last we broke up and launched the boat once more.

We were in a narrow channel, and before we could begin rowing there was suddenly no water to dip the oars into. With frightening speed the ice floes closed in on us, and we were lucky to save the boat before it was crushed by the screw ice. We put Mequsaq in the boat, since we had to move at a moment's notice because the screw ice was in violent movement all around us.

While we waited the ice seemed to grow around us. There was no noise, only an invisible relentless power beneath us. In a few seconds a tower of ice loomed above our heads, completely closing off our view. We no longer had to worry about the direction we were taking—our only concern was to save our lives. Samik, one of the men with a kayak, was making his way carefully across the ice to join us, carrying his small craft on his shoulder. Suddenly it was as if an unseen hand grabbed his kayak and pushed it under a block of ice the size of a small house. Samik did not move fast enough; probably the kayak had blocked his view. He wanted to save his craft and nearly lost his life in the attempt.

We had to ignore him for a moment while we struggled to rescue the boat, without which we would all be lost. When we looked at him again he was sprawled on his back, with one leg pinned under a mass of ice that moved closer to him like the foam on the crest of a wave. We ran and managed to pull him out from under the ice, but his leg was broken and his kayak was completely out of sight.

The screw ice seemed to boil around us, and we carried Samik back and lowered him into the boat. Mequsaq apparently drew new strength from this mishap, and as we could not carry both of them in the boat, he jumped out to help us, suddenly as strong and nimble on his feet as the rest of us.

After a while we could notice some sort of a system in the apparent chaos. The ice seemed to settle down in enormous stripes with narrow channels of open water between them. Only one such stripe moved at a time. After a while the stripe we were on calmed down and the movement traveled farther toward the shore. At the same time the whole mass of ice was moving out to sea, and each separate floe was spinning slowly around in the water like a merry-go-round. Several times there was open water all around our ice floe, but before we could move the boat and get it into the water the ice closed in again and piled up like a solid wall around us.

As soon as the ice wall receded, the floe that held us and the boat seemed frighteningly small. If we had not had a sick man to care for and a boat to hold onto in order to save our lives, we might have stopped to enjoy the splendor and beauty of this fantastic spectacle, the incredible power of the water hurling around icebergs like nutshells and shifting floes large enough to stop a ship and crush smaller craft.

The two kayaks we had left were thrown on top of the suffering Eskimo as the boat was tossed from side to side, no matter how hard we tried to keep it upright.

During the momentary lull we became aware of the wind and noticed the first clouds. A southwester was coming up, the prevailing wind in western Greenland. We could always tell a change in weather by looking at the two mountaintops behind Thule, the Pingos. Every morning we invariably looked up at the Pingos to see what kind of day it was going to be. Now the clouds gathered around them, indicating a strong southwesterly wind. The ice had already carried us beyond the mouth of the fjord, and now the wind began moving us north.

The southwester proved to be a blessing because it did not take long before we were close to the goal of our journey, Saunders Island.

Much of the ice had disappeared by now, and there was open water along the shore. We had no trouble rowing as the ice floes we came across were easy to get around, and we made good progress. Two men were waiting for us on the shore.

I could see at once that Navarana had been right—the strangers were not Eskimos. They were white men, and we were anxious to learn how and why they had come to Saunders Island, but to the Eskimos any show of haste would be unseemly. We made leisurely progress toward the strangers as I wondered who they could possibly be, what condition they were in and what assistance they would need.

Our visitors turned out to be five in number, not two. They had made camp quite a distance away on the shore, and these two had left their companions in order to climb the mountain and search for some birds. They had seen us on the ice and had been waiting impatiently for us.

They were all whalers who had been separated from their ship, we found out. They were stranded on Saunders Island, and their rowboat could take them no farther. The two men who met us on shore were Bill Rasa, the whaler's first mate, who was in command of the rowboat, and a Norwegian by the name of

Semundsen. He was a huge, blond man with an enormous beard.

I asked them first if the two of them were alone, and they explained that there were three more left behind in their camp farther up the coast. They were utterly exhausted and in need of rest. But above all they needed warm food, as they had nothing but raw seal meat to eat for a good many days.

They were all from the Scotch whaler *Horticula,* and they had lost their ship. It was the same old story: In their small rowboat they had left the mother ship and gone after the whales. Before they caught any, the fog set in—the terrible, heavy Arctic fog which can last for days. One can see the sunlight above the dense fog, and one can see the peculiar rainbow made by the ice crystals in the air. They had been helpless and could do nothing but wait.

In addition to Bill Rasa and Semundsen, they told me, there were three others—a Danish whaler by the name of Tom Olsen, a Portuguese by the name of Pablo, and Rockwell Simon, an American.

Semundsen and Rasa were in poor shape, and we made slow progress toward their camp as they told me the rest of their story. Left alone on a small ice floe, they had repaired the broken boat as best they could. The boat carried the usual tool chest, and somehow they had managed to rearrange and saw off enough wood to replace the broken sideboards. With great ingenuity and labor they had turned the boat into a smaller, clumsier craft which leaked like a sieve but could be kept afloat for a short while as long as three men kept bailing out water while the other two rowed. They would stay in the boat for nearly half an hour at a time before they had to get up on the ice again, and thus they had been drifting around helplessly.

At last they sighted the island in the distance. They had used their boat a few times to move from one ice floe to another in order to get closer to the distant shore, but they realized that they would never get there unless the ice carried them close enough. They had waited in a state of unbearable tension until Saunders Island was at long last within reach.

When they reached the shore the three other men had collapsed, but Bill Rasa and Semundsen had gone off in search of food. They had "heard" the bird mountain in the distance. There is always movement on such bird cliffs. Small and large pebbles and rocks, upset by the hundreds and hundreds of birds, start rolling down the cliffside, and the resulting avalanche can be heard far away. The rolling stones usually take some birds along on their way down. The birds get killed by the rocks and can be picked up at the bottom of the cliff. They are always freshly killed and can be eaten without danger, since they never remain on the spot for any length of time. It seems only a matter of minutes before foxes or the huge Arctic sea gulls pick them up. They appear to be on the lookout day and night; they rush to the spot so fast that there is usually a fight, with the fox most often carrying off the prize.

The two men had found two birds which I now offered to carry for them. They were tired enough to give them to me without a protest as we trudged along the shore. All my Eskimo friends came with me, of course, eager to help the strangers. After two hours of slow walking we reached the small camp and the three other men. One of them was livelier and smaller than the other two, and he got up to greet us:

"I am glad to see that there are other people in the world than the five of us," he said in a tired voice—and burst out laughing. The sound seemed loud and strange, and the man became embarrassed. He calmed down until suddenly his laughter turned into loud sobbing, and tears were running down his cheeks.

Tom Olsen was a giant of a man and did not act as if anything out of the ordinary had happened. He had been sound asleep when we turned up, and he greeted me like a long-lost friend. The last of the five was a middle-aged Portuguese, Pablo. He did not speak much English; in fact, he did not speak much at all, but from what little he said he seemed to be an experienced sailor who had come up to Greenland for many years.

The boat they had hauled on shore was in a sad state, but we could not help admiring their ingenuity. It had served them well even if it could not stay afloat for more than a few minutes. On their way across Baffin Bay they had had to be on the move constantly, changing from floe to floe as the ice broke up, and the craft had undoubtedly saved their lives. Now Bill Rasa agreed with me, however, that they had no further use for it. We cut it up and soon we had a roaring fire going. The five men gathered around it to keep warm while the Eskimos helped me prepare some food.

Once they had eaten and settled down by the bonfire, they all decided that the future was up to me. They gave me all responsibility and gladly put themselves under my command. I might have appreciated their touching confidence more if I had known what to do next. There were eight of us from Thule, in addition to the five men who could not talk with the Eskimos and who in their present state could not be counted on to provide any food for themselves. I had to take care of them all, and it might not be easy.

The Eskimos are masters at making a pleasant shelter with small means. They salvaged one half of the whaleboat which we did not yet need for firewood, turned it upside down and built a supporting wall of rocks around it. By extending the stone walls they made room enough for our five "guests" to stretch out under the boat where they were protected against the wind and the rain. The rest of us gathered around the bonfire trying to keep warm. Even if it was summer we were pretty far north and the sharp southwester lashing the rain in front of us was bitterly cold—the nastiest of all Arctic weather. We had been lucky for too long, and now the weather gods decided to make us pay for it.

The strong wind, more like a gale, brought the ice with it. The waters outside Saunders Island were soon completely blocked by ice as far as we could see. It was constantly churning and piling up, and the prospects were none too good. We could not get back to Thule before the ice cleared up.

We put my boat opposite the wrecked one and built a wall of rocks and turf between the two. Finally we put the mast crosswise from one boat to the other and hung the sail over it, weighing it down with rocks and large pieces of walrus meat to keep the violent wind from tearing it down.

We spent some hours building this elaborate house—always a pleasant task. In the Arctic I have sometimes spent hours preparing a good place to sleep, perhaps only to have no more than an hour or two left to sleep there, once the shelter was ready. The pleasure of making a shelter is often more valuable than the rest itself.

We had not planned on a long stay on the island and had brought no extra clothing—something we bitterly regretted during the many cold and rainy hours. Soon we ran out of wood, we did not have much left of the walrus, and our guests complained of the lack of tobacco, the first thing they had asked us for. In summer we had no tobacco until the first ship from the south turned up.

The gale continued, the rain never let up, and we were all impatient to get going, particularly the five whalers.

I had to explain my situation to them—that I lived alone with my Eskimo wife among the Eskimos in Thule. We would be very glad to take care of them and help them in any way we could, I assured them, but they had to realize that my wife who would be their hostess was an Eskimo—like every other living soul in Thule. And I warned them that they would have to treat the Eskimos the way Knud Rasmussen and I did—as their equals in every respect without any kind of discrimination or condescension.

Rockwell Simon, the American, answered for all of them. He was grateful for my assistance and hospitality, but although he had come to the Arctic to meet adventure he felt that he had had enough. He wanted to get home as soon as he could and would prefer to go south at once if I could lend them a boat. Rasa and the others agreed with him. They were in a hurry to return—if possible to their ship and if not, to their homes.

While we were still considering the best course of action, one of the Eskimos interrupted us:

"Sigdlartupok!" he cried jubilantly. "Change of weather, clearing up!"

He had been up in the mountains, and now we could see what he had discovered higher up. It did not look too promising, but the wind had died down. The rain was still pouring and the clouds seemed impenetrable, but there was one spot that appeared a little lighter.

The Eskimos made ready to break camp. They knew that the weather would be all right, and before long they had cleared up our shelter. The rain stopped and there was a pale glimpse of the sun. We finished our last meal of walrus soup and were ready to leave. The ice was still heavy, but we had no doubt that we would make it back to Thule now that the gale had changed to a sudden calm. We got the boat back in the icy water and somehow found room for everybody—the five strangers, my seven Eskimos, and myself.

The crossing took us more than twelve hours, but on the way the first hint of the warm southwest wind told us that the ice would soon again be on its way out of the fjord. We had been more often on the ice than in the water, and all of us had fallen into the icy fjord several times. When we entered the Thule harbor we were once more utterly exhausted, but the sight of our houses with the smoke coming up the chimney revived us. All our tiredness was forgotten when we saw the Eskimos standing on the Thule shore waiting for us—the children down by the edge of the water, the women in a group a little farther back, and the men at a proper dignified distance where they would not seem too curious.

As my wife, Navarana was the hostess in charge, and she

handled this sudden invasion with ease. The only problem was to supply the guests with the necessary clothing; otherwise their presence caused no immediate complication. There was food enough, and even if we did not have beds for them all, we had a large attic where the five whalers would be comfortable with polar-bear furs and caribou skins to keep them warm.

While I set about at once preparing for the long trip to Thom Island the five guests enjoyed their long-needed rest. The Eskimos were all disappointed because the whalers did not speak "the human tongue," as they called their own language, but they visited us every day and crowded into our small house, staring at the guests and asking questions about them.

The five whalers did not know their way about, and I provided a special guide for them, the young orphaned boy whom I had taken under my wing—Qupagnuk. Although he was still a youngster he was a master at handling the dogs and would see to it that the strangers did not get into any trouble with the huskies. The boy was originally called Ungarpaluk and was used for odd jobs by everybody in Thule. He had been left to fend for himself at a very early age. He was dressed in a curious collection of clothes. Someone might give him an old pair of kamiks, another would donate a worn-out pair of bearskin pants, and the boy was always so full of lice that nobody would have him in his house.

The boy did not care. He had a wonderful time and was everybody's friend.

If our five guests were at all tempted to get into trouble it was with Aloqisaq.

Aloqisaq was put to work preparing the skins and furs we needed to equip the whalers for the trip south. They all had to have new leather kamiks and pants, and Navarana was in charge of the sewing.

"It might be a good thing to have Aloqisaq stay in our house until the visitors leave," Navarana told me. "She has nobody to look after in her own house, and she can stay up nights with the sewing."

Aloqisaq was delighted with the arrangement, but she had a different program in mind for her nights.

"Remember that I am a widow," she smiled. "I have to be satisfied with the men who visit me occasionally, and I'll be glad to take care of the white men. I want to show them true hospitality!"

But Navarana was a firm guardian of virtue—not so much for moral as for practical considerations. She needed the widow to do the sewing, not to entertain the visitors at night.

I had made up my mind to take the whalers down to Thom Island, where we might be fortunate enough to meet the whaling vessels—if not *Horticula,* at least one of the others that might take the five men south.

With the five whalers and myself already in the party, I decided to take no more than three Eskimos along. The first choice was inevitably Mequsaq.

I discussed the second choice with Navarana and we agreed to pick Kraungak, an old childhood friend of Navarana's—the one who had cut off his toe. The third man I picked was Itukusuk.

With this crew I was confident that I could get to Thom Island. Mequsaq would be at the tiller, and the three of us at the oars. The five whalers were, of course, also used to handling an open boat. I had sails, but they would not be of much use because there would be too much ice for any convenient sailing even if the wind should be favorable.

When the time for departure approached, it was obvious that some of the whalers did not mind their stay in Thule at all. They had recovered sufficiently to have strong desires beyond mere survival, and they had evidently enjoyed the companionship of Aloqisaq the widow. She knew how to please them, and although some of the younger Eskimos were deprived of her pleasant company they did not mind this sacrifice on the altar of hospitality.

"The white men are strong and have great demands," Aloqi-saq explained. "Their long absence from women makes it our duty to pity them and be helpful to them!"

As we made ready to leave, Bill Rasa and Semundsen tried to thank Navarana for her hospitality and help, but an Eskimo woman does not want any gratitude. It would only embarrass her if the men should publicly acknowledge that the help of a mere woman had in any way been needed. She calmly urged them to get going and hurriedly gave their equipment a last-minute inspection.

When everything was checked I casually mentioned to Nava-rana that the weather seemed good for a little boat trip. That was the only good-by. The Eskimos feel that any sign of emotion may be a bad omen for the trip. Instead of saying good-by, Navarana smiled to me and said that she suddenly had a great desire for fresh salmon. She would go up to the lake behind Thule and try her luck, she told us, and while we boarded the boat she and the other women walked up the hill without a backward glance.

The men we left behind in Thule pretended not to notice our departure—as if we were just crossing the harbor. The only person to say good-by and wish us good luck was Aloqisaq and the Eskimos roared with laughter as she was left behind on the beach.

"Poor Aloqisaq," one of them exclaimed. "She forgets her manners because she is afraid she'll never again invite a white man to her bed!"

In Wolstenholme Sound outside Thule a breeze from the north enabled us to put up the sail and take it easy on the first lap of our long journey while we made things as comfortable as possible in the boat.

At first we sailed easily enough and made rapid progress. But then the ice began to close in all around us. Whenever Mequsaq saw some kind of channel ahead we had to row for all we were worth to get there before the ice closed in again. And once we moved too fast. The boat shot ahead with such speed that it crashed against the ice, and the kayaks caught the full force of the blow. One was ruined completely and had to be thrown away. The other was badly damaged and could not be used before it had a new cover. And this would have to wait until we reached Cape York, because preparing the skins for a kayak cover and sewing it is a job for women.

"What did I say!" exclaimed Thomas Olsen. "I told you we should have brought Aloqisaq along with us!"

He had been unable to forget the hospitable widow in Thule, but we reassured him that we would soon meet other women in Cape York who would be able to repair the kayak for us. And the Cape York women were hospitable, too, Mequsaq promised him. They might do more than repair a kayak in order to please the white men.

As we moved slowly south the floes and icebergs got so large that they hit bottom before they reached shore and thus left a channel of open water close to the beach.

By now we had very little food left and our evening meal consisted of seal fat and tea, but I think we were all too tired to care. And we were quite glad to spend the next day in Kangek, resting and stocking up on food. We caught a few of the large Arctic sea gulls and some rabbits.

I was glad that there was nobody in the settlement when we passed by Sarfarik, and I was glad to leave Parker Snow Bay behind. Although the wind was not yet very strong it brought mild weather, and that night we reached the famous Agpat cave, the halfway mark between Thule and Cape York. On Conical Rock just outside the cave we caught several eider ducks and had a luxurious evening meal. Before settling down for the night Itukusuk and Kraungak set out on an inspection tour and soon brought back the report that there were strangers in the neighborhood. They had found well-stocked meat depots which had been built since the last frost. The strangers could be only a few hours away.

"We are likely to meet Kridtluqtoq tomorrow," Itukusuk announced.

"Why Kridtluqtoq?" I asked. "How can you tell who has built the depots?"

Kraungak explained that every man builds in his own peculiar way and might as well leave his name behind because his identity is clearly revealed by the depots.

We broke up early next morning to see if they were right. We seemed to inch our way down, and Mequsaq made us follow the shore as closely as possible. He had the fear of the old kayak man for the open water. If we forced him, he would reluctantly cross a bay or an inlet, but when we did not watch he followed every small indentation, every zigzag in the shore line.

Some hours beyond Agpat we came across a small camp, just as the Eskimos had predicted. In a narrow valley with a steep glacier, Kridtluqtoq had settled down, and I had the impression that he had recently moved away from Cape York to this remote and lonely spot where nobody ever stayed. We did not ask him why he was there, and all he volunteered was that he had obviously chosen his campsite wisely, since it was honored by a visit of white people. This rather far-fetched explanation of his choice sounded more like an apology to his wife, Arnaluk, who was still young and gay and good-looking. She probably hated living in such a lonely place.

They had two small children with them, and Kridtluqtoq had brought along old Semigaq.

I was surprised to find something odd in Kridtluqtoq's manner. He seemed to be on his guard, and if I had not known him so well I would have said that he was afraid of something At first I thought it was simply the strain of this sudden meeting with his beautiful wife's first husband. (Admiral Peary had given her away to Kridtluqtoq while Itukusuk was away with Dr. Cook.)

I told the whalers about the situation, and they were eager to see how the main actors in this Arctic triangle would carry it off. The men were too tactful to refer to the old conflict, but old Semigaq had no such restraint. She was bursting with excitement and eager to fan the flame. When the men had greeted each other politely she was quick to speak up:

"In a dream last night strange things were predicted, and now they seem to come true! A man has come accompanied by strong friends in order to get his woman back. Since she has proved herself able to bear sons there is likely to be a fight in this valley tonight!"

This insolent challenge went unanswered by the men, but Arnaluk seemed pleased and flattered by the prospect of a fight between her two lovers. She studiously ignored them and pretended to find the view particularly fascinating as if she had never before seen the icy fjord.

The Eskimos were getting tense, but Rockwell Simon, who did not realize the seriousness of the situation, pointed to Arnaluk and made some remarks to the other whalers. Arnaluk took this as a sign that she was now the center of attraction. She felt compelled to follow Semigaq's lead and fan the flames of desire still further.

"One is not used to being the only woman among so many men," she said with a bashfulness that was not entirely convincing, since she was obviously enjoying herself. And then, with a quick look at her two men: "But nobody here bothers to notice a mere woman, of course, particularly such an ugly one as I!" And turning to Semigaq: "Such great men will hardly notice whether a woman is here or not. She might just as well not be here."

To her obvious regret there was still no reaction from the men, but her bold words demanded action. Reluctantly she turned to the tent and disappeared, followed by the excited old woman. In the silence that followed I tried to relieve the tension by telling Kridtluqtoq about the ordeal of the whalers and the long journey ahead of us to Thom Island. Kridtluqtoq was an experienced traveler, and from his trips with Peary he had learned some English. He told us that he would have liked to go with us across Melville Bay and that he was sorry he was encumbered with a family he could not leave behind. He asked us to stay overnight in his camp and not leave until high tide the following morning. He had recently come up from Cape York and assured us that the ice would not cause us much trouble from there on.

When we had finished the substantial evening meal he served us and there was still no hint of a fight between the two Eskimos, the whalers asked me if they could spend the night in the tent in order to get a comfortable rest for once. Since the main attraction in the tent obviously was Arnaluk and not the prospect of sound sleep, I told Rasa instead to take his men down to the boat and spend the night there.

Kridtluqtoq seemed more relaxed once we were alone, but the Eskimos were still waiting to see what would happen between the two men. I tried my luck as a peacemaker.

"There is a pain in my ears," I told Kridtluqtoq. "They still hurt from the stupid words of your old woman."

Kridtluqtoq looked quickly at Itukusuk but said nothing. Mequsaq and Kraungak were still apprehensive until Itukusuk finally broke the silence and decided the issue:

"It gives me cause to wonder, Pita, that you can still feel pain. There must be a long memory in your head. Even if one could understand the idle chatter of an old woman, her words are long since forgotten!"

Once more the good man had preferred to keep the peace. He was not going to fight for Arnaluk, and we could all relax. I mentioned to Kridtluqtoq my surprise at finding him in this lonely spot. But he had been wise to stay by himself since such a great hunter never left any catch for other people, I said, intending to flatter him. He was known to kill anything that crossed his way.

He did not like my words and looked at me nervously as if he had found some hidden meaning in them.

The next morning ice conditions had improved greatly. Kraungak climbed up the mountain for a good view and told us that there was open water or at least ice-free channels all the way down the sound. We said good-by to Kridtluqtoq and his women and left with the high tide.

Our host was still nervous, and I noticed that he never let go of his gun as long as we were on shore. He did not relax before we had all boarded the boat, and I wondered if he was still afraid that Itukusuk had designs on his wife. Many months went by before I finally discovered the reason for his strange attitude —and the explanation was much more dramatic than I had imagined.

Admiral Peary had great faith in Kridtluqtoq because of his many outstanding qualities: he was a good traveler, he had great stamina, knew some English, and was exceptionally good-natured and helpful. When Peary made the final preparations for his dash to the North Pole he put Kridtluqtoq in charge of the Eskimos going with Professor Ross Marvin to establish food depots for the return trip. This team under Professor Marvin had to go up to the last outpost before the final journey into the unknown and leave vital supplies there to keep Peary and his companions going on the way back from the Pole.

Professor Marvin was not well liked by his three companions —Kridtluqtoq and Aqioq, who were both seasoned travelers, and Inukitsorkpaluk, a much younger Eskimo (and cousin of Kridtluqtoq) who made up in strength and toughness for his lack of experience.

Many times the three Eskimos wished they had been in another team, but they realized that Marvin himself was also unhappy on the trip. He had no one to talk to. He did not understand the Eskimo language, and Kridtluqtoq had only a limited and strictly utilitarian vocabulary in English. Whenever the Eskimos talked together and laughed, Marvin would ask what they were laughing at. Since Kridtluqtoq was unable to translate he shrugged his shoulders and told the poor American that it was a trifle too unimportant to be translated.

On the return trip they ran into several fresh wide cracks in the ice. They were usually covered, since it was extremely cold, but the ice was not always thick enough to carry them. Marvin knew nothing about the dangers of such fresh ice. A few times the Eskimos stopped and explained to him that it would be dangerous to continue and that they had to either detour or wait until the ice was more solidly frozen. Marvin got angry and insisted that the ice was strong enough. He was convinced that the Eskimos were simply lazy, and he urged them on with angry words. When they had their first argument Marvin finally gave in, but the next time he wanted to demonstrate to them that they could not possibly judge the safety of the ice simply by looking at the color. He left the Eskimos behind and walked boldly out on the black ice. He had walked only a few steps when he crashed through.

The Eskimos pulled him out without difficulty. Marvin did not say anything further about the ice. He was satisfied to let the Eskimos build an igloo and remain there until they could proceed safely. The following day they ran into more fresh ice, but Marvin had apparently not learned anything from his experience. Once more he impatiently urged the Eskimos on until Kridtluqtoq found a safe passage by detouring the crack, and Marvin reluctantly accepted the compromise.

They quarreled again several times during the day, and there was not much left of the team spirit that night—when Inukit-sorkpaluk fell sick. He could not digest his food and was very weak in the morning. Kridtluqtoq knew that he would be all right in a day or two and explained it to Marvin, but he refused to stay over. He ordered the Eskimos to let the sick man stay behind. They could leave his food rations with him in the igloo, he said, and as soon as he regained his strength he could follow their tracks. If he did not recover . . . well, then he had to die alone in the igloo. And since the man would be unable to handle a dog team Marvin would take his sled from now on.

At first the Eskimos could not believe that he was serious. When Marvin began loading the sled of the sick man, they were finally compelled to realize that he meant what he said.

Kridtluqtoq did not waste another word. He walked over to his own sled, pretended to rearrange his load, and when Marvin did not watch him he got out his gun. Without further argument he shot Marvin through the head.

The Eskimo left the white man where he fell. He calmly returned to the igloo and told the other two that a man was going to be left behind in this camp—but a white man, and not an Eskimo. They decided to tell the Americans that the professor in his ignorance had tried to cross dangerous ice, had plunged through and drowned before the Eskimos could help him. It might well have happened that way, they assured themselves as they tied Marvin's gun and scientific equipment to the body, made a hole in the fresh ice and watched the weighted body sink rapidly.

The three Eskimos settled down in the igloo, fell asleep at once, and slept all through the day. When they awoke they had a substantial meal, eating more than Marvin had ever allowed them to, and fell asleep once more. In the morning a blizzard raged outside and they had to stay over another day. The rest and food gave Inukitsorkpaluk new strength, and as soon as the storm abated they were ready to leave.

When they approached the ship at last, they had to honor the dead man and announce his death in advance. As soon as the ship was in sight Kridtluqtoq began beating his dogs to call attention to their arrival. When the Eskimos in the distance could be seen running out on the ice they knew that they had been discovered and the three of them sat down on their sleds with their backs to the people who came to meet them. In this way they made it clear that someone in the team had died.

The man in charge of the base camp in Peary's absence was Bob Bartlett, "The Great Captain." He asked them at once what had happened to Professor Marvin. Kridtluqtoq spoke for the three, since he was the oldest of them and also because he was the one who had saved his cousin from being left behind on the ice. He explained to Bartlett that Marvin had insisted on crossing the thin new ice in spite of numerous warnings from the Eskimos. At last he had fallen through and before the Eskimos could reach him the poor man had drowned.

Bartlett was very angry with them and refused to believe their story. A man falling through the ice would not sink so quickly, he insisted, and he accused them of having caused Marvin's death deliberately. He knew, of course, that the dead man had not been especially popular with the Eskimos.

The Eskimos had all been told the true story, and they agreed among themselves that Kridtluqtoq should stick to his official version. If he changed his story and explained to "Piuli" that they had shot Marvin in order to save Inukitsorkpaluk, the white men would say that the Eskimos no longer knew the truth and then they would no longer visit this part of the country.

Kridtluqtoq was praised by all the Eskimos for the brave way in which he had saved his cousin.

Soon the triumphant Peary returned with his companions and told of his successful trip to the "Navel of the Earth." He left Greenland shortly afterward, never to return to the Arctic, and the truth about Marvin's death remained Kridtluqtoq's secret for a number of years.

I did not know all this when I met Kridtluqtoq that fall on our way to Thom Island with the five whalers. I was only bewildered by his odd manner. He seemed nervous and restless as long as the strangers were around, and he kept his gun close at hand. The poor man had obviously been afraid that the white men were going to take revenge. He must have been greatly relieved to see the last of us as we went on our way down the sound toward Cape York.

We reached the wide open sea outside Cape York where winds and currents are always unpredictable and treacherous. A sudden violent gust had shifted the boom, and we could hear splintering wood as it hit the water on the leeside. The heavy boat settled down so the water came pouring over the side. Even after the boat righted itself every wave drenched us and added to the water we were desperately trying to bail out. The sea that had been so calm minutes before was now churning viciously all around us. There was no more solid ice in sight, but there were enough floes to make it dangerous to race as fast as we were going. Mequsaq clung to the tiller, but he had not the faintest idea how to handle the boat. As long as he was there, we were at the complete mercy of the wind.

It was my boat, I was technically in command, and I thought that I had better take over, although I was no expert sailor myself. The wind seemed to increase every minute, and while I was still debating with myself what to do Thomas Olsen suddenly and dramatically relieved me of further responsibility.

Seemingly in one single movement the otherwise quiet Dane moved from his seat, pushed old Mequsaq aside, took the old man's seat and grabbed the tiller. Just looking at his sturdy hand and the way it took hold of the tiller gave me confidence. He sat there as solid as a rock, and it was obvious that here was a man who was used to being in command.

In a booming voice he ordered us about, and without the slightest hesitation or indecision he told each man what to do. Automatically I obeyed as he roared at me to let go of the mainsail line. Keeping up the sail with a broken boom in that terrific wind was sheer suicide, but no one had thought of doing anything about it. I let go of the line, but the mainsail would not come down. We had strengthened the mast with a couple of guy wires, and the canvas got entangled in them. Willing hands were ready to obey his angry orders and somehow got the sail out of the mess before it could cause any more trouble.

The jib was being whipped by the wind and looked as if it

would be torn to shreds any moment, but Olsen got the boat under control, came about and sailed with the wind as long as the boat was so dangerously low in the water.

The gale was of incredibly short duration. It disappeared as suddenly as it had come, and when the wind calmed down Olsen told us to hoist the mainsail again. We had to get it up fast if we wanted to stay afloat, he warned us. He alone had realized that the boat was leaking badly. During the storm we must have been hit by an ice floe which had broken one of the clinker boards, and the water was still coming in as fast as we could bail it out. We covered the damaged part with hunks of seal meat and let two men sit on top of them. In the meantime Bill Rasa and Semundsen had managed somehow to splice the splintered boom. We got the mainsail up, and with Olsen in command we headed for the cape so many sailors had used for a landmark, the profile that is always etched in the memory—Cape York.

The sun was low behind the mountains when the dogs in Cape York discovered us. They set up a concert of howls that brought all the Eskimos from their tents to welcome us as we approached the shore. I was surprised to see nothing but women in the settlement—although the sight of them seemed most welcome to some of my whaler friends. Apparently all the men were out seal hunting, and the only male left was poor Usukodark, who was deaf and dumb. He was the most useless man in the tribe, since his double handicap kept him from all hunting.

The seal hunter must be able to hear the animal approaching the breathing hole, and he must not make any sound to scare away the seal. Usukodark could not tell whether he was making any sounds or not, and he was unable to hear the seal. He could not be used in a kayak, since he did not realize that the sound of his oar hitting the water might be enough to put the game to flight. The poor man could not even join the children in their rabbit hunts. Usukodark made so much noise that the rabbits were warned off long before he could catch sight of them.

Now that all the men in Cape York had gone away Usukodark was left behind, as usual, and he was delighted to be the host and the man in charge. He motioned to the women to bring us food, and he made some incoherent sounds which the women strangely enough understood and quickly obeyed. They lit a bonfire outside their tents and served us an overwhelming meal. Due to the presence of so many white men, the women even obeyed him when he motioned them to retire and not offend the great guests by sitting down to eat with them.

We had to stay overnight in the settlement—to the delight of the whalers and the women of Cape York. I was determined, however, to leave the next morning no matter what urgent reasons Pablo and Semundsen and the rest of them might find for staying on.

The whalers were most reluctant to leave in the morning, but I got them together. They had to say good-by to the hospitable women, and we were off once more. We were already a distance away from land when I suddenly noticed that Usukodark had casually settled down with us in the boat. I wanted to return to get rid of the poor man, but he protested so vigorously in his own peculiar way that I gave in.

After a few days' easy traveling we were once more surrounded by moving, cracking ice. Just then, Usukodark saw a seal and got wildly excited. We were tired and had no need for another seal, but he would not give up. If we would not kill it for him, very well—he would do it himself.

He ran up to me—his good friend Pita who always spoiled him—and grabbed my gun. In his sign language he explained that he wanted to shoot the seal, and to humor him I gave him a couple of cartridges. He had never fired a gun before, but he had seen others do it and apparently was confident that he could do as well.

He walked off and we forgot about him. Once again all our attention was focused on the ice. The wide rift which we had crossed with so much trouble closed again. The ice was rumbling and groaning all around us; the pattern changed; existing channels disappeared; new ones opened up. One of these new rifts approached our boat, and we had to interrupt our meal to pull the craft further back on the ice and throw all our belongings into it before they disappeared in the water. We slaved over the heavy boat and did not remember Usukodark until there was a thunderous noise from his direction.

Heavy ice from the south was pressing relentlessly forward, pushing small and large floes in front of it. Some of them were piled up in a horizontal position before they crashed down again. We saw Usukodark outlined against the backdrop of such an ice floe. He could, of course, hear nothing. He was solely concentrating on the seal he was going to shoot. We saw him lift the gun to his shoulder, his back to the ice mass towering above him. My dog stood next to him, equally intent on the animal in front of them. Instinctively we shouted to him at the top of our voices, forgetting that the poor man could not hear us.

There was nothing we could do, the tragedy was unavoidable —although another man could have saved his life simply by running a few steps. He gave us a look over his shoulder and saw us waving to him. Apparently he thought we were cheering him, praising his ability as a hunter. He gave us a happy, proud smile and turned back to the seal. That was the last we saw of him. The ice mass crashed down. One moment he was there with the gun to his shoulder—the next there was only ice. When we reached the spot there was nothing but water where Usukodark and the dog had been.

Usukodark probably died at the happiest moment in his life. He drowned as a proud hunter with a gun to his shoulder.

Mequsaq had been helpless all by himself. He was now busy trying to save all the equipment we had left in the boat while the ice was slowly but surely enveloping it. The entire rear of the boat was covered, the ice moved forward, imperceptibly but with relentless pressure. There was nothing we could do to stop it. When we reached the boat, or what little was left of it above the ice, Mequsaq had saved most of our clothes, food and equipment.

"An old man could do very little alone," Mequsaq apologized, and smiled. He was not greatly upset. He was a fatalist; he took things as they came, and he had often before in his life been stranded on drifting ice without a boat. Most of us had not, but we tried to take it as graciously as Mequsaq.

"Well," Semundsen sighed. "We are right back where we started when you found us—except that now we don't even have a boat!"

I decided I would try to take us first to the only island close by—Bryant Island, an isolated dot in Melville Bay, hardly more than a single huge rock standing straight up from the ice. We would be safe there until we formed a better idea of the weather and ice conditions. I explained my plan to the others and told them that I thought we should split our forces. We might have to walk for hours through the ice field before we reached the island, and I felt we would do better if we walked in three separate groups rather than all nine of us together.

I decided to keep my wife's grandfather with me on this hike, and asked Thomas Olsen to join us. Bill Rasa and Pablo would go with Kraungak, and Semundsen and Rockwell Simon would team up with Itukusuk. Traveling in this manner, we had one Eskimo in each group. We would stay fairly close together, I explained, but we would obviously have to take different routes from time to time, and the two white men in each group should stick with the Eskimo.

Finally we divided all our belongings, leaving behind the things that were useless or too heavy to carry. Each group had a makeshift toboggan consisting of sealskin and pulled along with lines taken from the boat. On these toboggans we piled as much as they would carry. The rest we made up into bundles that we carried on our backs. The harpoons, although heavy and clumsy, served us as walking sticks, very useful to test the ice as we went along.

We kept walking for several hours, but the ice was by no means like a skating rink. For a few minutes at a time it might be level, but most of the time we had to travel across rough screw ice, climb uphill and slide or crawl downhill. Once in a while we had to scale icebergs so steep and high that we thought we would never make it. And every now and then we had to walk around open water—if we discovered it in time. Sometimes thin, new ice that was not solid enough to carry our weight would cover the water. Twice Olsen stepped into slushy snow and ice that turned out to have no foundation, and plunged into the water below. We were right behind him and got him out before he suffered any ill effect—except for his soaking-wet clothes which we could do nothing about.

As we came closer to Bryant Island we had more and more trouble with the water. We were forced to make long detours to work our way around wide rifts, and soon the solid ice changed into loosely packed ice floes growing smaller and smaller in size as we approached the island. We were in for one more disappointment before the hike was over. Between the ice and the shore there was open water, several hundred feet across. We had been jumping from floe to floe for the last hour; now it looked as if we were finally going to be stopped by water, but Itukusuk took command.

He was an experienced ferryman, and he did not hesitate to take us across on an ice floe. All nine of us gathered together on one floe that was barely large enough to hold us and began peacefully rowing across. The sun was very low on the horizon, it was probably close to midnight, and we were utterly exhausted but in surprisingly good spirits. I think we all had a feeling of pride in our accomplishment, our successful crossing to the island.

Rockwell was in top form. He sat quietly for a long time, lost in contemplation of the Arctic scenery, and finally he sighed deeply and said:

"This is even better than Arizona. And I always thought Arizona was the most beautiful spot in the world!"

The final crossing was strenuous, but compared to the rest of our long journey from Saunders Island it was an anticlimax. We split up in three groups as we had the previous day, but we moved with considerably less speed—partly because we were in poor condition but mainly because of our feet. The many hours on the ice had ruined our kamiks. Some of them had sizable holes in their soles. Every now and then we had to stop and cut out small pieces of sealskin to put inside the kamiks. They protected the feet for a while, but they never lasted long and could not keep the water out. They had to be changed constantly, and all this patchwork on the kamiks delayed us.

Once again we were stopped by water, an open rift stretching in both directions as far as we could see and much too wide to jump across. The ice was thick and smooth, the edges sharp and clean, with no small ice floes broken off to be used as a ferry. Our goal was clearly visible within a few hours' walking distance, but we seemed to be stymied.

Farther out in Melville Bay the rift probably ended in open water. How far it reached we had no way of telling; there were no icebergs we could climb for a better view. If we had to detour in the hope of getting to the end of the rift we might have to walk for days. We might also stay where we were until the rift closed again, but that might take hours or days and we had no assurance that the ice would remain stationary. We might be carried with the ice back to Cape York!

Suddenly Kraungak called out to me. He was running along the rift with Itukusuk, and when I caught up with them I realized that they had sighted a polar bear. I could not quite share their excitement but was nevertheless ready for a bear hunt. It would at least make us forget our predicament for a while.

The bear was on the other side of the wide rift, beyond the range of our one remaining gun. The huge animal had seen us and was very curious, like most bears. The only way to lure it within range was to take advantage of this curiosity, as I had done so often before. I flopped down on the ice close to the water, waved my arms, and kicked my legs wildly. The bear stopped at once, watched me for a few minutes and decided to investigate further this strange creature on the ice. Gently it slipped into the water and began swimming across the rift. Apparently afraid that I would try to escape if I became aware of the approaching animal, the bear swam slowly, mostly under-water and practically without a sound.

At last Itukusuk could wait no longer. When the bear sur-faced for the last time the Eskimo sent a bullet right through its head. Never have I seen a bear with such shocked astonishment so clearly expressed in its face, and we could not help laughing as the proud animal sank. In a moment it came up again, float-ing, like all dead bears. This one was a very fat specimen and was high in the water.

The sight of the floating animal gave me a great idea, prob-ably the only good one I had on the entire journey. We did not yet have to admit defeat. The polar bear might ferry us across the rift!

I did not tell my friends what I had in mind. I asked them quickly to gather our belongings which they had scattered all over the ice when we were stopped by the rift. Kraungak brought his harpoon, and I used it to pull the dead bear close to the ice.

We still had the two oars we had used for our makeshift toboggans. I now put one on each side of the bear, tied the front and hind legs of the bear to the oars, and thus had a fairly stable "ferry."

When I had completed these preliminaries I motioned to the others to stand aside, pushed the bear halfway out in the rift, and stepped back a few yards from the edge to gather enough speed. I started running before the others realized what I planned to do, took off from the edge with all my strength—

and for once thanked the Lord for my long legs. I landed with one foot on the floating bear and hurtled off again, the wildest jump I ever made.

I stumbled on the ice, rolled over several times, but I made it without touching water. When I got to my feet the others were cheering me.

Itukusuk was the first one to follow me. The bear sank deeper under the weight, but it carried him and I got him safely across. When he jumped off he was soaking wet up to the hips, but I was vastly relieved to have at least one companion—and an Eskimo is used to being wet.

The oldest white man among us, Thomas Olsen, was next to cross over. While the others continued chopping through the ice, he calmly began undressing! When he had removed every stitch of clothing and stood naked in the snow he bundled up his clothes, held them tightly on his shoulder with one arm, and jumped on the bear ferry. Clinging to the neck of the bear with his free arm, he shouted to us to pull as fast as we could. The crossing did not take very long, but he was half-frozen when we pulled him up on the ice on our side and put him down on a sealskin to keep his feet warm and dry. He quickly dressed and assured us calmly that he was now really warm for the first time in days.

Rockwell Simon was ready in his birthday suit with all his clothes on his shoulder. Again we pulled, but were interrupted by a wild shout from Itukusuk. The Eskimo had used his eyes while all the rest of us were watching the ferry, and he roared with laughter as he looked at the rift a little farther out. While we were frantically trying to complete the crossing the rift had closed again a few yards away from us.

We were furious because we had not had the patience to wait, but we laughed with relief—and promptly forgot about Rockwell Simon, who was still clinging to the bear halfway across. We watched the other four men walking down to the covered passage until Rockwell screamed at us. As soon as we stopped pulling the line the ferry sank still deeper and the poor man was just about going under when I began pulling again. The water reached up to his neck, and he held his clothes on top of his head. As soon as he was close enough I relieved him of the bundle on his head. I meant well, but the immediate result was that Rockwell lost his precarious balance and plunged into the water.

When we pulled him up his naked body inevitably scraped the sharp ice. When he finally stood up he was bleeding from cuts on his chest and stomach, hips and thighs. They were only surface cuts, but they must have hurt terribly in the icy air, and he looked quite a sight.

The poor man swore and cursed. He threatened us with the most vicious retaliation for leaving him in the water, and he was so infuriated that he forgot to put on his clothes. Naked and bleeding, he danced around on the ice, shouting and screaming at us. He became even wilder when I suggested that he put on his clothes before he froze to death.

"That's none of your damned business," he yelled. "I'll get dressed when I'm good and ready!"

I could not help laughing at his helpless fury and his refusal to dress. The others joined me, and after a while even Rockwell realized the humor of the situation. He howled with laughter while we helped him to get dressed. In a few minutes we were joined by the others, who had calmly detoured and walked across the ice while we nearly lost our lives in the water. As soon as we had skinned and cut up the bear we were ready to cover the final distance to Thom Island without further interruption.

We were triumphant when we stepped ashore. We felt as if we were already in safe harbor with all our troubles behind us, although we had no good reason to believe that we would be any better off on the island, or that any ship would call for us. My only thought was a certain satisfaction because we had accomplished the seemingly impossible: losing a boat in the middle of Melville Bay and crossing safely on the ice in the month of September when the sea should normally be ice-free. I do not think it had ever been done before, and I doubt if anyone has ever done it since.

After many days of waiting a ship finally arrived and we said good-by to the five whalers. To tell the truth, I was not too unhappy to see the last of them.

Love and Marriage

One of the most difficult things for anyone to grasp is that sexual morality and family law anywhere in the world can be different from our own without being necessarily degrading or evil. The result is that such morality is seldom described calmly or objectively. One of Freuchen's great contributions is that he wrote about Eskimo traditions and behavior not only with good humor and from a wealth of personal experience but with great understanding and sympathy, too.

The girl he left behind in Denmark, whom he mentions so briefly in his discussion of family structure and morals, was Michelle Erichsen, a lovely young woman who had been genuinely helpful in getting the Freuchen-Rasmussen partnership launched successfully. In their later correspondence, Peter had been encouraged to hope that she would be willing and able to share his life in Greenland, although he was careful never to urge her. At last in one letter she said she actually was sailing on the little schooner which brought supplies to Thule.

Only after he sailed part way across Melville Bay to meet the ship at Saunders Island, where he found the whalers, did he learn that she had changed her mind. Much later her awkward letter in which she said that at the last moment she could not face the prospect of Arctic life reached him at Thule. In his heart he had known it was expecting too much of a gently reared Danish girl to embark on such an adventure, he said once, but that did not cushion the blow at the time.

Whether or not this rejection led him to become more of an Eskimo than ever—readers can judge for themselves from this ac-

111

*count of what followed—his acceptance of Arctic life became vir-
tually complete. His own marriage somewhat later was a singularly
successful one, and the wisdom of his wife gave him an even keener
appreciation of the people of whom he had grown so fond. One
may mention here that they had two children, and it is perhaps
significant that their father gave them both Eskimo names. His
daughter, Pipaluk, has become Denmark's popular writer of children's stories, and his son, Mequsaq, was named for Navarana's
grandfather.*

Family Structure and Morals

Life is so hard for the Eskimos, and the different chores they
must perform are so specialized, that each man must always
have one woman to take care of his skins, his clothes and his
food. Through necessity as well as an ancient custom, which
in many cases amounts to a taboo, all work is rigorously divided
between man and woman. Even so, both of them have plenty
to do.

The man has the more heroic tasks of fighting the polar bear,
harpooning the fierce walrus or outsmarting the tricky seal.
Sometimes he must endure the long wait at the seal's blowhole
for many hours during the cold nights. In the springtime, when
the sun is in the sky day and night, the man must seek out every
opportunity to catch game. Not only must daily needs be taken
care of, but meat caches must be built and filled for the coming
winter. So when the weather permits, he hunts continually,
sleeping and resting as little as possible, wandering around in
the open with the dog team.

The woman with her children and her needlework stays at
home. She has to scrape the animal skins and prepare them
while they are still fresh. She sews the clothes of the entire
family, cooks and keeps the house warm. Also, meat must be
laid out on the sunbaked rods and dried for traveling provisions. The man cannot sit there looking out for the birds

that come and want their share of it: this is the woman's work. And the woman is expected to do this and many other things at the same time as she is chewing the skins or sewing garments.

If a man loses his wife, he is immediately destitute. He can no longer claim a household of his own, and has to move into the home of a married couple to have his clothes dried and mended, his boots softened by a woman's chewing the soles, and his stockings turned inside out every night, and to be supplied with fresh dried grass in the morning. In return for taking care of his needs in such a case, his hosts claim all his catch.

On the other hand, a woman who loses her husband, and who is not taken to wife by another hunter, is reduced to the state of a beggar. She must live on the mercy of other people, only now and then trapping a fox or fishing some trout. She has never learned hunting, since, Eskimos believe, "the great animals would be offended and go away from our shores if they were hunted by women." And if the woman happens to lose her husband during travel in desolate places, she frequently starves to death along with all her children.

Thus man and woman stick together as a close unit, and the woman's work is considered just as essential as the man's. This, of course, is not official; the man is reputed the stronger one, and his physical prowess makes him feel far superior. To regard a woman as having anything to say would make a man ridiculous, and he never lowers himself to mention his wife when he is out hunting with his fellows. For if by chance or mistake he mentions her name, everybody will laugh and shout at him: "My, my, here's a fellow who is longing for his wife! Why don't you quit and go home to her instead of exposing yourself to the cold and the difficulties out here!"

But in reality women have great power, as in our society. If you want a man to do something, to go traveling with you or to do some job, your surest bet is to get his wife interested! You can be sure that the man will come along if the wife wants it, although officially she has nothing at all to say. An old friend of mine, Odark, once admitted to me: "People travel according to women's wishes, never according to their commands!"

The fact remains that man and woman are indispensable to each other; they form a basic economic unit. Consequently, marriage between Eskimos is usually a matter of mutual interest and sheer necessity rather than of love in the sense in which we use the term. On the other hand, married people are generally very devoted to each other and as a rule remain faithful to each other throughout life. But Eskimo love for—or rather devotion to—each other has very little to do with sex. It is considered rather ludicrous if a man can find pleasure in only one woman; as for the woman, it is considered a great honor if she is desired by many men and can give them pleasure. For this reason, Eskimos have never understood why white people put so much significance on their so-called *wife trading*.

The Eskimos' rather free sexual mores are based on the necessities of their way of life as well as on their point of view concerning marriage. Consider first the impossibility of washing clothes in the low temperatures of the north, along with the fact that Eskimos rarely have a second set of clothes. As a result of this situation, people are used to going naked inside their houses while their clothes are being cleaned. This is not only to get away for a time from the warm skin clothing and to get fresh air for their bodies; it also allows them to pick out the lice from the garments that are bundled together and hung up by a string from the ceiling. An old adage has it that "we would rather be a little chilly and be the only ones in our clothes."

From their childhood, therefore, Eskimos are used to seeing men and women in the nude, and absolutely no shame is connected with the human body and its needs. This is not to say that wherever Eskimos get together there is promiscuity. On the contrary, if several families should happen to occupy the same house, there is strict order in the sleeping arrangements. All lie in a row facing in the same direction. An older daughter will usually be closest to the wall. Then comes a younger daughter or two, then the mother. Next to her sleeps her husband, and beside him the boys. Then follow the boys of the next family, their father, their mother, then their sisters, etc.

More important in understanding the Eskimos' sexual ethic is their point of view that sexual desire is entirely natural and normal, something like the desire for food and sleep. White people, seeing that Eskimo sexual morality is quite different from their own, have tried to change it, or to take advantage of it, at the same time calling the Eskimos "heathen pigs." But there is this much to say for the Eskimos: they stick to their unwritten laws very strictly, and any digression from the rules will be reported and retold and commented upon—and very often punished.

When an Eskimo goes on a hunting trip, it is essential to his success that he take a woman along with him. When I drove with Eskimos from Thule across to Ellesmereland to hunt musk oxen, in my earlier days, women were absolutely essential as traveling partners. Musk oxen are hunted early in the spring when it is still cold; and it was very practical, when we came to the place where we intended to camp during the hunt, to build an igloo and install women to make it habitable, if not comfortable. When we returned from the hunt to get food and rest, they would have ice chopped and melted for fresh water, and the igloo was warmed by their blubber lamps. Further, they had dry stockings, mended mittens and other clothes completely ready. And if we were lucky enough to bring in the raw skins, they stretched them on a frame, scraped them and dried them. In this manner, we were able to bring thirty or forty large musk ox skins home on our sleds after each trip.

If, however, we had been alone, we would have had to stop hunting early at night to return to the igloo to light our fires, melt ice for water and boil meat. We would have had to bring spare boots and mittens from home, as there would be no time for drying them. The musk ox hides could not be scraped or thawed out; they would have had to be brought home raw and frozen, and we could have carried only ten or so in our sleds, as they weigh so much more in that condition.

Now perhaps a man intends to go musk ox hunting, but his wife is unable to go along. She might be advanced in pregnancy or have a very small baby, or she might be sick. In such a case, the problem is solved by leaving her with a neighbor, who graciously consents to let his wife go along on the hunting trip. Another case might be that a woman wants to visit some relatives far away, and for some reason or other her husband has other plans. It might then be arranged that she go with some other man who is headed that way—provided that this other man will leave his wife behind to do the housework.

Thus one may often see men with women other than their wives. This does not necessarily mean a divorce or lack of harmony between husband and wife. People look very liberally at such arrangements. As a matter of fact, it would be difficult to find a more tactful people than the Eskimos. If anyone sees a man and a woman traveling on the same sled, it does not concern him the slightest bit whether they are married for good or just for a short time. When it started, or how long it might last, does not matter to him. Nobody asks questions—that is considered rudeness in the extreme—and everyone treats it as the most natural thing in the world. Wherever the couple happens to visit, the woman is given the same status as if she were the hunter's real wife.

I myself, during one of my first visits to Thule, had occasion to appreciate this Eskimoic tact. I was expecting my Danish girl friend, Michella, to join me. But the ship that summer brought no Michella, only one of those clumsy letters it is as embarrassing to write as to receive. She was not coming, and I hardly found life worth living any more. But then, some weeks later, I was active again, trying to forget as I made plans for a trip up north to hunt walrus. An Eskimo, Tatianguaq, came and wanted a word with me.

"It appears that you are without woman's companionship," he said. "My poor wife wishes to see her family up north. It is not impossible that one would benefit a little bit from her company. It is supposed that she knows the best way to travel; she can help set up camp and dry clothes. Also, a man's pleasure at night is increased by the presence of a sensuous woman in his sleeping skins!"

In this modest way, Tatianguaq let me know that he knew my problem and wanted to help. There was, of course, another side to the coin: he had for some time been having a little difficulty with Ivalu, his beautiful wife. She had been on board Peary's ship and there learned to like the white men's form of courtship. A temporary separation might set matters straight. As for me, I was more than ever—due to my keen disappointment—feeling akin to these kind and carefree people, and I was ready to adopt their way of life. So Ivalu and I started north.

But not without the comedy that was expected in such cases. I had my sled packed and loaded on the appointed morning. The arrangements had been made with the husband, and Ivalu had not shown her face at my house while the negotiations were taking place. When I started out and turned down past the Eskimo houses to get my companion, not a soul was in sight. Ivalu wasn't up yet. I called her; nobody answered. "Ivalu, Ivalu! What is the matter? Come out, we are going on a trip visiting!"

"Somebody sleeps, why go on a trip? Don't speak to a poor woman!"

I entered the house and saw immediately that a new foxskin fur coat had been sewn, and new kamiks were laid out. Ivalu was on the bed, about to lie down for more sleep. Tatianguaq sat by the wall and looked at me with an embarrassed grin.

"Women have women's minds," he said.

I wasn't sure whether this meant that our agreement was canceled and that a retreat was difficult to perform. Besides, I really needed someone who knew the way across the glacier.

So I insisted that she was to come—now! An old woman was lying farther in on the bed reminiscing about the days when men had fought for her and desired her company on sled trips. She got quite carried away, and Ivalu seemed determined to stay in bed.

"Hurry up, my dogs are waiting!"

"Let them wait. A woman is without knowledge of your dogs' decision."

"The decision is that we are going north to the settlement."

"You are witless! Listen to a man speak without meaning! No journey has been decided for me."

"Nonsense, you are going with me. Hurry to get dressed!"

Several visitors had entered the house now, mostly women who followed the developments with ill-concealed interest. Ivalu enjoyed her triumph and tried to prolong it as much as possible. "Take another woman. I have no desire for journeys in the cold, and others are better than I to help a man!"

The situation was embarrassing, and I turned to Tatianguaq saying that I didn't like to force his wife, and hadn't we better give up the whole thing?

Ivalu became attentive immediately. It began to look like a victory she didn't want. Here she had been advertised as the one who had conquered this strange white man whose whole desire had been for one woman who never came. She had been looking forward to entering settlements in triumph as my companion. But on the other hand, with so many spectators, she couldn't very well give in as if she were destitute for men's attentions.

"I don't want to go with you. Also, it is not supposed that you would want me along. [Pause.] Of course, you could trust that I will run between the stanchions of your sled to lighten it, and I will take care of your clothes if you force me against my will!"

But Tatianguaq was getting impatient. It was early in the morning, and he had to go sealing.

"Let my kamiks be supplied with grass under the stockings; since my wretched wife seems to be leaving my house for a while, it is expected that Ilaituk will take care of things!"

It had been Ivalu's hope that I would use violence to get her on my sled, so that she could attract the whole village with her screams. But I just went out, saying that she had to make haste. The last I heard as I crawled out was her opinion that I was without my wits and that I would never get her down to my sled. I cleared the dogs' traces, got other things ready, and pretty soon Ivalu appeared, dressed in her new traveling finery.

"Come and sit on the sled, we have to leave!"

"I am not coming down to your sled. What do you want with me? Others can serve you better!"

"I said that you were to hurry!"

"Some words were spoken into the air!" she called back.

She was beautiful and enticing to behold. Some people had crowded up to watch, but nobody wanted to appear to be listening. It was mostly women who had gone outside to pee—a business that can be prolonged interminably—and everything could be seen and heard. Finally I ran after Ivalu; she tried to evade me, but without any great haste.

"Is your traveling gear ready?" I asked.

"What traveling gear? I don't know what you are talking about. Why are you saying this to me?"

"Because you are going with me on a trip."

"Take somebody else who might possibly want to go. Not I! Go away from me. My husband will shoot you. He is already making his gun ready."

Then I caught hold of her and lifted her up. She kicked a little and cried out that the lot of women was an unhappy one. And if only she had a husband who dared to defend her, for this was very distasteful! We reached the sled, and the dogs saw me carrying something; it was half dark, and it was natural for them to suppose that it was something to eat. So they crowded around us, and I had to put Ivalu down to bring them to order.

Now, of course, I was afraid that she would run away while she had the chance and make a show of us once more. But not at all!

"Oh, you fool at training dogs," she said. And then she took the whip and swung it with a talent I myself didn't possess. She scolded and shamed the dogs, and then she gave them the starting signal. I pushed on the stanchions to get the heavy load going, and the dogs rushed off at full speed, gay and yapping with anticipation. I could hardly keep up with them. But Ivalu jumped up on the sled and made herself comfortable. I saw her wave to her husband and to the other women. She was now sure that the event would be related to everyone in the tribe and that her role as an honorable and reticent woman had been carried out to the extreme.

We drove across the Wolstenholme Fjord and into Granville Bay. When the excitement at the departure had dissipated, I asked her if she had sleeping skins with her. "No," she said, "but I suppose you have. It is to be hoped that we are not going to sleep on the sled until we reach the houses of people again?"

What do you say to your lady on a sled trip? I tried a lot of things, but it was like water on a goose. First I said that I was happy to have her along. No answer.

"Aren't you happy too to be along on the journey?"

"No, no joy is felt," she said sullenly.

I tried something else. "Do you know the way up across the glacier?"

"It is not desirable to drive across the glacier. There it is always windy and cold."

"Yes, but there is no ice to drive on around Kangarssuk!"

"You are saying senseless things. What you said is known by all. People are not without thoughts."

"Yes, but it was just to talk some words to you."

"Let men speak to men, and be silent when they are with a poor woman," she said. So we were silent for a while. Not for long, for I have always been a talker, and I wanted, like any man, to feel that I was master of the situation.

"Are you afraid of me?" I asked.

"Certainly not. What should I be afraid of? Hold your speech when nothing sensible is being said!"

This was a conversation to cool the passions, particularly since it was twenty-five below with a cold gale blowing from the north. But the journey became smoother; the dogs adopted the trot that is natural to them—that is, too fast for man to walk, and too slow for him to run. I jumped off the sled and practiced the two paces walk and one pace run that is required. But the girl sat and shivered in dignity. Every time I asked if she was cold, I got the same answer: "Be silent, somebody is thinking."

I was hoping that the thoughts were about me and our imminent adventure, and I asked several times to find out. At first she didn't answer, but later her mood became somewhat warmer.

"Somebody is thinking of meat," she said suddenly, as if wanting to be friendly, perhaps also to make me stop and prepare a meal. But it was too early for that, and I wanted to get to Granville Bay without stopping. When we had been driving along for some hours, she again said she was beginning to feel a little desire for food. She had not eaten that morning. Why? Because she had been nervous anticipating what was to happen.

Only then did I feel a little pride. I had been very much in her thoughts. Silently we went on, and I decided to reveal more of my personal affairs to her and make her understand—what she was to understand I didn't know. Nothing came of it, for when I had been lecturing for a while without getting the usual conjectures about my stupidity and lack of rational thought, I turned to her and discovered that she had fallen asleep sitting on the sled.

I had been thinking that I could find a soul to relieve my desperation. I was even intending to nobly bring her back to her husband untouched by me and completely like a sister who had been with her brother on a trip visiting people. I had been thinking of her as one trembling bundle of nerves, horror-stricken at what was in store for her.

And then she was sleeping quietly and without apparent feelings of any kind. An Eskimo woman can lean on the stanchions and sleep calmly. She follows the movements of the sled with her body, and when she has had the sleep she needs she wakes up, as quietly as she fell asleep.

But let us draw the veil of discretion over the rest of what transpired between Ivalu and me, and say only that it was a satisfying journey for both parties. When we returned to Thule after an absence of almost three weeks, she jumped off my sled while we were still driving up the frozen beach. Without a word or a smile of good-by to me and our now ending love affair, she ran up toward her house, laughing and shouting to everybody as if she had left them only an hour ago and nothing at all of importance had happened.

Besides exchanges of wives for practical reasons, the Eskimos practice a more casual exchange—sometimes just for the fun of it, sometimes as a means of persuading nature. In the first instance, it might happen when men are out hunting—Eskimos hunt together, as a rule—that they decide to visit each other's wives the following night. They consider it a marvelous joke, and they keep their plan secret from their wives until it is time to go to bed. Then each husband goes outside and enters the other's house.

The women are always supposed to accept the one who comes. I have heard of a case where a woman refused to give herself to the visitor. In the morning, when the men came out, the "betrayed" man complained to the husband and said to him: "Now you have enjoyed my wife, but I was not allowed to come near yours." The husband felt that the honor of his house had been spotted, and to make up for it he beat his wife thoroughly in public. It only made her more stubborn, and the same occurrence took place the next night. More complaints

ensued, and more beatings, until finally the man with the presumably low sex appeal felt that it was below his dignity to give
a woman and her behavior such great importance. So he told
the husband that he could have her, that she had no attraction
whatever.

As a means of persuading nature to greater generosity, wife
trading was, in earlier days, often ordered by the *angakok,* the
local conjurer. When the hunting had been bad, and starvation
followed, the absence of game was thought to be caused by certain evil spirits, and it was up to the wise man to find out why
they were offended and to try to appease them. Often he ordered
a common exchange of wives. This indicates, of course, that
sex plays a role in the Eskimo supernatural world—a thing
which they themselves would not readily admit.

The angakok would then designate which wife was to belong
to which man, and if, in the course of some days, still no game
had been caught, he would try another combination, and wait
a few more days for success. If thus all the men in the village
had visited all the women, and it had not improved the hunting
luck, the angakok had to find some other means of persuading
the great woman who lies at the bottom of the sea and who
sends out the animals to be taken for food.

There was also the rather popular game of "doused lights."
The rules were simple. Many people gathered in a house, all
of them completely nude. Then the lights were extinguished,
and darkness reigned. Nobody was allowed to say anything, and
all changed places continually. At a certain signal, each man
grabbed the nearest woman. After a while, the lights were put
on again, and now innumerable jokes could be made over the
theme: "I knew all the time who you were because--"

Several old stories deal with this popular amusement. It
should be said that, crude as it may seem to us, it often served
a very practical purpose. Let us, for instance, say that bad
weather conditions are keeping a flock of Eskimos confined to
a house or an igloo. The bleakness and utter loneliness of the

Arctic when it shows its bad side can get on the nerves of even those people who know it and love it the most. Eskimos could go out of their minds, because bad weather always means uncertain fates. Then suddenly someone douses the light, and everybody runs around in the dark and ends up with a partner. Later the lamp is lit again, the whole party is joking and in high spirits. A psychological explosion, with possible bloodshed, has been averted.

Other old stories tell of occasions when animals played a role in the exchange of wives. Hudson Bay Eskimos told me the following tale about "wife trading and the whale."

Once upon a time, the men at a settlement decided to swap wives, but one of them, who always had odd ideas, proposed that they should not do it the usual way with the men going to the women. This time the women were to leave their tents and go to the men they were told to visit.

When the women were kicked out from their tents, they stood there feeling very embarrassed, as they were shy to go visiting each other's husbands by themselves. Now, it must be told that at that certain place the whales used to come very close to land. A big harpoon was attached with a strong line of walrus hide to a rock on the shore; thus there was no waste of time when a whale came near. While the women were standing there, telling each other that this was a most awkward situation, a whale came running in spouting right under the cliff. One of the women shouted in great excitement: "If women must act like men in one way, let them do it in another way, too!"

And with that she ran down and grabbed the harpoon and hurled it, and it fastened in the whale's blubber. The huge whale got very offended at being harpooned by a woman, and he ran at full speed away from the coast, broke the walrus line, and disappeared out to sea.

For many, many years after that no whale came close to the coast again—until a great angakok conjured up the soul of the big whale and promised that no woman should ever be present at a whale hunt. At that same time, it was promised that women should never again be forced to visit other men— the men should always come to them.

The Eskimos around Hudson Bay offered me this story as an explanation of why they always locked their women up in tents when they went whaling. There was a strict taboo against women even looking at a whale hunt.

At Hudson Bay, I once traveled with a married couple, Aguano and Qinorunna; they were en route to Pond Inlet to meet another couple, with whom they had a strange arrangement. The two couples met every spring and traded partners. Aguano had had Qinorunna for a whole year, and now he was going to give her to his friend and receive the other wife in exchange. This had been going on for several years, everybody was very satisfied with it, and I could get no other explanation than that "it was because of a certain idea."

I found out that the two men had been friends from childhood, and it must be said that none of the women had any children. Here we come to an important factor in the family life. Quite a few women are sterile (it has erroneously been supposed that it is because of the early start of the sexual life), and as all Eskimos love children, and also need them to give support to their old age, it is considered a great misfortune for a woman to be without children. I have known cases where men have divorced sterile women and remarried in order to have children. In some instances this has brought forth tokens of real love in the sense that we know it in the Western world.

I remember a man, Samik, whose wife did not bear him any children. After a while, he chased her away and married a young girl with whom he subsequently had three children. The first wife was inconsolable. Time and again she returned to Samik's house, only to be kicked out, beaten and mishandled. She kept coming back, and for a long time she refused to have anything to do with any other man.

A couple of years later, though, she married a young hunter, and now positions were reversed. For she lived very happily with the young hunter who, although she was much older than he, appreciated her because of her great abilities in tanning skins, sewing clothes and keeping house. And now Samik turned to her with his old affection—and she refused him flatly. He tried to surprise her when she was once looking into her fox traps. He entered her house when he knew the husband was out hunting, but she would not have him. She told me that she had once been so much in love with Samik that the fact that he had preferred someone else to her had hurt her too much; she could never be happy with him again.

Visiting a wife behind her husband's back just isn't done. It should be clearly understood that, in each case of wife trading or wife borrowing, it is strictly an arrangement made between the men. The wives have little or nothing to say in the matter. The man who dares to visit a woman without her husband's express consent not only delivers a mortal insult to the husband, he also becomes an eyesore to his tribesmen, being guilty of a serious breach of all good rules. His behavior is related with the utmost contempt, and, in many cases, it calls for decisive action by the husband. In order to save his honor, he might drag his wife out and beat her in public—whether the affair be her fault or not. He might seek out her paramour and take his revenge upon him. Among some Canadian Eskimos, fist fights take care of the matter, but in other tribes, as the Polar Eskimos, blood revenge was quite common, and everybody would consider such a killing justified when there was no other way of saving the husband's honor. But, conversely, it could also be a dangerous insult to a man to refuse to partake of his wife's embraces when he had clearly indicated that it was permitted. It was like saying that what the house had to offer was not good enough.

Eskimos have no such thing as servants, but the man is master in his house, he makes decisions for everybody; everything that is brought in by those living in his house belongs to him, and his wife does the sewing and cooking for them. From this stems the fact that it is regarded as unfaithfulness in the extreme if a man catches his wife doing some sewing for another man without his permission or, rather, his order. He will immediately tear the clothing from her, cut it to pieces and beat the wife terribly outside the house, and not only will the story be told to the neighbors, but it will run up and down the coast as a sensational scandal worthy of many comments and explanations.

Sometimes you will find a hunter so mighty and strong that he can afford to keep two wives. He will claim to have so many skins to prepare and such a great supply of game that it would be too much work for one woman, but this might, of course, in some cases be only a subterfuge. He might have fallen in love with a young girl while his elderly spouse, even if she no longer attracts him physically, still is a good housekeeper, and it pays to keep them both.

It is rather funny to visit a man with two wives. When you come into his house, one of them will do all the talking, welcome you and tell you to give your outer clothes to the other one, who will mend them and dry them and otherwise be of service. You can then be sure that the husband is sleeping at the former's side of the house. Each of the two has her special side of the house and her own lamp to take care of.

Next time you come, you may find that the other woman is the ruler of the house and orders her co-wife to please the guest. Then she is being preferred, at least for the time being. They always know exactly where they stand, for when the husband returns from the hunt they will spot his sled from afar, and they will both run out to meet him with dry mittens, a choice morsel of food or some other thing that can show their affection. He then takes great delight in just dropping the gift offered by one of them while he accepts and enjoys what the other one brings, takes her up on his sled and lets her co-wife walk to the house.

Because of the general scarcity of women among the Eskimos, polyandry is quite common. In such cases, people live in a triangle so that a woman enjoys two husbands. Nothing can be more delightful for a woman, for then she sleeps in the middle of the igloo while the two husbands have their places by the cold snow walls. She never has to carry ice or water into the house. As soon as she expresses desire for something to drink, her two beaus will start a race to be the first to bring it to her. They have to mend their own stockings and mittens, and they are in every way competing for her affection and sympathy.

When they are out hunting, they have to think of their wife. While we free men with just one wife always eat the tongues and the hearts of the caribou right away, the two co-husbands will always tuck the best parts of the game away to bring home to their wife. They thus maintain a permanent rivalry, so to speak, being all the while the very best of friends.

The scarcity of women among the Eskimos has one very definite reason: girl babies are considered less desirable than boy babies and are often strangled at birth or left out to die from exposure. This would seem like extreme cruelty to us, and in modern times it hardly takes place any more. But in former days it was often a matter of pure necessity. Consider a country where you have no insurance for old age and no way of gathering a fortune of any kind, where life is difficult, and the only way you can protect yourself against sure starvation when you are too old and weak to hunt is to have sons who will take you into their houses and let you live out your time in contentment. It is an old Eskimo saying that "a son is a better provider than a son-in-law." As soon as a daughter was married, her skills were lost to her parents. She would go with her husband's parents and owe them all her loyalty and support.

An Eskimo woman never weans her baby until the child is

three or four years old, often later. There is then a lapse of at least three years between pregnancies. It follows that, in order to get a son, a couple would often have to let a newborn girl die, always right after birth before "they would get too fond of the child," so that the woman could become pregnant again sooner. It was, in fact, often out of courtesy to a friend or neighbor with a son that Eskimos let a little girl live; she would later make a wife for the boy. The couple were then regarded as married from the time of the girl's birth, and almost always respected the plan of their parents, marrying when they came of age to do so.

Since the Eskimos take such a natural attitude toward sex, it would seem that sexual perversities are rare among them. From the time of the wars with the Indians, they have strange tales about unnatural practices which they claim are rather common among the Indians, though they say it is unusual to find such things among themselves. It is true that I have no recollection of hearing of them among the Polar Eskimos. But among the Hudson Bay Eskimos, I heard about some pretty startling things. Here are a few samples.

One case of homosexuality was mentioned, that of a certain Panimuaq, who was said to have had relations with his adopted son. But it was said that he hanged himself out of shame.

Relations with dogs were apparently not uncommon, and no shame seemed to be attached to it. The same was the case where dead caribou and seal were involved, although it must be said that men who resorted to this procedure were thought to be rather ridiculous.

Copulation with dogs must always take place out in the open. The only place where cover might be sought was where two ice floes in the pack ice stood up against each other, so as to form a small shelter.

Then there is the age-old tale of another woman, who had relations with her dog and bore young which were dogs with human hands and hairless bodies. She had been confined in the open air in the shelter of some rocks, but her fellow-villagers had been ashamed of her and had pushed stones down over her and crushed her and her brood. The Eskimos believed firmly in the truth of this account.

Sometimes, sexual abnormalities were believed to give magical powers, as in the case of the man who was believed to be a great shaman because he had relations with his mother.

Incest was frowned upon, but in all cases of sexual deviations it was the rule that they were not to be concealed, that they had to be confessed openly. Only when the doer kept it a secret to himself was he believed to be possessed by an evil spirit (our equivalent of being sinful). As long as he talked openly about it to other people, it was considered to be a matter of no great consequence!

The Eskimos have nowhere mixed with the Indians nor with the primitive races that neighbor them in Siberia. Yet they do not seem to mind interracial marriages. Many Greenlanders have Danish blood in them. Admiral Peary had two sons with Alakrasina, and Matthew Henson had a son with Ivalu, and these three young men grew up to become the best and most intelligent hunters of the tribe. In recent years, intelligence testing has been carried out in Greenland, and it shows that the mixture between Eskimos and white people is fortunate, since those with mixed blood tested fully as intelligent, on the average, as white people, and are physically probably superior.

An Eskimo Wedding

An Eskimo wedding does not always mean that the young couple will establish a household of their own or that they are able to support themselves. The newlyweds almost always join the household of either the boy's or the girl's parents, most often the boy's. This is necessary, first, because the young bride still has to learn the more difficult domestic chores, such as how to cut out the various skin parts for clothing and how to sew them together. The young man on his part must continue to learn from the older man about hunting, trapping and the like. In the second place, it might be several years before the two have collected enough tools, cooking pots, skins and bedding to build a home for themselves.

In the meantime, then, newlyweds stay with their family or other people. Whatever game is caught, whatever is earned by the young man, belongs to the owner of the house. Separation from the parents' house is effected gradually, just like independence from the parents themselves: the young couple will go on hunting trips alone, live in an igloo or a tent by themselves, and stay away for longer and longer periods at a time.

The groom's very first task is to dress up his bride, for it cannot be too much emphasized that a wife makes the reputation of a house by her looks and her apparent comfort. Among the Polar Eskimos, fathers always let their young girls go around in miserable old rags. In southern Greenland, it is just the opposite: young beauties are dressed in gorgeous colors, are given bead embroideries and what not. They shine, they entice the male population in every possible way. But later, when the church has given its blessing, and the holy rite keeps the two parties nailed down in matrimonial bliss, wives gradually become sloppy. After an absence of a few years you may see young women who used to charm you out of wit and senses looking slovenly and indolent.

In northern Greenland around Thule, still another practice prevails.

There, a father, no matter how wealthy he is, will not waste good skins on a marriageable daughter; it is up to the groom to dress her up, and you may be sure that he wastes no time in doing so, for she is his publicity, and it is a man's pleasure to see his wife neat and content.

At the Thule settlement near my trading station, I began to

notice a little girl who was wretched to look at—dirty, and with clothes made partly of dogskin, partly of worn-out hand-me-downs. Her mother, Kasaluk, had had two children with her first husband. The one, a little boy, she had to kill during a hunger period, but the girl, little Mequ, had "found life sweeter than death" even under those circumstances, so the mother allowed her to fend for herself. She survived and later had gone to live with her grandparents up north. Then Kasaluk was married to Uvdluriaq, the great hunter at the settlement, and Mequ had been brought down to take care of her younger half-brothers and half-sisters.

The little Mequ had only rarely visited our house. But once while she was there I gave her some bread, which was a great delicacy to her. She was happier than any Eskimo girl before! And a few days later, she came with a pair of mittens she had sewn for me. She just laid them down in front of me and said: "To express thanks for the bread!" Then she was gone again, as quietly as she had come! She was shy and not used to speaking to important men without being asked!

During that period I had become more and more Eskimoic. Once Ivalu had come to visit me and stayed overnight, and I can't even maintain that she was the only woman I had pleasure from when my travels took me around in the district, or when I—while fox trapping—camped in igloos or caves with members of the fair sex.

One day, when I passed by the tents with Knud, Mequ was sitting outside with her little brother.

"How sweet she is, really," said Knud. "If I were ever to marry up here, she would be the only one along the whole coast, from the south and right up to here, that I could imagine would be intelligent enough, and clever enough, and beautiful enough!"

I didn't ponder the matter; but for the first time the thought of marriage occurred to me. Knud was right. This business of borrowing another man's wife was not exactly what we ought

to promote in the district, and therefore we shouldn't partici-
pate in it, either. It never came into Knud's mind to reproach
me about the conduct of my private life, but his remark hit
home with me. This little girl, just reaching the marriageable
age, seemed really so pure and fine to me—in spite of her dirty
dogskin pants and the torn kamiks. Her smile and good cheer
covered it all. Also, it was known that her stepfather could
furnish her with magnificent skins if he wanted to. But this
just wasn't done. Because of the hunger period some years before, during which many girls had been killed, there was a lack
of women among the Polar Eskimos and several young men had
already been to see Uvdluriaq.

One day we heard that Samik, a feared and often wrathful
man, had raped Mequ while his wife happened to be visiting
us. It caused quite a bit of excitement, but nothing could be
done. The missionaries remained silent when their own little
flock wasn't concerned—but it happened to be one of them, a
man named Seckman, who brought me the bad news. He asked
if we shouldn't do something. We then went to see Uvdluriaq,
but he didn't think that any harm had been done. He had no
intention of starting a feud with his neighbor. Shouldn't people
rather laugh at such a witless hunter like Samik, who preferred
an immature girl to his own excellent wife?

Later that winter, I was staying alone in our house with a
servant woman, Arnanguaq, who took care of the lamps. Everybody else was away on trips. Arnanguaq was married to our
handyman, Minik, who happened to take the position that "he
did not want to make appointments for exchange of women"
with anybody. But even if Arnanguaq did not fear any attack
from my side, she invited Mequ down to the house for the
night, so that she wouldn't be alone with me.

We undressed and went to bed. Our lamps were burning low,
the wicks had been made small so that the blubber could last
until morning. Suddenly, in that romantic half-dark, I was
possessed by a power stronger than myself. I threw my skin

covers aside, reached over and grabbed the young girl, and swung her over to me on my bunk. She didn't say a word, and neither did Arnanguaq.

Thus I was married and, to the extent possible for an explorer, settled down. Mequ was so small and fine of build. Her hands were soft, as if she had been manicuring them all her life. But the night of our marriage she had had to do a lot of dirty work, and her entire body was filthy, her clothes too miserable for description. My remembrance of the night is somewhat misty, but in the morning I told her that I didn't intend to let her go home, that I wished to keep her with me.

Her reaction was a little less lyrical than I had expected: "Then somebody else must bring my mother the needle that I borrowed from her!"

She pulled a needle out of her hairtop, where she had kept it tucked away. Possibly it was only a message; Arnanguaq went with the needle. In the meantime, we went to the big house to have breakfast. Emilie Rosbach, the missionary's wife, had the food ready. Naturally, she was much too well-bred to say anything. I put Mequ down at the table by my side, and there she sat, for she didn't dare to move. She got a fine cup, she got bread and tea. There was sugar to put in the tea, but as she didn't seem to think that it was proper for her to take any of it, I put two teaspoonsful in her cup. In those days a clearer announcement of marriage couldn't be made in Thule.

I was aware that I had to guard Mequ for some time. Since I had not abducted her properly, as any decent groom would, it would be a while before people realized that it was a permanent arrangement. So she went with me wherever I went, except that I couldn't take her with me out to my caches to fetch supplies; her clothes just weren't good enough for even short sled trips. Pants of dogskin, the greatest shame to a man! But it didn't take long to make up for that, for we had plenty of fox-skins. I didn't have any sealskins for kamiks, however, so she had to go to her mother to get them. She went with rich gifts:

the little children got canned milk, the mother became the proud owner of a beautiful pair of scissors and a royal supply of thread. Mequ was now completely rehabilitated after her former miserable state—which was by no means due to Uvd-luriaq's stinginess, only to custom. Besides, her husband now had the joy of seeing his little wife grow more well-dressed and civilized from day to day.

She had, of course, a lot to learn. I remember clearly one thing which became the cause of much amusement. It happened on the second day she was living with me; we lived in the little house, where it was cold, and in the morning—when we had entered the big house to eat and warm ourselves—I told her that she had to be washed.

She looked at me in great astonishment: "What are you saying? Don't you remember that I washed yesterday?" When I then said that in the future there was to be washing and bathing every day, she almost feared that she had been seized by a madman. But later she became one of the great agitators for personal hygiene in Thule.

There was no great excitement until Knud returned home. Rasmussen wasn't a man to let a wedding just pass by. He sent word north and south, east and west, that with the next full moon the wedding would be celebrated in the grandest manner. This was a little against people's taste, though. They found it immodest and a little bit tactless to blazon abroad that two young people now had agreed to stick together. What concern was it to others?

But the feast had to be great. I was myself ordered to deliver everything I could, especially eggs from my caches. So I made my first sled trip with Mequ, and we stayed away for a few days. Only then did I discover what I had been missing. On a sled, a Thule woman is as good as a man. She arranges the dogs, she swings the whip expertly, and she helps to pack and secure the load. Her cheer lights up the darkness! We were staggering around in the Polar night to find my depots, but we had a wonderful time. For Mequ it was the introduction to an entirely new life in which she, for the time being, remained a bit lost, but was very happy.

Once my axe slipped down from the sled, and it was impossible to find it again. When I expressed my annoyance at the loss, Mequ asked if it meant a lot to me. I said that it was bad luck for a man to lose his axe. "Will it be the right thing to show understanding of the loss by crying a little?" she asked. But then I said that she shouldn't worry, for at home I could get another one from our stock.

"It is unknown to live under conditions where belongings are so numerous that they decrease in value," said Mequ.

She was learning, and before long she was running our house with great administrative ability. She became the first lady of Thule, even deposing such authorities as our housekeeper from southern Greenland, Vivi, and Emilie Rosbach, and her own mother, Kasaluk.

Our wedding feast was a great success. Knud had announced that he wanted to see who could bring the most and the best, and the celebrations finally amounted to several days' sumptuous eating. It wasn't quite easy, at first, for Mequ to be hostess to older women who had known her since she was born. She had been fatherless, and even if she lived with the old Mequsaq, she wasn't as well protected as were the children of great hunters. Now she was the one who had the right to call out that boiled meat was ready and to say that she hoped the guests would eat well to get her pots empty, so that she could fill them up again. Vivi and Emilie, two mature women, had to step into the background, and there were some frictions.

During that first year of our marriage, we actually had it best when we drove away and took it upon ourselves to visit people all over the district, taking part in the hunt or bringing them supplies so that they could make more out of the fox trapping.

Mequ's intelligence and authority became more and more apparent, and she called upon them almost as if using magic.

The Eskimos commonly have several names, of which one is the calling name. Often the calling name is changed in order to mark a great event or turning point in the person's life. At Christmas, shortly after our wedding, Mequ decided to use one of her other names; she was now to be spoken of as Navarana— "in order that some greater ability, hitherto concealed," might appear in her.

From then on she was called Navarana. After Christmas, we drove south to Cape York to see people there. There had just been a violent gale from the southwest which had broken up the ice around Parker Snow Bay, so we had to go behind the Cape and up across the glacier there. It was a hard turn, and I didn't think the dogs were able to drag the sled. Navarana walked quietly between the stanchions while I yelled and shouted and beat the dogs—with little result. She must have thought strange things, seeing my impotence. Then I got the idea to walk in front of the dogs, enticing them to follow me; I gave the whip to Navarana and proceeded out front. But then I saw something new. Navarana let a tempest break loose. She started to use the long whip as it had never been used before, letting every single dog feel the smart on its back, and her encouragements rained down over them in one fury. At first, they didn't quite understand that a new partner had joined the firm.

"Oh, you strange dogs who are not ashamed to be lazy, you whom a mere woman must remind of your duty. Run forward quickly if you want to avoid the lash. Hurry up, dogs! Hurry up, dogs!"

The dogs howled and began immediately to fight, the stronger ones falling upon the weaker. But that only resulted in more pain and more smarting cracks over them. There was nothing else to do but to move along; it turned out that they could very well pull the sled when they wanted to. Up they came, past me, walking there to entice them. Navarana didn't stop because she passed her husband. She was moving now, and she wanted to move faster. I tried to run after the sled but couldn't catch up. She carried on so that I almost became afraid of the devil that had been hiding behind her quiet demeanor.

Only when she had reached the ridge of the glacier did she let the dogs stop and wait for me. I struggled up at last, and there she stood by the stanchions, smiling. She had already cleared the traces, and now she handed me the whip.

"It is difficult to mount the steep side of the glacier. It so happened that a woman forgot how hard it is to move when the hands are not at the stanchions!"

I asked if she wouldn't rather continue the driving, since she did it so much better than I.

"Can a poor woman get dogs to obey? A man's dogs know only his command words!"

Down from the ridge was easy, but it became more and more precipitous. She then taught me to put the dogs behind the sled, while we sat down on it and hit with the whip out back; thus the dogs worked like brakes. It was the first time I saw this method, and I was to use it a lot later on.

Down on the ice we ran into another snowstorm and had to give up. The snow was too loose to build an igloo from, and we couldn't reach the cave at Agpat, since the ice was all broken up. Navarana again had the solution to our problems. She told me to turn the sled over so that it made a shelter. Behind it, out of boxes and other baggage and our skins, we made a cave and crawled into it. We were laughing very hard because we, who had a big and wonderful house at home, and who intended to go see friends in warm shacks at Cape York, now had to let ourselves be snowed under. We were talking about how wet and cold our clothes would be in the morning because we had slept in them, about how hungry we were, and about how we couldn't boil meat. These things showed how completely witless people are and worthy of ridicule.

We then fell asleep in our strange lair while the storm raged around us. The next day it was the same thing; we couldn't see three feet ahead of us for drifting snow. Wet and cold, we stayed right where we were, and I don't know how long we remained so. Suddenly the storm quieted down. We could see the moon, and we got up in a hurry. The cold went to our bones, but we had plenty of work digging the baggage out of the snow, getting the dogs ready and getting everything cleaned of ice and snow. All the while the moon was shining down on us, and I asked Navarana if she could see the mountains by their shadows, for the moon was in its third quarter.

"The mountains?" she asked. "What mountains?"

"The mountains in the moon."

"But isn't it a man, then?"

I started to explain that the moon was a cold globe, that irregularities in its crust could be seen clearly and that even the single mountains had been given names by people on earth.

This was completely new to Navarana. She told the old tale about the sun and the moon being brother and sister pursuing each other, but never able to meet. I explained how unreasonable this was, and defended my ideas, which were founded on scientific observations.

Navarana looked very serious: "Yes, I have been thinking that the woman who is taken by a white man must assume his beliefs. Is that what the minister is talking about on Sunday?"

I said no, it had nothing to do with religion.

"Yes, but my grandfather has told me about the creation of the world, about the sun and the moon, and about the earth's creation. It sounds unreasonable, I know, but we people think only weakly, we see only close by. Outside our thoughts there is only mist. But now I will take up your beliefs, and it now happens that a woman forgets the man in the moon!"

In this manner we discussed things during our trips. I was by no means smarter than she was; it was only in certain fields that I could make up for the knowledge she gave me.

We arrived at Cape York, and Navarana was now a lady of high rank. We moved in with Krolugtinguaq, chief hunter of the settlement, and one festive meal after the other was arranged in our honor. In the meantime, Navarana was playing with the other young people and having the time of her life.

We couldn't stay long, though, and we would now try to get over the ice around the Cape even if it was still unsafe for our return trip. We found several times that between the ice floes there was thin ice that couldn't hold. The storms and the strong currents cut the ice up from beneath.

"Are you afraid?" I asked one day, when we were driving over ice where the dogs got their paws wet every minute.

"Is a woman afraid when she is traveling with her husband?" she said. "Women leave the care and the worry to the man when they are on his sled."

Such words made me proud and strong.

When we arrived home, I was informed that the strong gale had broken the ice around Dalrymple Rock. Now that it was about to settle again, there was a chance of a good catch of walrus, because these animals could get closer to Saunders Island, where there are mussels and where they like to stay. Consequently, I left Navarana at the settlement and joined the hunters on the ice. It was a healthy life, but somewhat dull in the evenings when we were running around playing to keep ourselves warm. One day, a fresh young man had a bright idea.

"Somebody got the desire for eggs," he shouted. "There are eggs on this island. Let us go get eggs!"

The others seconded his motion, and the whole crowd scurried up to get—my eggs. It so happened that I was the only one who had collected and cached enough of them, and I had sneakily counted on them for myself and my guests. As a man of honor, I could, of course, do nothing but join the chorus and express my satisfaction that my wretched eggs were allowed to be included in the meal. They came down with bags filled with the stone-hard frozen eggs. Some were gnawed on the spot, like apples, others were put in the pot until it was filled up with eggs. Nobody gave it a thought that these eggs belonged to me.

Had I owned the eider ducks? Had I done anything but hide the birds' eggs? Nobody in this country knew how to be content with an egg or two. Here the fun was to see how many could be downed. And every man had ten fingers and ten toes, that was enough to count on. We filled the pot several times.

When I returned home, I told Navarana of my experience with the eggs. She said immediately that she would take care of that, since I seemed to be so fond of eggs. I told her that she was not to ruin my good name and reputation as a hunter by passing my complaint on to the others. She turned her big black eyes toward me and looked at me as if I had wanted to avert a misfortune or heavy insult to both of us: "Do you really think that I could do that to you?" she said seriously.

She went down to her mother and said that she felt sorry that it would not be possible to treat guests to eggs this year, since the hunters had used them out on the ice and didn't leave any to take home to the women.

The next day, Kasaluk told her husband that she strongly feared that the walrus hunt would be of short duration this year. In her dreams, she said, she had seen that the ice was strewn with eggshells, and in the same vision she understood that this insulted the walrus so that they would decide to go elsewhere. The hunters talked the matter over. They agreed, of course, that a mere woman's dreams should have no influence. But for the sake of all eventualities it was decided that it was better not to eat any more eggs as long as the walrus hunt lasted. As a result, plenty of eggs were stored up in my quarters.

Such a clever and precious person was Navarana. She gave me some of the happiest years of my life, until the Spanish flu took her away in 1921. And she bore me two children, a boy who was named after his great-grandfather, Mequsaq, and a girl, Pipaluk, who is now a well-known writer.

Eskimo women used to talk about giving birth as being "inconvenient." This is not to say that it was any fun, but they had a remarkably short period of confinement. The women used to sit on their knees while giving birth. If the woman was in a tent or a house when her time came, she would most often dig a hole in the ground and place a box on either side of it to support her arms, and then let the baby drop down into the hole. If she was in an igloo, the baby had to be content with the cold snow for its first resting place. If the birth seemed to take long, the husband would very often place himself behind his wife, thrust his arms around her, and help press the baby out.

Among the Hudson Bay Eskimos, things were a little more difficult. In that community, childbirth was surrounded by a number of taboos that virtually isolated the poor woman. Nobody, for instance, was allowed to touch her. So if the husband had to help her, he would place a strip of skins around her just above the fetus, tie it with a loop at her back, and pull it tight. The baby was immediately wiped clean with a piece of skin and placed in the amaut where it would spend its first year. The skin piece was guarded as a precious amulet to ward off evil.

At Thule, in one case, I gave some skins to a woman to prepare in the morning. She brought them back in the afternoon deploring that it had taken so long, but she had had a baby in the meantime!

Another time we were traversing a glacier while traveling in the company of an Eskimo couple. While up there, the husband came and told us that his wife was going to give birth. I told her that this was very inconvenient, since there was no snow from which to build an igloo. Couldn't she wait? She said she might, and in two hours we managed to get down from the glacier, and we all helped build the igloo while everybody joked about the event.

As soon as the igloo was finished she went inside with her husband, and we waited about an hour. Then the man came out and told us that he had a son. But the mother was a bit tired, and they had decided not to go any farther that day. We went across the bay, and the next morning, when we woke up, there were the happy parents with their newborn child waiting for us.

Navarana was true to form regarding these things. One day, while I was sleeping she came to tell me that Itukusuk had caught a narwhale. Did I want to go down there and eat mattak? I said that I was sleepy, I had just returned from the hunt, but I would come later. It was during the summer, daylight lasted through twenty-four hours, and every man had his own sleeping period in that part of the world. Later I woke up again when she came back home. I asked if the mattak feast was over already, but she said that she had an upset stomach, and so she had come home to sleep. She went into our other room, and I resumed my sleep. After a while, Arnanguaq came to report that Navarana was in labor.

I became very excited and called Knud, who was sleeping in the loft. He had himself taken an Eskimo wife. His wife had borne him two girls; he had experience in those matters, and I wanted to ask him what to do.

He said that, as far as he knew, coffee had always played a role in the proceedings. It was during the first World War, and we had not received supplies (especially coffee) for a long time, so I said that this was quite impossible. Knud then revealed that he had preserved some coffee beans tied up in a piece of cloth for the occasion. Consequently, we resolved to go to the brook for water.

Before we could leave the house, though, we heard a loud yell: "Anguterssuaq! A big boy!" It was Arnanguaq, acting as midwife. Somewhat dazed, I went with Knud for the water, and when we returned, we went inside to see Navarana. She said that it was more tiresome than she had imagined to bear boys and so she wanted to be left alone. It was only three in the morning, she still had time to get a nice sleep.

Knud was sleepy too, and the coffee was forgotten. I was too happy to sleep. I went outside and sat down on a rock and started laying all kinds of plans for my boy. I resolved to stay in Thule the rest of my days, to teach him hunting, economy and industry, and to be to him everything that a father could be.

He was to avoid all the stumbling blocks I had run into myself. In short, I sat there daydreaming about my newborn boy that I hadn't even seen. And I stayed there until Navarana came out herself and told me to come in and see him. She got out of bed at the usual hour and tidied up the house.

In the evening, Knud threw his coffee party. The entire Thule population was there, of course, and he opened the dance with Navarana. She didn't stop dancing till very late. Our first-born had arrived in style.

When our boy was five days old, Navarana put him in her amaut and mounted the Thule Rock with him to show him his future hunting grounds where he was to perform great deeds and bring much game to the house—and whatever else an Eskimo mother wishes for her child.

An Eskimo mother doesn't wean her baby until her next pregnancy sets in, however long that might be. If she does not become pregnant again, she often nurses her lastborn for many years. It is considered a sign of a woman's youth and agility that she still has a child to nurse and milk to give, and only when she had finished her usefulness to her children is she really old. I thus saw several times, among both the Hudson Bay and the Polar Eskimos, and even in southern Greenland, mothers giving the breast to fourteen-year-old boys who were already ·sporting in kayaks and taking part in the hunt.

Otherwise, the mother doesn't interfere much with the children once they can walk and run around. Under her watchful eye, they are allowed to play freely around the tents or houses and even with the dogs. Instinctively, they show no fear of the dogs, and it is amusing to see how these otherwise so ferocious beasts are completely complacent when it comes to children. They will gladly tear a bear or a fox to pieces, but when a little tot starts pulling their tails, poking their eyes or riding on their backs, they suffer it in quiet dignity.

Our children didn't get any education, as such, at Thule. Once, on a summer day, I was busy in the shop, and Mequsaq and Pipaluk were playing outside with their little friends. Their game was to crawl up on a big slanting rock and slide down its smooth side. Up and down they went in one wild tumble.

Then I heard their grandmother, Kasaluk, come out and shout to them: "Oh no, dear children, don't do that! Think of your poor father who has to drive long stretches in the cold and dark to get skins for your pants. Now you are wearing off the fur. It is unreasonable, you must not do it!"

Then she went back inside, and the children resumed their sliding down the rock, a wonderful game in any latitude!

After a while, the same amiable woman came out again: "But dear children, now you are still sliding down the rough stone. Please remember that your father has to provide all the foxskins and bearskins that you are wearing out. There won't be any seats left in your pants. You must stop that immediately and show that you are sensible and economical children!"

Whereupon she went into the house again, and the children continued their fascinating game. A third time Kasaluk came out: "Oh, dear children, now I must admonish you to stop this game. Think of your poor father! He has to drive around in the cold of winter, fighting the bear and looking to his fox traps, so as to get new skins to replace those you have worn to pieces on the rock. Children, please think!"

It was finally dawning on me that the children were disobedient and also extravagant with their pant skins. I found that the moment had come to show up in parental dignity and demand that the respect and the economy be maintained in full. So I went out there.

"What is going on here?" I asked sternly. "How remarkable!" I tried to speak my finest Eskimoic so as not to make myself ridiculous just by using wrong words. This was a serious affair!

The grandmother concurred, very pleased. "Yes, truly remarkable," she tuned in. "Very remarkable! How one must rejoice in this sad sight!"

Her words seemed confusing to me, and I asked for an explanation.

"Yes, it is very clear that no pants can stand for this sliding down that rock. Those children ruin a lot of things. That can only please us older ones!"

I didn't think so at all, but the woman was my mother-in-law, the incarnation of an international authority who understands all things and who must command respect. So I said petulantly, "No, I don't think it is so wonderful. I have to drive around in the cold and the dark, hunting the bear and looking to fox traps, and now they are wearing the fur off their pants by sliding down this stone!"

"Yes, but you see, nobody can help thinking by seeing this foolishness. Children ruin things without giving it a thought; they have no cares. But every day of their lives they become wiser and wiser. Soon the time will come when they never will do that sort of thing. They will remember their unnecessary wear on their pants and regret it. Everyone must rejoice by recalling that we start out as thoughtless children, but with every day the good sense increases in us. At last we become old and sage. Just imagine if it were the other way round, so that we were born clever and economical, and our wisdom decreased with time. Then misfortune would dwell with people! Therefore, it is joyful to watch children's careless play!"

There was the Eskimo educational system in a nutshell. They had invented progressive education long before others. In their defense, it must be said that their stern and barren country had of itself forced its stern rules upon them; their ethics were so strict, their ways of disapproval so definite and so pitiless, that the youngsters quite automatically grew into upright members of society.

And they loved their children. A man would lose his honor if he hit a child. The father of a flock rarely had a leisure hour with his family in which he didn't take out his knife and carve out of bone or wood dolls for the girls and animal figures for the boys. One thing that Eskimos developed to perfection was the bull-roarer. These artfully carved thin blades of bone or wood, sometimes ornamented, had little cuts along the edges at regular intervals. They were attached to a string, and when the child swung them in the air, they would give a delightful humming sound. Sometimes the bull-roarer would have two holes in the middle; a thread was passed through them, and by pulling with both hands the string would get more and more twisted, and the bull-roarer would go like a propeller and make almost as loud a sound.

Other games popular with the children were various versions of "house," "hide and seek," "tag," "hopscotch," just as in other civilizations all over the globe. As already mentioned, the children played freely with the dogs, and both boys and girls were expert trainers and drivers even before they became of age to use a sled.

The girls were made to help their mothers very early, for it took a long time to teach them the many chores a woman must do. As for the boys, they were always encouraged to play with toy harpoons and other tools, for soon they would have to go out with the men on the hunt, tagging along with their undersized instruments; and by the time a boy was fourteen he was usually expected to have brought his first seal home. This, of course, called for a celebration; everybody from near and far was called in to take part in the young hunters catch. To an Eskimo boy, this was the introduction to the ranks of the grown-ups.

Another event that called for a big eating feast was when a tot had worn out its first pair of kamiks. The happy parents would throw as big a party as they could manage, and among the Hudson Bay Eskimos, particularly, the little kamiks were kept as invaluable talismans.

The grownups had their games, too. Among the women, making figures with a string was often used to while away hours that because of the weather or other circumstances couldn't be passed in any other way. A sinew thread about three feet long would be cut off, and the ends tied together. A woman would stretch it out with all her ten fingers, tying it in a certain pattern. It was now up to the next woman in the circle to pick up the string with her fingers in such a manner that it would form a new figure. Thus the most intricate figures would be formed, many of which had names and originated in a long-forgotten past. Learned men have written whole volumes about the intricacy and the symbolism of this strange pastime.

In Greenland, both at Thule and down south, a kind of soccer was sometimes played. The ball was sewn out of walrus skin and stuffed with grass or feathers. The participants were usually divided into two teams, and often there were tournaments between settlements. At other times, the players were divided into couples, each couple against all the others, and it could develop into a real brawl. There were no rules to the game, anything went, and there are records of injuries and even fatal accidents during particularly heated games.

Eskimo Courtship

Eskimo girls marry so very young that a girl will often continue to play with the other children right up to the time of her first pregnancy. A boy, on the other hand, has to hunt well for many seasons before he has accumulated enough property to establish a home, so the husbands of the twelve-year-old brides are frequently grown men, two or three times as old as their wives. Only when a young man is a member of a well-to-do father's household can he afford the luxury of marriage at the age of eighteen or twenty.

Among the Eskimos, sexual life is not directly connected with marriage, and the simple biological need for the opposite sex is recognized in both men and women, young and old. Toddlers of both sexes are encouraged to play together with a freedom that would outrage a mother in other countries, and the game of "playing house" can, among Eskimo children, assume an awfully realistic appearance. The mother of a six-year-old girl once confided to me: "You should see my daughter and that little boy next door. They're as cute as they can be, just like husband and wife. But I wouldn't for anything let them know that I was watching."

Parents never worry when their teen-agers fail to return home at the usual hour. They take it for granted that the young people have found a vacant igloo nearby and are spending some time there, either as a couple or as members of a larger party. In fact, at a larger settlement there will always be a house called the Young People's House where young people can sleep together just for the fun of it, with no obligation outside of that certain night. Nobody takes offense at this practice, for no marriage can be a success, Eskimos believe, without sexual affinity.

But a good hunter has additional considerations when he is choosing a bride. To an Eskimo, a wife is more or less an advertisement. The degree of ease and comfort in which she seems to be living is the measure of his ability as a hunter and provider. Although she has a thousand tasks to perform, she is never required to do any heavy or dirty chores. Her value to him lies in how neat, gentle and loving she can be; hard work would only weaken her for love-time. Chewing skins and sewing are the woman's job, but flensing the animal is the man's job; cooking the meat for the guests is the woman's task, but taking it down from the meat rack, chopping it up and bringing it into the house are the man's. The wife's composure and attractiveness tell the guests of the husband's wealth. It follows that a girl who shows industry and talent, and who keeps herself neat, is much desired for a mate.

On the other hand, the busier a hunter keeps his wife sewing, entertaining guests and bearing children, the prouder she is of him. Coquettishly, she calls him "the terrible one" because he keeps her in such slavery, and it is every girl's dream sometime to be able to shout: "Oh, a poor woman does not have the ability to prepare all the skins that a man can bring home. How I envy those women whose husbands give them only a few skins to prepare!" With such a speech, she can make the other wives green with jealousy.

If such a neat and clever girl should also happen to be fat, then she is really the village belle. An Eskimo cannot give his wife jewelry, new hats or other things that will demonstrate his wealth; nor can wealth be demonstrated in clothing: all the women's apparel is pretty much alike. It is therefore essential that she appear well fed! As a result, there must always be lots of food—and fattening foods, too—at his house, and his family will enjoy respect and a good reputation. A fat girl is always popular because, as a wife, she will be easier to keep in style, and stoutness is identical with beauty among the Eskimos.

This reminds me of Inuiyak, who was one of my Eskimo helpers during the Fifth Thule Expedition and whom, when I was about to return to Denmark, I paid with such gear as I was not going to use any more. He got sled and dogs, axes, knives and a gun. All of a sudden he became a tycoon among his people, and his first thought was to get a wife. In Repulse Bay he asked for a few days off, and came back with a bride. Being so rich, he had, of course, no difficulty in getting the fattest one in the place. When Inuiyak came driving up with her on his sled, he made a big to-do out of puffing and panting so that we all could see how hard he had to push. We gave them a celebration, but the next day we regretted it. We had counted on Inuiyak to take a load on his sled for us on the month-long journey we still had left. But he was no longer the same man!

"My wife is so fat," he bragged. "No dogs can drag this heavy burden. She is too big to run, so others will have to take those boxes!"

This was shouted in a loud voice so everybody could hear it. The intention was to flatter the beauteous lady; being in love has strange effects on people. So Inuiyak wasn't very useful to us any more.

Another standard of beauty among the Eskimos is the nose. Once, when I was a contestant on "The $64,000 Question," quizmaster Hal March asked me why Eskimos rub noses. I said that the custom was of no particular significance, other than olfactory. But now I'd like to modify that statement. Although white people are much too fascinated with this business of rubbing noses, it is a fact that noses *are* important to the Eskimos, and perhaps in a sensual way. A girl must have a petite nose, and if a man really wants to deliver a well-styled compliment, he will tell her, cooingly, that her nose is so little that it completely disappears between her broad flat cheeks.

Fifty years ago, when I first visited Greenland, I stopped overnight at a settlement where there was a girl with an unusually large nose. Her mother took one look at me and almost kissed me. At last, she said, there was someone in the village uglier than her daughter. I say "almost kissed" because Eskimos don't kiss. They bump noses together momentarily in greeting, but there is never any pressing lips together, not even when boy meets girl.

Unlike almost all other primitive people, the Eskimos know nothing of cosmetics, probably because in most places the vegetation is so scant that vegetable dyes were not developed. Still, I came across a couple of cases where women thought of "helping nature," almost causing unhappiness and dire disaster.

One incident took place in the northern part of Greenland's Upernavik district, which at the time was Christianity's outpost. The boy was a prominent figure in local life, son of a Dane who had married an Eskimo; he had learned the trade of carpenter, which put him in the upper class. Because of his strangely indistinct features he was usually called "Snotface." The girl's name was Bala: she was daughter of a great seal hunter and known for her domestic ability, but above all she was noted for her enticing chubbiness. Her clothes were well-sewn, and her sealskin pants were of a particularly miraculous fit, clinging tightly to delicious curves. There was mass, and there was fullness of form. "Snotface" started sleeping poorly at night, dreaming about this female horn of plenty. The two had met several times at informal dances at the settlement, and finally "Snotface" proposed. Her answer was yes, and a letter was sent off to the minister to please perform the wedding on his next inspection tour.

I happened to be on the same boat as the minister, and that automatically made me a guest at the celebration. A feast to remember! The groom himself was colorful as a Christmas tree: white anorak, blue pants, fancy kamiks, green scarf, red hair, and strings of beads and colored pictures on the cap—Raphael's angels and other such things. The dinner was delicious and the food plentiful. The bride served us, and the groom presided at the table, expressing his satisfaction both with the meal and with his imminent fate.

We continued our journey the next day; the minister had many chores of baptizing, preaching, marrying and giving last rites in his vast district. But at our next stop we were met by a dogsled—an express sled, I might add. The man on it shouted aloud that he was looking for the minister. His entire being was shrouded in the dignity the importance of the occasion gave him. For here was a letter, and it was sealed with lacquer. Solemnly he handed it to the minister, who hastily broke the seal and read. Accidents and death are everyday business so far north, and there was reason to fear the worst. But the tragic message turned out to be that of a soul in torment. "Snotface" wanted an annulment. His bride had been revealed as the daughter of deceit personified. His love had turned into hate. A divorce was demanded. Most Respectfully Yours.

So it was bad work the minister had done, but he defended it bravely. That same evening he wrote an admonishing letter: What God hath wrought one day cannot be sundered by mortals the very next. Time will even out all differences. Remember the holy rite, the vow before the Lord's altar. No, he said, he could not agree to a divorce. With kind greetings in God. Yours Truly.

The next day's travel carried us even farther away from "Snotface's" woe, but even so, another express messenger with a letter caught up with us in the evening. Daily mail delivery in Greenland! This was very extraordinary indeed!

"Snotface" was giving his explanation in intimate detail this time. He insisted that the marriage was built on a foundation of falsity, and that his life's happiness was forever lost. Bala's deceit had, literally, been unveiled. "Snotface" expressed certainty of the fact that he could have had any girl he wanted. But now he had been betrayed and gypped.

It appeared that Bala had falsely been wearing panties that she had fabricated out of her father's thick knitted sweater, and which, moreover, she laid double! Here she had been promenading borrowed magnificence, her bulging shapes had charmed "Snotface" out of his wits and aroused his soul's most beautiful dreams. Now that the vow had already been given before the altar, he had discovered that leanness incarnate and bony angles were hiding under the ostentatious exterior. "Snotface" gave vivid expressions of his hatred of vanity and woman's propensity to fraud.

It cost the minister an extra trip and numerous Bible quotations to maintain the sacred alliance. But, I am happy to say, he finally succeeded.

Farther up north, among my wonderful Thule Eskimos, where choosing and discarding a bride were a much simpler matter, I never thought that vanity could wreak such havoc. But there lived a man, by name Napsanguaq, who had a daughter, Arnanguaq, who was a lovable woman, delightfully plump and clever at sewing. But she was not married, even in a country almost destitute of women. Alas, she did not have enough hair on her head for it to be set up in a top such as women must have to look neat. The hair hung like miserable little wisps around Arnanguaq's pretty face. Whoever would take such a girl as wife and expose his house to ridicule?

Napsanguaq was really worried. The daughter was a wonderful help in the house, but a son-in-law would be better. Napsanguaq needed a hunter to help out, now that he was growing old.

They went musk ox hunting in Ellesmereland, very far away. A whole year elapsed before they came back, and their return made a sensation. Not only did they have many skins and much news to tell, but Arnanguaq had in the meantime grown hair on her head so magnificent and abundant that the other females almost went mad with envy.

The young men in the tribe responded splendidly to the new challenge, and so violent was the sled traffic to and from Napsanguaq's domain that the track through the snow assumed the looks of an icy highway. The courtiers brought gifts, and the game they caught went to the household as long as they were guests. Things were really looking up, and one fine day it was rumored that a handsome young buck named Aqioq had been preferred. The girl was betrothed, and not much later I heard that the young couple were spending their honeymoon on a lonely little island. I transferred their names to my list of married people, keeping the statistics up to date.

One day we heard the baying of dogs as if a sled party was approaching, but it turned out to be just one traveler, Napsanguaq. He was alone! No family, no festive crowd packed together on one sled, no dashing son-in-law tagging along! One very quiet man drove up, greeting nobody. Something was the matter, but since he hadn't stopped out on the ice, it couldn't be a death. I was mystified, but among the Eskimos discretion is a must. It is rude to ask questions that could embarrass another person.

I did the trading with Napsanguaq, and he informed me that he would be leaving again the next day. This was so unusual that I could allow myself to ask the reason.

"Alas, it so happens that the sight of other people's faces is not desired. These things were badly needed; if not, I would have stayed home."

"But what is wrong? What has happened to make you leave both your happy face and your family behind?"

"The lie has entered our lives. It has been the cause of comments among people that a young woman was different from what was expected and desired!"

I had to *drag* Napsanguaq into the house, we sat down alone in my room, and he confessed all.

Arnanguaq's coiffure had attracted the eyes of men, their senses had been inflamed, and a state of happy excitement had ruled the settlement. Aqioq was the swiftest hunter; his catch would add greatly to the supplies of meat and skins in the house. So he got the girl and carried her away to the little island where their young love could bloom in peace.

But unfortunately there is only one room and space is scarce in an igloo. It is difficult, even impossible, for a lady to guard the secrets of her toilette. It soon turned out that Arnanguaq's crowning glory was a swindle, a deceitful masquerade! It was black musk ox hairs she had combed into her own sparse strands. She had matted them together artfully, but it does happen that hair has to be reset. In order to look passable she couldn't very well let it go for more than eight days or so. The groom discovered the trick, and in that instant his love was gone. What he saw would inevitably be seen by many others, and then the laughter would resound, derision would fill his house, they would even make taunting songs about it. The scandal was certain, and Aqioq wanted none of it.

He drove the girl back to Napsanguaq, threw her off his sled, and said thanks for the loan, but he had had enough. A woman whose hair reminded him of a man's was not to his taste. Aqioq drove south, and Napsanguaq was left behind with both his daughter and the shame. Arnanguaq herself was even worse off than she had been originally, for, matrimonially speaking, she was now a "reject."

My heart was bleeding for her. Ever since I had set foot on Greenland I had time and again been called upon to straighten out other people's love affairs. I don't know why people showed me this extreme confidence, which many times made me feel like a roving "Lonely Hearts" club. Anyway, I was getting to be an expert in the field, and in this case I went all out. I felt strongly with Arnanguaq in her heart's yearning for nuptial bliss, and she had to be saved for marriage.

When Napsanguaq went home, I went with him. Most of the houses in the settlement were being lived in at the time, so I got the audience that was necessary for the success of my mission. I started to give them of my rich experience and wordly wisdom. After the meal at Napsanguaq's house—in which the whole population, as was the custom, took part in honor of me as the guest—I found a convenient moment in the conversation to start my speech.

"I have seen instances of this sort in many countries," I said. "Women wish to be attractive to men, and who are we to blame them for it? Among white women—even among the wives of the best hunters in that faraway land—I have seen those that improved upon their looks."

An elderly woman cut in excitedly: "Yes, but here we are dealing with a woman who wished to be more beautiful than it was nature's intention she should appear to be before people!"

"Yes, that is very true. But I know women in many places who add to nature's intentions and subtract from them almost at will. Women who add a little hair where it is needed, color where it is lacking, and even replace teeth that have fallen out. Nobody censures them; their reputation is the very best!"

My listeners were gaping in utter amazement, but to doubt the reliability of the speaker didn't enter their minds. It had to be so.

"Yes, but if the husband sees it, what then?" asked several.

"He is pleased that his wife will look nice and happy and show that she is comfortable and well-treated in his house!"

This started them thinking, I could see. The publicity value in the case was now beginning to appear to these people north of everybody and everything. And I continued exposing the methods and wiles of civilization to them. A little color makes a woman look well rested, a little hair shows her younger and more attractive, so that her husband is envied by strangers. I talked and talked, and Aqioq listened. He understood that the pride of a man is demanding. In this, as in so many things, the woman is his help and support.

And during the night he sneaked up to Arnanguaq while her parents discreetly looked away. The marriage was again in effect.

Another time, I had the opportunity to be counsel to Apilak, whose fame is based on the fact that he accompanied Dr. Cook on his ill-fated North Pole journey. Apilak was married, but his heart was big enough for two wives, and so was his wealth. He had, however, fallen in love with a girl who was absolutely impervious to his advances. Apilak—who ordinarily was a loving father to his children and a good provider—was beginning to go off the deep end as the lady turned a deaf ear to all his prayers. He sent out invitations to sumptuous banquets, using up all his meat stores. He sang lustily and long to the accompaniment of the drums, but his ladylove remained cold.

One day, Apilak killed one of his best dogs right outside her house. The intention was to show her that his most valued possessions meant nothing to him when he thought of her.

Two days later, he stuck his knife twice into his little daughter's leg so that she screamed with pain. The idea was to show the girl once again that nothing else in the world meant anything to him; he had even forgotten his children.

But nothing happened, so something extraordinary had to be done. One day, when there was a big village gathering, Apilak rolled his sleeve up to his shoulder, took his powder horn and poured out a streak of powder—from the shoulder to the hand, making a little heap in the palm. He lit the powder, and searing flame ran up and down his arm while his face never moved a muscle. But all that happened was that the women became frightened and ran off.

I arrived at the settlement a couple of days later. I had heard about Apilak's behavior, and now I was told everything about his strange courtship. I had come with the intention of walrus hunting, and I urged all the men to accompany me out on the ice. Most of them did, including Apilak.

When we wanted to rest during the hunt, we built an igloo. At night, while the others were asleep, Apilak and I lay awake. Things were still bothering him, and finally he started talking about his elusive beloved.

I took the occasion to scold him for his cruelty to his little girl. I looked at his arm that was festering. The sores in the hand were constantly breaking anew when Apilak threw his harpoon, but as a man with dignity he made no complaint. While I bandaged his sores, I spoke to him of my personal experiences; I informed him of my opinion of women and the best way to win them. You can't succeed by beating around the bush, the personal element is the great appeal. Go to the girl herself, talk to her, influence her heart, I told him. I talked enthusiastically, and my words sounded convincing—or at least I thought so.

Soon after the ice broke up, the chances of getting any more walrus were gone, and we returned to the settlement, where we spent the time visiting, eating and talking, as one usually does when the time is inopportune for hunting, just letting the hours slip by as easily as possible.

Suddenly we heard the screams of a woman, the cries of children and many excited shouts. We rushed out to see what was afoot.

It was Apilak, the great lover, who was busy with the

"personal element" I had recommended. But with his own interpretation of it: He had grabbed the girl by her hairtop and was swinging her around in a circle, while she was stumbling and crying and screaming loudly. I ran over to them, but the lover had finished and stood beside the girl, who lay sobbing on the ground. From their talk I could tell that personal matters were being discussed. So the rest of us withdrew. Soon it was announced that Apilak had left the village with his beloved on a sled—a little trip away from other people where, alone, they could exhaust their passion for each other.

The final result was that Apilak had two wives. In the long run, the girl could not resist him. This showed that even among the Polar Eskimos, where women are not supposed to have a mind of their own, it pays to go directly to the heart of the matter.

But let us consider the case of an ordinary young hunter who wants a certain girl as bride. Maybe he has been with her in the Young People's House, or just the sight of her and her good reputation have made up his mind. It would be beneath his dignity to go up to the girl and propose, and it could also be embarrassing if her answer was no. So he starts visiting her house, or rather, her father, and sits and talks with him or eats with the family. The girl can then reveal to him a lot about her like or dislike of him by the way she takes his outer clothes and takes care of them, by the way she serves him food, etc. But she says nothing, and he only talks to her father and her brothers about the hunting and such matters as silly women know nothing about.

He may then start bringing presents for her. He would not give them to her directly, but he just casually "forgets" them when he is leaving. It might be a choice piece of fur, a piece of ribbon or a mirror from the trading post, or the like. If she ignores the gift, or even throws it out of the house, saying something like, "Something was forgotten which is too good for a poor woman to use," then her feelings are cool. If she should go to the extreme of cutting the fur or ribbon to pieces in public outside her house, then his case is hopeless. But suppose she accepts his gift and uses it conspicuously: that amounts to a public declaration, and the young man's next step will be to ask her father's consent. Very often the father makes his decision according to his friendship or esteem for the young man's kin. Officially, the girl's mother has nothing to say, but she is actually an active agent in persuading the father one way or another, and just as often as not the marriage has already been "arranged" between the two mothers before the developments have reached this stage.

If the young man gets the approval of the prospective father-in-law, he has permission to take the girl, and that's all. And I mean just that: he takes her.

First Thule Expedition

Not long after Peter and Navarana were married, the infrequent mails brought to Thule an old Danish newspaper which reported that Ejnar Mikkelsen, a Danish explorer of some fame, accompanied by one companion had started on an expedition along the east coast of Greenland to the island's northern tip, then a virtually unknown territory. The article added that the risk had been minimized because Freuchen and Rasmussen were on the island and could help if needed.

Neither Peter nor Knud had heard anything else either directly or indirectly, but they knew enough of the country to be sure that anyone engaged in such a venture could use a little help and probably would need it badly. Peter undertook a long, dangerous, bitterly cold trip to the nearest post which boasted a Danish manager, only to find that no word had been received in Greenland from or about Mikkelsen.

Freuchen and Rasmussen were aware of the fact that Mikkelsen had had little experience of Northern Greenland. They also felt that if he had been successful in what the newspaper said was his objective, he should have turned up in Thule by this time. As it was, he could hardly have crossed the Humboldt Glacier, Peter thought, and a rescue attempt seemed clearly indicated. So, with no further information to go on, either as to Mikkelsen's whereabouts or his needs, the First Thule Expedition, as it came to be known, was launched.

Later Peter called it "one of the strangest expeditions ever undertaken in the Arctic." His account of it, given here, explains why. What he does not tell is that its success would be dependent upon

161

*his skill as a navigator because no other in the small party knew
how to chart a course across the ice.*

*When one looks at the map of Greenland, one marvels that two
men of such experience should set out with so few solid facts in
search of another of whose plans they knew so little. But in fact
both Freuchen and Rasmussen regarded any excuse for an exploring expedition as better than none. Their curiosity about the Arctic
was insatiable. If they could partly satisfy it even at the cost of pain
and hunger and suffering, they never hesitated. They were inured
to all the dangers and hardships.*

We were to take with us my father-in-law, Uvdluriarq, and a
fine young fellow, Inukitsork. They were the best men available
and both volunteered to make the trip, not as hired men, but
as Greenlanders whose unique privilege it would be to take a
look at the other side of their country, and make their own
observations.

We planned to follow the sea to the north coast, and then go
east until we met Ejnar Mikkelsen, or came upon traces of him.
We would return—well, when we returned. We might be forced
to spend the winter on the other side, but what of that?

The day before we intended to leave I was called to a conference. Uvdluriarq had been looking at the map, along with a
number of the other natives who had been with Peary, and he
thought it would be a waste of time to follow the coast around
to the east.

"Why can't we go straight across?" he asked. "It looks as if it
would be a shortcut."

I tried to explain to him that such a course would lead us
directly over the ice cap—that we would encounter no land and
no game!

The interior of Greenland is covered by an enormous sheet
of ice burying all valleys and mountains far below its surface.
Its area is 727,000 square miles, and it is the greatest glacier of
the northern hemisphere.

"The ice cap is only a road without rough ice," Uvdluriarq persisted.

We all talked it over and argued the possibilities. Then Knud joined the discussion, and asked me if it would not be possible.

There was nothing to prevent our trying it, except that we had insufficient provisions, no goggles to prevent snow blindness, and we knew we would find no wild game until we came down on the other side.

"If you can navigate us across," Knud said, "we'll look out for the food!"

And so it was decided.

We started out on April 8, 1912, with thirty-four sledges, most of them loaded with meat, and three hundred and seventy-five dogs. Our plan was each day to send some sledges and drivers back as we gradually made room on our four sledges, by feeding our dogs, for the extra meat they hauled.

The first day we did not go far. Wise men of the tribe told us to ascend the ice cap via Clements Markham's Glacier—named for the old English admiral whose splendid explorations had been made near Nekri. The glacier was steep, and the humidity and heat were exhausting. The thirty-four sledges stretched back from us in a long, ragged column. The teams were eager to overhaul each other, even our own dogs who did not realize they had so far to go. We had used an old trick to advantage here—harnessing the bitches in heat among the forward teams; then the male dogs would haul any load in order to catch up with them.

Attached to my sledge was a hodometer—a wheel that runs between the uprights and indicates the distance covered. It was scaled in kilometers, but it is impossible to travel in a straight line with dogs, and we could not figure the distance exactly. Nevertheless, it was better than nothing.

The glacier was surfaced better than any I had ever seen. It was slightly uneven in places, with a few boulders of ice caused by running water the preceding summer, but there were very few crevasses, and none large enough to swallow a man.

We did not feed our dogs the first night, so we had the whole crew with us another day. Next morning soon after starting out we reached a spot where the going was terrible. All the snow had blown off the ice, leaving no foothold for the dogs. We had to unload, drive on with half our loads, and return for the rest. Late in the afternoon we reached snow again and kept on until our dogs were exhausted. But by the third day there were only twenty-seven teams left, and we sent more home each day as our dogs consumed the walrus meat. After three more days we reached the interior dome of the ice cap, and bade good-by to all our helpers.

We were at last at the spot where the success or failure of the expedition would depend upon our speed. And our speed depended upon native methods, which no expedition of whites had ever used before.

The ice cap is especially difficult to traverse because of the soft dry snow through which the runners cut easily. We had brought along from Nekri walrus hide sliced into long strips as broad as the palms of our hands. These we fastened beneath the runners of the sledges. Then we melted snow with our Primus stoves and poured the water over the long strips, letting it freeze. It took us twenty-four hours to prepare the runners, but when we finished, the sledges were almost as easy to shove as a baby carriage. With such runners much greater loads can be hauled over loose snow, and we had the advantage over sea-ice travelers that we could spread out our load without danger of its catching against ice hummocks.

At three o'clock on the morning of April 14, 1912, I took the hour angle, and we set out. Our course lay east-northeast, and it was no task to hold the direction so long as we could see the sun. Later on we shifted to northeast, so that we had the sun directly in front of us every morning when we set out.

Inside the ice cap the snow drifts constantly. Even when

one is unaware of the wind, dry snow sifts through the air covering everything, like flour in a mill. In no time the sledges were white, and the loads saturated with the stuff. We looked like ghosts driving ghost dogs. When we put our hands in our pockets we even encountered the snow dust there, and it was not very pleasant.

My special job, of course, was taking observations. So far as I was concerned I did not mind this task—at first. My talent made me especially valuable to the expedition, and in the evenings when the others were cooking I could figure out my observations. But in the mornings it took me a long time to get the hour angle, take the temperature and pack my instruments, and do all those tedious little things which are annoying for others to watch. They always drove on without me. I had a number of bad frights when the drifts had covered their tracks before I was ready to follow, and once, when they had gone far out of the prescribed course, it was only by chance that I caught sight of them through the valley between two drifts. Of course, we all had enough common sense to realize that in case we were separated, the only thing to do was to lie down and wait for calm weather before we tried to find each other.

Knud's energy drove us on. Early every morning, while we lay freezing on the ice in our sleeping bags and dreaded the thought of going out into the cold and driving snow, Knud would sing lively songs and ditties for us. He cheered me up with the words and the Eskimos with his buoyancy.

Every evening, while we were building a shelter, he would begin to heat water from snow in a little shelter made of blocks of snow. One gets terribly thirsty up there in the snow, and he would always give us the first lukewarm water from the pot. We took our turn at the spout, and only after we had slaked our thirst did he drink. Then he would make tea, and the daily strife would begin, because he never learned how to make tea properly! I traveled with Knud for fourteen years, and I never had a cross word with him except on these daily occasions. He thought that tea should be *boiled,* and of course that's wrong. Hence I got the first cup of tea, before he had boiled the essence away, and he served the resultant slop to the others. But in that way I got only one cup, and that annoyed me, because there was always enough for two cups for the others, who didn't care what they drank.

Until we reached the center of the ice cap the wind was in our faces, but when we came to a large area in the very center there was no wind at all—apparently there is never any wind there; the snow was so soft that we could not cut it into blocks for igloos and had to use our tent. It was constructed of fabric not much heavier than bed sheets, but it lasted the whole time, and it served as a home for us during the summer. We anchored it in the snow, and even when it was really cold, we were so fagged out by night that we never again made igloos during the whole trip.

The dogs began to be unmanageable, and we had to resort to whips. We realized that they had to be fed oftener than we had planned on, and we saw our supplies running out faster than we had anticipated.

Our only hope lay in getting down to land where there were musk oxen before we had to eat any of the dogs; then we could find something for them—and us—to eat. But they grew lean, and so did we. We had overestimated our endurance, and there was nothing for it but to go on to the end.

The worst calamity of all—for all of us—was that I was slowly falling a victim to snow blindness. Unless a person has experienced it, he cannot appreciate the torture. Your eyelids feel as if they are made of sandpaper. Knud Rasmussen, who had much dark pigment in his eyelids, was not troubled, but I am rather light. Added to this, I had to take all the observations. Now that we were nearer land, it was all the more important that we know our approximate position.

Finally a day came when I announced that tomorrow we would sight land. The ice cap was now definitely dipping toward the sea, and the going was easy except for the snowdrifts. We were hardened against everything, cold and wind and pain, and there was in us only a concerted drive to reach land again— and fresh food. Suddenly I heard a shout and pried my eyelids open. There before us, between the drifts, were mountains! We were as happy as if we had found an unexpected cache of provisions. Now we had hard ice to drive on. We had no more use for our walrus-skin runners, so we took them off and chopped some up for dog fodder, saving the rest for ourselves.

Descending from the ice cap is always more precarious than climbing onto it, for one cannot be certain what he will find at the foot. When we were close enough to the edge Uvdluriarq went ahead to explore. We waited for him, I with my eyes closed and my coat over my head. He was gone for hours, but when he finally came back he said that he thought he had discovered a route down.

Once again we started the dogs, and this time the ice was so smooth and the slope so steep that the sledges ran up onto the dogs' traces. Knud's sledge ran over the neck of his left wing dog and killed it on the spot, but we could not even stop to pick it up and save it for food. There was no controlling the sledges, and I had to open my eyes regardless of the pain. The sledges chose separate routes down—there was nothing we could do to guide them—and I wondered whether we could stop them in time to avoid their crashing off the final drop onto the hard ice of a lake at the foot.

The wind was strong at our backs, and occasionally I caught a glimpse of my three mates whizzing along amidst a scramble of tumbling, snarling, yapping dogs. Then suddenly our paths converged in a kind of glacier river bed, and we all drew to a stop and unscrambled our dogs.

We looked about us, and found that we had stopped just in time. The glacier dropped in a perpendicular wall fifty feet to solid ice below—and there was no mattress to land on!

We tied our three harpoon lines together—it was impractical

to detach the points from the lines, as they were fastened on with leather stitches—and figured that they would reach the bottom. It was hard to get a foothold on the smooth ice at the top. We chopped holes to make it rough, and dug a couple of deeper holes for leverage. We also had to have a double line so that the last man to descend could, by a hazardous process, bring himself and the lines down together.

I was to go down first, since I was the heaviest. If the lines would hold me, the rest could descend safely. The idea was not particularly gratifying to me, but there was nothing else to be done.

A sealskin line is slippery and hard to grip, so I had to wind it once around my thigh. I lowered myself carefully over the edge, and started down as slowly as possible. Everything seemed to be going well until I happened to glance down. Within two inches of my thigh was the point of the second harpoon. I tried to grasp the line tighter with my mittens and hold myself up. I screamed, but they could not hear me above; even if they had heard me they could have done nothing. I had to make my way over the point somehow.

My hands continued to slip, and I felt the point penetrate my pants, and then my flesh. I kicked and finally got the loop free of my leg. But the harpoon point was already well into my thigh, and in coming out it tore a long, deep gash. It was over in a moment—I was rushing down now holding the line only by my hands—but I had time to realize that it must be rather unpleasant to be a seal. My swift descent was stopped when I struck the first knot below the point. I fastened the line round my leg once more and continued slowly to the bottom.

My entrance into the new country was not auspicious. I tried desperately to stop the blood with snow and my inner mittens. It was cold, especially with my pants torn and soaked with blood, and now added to the pain in my eyes was the sharp throbbing of my leg.

I could do nothing but wait for the others. They lowered the sledges and dogs, three at a time, but some of the dogs at the top grew panicky and jumped—beautiful flying arcs that ended in death. The men were the last to descend.

We chopped up more of the walrus-hide runners and cooked them for ourselves; then brewed some tea. We tied the dogs; the three that were dead we chopped up for their teammates. The dogs did not eat them at once, but next morning there were no signs of the carcasses.

Unfortunately I was now in such a state that I could do nothing. My eyelids were as thick as my lips, and I could only pry them open with my fingers. I could not walk without re-opening the wound in my leg, and so there was nothing for me to do but lie quiet for a few days while the others explored the country and procured something to eat. They left one dog behind with me to warn me of bears or wolves.

All I wanted to do was to crawl head first into my sleeping bag and get away from the everlasting glare. I wanted no food but fat, and there was none. I wound my watches, but I did not look at them—I felt the need of complete relaxation for my eyes after nineteen days of observations on the ice cap. We had actually traveled for only eleven days, but sometimes for more than twenty-four hours at a stretch; the rest of the time we had been laid up on account of storms.

As soon as I had recovered somewhat, Knud urged us on. He never lost his high spirits and was always the one who woke us every morning, or rather, after we had slept the allotted number of hours. After all, it was light night and day so we could not observe the normal divisions of a day.

The dogs got steadily fewer and fewer in number. Some had died of exhaustion, and two had been washed away by a raging river we had to cross.

After two or three days, they would go no further, and we were forced to butcher the poorest ones and throw them to their fellows.

Some days later we decided to cut the expedition down to

three teams, using the fourth sledge for firewood. We butchered
the four scrawniest dogs, and fed them to their teammates and
ourselves. Dog meat is not too bad when the dog is young and
fat, but ours were half-starved and worn out with fatigue. Still,
the meat was filling.

Next day we went out in scouting parties—Knud and Uvdluriarq to the east, Inukitsork and I to the west. We shot a rabbit
and ate it raw, but on the second day we returned to camp,
realizing that this was no place to stay—no musk ox tracks, no
sign of big wild game anywhere.

Knud returned after four days with news that he had seen the
sea. (He also brought three rabbits and six ptarmigans—he and
Uvdluriarq had eaten three of the latter already.) We looked
at the map, and Knud was positive that what he had seen was
Independence Bay, and the land across it, Peary Land.

If that were the case, then my calculations were incorrect.
If we were only as far as Independence Bay, we had a long way
to travel before we reached Denmark Inlet, and the country
looked anything but promising.

Unfortunately Inukitsork had a touch of snow blindness, and
we could not go on until he was better.

While we waited for him to recover I made sufficient observations to prove that we had reached Denmark Inlet, not Independence Bay. Our journey down to it, via what we named Zigzag Valley, had cost us more days and dogs than the whole
journey over the ice cap.

As soon as Inukitsork was fit to travel, we lost no time in
moving on. The feel of the tough salt-water ice under us once
more was good.

Soon we sighted signs of habitation on shore, and when we
drove closer we discovered that it was actually the summer
camp of Mylius-Erichsen, Hagen the soldier, and Jörgen Brön-
lund, Knud's old friend who, we later learned, had succeeded
in bringing back the records of their explorations at the cost of
his life. Their camp had been made in a most desolate spot.

There was no game for miles around, and during the summer no possibility of getting away. Nothing to do but settle down to a lingering, horrible death.

Nearby they had burned a sledge—the ashes were still here. One of the iron runners was stuck in the ground to attract any travelers who might pass later. The dung of the dogs contained innumerable pieces of cloth, wood and rope, which indicated that they had consumed anything and everything. There were also bits of clothing.

The men had built a cairn, but there was no written message in it or any indication of where they had gone. Later on we learned that Ejnar Mikkelsen (the man we were looking for) had been here before us and had taken the script in the cairn without leaving any word of himself.

However, we assumed he had never been here and wondered whether we should go northwest in search of him at Independence Bay and the Peary Channel, or turn south along the east coast. Our equipment was equally inadequate for either venture. We decided first to head north, and rounded the northeast corner of Greenland—Cape Rigsdagen—named for the Danish parliament.

It is not a very conspicuous mountain, but I was determined to climb it, as it offered the only vantage point in the vicinity.

The coast looked none too inviting, so we crossed over to Peary Land. We had heard of this locality from the leader of the only expedition that had yet been there, I. P. Koch, and we expected much of it. We were not disappointed.

From the sea we glimpsed a herd of grazing musk oxen—it is always a good omen for hunting when you sight game before touching shore. We pitched our tent again and cooked a fine meal. Then we slept, and three of us went out hunting while Knud stayed with the dogs and patched his underwear. He hated sewing for himself, but there was no one to do it for him, and I made fun of the picture he made sitting there with needle and torn garments slung over his knee. He took his revenge on me by using for patches the great blue handkerchiefs my mother had sent me.

We shot the oxen and had to make a number of trips to carry all the meat to camp. These remarkable animals are peculiar in that they never run away, so that one has to shoot the entire herd, because the living oxen remain to defend those that have been shot.

Our plan was to follow the coast down to the Peary Channel and then, if we did not find Mikkelsen, take it for granted that he had retraced his trail down the east coast. Later we learned that this was, indeed, what he had done.

As we progressed up the bay the ice changed from bad to worse. I made short observation trips into the hills at the side, and one day I came back to the party with some information which no one would believe: there was no such thing as a Peary Channel between Greenland and Peary Land. I had discovered that a glacier came down to the head of the inlet, and there would be no chance of our going much further on sea ice.

Knud and our Eskimo friends would not believe me. Knud thought me an incurable pessimist anyhow, and besides, what Peary had said was good enough for him.

We went on up the bay slowly. It was now the middle of June, and the brooks were swollen with water. There was no breeze to cool us off; the sun beat down ceaselessly, night and day. Our feet were sore, and the ice under us was a path of needles which bit through our soles. It was too warm at night to sleep in our bags, and we merely took off our footgear to try to get them dried. And they never dried.

The further we progressed the more evident it became that there was no Peary Channel—nothing but a high glacier awaited us at the head of the fjord.

Our dogs were in wretched condition, their paws cut by the sharp needles that form at the bottom of all the shallow ponds. We had to make footgear for them, adjust them every morning and take them off every night—if they are left on, gangrene is apt to set in because the tightness of the strings prevents adequate circulation.

We had eaten freely of our supply of meat, and the last few days had caught no seals. There were a number on the ice, but they were wild, and when we went after them we often had to swim across pools of open water.

There were twenty-five dogs and three sledges left. If absolute necessity faced us we could kill some of the dogs, eat them and feed them to their teammates. We could last about a month in that fashion. The only thing to do was to try to hurry home via the glacier. If we got only one musk ox we thought the journey would be possible. Our immediate problem was to find an approach to the glacier, which we named for our friend Nyboe. Uvdluriarq was elected to climb it and find a route back of it, which he did.

Before we ascended the glacier I tried to teach Knud how to secure the hour angle in case I should go snow blind again. But he was a strange man. Possessed of a marvelous brain, he still had made up his stubborn mind that he could never learn how to do it. I tried to teach him, but we both got angry and gave it up amidst hearty laughter at our own sensitiveness. Then Knud celebrated the occasion with tea and pudding. Astronomy had always been a nightmare to him, and now he decided to give up its study once and for all. This, for Knud, was sufficient occasion to celebrate.

I remember the five days it took us to ascend Nyboe Glacier as the worst in my life. It meant pulling our heavy sleds thousands of feet up the side of the steep mountain. I had to admire Knud. I was bigger than he and could lift heavier weights than he could, but it was impossible for me or for any of the others to do what he did.

He carried his heavy sled in a sling which he fastened around his forehead, and got up to the top of the glacier without resting. This was a climb of seven hours, and when I arrived with my burden, which I had made lighter by twice loosening the sling and setting the sled down, I realized that I had found my master.

Our meat was gone, but we had to forge ahead, and our provisions consisted of fifteen pounds of oatmeal in an old pillow case. It could not be touched. It was our only reserve.

We wore holes in the soles of our boots, and we wore out our neck muscles. But when we reached the top, Knud shot a hare which had recently borne young and therefore had milk in its udder.

"Sleep is milk, and milk is sleep!" was Knud's old motto, and we chewed on the udder and got the taste of milk in our mouths. And we went on.

A few hours later we shot some more hares, so many that we could give the dogs half of them, and we also shot some game birds for ourselves. At last we got across a foaming river and entered the Valmue Valley, where we rested.

Here were a great many musk oxen, and we began to dry meat for the return trip; wonderfully fat ribs were laid out on stones, and while we collected provisions and made observations, our stores increased and our dogs put on weight.

Tying our three sledges together, we continued on across rivers of ice. One day we encountered nine musk oxen. Knud and I had seven bullets in all. With these we managed to kill five. The rest were heifers, and we tried to scare them away. We were not successful, and then Knud got the idea to try his skill as a toreador.

I had a dagger which fitted into the barrel of a rifle, and with this weapon he killed the animals by charging them while I attracted their attention by throwing stones at them. I'll never forget Knud as a toreador. He rammed them precisely between the shoulders, and they fell dead at once.

As we returned to our tent we figured out that for two months we had eaten nothing but the meat of musk oxen, and then Knud said:

"If you could choose and could have anything in the world, what would you like to have for dinner tonight?"

"Well, I don't know; I really don't know. It's hard to say."

"What would you say," said Knud, "to a delicious piece of boiled musk ox meat? Could you imagine anything better?"

"No," I said, "not really." For that is how musk ox meat is, and that is how Knud was.

One morning Knud complained of a pain in his left leg. He limped slightly during the day, and when we packed meat I noticed that he carried less than the rest of us. That was not like him. In the evening he said he thought the pain had come from sitting on cold, damp stones, and he remembered that Harald Moltke had been ill all his life from sitting on cold stones as he sketched.

During the night he woke me up and said there must be a rock under his sleeping bag. I knew then that something was wrong; no man would wake a friend on such a slight pretext. He could not sleep, and he said that the worst thing that could happen to us was for someone to be taken sick. Somehow we had never taken this possibility into consideration.

Next morning Knud could not walk. He looked bad, and evidently ran a high temperature. There was no doubt that he had sciatica in a violent degree—caused by his having been wet the whole summer. Just as Knud Rasmussen always exerted himself more violently than anyone else in anything he undertook, so he was always sicker than anyone else when something was wrong with him, no doubt because his boundless energy kept him from giving in until he was absolutely forced to. He hated to be sick. But here in Great Wildland his pains were so fantastically great that he lay awake for many days, biting a piece of hide in his pain. His concern for the expedition was not affected, however, and one day he told me that he considered it essential that I should return home. Since he was unable to travel, he would remain there over the winter with one of the Eskimos and would return to Thule the next spring.

However, we opposed him, and the decision was postponed for a week. But then he suddenly recovered to the point where he dared to undertake the return trip. We had only two sleds left, and thirteen dogs. I have rarely seen a face so twisted in pain as Knud's on that return journey. I went ahead on skis, then came Uvdluriarq with Knud on the sled, using seven dogs, and behind him Inukitsork with six dogs. Knud lay on his back on top of the load, with his feet hanging out over the uprights, his face white as a cloth, his mouth pinched tight, and his eyes closed. Only when he got to an uneven stretch, where we all had to lend a hand in pulling the sled and it would bump and shake a great deal, would we see his eyes pinch a little tighter, but no sound would come from his lips. A couple of times the sled turned over, and he fell off. Then he would only say, "This is unpleasant!" so quietly and in such a way that we almost had to laugh at the incongruity of it all.

But fortunately he got better on the way. We made the trip in twenty-five days with quite a bit of difficulty, and when we finally reached the west coast near our settlement at Thule he was so strong that he made the last fifteen miles, which we had to cover on foot, faster than the rest of us. My feet were tender from many days of skiing, so that I fell behind, but when we reached the crest of the last hill, from where we could see our houses, Knud was sitting waiting for us, and the four of us came down with our last five dogs; the rest had been killed for fodder.

And then there was feasting in Thule! All-night dancing and heavy eating! People came running with huge slabs of whale hide and rotten bird meat and other kinds of delicacies, and Knud dissolved all of the journey's difficulties into laughter and gay stories. How the Eskimos grinned at the thought of our going hungry and carrying our sleds up the mountain while the meat of many walrus rotted in our cellar in Thule! And the women howled with scorn when Knud told of my clumsy attempts to resole our boots during the summer.

A Hudson Bay Expedition

The travels which are the subject of this selection originated in a proposal by Knud Rasmussen that he and Peter study the customs of the Hudson Bay Eskimos and map some of the area's still poorly charted coasts. A ship was built for the purpose in Denmark, and it was planned that Navarana would go along. But while she was getting the necessary clothing together and Peter was in Copenhagen in 1921, she felt ill. She died shortly after his return, her hand in his.

He tried to work out his grief in furiously active preparations for the Hudson Bay Expedition, of which he was Rasmussen's second in command. He was Captain of the new ship as well, so there was plenty for him to do. Also in the party were Jakob Olsen, a great hunter who, like Rasmussen, had been born in Greenland; Dr. Therkel Mathiassen, an archaeologist for whom Peter had much respect; Dr. Birket-Smith, an ethnographer, and Helge Bangsted, a poet whom Rasmussen had picked up in Denmark and of whose qualifications for Arctic travel Peter was a bit doubtful.

It was on this expedition that Freuchen lost his left foot, and his description here of how it happened is one of the classics of Arctic adventure. He used to say, too, that this is what turned him from an explorer into a writer. The Magda of whom he thought and whose name meant so much to him was an old friend in Denmark. They had met again during his last visit there, and he got a letter

177

from her when mail finally reached him after the operation on his foot. This missive made him realize, he said later, that she was the one he wanted to share his life, now that he had lost Navarana. He wrote to tell her so, and they were married when he returned to Denmark.

Knud had brought three families of Eskimos down from Thule to be our helpers on the Hudson Bay Expedition. They were all curious about their Canadian cousins and were fine men and women, but they fell sick, probably infected by the same germs which had slain Navarana, and now were also victimized by the itch. That was a pest we never had at Thule while we were there, but recently the bugs had infested Lauge Koch's camp, and no one knew where they came from.

Knud thought it would be a fine idea to take along a native secretary to help tabulate the traditions and folklore of the Central Eskimos. As the missionaries said that they would be delighted to have one of their number with us to scatter the seeds of religion among the heathen, Knud decided to combine the two offices in one man, Jakob. He was strong and intelligent and willing. He was also an excellent hunter, and even though he did disappoint the church (he had no inclination or interest in the missionary portion of his labor), we put him to good service on the expedition. He spread considerable seed among the different tribes, but not quite the sort the church officials in Greenland had anticipated.

The natives with us began to recover almost as soon as we sailed out of Godthaab.

Finally we sailed out of the western end of Hudson Strait, setting a course to the north of Southampton Island, and thence heading straght for Lyon Inlet where we planned to make our headquarters on Winter Island, the place where old man Parry had stopped a hundred years ago.

But we ran into bad ice—heavy and sluggish. The ice one

finds around Greenland, on both east and west coasts, is treacherous and never to be relied upon. It grips the traveler, holds him, carries him about and smashes him. We made slight progress. Resorting to all the tricks we knew, we accomplished only a few miles a day through the jungle of ice. It was also difficult to ascertain our direction, for the clouds blanketed the sun and our compasses were entirely useless so close to the Magnetic North Pole.

And then one day sure enough there was land ahead—a low range of mountains materialized through the fog. I did not know where we were, nor did anyone else, but as we approached it looked like Winter Island as described in Parry's book, and the fjord had the appearance of Lyon Inlet.

The motorboat was lowered into the water and the dogs hurried to land. They were so filthy and so lean that they scarcely looked like dogs. They made a beeline for the pond and drank till their bellies bulged. Not until then did they stop to sniff and explore the place on legs stiff from long disuse.

We shared the work as usual. Knud took the natives with him and set out to determine the location of the land we occupied and also to secure meat for ourselves and the dogs. He was always lucky and I never was; therefore, I remained at home and built our house.

To tell the truth, I was a little annoyed because Knud had left me with only two scientists and a young man named Helge Bangsted, whom Knud had hired as a handyman, as helpers. They were not much help. They pounded their fingernails instead of the nails, and their backs were too weak to lift a hundred pounds unless they emitted frightful groans. Still they were so kind and interested in the task that during the whole expedition we had no quarrels and remained until the end the best of friends.

According to the map, we were building a house on the open sea. We knew, however, that there was earth under us and that the map must be wrong.

Knud returned finally with news and provisions. He had discovered that we were situated on a tiny island, and the mainland near us supported herds of caribou. He had shot twelve and a number of seals. There were also many walrus in the sea outside, so we were assured that we would not starve.

As soon as the ice was hard Knud and I and our adopted boy, "Boatsman," left to discover the native Eskimos—if any lived about. We traveled up the fjord and came to a narrow sound through which ran a swift current. It was, we later learned, Hurd Channel, which never freezes.

The next day we set out again as soon as it was light, and before long we came upon tracks of a sled. From the tracks we could see that the sled itself was very narrow, the runners broad. Far in the distance were black dots moving through the snow.

We urged our dogs to their greatest speed in order to arrive among the natives in an impressive manner. The Eskimos stopped when they saw us coming and grabbed their guns. I was a little frightened and shouted to Knud. He yelled back that he would go ahead and meet them first.

He took off his mittens and raised his bare hands in the air. We followed his example. Instantly the natives dropped their weapons and stuck up their hands. We halted our dogs and stood quiet a few moments to give them time to look us over.

After a little while the chief stepped forward and said:

"We are only plain, common people."

"We also are only plain, common people," said Knud.

They had thought, because of our white clothes and sleds, that we were ghosts, and our whips had frightened them still more. This was the first step toward a friendship of four years' duration between the natives and ourselves. The chief's name was Pappi (The Birdtail), and the three families with him belonged to the Netchilik tribe.

It was no great treat to visit this tribe, for they had no food whatever. We brought in some oatmeal from our supply, and the woman of the house, whose body was tattooed all over, simply dumped it in her pot of old soup. The mixture was terrible to the taste. I noticed that she herself ate nothing, but she later explained to me that she was pregnant and therefore not permitted to eat from the same pot as the rest of us.

Later, when we arrived at the little post at Repulse Bay, we were greeted by a number of natives obviously cleverer and much less frightened than the Netchiliks had been. As soon as they heard us speak in their tongue they were won over. It was a surprise to them and to us how easily we could converse, and we had little difficulty in explaining to them where we had come from.

Captain Cleveland—Sakoatarnak—was quite a person and not without merit. He lived there, the only white man, and his word was law over a district larger than many states in the United States. He ordered the natives to cart our belongings from the sleds to his house and to feed our dogs. Then he asked us if there was anything else he could have done to please us. We said no, very much impressed with his grandeur. The great man then turned to the natives waiting at the door and, speaking in a soft, mild tone, said: "Well, then get the hell out of here!"

The Eskimos understood and scuttled away, leaving us alone with Cleveland.

Cleveland was a great character. When we asked him, during our first meal together, whether he would object to our bringing out a bottle of our famous Danish schnapps, he assured us that we could make ourselves at home in his house as long as we desired. "In fact," he assured us, "liquor is my favorite drink— any kind and any brand."

He was limited to six bottles a year "for medical purposes." But, as he was usually ill the very day after the ship arrived with the year's supply, he almost never had any left over for subsequent illnesses. After he had appropriated our bottle he opened up and confided his troubles to us.

His troubles had to do exclusively with women. "I have," he

said, "been too kind to too many." And now he could not get rid of them. They hung about, their husbands were insolent to him, and the women themselves were most expensive to keep. Now if we could use a few women on our expedition he was the man to recommend some very good ones. It would also be a great relief to him to be rid of them.

There was another expedition in the district. This one, said to be under Captain Berthie of the Hudson Bay Company, was to explore Committee Bay and Boothia Felix next spring. The members of it had been caught by the winter and were lying over at an occasional harbor in Wager Inlet.

I decided to drive down and see the leader.

Berthie received me royally, as did the natives. They were vastly interested in my stories and my clothes and my outfit as a whole. They questioned me endlessly. They wanted to know if all the inhabitants of Greenland had whiskers like mine. They could hardly believe that the sun disappeared during the winter entirely, and they asked whether the Greenlanders were cannibals and did they speak the same language.

Finally one of the men asked whether the natives there conceived children in the same fashion as they did, and when I assured them that there was no difference they came to the conclusion that perhaps theirs was not the only civilized country in the world.

In the evening there was a dance, and the girls came dressed in some of the most horrible costumes I have ever seen. They were made of gingham, and apparently designed after a pattern in vogue a century before. The girls were not bad-looking, but their tattooing and the gingham dresses, which they wore over their fur clothes, made them appear monstrous.

When I returned to Repulse Bay I found both Dr. Birket-Smith and Dr. Mathiassen there. Knud had thought them in condition by now to make a visit to Captain Cleveland and secure information from him in order to plan our work for next spring.

They were both overcome with joy as I met them. "He is the most amazing man!" they said. "He knows everything! He's worth his weight in gold!" They had their notebooks in hand and jotted down every remark he made.

They were both great scientists, and suspicion was not in their trusting souls. Unfortunately I have never been a saint, but I was saved by experience from believing in the old man, and I told them that he was a damned liar, and nothing else. I recognized the stories he told as the same old ones that were always used in the North to impress greenhorns. Later I learned from the natives that Cleveland had never been north of Lyon Inlet.

On our island—Danish Island, we called it—we prepared for our spring journeys. I was to go north on a mapping tour while some of the others were to drive south and inland in order to visit unknown tribes.

Dr. Mathiassen was to accompany me and assist in the survey- ing and mapping. We divided the wasteland between us and Fury and Hecla Strait so that he should go up Admiralty Bay and I through the strait and along the west coast of Cockburn Land.

We traveled with an old couple, Awa and his wife, and their adopted boy, a child who had to be fed crackers and sugar con- stantly so that he would not yell and annoy us.

Then one day a man named Kutlok (The Thumb) returned from the south where he had gone to deliver a letter. The man to whom the letter was addressed had moved, it seemed, and Kutlok had spent more than two years completing his mission. While in the south he had visited a school and received a taste of the Christian code of morals. The day after he returned home his wife gave birth to a child.

So he became a teacher. In a short time he had won over all his people to Christianity. The conversion took place at a meet- ing, and immediately all the old restrictions fell by the wayside.

In fact, it was a great relief to the natives to be able to sew all sorts of skins at any time of day or night, to be permitted to hunt whichever animals they needed, etc.

On the other hand, there were a number of beliefs and rules which it was difficult for them to grasp. It was said that the missionaries did not favor wife trading, and that would have to be stopped.

However, not to make it too dull for the poor ladies it was decided that Kutlok and a few of the mightiest men of the tribe should have the privilege of entertaining the girls, as it was considered healthy for the women themselves and also for the children they would bear.

In our group were also Aqioq and his wife, Cape York natives who had come down to Canada with us. We made good progress up the coast.

It was a joy to travel with Dr. Mathiassen. He could not drive dogs, so he walked. His speed was an unvariable three miles per hour. He started off early in the morning, and when we caught up with him he rode for a short distance. Whenever we stopped he walked ahead, and toward evening he dropped behind and caught up with us after we had camped.

We also met a party of natives on their way south to trade. Aqioq and Arnanguaq, his wife, were interested in talking with them so that they might return to Greenland and recount it later in their igloos. These natives were the same mild and understanding people as those of Greenland.

A number of small boys played outside, sliding down a slope until their clothes were filled with snow and the hair worn off their pants. The old wife of Awa asked them a couple of times to stop: "Don't you think of your old grandfather who has to walk around and hunt and hunt to fetch those skins for you? Or of your old grandmother whose eyes hurt when she has to sew pants for you?"

The children laughed and kept up their destructive play.

"Oh, how pleased one feels watching them play," she said.

"It makes one think of the time when they will be older and learn how to think and behave. How wonderful it is that foolish little children turn into intelligent grown-up people who know how to care for their things."

The natives of northern Canada have developed a fine method of making their sleds easy to haul. In the first place, the sleds are quite different from ours—long and narrow, and heavy. The runners are at least two inches broad with the crossbars fastened on clumsily. The most surprising thing is the treatment of the runners: they are made of frozen mud!

If such a sled hits a stone the frozen mud may crack, but it is marvelous how much punishment a mud runner will take. It can be repaired with a piece of chewed meat plastered on the crack.

When we came to Hudson Bay we knew nothing about this practice, and though we had better dogs, our old-style iron runners made it impossible for us to compete with the Canadians on the trail. We had no mud, but we found that frozen oatmeal or rye meal would serve just as well. I made a dough of the stuff and plastered it on the runners.

Later on in the spring when the rye meal was of no more use on the runners I made pancakes of it. As I said before, however, we were rather careless of what we smeared on it, and I gladly dispensed with my share of the pancakes.

We reached Igdloolik after a number of exciting hunting adventures along the way. This is the center of population in the northern reaches of Hudson Bay, a small, flat island at the eastern outlet of Fury and Hecla Strait. The Parry Expedition explored it when it was still believed possible to find a route north of the American continent to China and India. The land is all flat and almost at sea level and the waterways almost impossible for a skipper to navigate.

There for the first time we saw houses made of ice slabs. The natives had built them near a lake where they fished for black

salmon before the snow was in the right condition for construc-
ing igloos.

At Igdloolik, Dr. Mathiassen and I parted, he to go straight
north across the land to Admiralty Bay, and I to follow the coast
along through Fury and Hecla Strait and up the west side of
Cockburn Land to the north, a stretch never before seen or
mapped by a white man.

I was to take only one boy with me, while Dr. Mathiassen
took Aqioq and Arnanguaq and some local natives. Unfortunately I let Awa make the choice for me, and he recommended
a certain Kratalik as my companion.

Kratalik was young but said to be very clever and had only
recently married. He was the son of the chief at Igdloolik, a man
with two wives. Kratalik also had several brothers, and they
planned to follow along after us for three days or more to an
open hole in the ice where there were so many seals that one
had only to stand by and slaughter them.

We reached Ormond Island to the west, the farthest point
visited by the Parry Expedition. I climbed the mountain on the
mainland and discovered the cairn left by Parry a hundred years
before.

From Ormond Island we were to go on west. Fury and Hecla
Strait, named for the two ships belonging to Parry, was filled
with ice many years old, and it was plain to see that it could not
be navigated.

The older brother, Takrawoaq, dropped his load at Ormond
Island and set off for Igdloolik. I was occupied at the time making observations on a small island nearby, but when I returned
I found my proud Kratalik weeping furiously and crying
through his tears: "Look! Look! There he goes. I am alone with
you and afraid to go on."

Then I made a great mistake. I should have realized that he
was impossible as a helper and turned back for another man.
But I thought I could manage him, and we went on. We had
only one sled and my own dogs, which I drove. I also had to

build the snow houses every evening and cook the meal, besides observing the landscape and caring for the dogs. Kratalik did nothing but weep. He was the worst fellow I ever had to travel with, and added to it all, I went snow blind.

Kratalik then thought he could take command, and ordered me to turn back. He would leave me if I did not. I made a few pointed remarks, but Kratalik grabbed a gun and said that if I did not obey him he would shoot me. At this I had to open my painfully swollen eyelids, take the guns away from him and hide them in my sleeping bag. He only sobbed the louder and stayed with me.

We advanced along the coast and I found a new island which I named for the Danish Crown Prince, Frederick, and also a number of unknown fjords and traces of ancient settlements. But we bagged no game whatever.

Our meat supply was running low, but every other day I cached a part of the fast dwindling supply in the igloo we deserted, so that we would have a means of returning the same way we had come.

When we turned around, Kratalik became snow blind. I bandaged his eyes. Every time he got off the sled for exercise I had to lead him, and he cried out with pain, believing he was going to be permanently blind. I applied a compress of tea leaves, and that helped him.

When we reached the first igloo on our way back it had been smashed in by a bear, and our meat, as well as a spare harness, was gone. The kerosene can we had left there was upset and the contents drained.

The next caches had been visited by wolves—the meat was gone. Then we struck the track of a wolverine, the most annoying animal in the Arctic. These overgrown weasels are persistent devils, and this one had lived up to his gluttonous reputation. He had consumed the meat in one igloo, then slowly, as is usual, followed the track to the next igloo and finished the cache there.

We did our best to map the coast on the way back to Danish

Island—fortunately we had made a preliminary survey on the way up and recognized points we had passed. This land, however, can be accurately charted only from an airplane. From a sled it is impossible. Sometimes we thought we were well out over the sea, only to notice grass poking up through the snow. It was difficult to tell which was land and which was water.

When we got back to our camp the house was completely buried under the snow. By the use of our snow knives we cut a passage into the store and found spades to dig out the door of the house.

Boatsman scouted about to find the natives we had left to guard the house and soon ran back to tell us that they were alive, but buried under the snow.

Sure enough, Patloq, a highly esteemed medicine man, was buried in his igloo. He was, as his wife said, not a great man for talking and working, but he was a terrible man for thinking, and he took his time when he indulged in his specialty. He had plenty of meat in his house, as well as tea and sugar and flour, so he need go outside for nothing. This seemed as good a time as any other for thinking.

A heavy snowstorm had come up and the snow had buried everything including Patloq's house. But Patloq knew that someone was likely to return home soon, and they would find it much easier to dig him out than he himself would, so he decided to wait.

Our camp attracted neighboring Eskimos, as usual. Among those who settled down near us were a tall man, Akrat, and his wife and little daughter. He was an elderly man and the best igloo builder I ever met, constructing some snowhouses large enough for dancing. Another native, Anaqaq, a man with a past, determined to settle with us too.

Anaqaq was a Netchilik and came from a distant tribe whose ways were foreign. Over at the Magnetic North Pole the women are scarce, and it is considered a luxury for a man to have a wife to himself. Instead the men club together to support one woman —and the women love the idea. When a girl has two husbands she is the ruler of the house. She sleeps in the middle of the igloo, which is warmest and coziest, and she does very little sewing.

Anaqaq had been happy, but since faithfulness was one of the tenets of married life there, as everywhere, and two-thirds of his household did not observe the rule, he grew angry.

Anaqaq was both medicine man and physician. His specialty was curing indigestion; when the caribou migrated from the north in the fall many of his patients ate too much and his services were required. Which, of course, kept him away from home much of the time.

While he was absent the co-husband rented out the wife and was paid for her services with caribou tongues, marrow, etc. The co-husband and wife kept this breach of trust a secret from Anaqaq, but the neighbors told him—they always do—and he was deeply hurt. There were but two things for him to do to restore his honor—kill the man or go away. Anaqaq was a decent sort of fellow and chose the latter course.

He merely wandered away, becoming an Arctic nomad, strolling from place to place, suffering cold and privation and loneliness. He visited various tribes for a few days at a time, and then walked on again. He could keep alive by spearing salmon in the lakes and rivers, and he caught an occasional ptarmigan, but it was a hard life. Finally he reached Repulse Bay—he had then been walking for two years.

We always had enough to keep an extra man busy, but for a few days I let Anaqaq idle about acting the summer guest. Then when the time was ripe I gave him little duties. I returned in the evening from a day's hunting and saw Anaqaq, as usual, walking about and smiling. I asked him why he had not done his work, and he answered, in a very friendly manner, that as he was an angakok he was so holy that he was not permitted to work at all.

I had to fight fire with fire. I said that I, too, was an angakok. Recently I had met a number of ghosts who foretold Anaqaq's arrival, and they also said that while ordinarily he would not be permitted to work they would especially appreciate it if he tried to be as helpful and industrious as possible while we were in the territory.

Anaqaq and I believed each other, and he plunged into the work and was most helpful. In the latter respect he was quite different from my personal servant, Inuiyak, who was the most devoted and most stupid gentleman's gentleman I have ever seen. The man was a miracle of dumbness, but I liked him. He had been a poor native when I arrived, and he would doubtless be poor the day after I left.

He was a master sleeper. No one else in the world could sleep so long or so often as Inuiyak—and it was impossible to wake him. In all fairness I must say that he was also a great worker. If neither intelligent nor fast, he was at least persevering. I told him to shovel the snow away from the front of the house. He made various objections and excuses, but I finally got him started and merely told him to keep at it until I stopped him.

Dinnertime came and passed, but Inuiyak did not appear. The cook supposed he had gone hunting, and thought nothing of his absence. After dinner I walked outside to take my observations, and after working out the results went to bed. I completely forgot about Inuiyak.

Next morning I saw, far out on the plain, someone shoveling snow like a wild man—Inuiyak. He had shoveled a trench extending hundreds of feet from the house.

I hurried out and asked him what in hell he was doing.

"What you told me to do," he answered.

"Why didn't you come in to eat?"

"Because you said I was to keep on until you told me to stop."

We spent the fall of 1922 in traveling among the natives in the district and in transporting our collections to Repulse Bay where they were to be picked up by a schooner early in 1923.

I planned to make an extensive foray into the field, mapping the north reaches of Hudson Bay east of Igdloolik along the coast of Baffin Land. With me were Helge Bangsted, as assistant, and Aqioq, as headman. We were to pick up more native guides and hunters en route.

We set out immediately after the first of the year, 1923, in a terrific cold spell with the temperature hovering around sixty below zero. Unfortunately we had no concentrated dog food for such a trip, and our sleds were heavy. Our faces had become softened during the Christmas celebrations, and the north wind burned into them. This wind never ceases during the winter months.

We were about a week out of camp when we reached a spot where it became necessary to desert the sea ice for the land. The snow was soft for many miles, and we had to whip our dogs cruelly. Both men and dogs did their utmost, but it was clear that the loads were too heavy—we would have to throw off part of them and return for the stuff later.

After we had cached it the snow soon grew hard under a thin soft layer, and we managed to complete a reasonable distance. I was disgusted at the delay our dropping the loads would necessitate, and I decided to return for it myself while the boys made camp and built an igloo. I thought I could be back before they got up in the morning, and thereby reclaim a wasted day.

My dogs were none too pleased at backtracking when they had expected to sleep. They were entitled to their rest, but I was tired too and even more stubborn than the dogs, so I set off.

I made the trip well enough and loaded the boxes on the sled, but shortly after I had turned about the wind started to blow harder, howling like a fiend. The drifts were alive under my feet, and it was impossible for me to follow the tracks. The wind turned into a storm, the storm into a gale.

I was lost. It was impossible to determine directions, as I could not see the hills. I was growing more tired by the minute, but the dogs understood me now. I dropped my load again, keeping nothing but my sleeping bag with the extra kamiks and a small square of bearskin. I walked ahead of the dogs and they followed along after me. With no load I ought to be able to get back to camp.

I had to stop now and then to turn my back to the wind and catch my breath. It was so bad that I could scarcely stand upright, and finally had to go back to the sled and hang on to the upstanders. I could not swing my whip against the gale, and the dogs refused to go ahead.

By this time I could not be far from the others, and I decided that it would be better for me to stop than to run the risk of passing them. I was hungry, too, and when I reached a large rock behind which the wind had hollowed out a depression, I stopped. The dogs dived into the hole, and I decided to spend the rest of the night there.

I set about building an igloo, but for the first time in my life I found it impossible to cut through the snow. It had been packed solid by successive storms, and I gave it up as a hopeless task. But I made up my mind to stay awake and wait for daylight.

At first I kept awake by walking back and forth in front of the boulder. When this got too boring I tried the old trick of walking with my eyes closed. I walked ten paces straight ahead, turned right, ten more paces and another right turn, another ten paces and the same thing a fourth time before I opened my eyes to see how far I had strayed from the starting point. But for once this game proved too cold, too windy, and too uncomfortable. I felt an unbearable desire to lie down and saw no reason why I should not do so without risk, and I decided to make a small cavelike shelter where I could stretch out.

I began digging in the solid snow and soon I had a depression long enough for me to lie down in. I put my sled on top of this strange bed, then I put all the lumps on top of the sled and around the sides. I had built my bed in such a way that the end opened into the cave where the dogs were asleep, and I left this side uncovered, since it was well protected by the large boulder.

On my sled I had the skin of a bear's head I had killed some days before, and I took this along for a pillow. Finally as I crawled into my snug little shelter, I pulled my small sleeping bag in place with my foot, so that it covered the opening like a door. It was a little like a berth on a ship—rather more cramped, but I had room enough to stretch out.

I was well protected against the subzero temperature, dressed like an Eskimo in two layers of fur—one with the hairs inward against my skin, the other facing out. I had heavy boots and good gloves. Strangely enough I have never been bothered by cold hands, not so my feet.

Warm and comfortable at last, I soon fell asleep. I woke up once because my feet were cold and I tried to kick out the bag which served as a door. I wanted to get out and run around to increase my circulation, but I could not move the bag. It was frozen to the sides of my house, I thought. In reality there was an enormous snowdrift in front of it. I was annoyed but not enough to keep me from going back to sleep.

When I finally woke up I was very cold. I knew I had to get out and move about at once. What worried me most was the fact that my feet did not hurt any more—a sure sign of danger. To get out I had simply to crawl out through my little door, I thought, and I inched my way down to the bag. I could not move it. I used all my strength, but it was obvious that I could not get out the way I had come in. I was not worried because I expected to turn over the sled which covered me and get up that way. And I managed to turn over and lie on my stomach so that I could push up the sled with my back. There was not room enough to get up on my knees, but I pushed with my back the best I could. The sled would not budge!

At last I was really worried. My friends would soon begin to search for me, of course, but the question was whether I could survive until they found me. Perhaps I could dig my way out.

But the snow surrounding me was now ice, and it was impossible to make the smallest dent in the surface with my gloved hands. I decided to try digging with my bare hands. My hand would freeze, but it would be better to lose one hand than to lose my life. I pulled off my right glove and began scratching with my nails. I got off some tiny pieces of ice, but after a few minutes my fingers lost all feeling, and it was impossible to keep them straight. My hand simply could not be used for digging so I decided to thaw it before it was too late.

I had to pull the arm out of the sleeve and put the icy hand on my chest—a complicated procedure in a space so confined I could not sit up. The ice roof was only a few inches above my face. As I put my hand on my chest I felt the two watches I always carried in a string around my neck, and I felt the time with my fingers. It was the middle of the day, but it was pitch black in my icehouse. Strangely enough I never thought of using my watches for digging—they might have been useful.

By now I was really scared. I was buried alive, and so far all my efforts had failed. As I moved a little I felt the pillow under my head—the skin of the bear's head. I got a new idea. By an endless moving with my head I managed to get hold of the skin. It had one sharply torn edge which I could use. I put it in my mouth and chewed on it until the edge was saturated with spit. A few minutes after I removed it from my mouth the edge was frozen stiff, and I could do a little digging with it before it got too soft. Over and over again I put it back in my mouth, let the spit freeze and dug some more, and I made some progress. As I got the ice crumbs loose they fell into my bed and worked their way under my fur jacket and down to my bare stomach. It was most uncomfortable and cold, but I had no choice and kept on digging, spitting, freezing and digging.

My lips and tongue were soon a burning torture, but I kept on as long as I had any spit left—and I succeeded. Gradually the hole grew larger and at last I could see daylight! Disregarding the pain in my mouth and ignoring the growing piles of snow on my bare stomach, I continued frantically to enlarge the hole.

In my hurry to get out and save my frozen legs I got careless. I misjudged the size of the hole through which I could get out. My hand had, naturally, been able to move only above my chest and stomach, and to get my head in the right position seemed impossible. But I suddenly made the right movement and got my head in the right position.

I pushed with all my strength, but the hole was much too small. I got out far enough to expose my face to the drifting snow. My long beard was moist from my breathing and from the spit which had drooled from my bearskin. The moment my face got through the hole my beard came in contact with the runners of the sled and instantly froze to them. I was trapped. The hole was too small to let me get through, my beard would not let me retire into my grave again. I could see no way out. But what a way to die—my body twisted in an unnatural position, my beard frozen to the sled above, and the storm beating my face without mercy. My eyes and nose were soon filled with snow, and I had no way of getting my hands out to wipe my face. The intense cold was penetrating my head; my face was beginning to freeze and would soon lose all feeling.

Full of self-pity, I thought of all the things in life I would have to miss, all my unfulfilled ambitions. With all my strength I pulled my head back. At first the beard would not come free, but I went on pulling and my whiskers and some of my skin were torn off, and finally I got loose. I withdrew into my hole and stretched out once more. For a moment I was insanely grateful to be back in my grave, away from the cold and the tortuous position. But after a few seconds I was ready to laugh at my own stupidity. I was even worse off than before! While I had moved about more snow had made its way into the hole and I could hardly move, and the bearskin had settled under my back where I could not possibly get at it.

I gave up once more and let the hours pass without making

another move. But I recovered some of my strength while I rested, and my morale improved. I was alive, after all. I had not eaten for hours, but my digestion felt all right. I got a new idea!

I had often seen dog's dung in the sled track and had noticed that it would freeze as solid as a rock. Would not the cold have the same effect on human discharge? Repulsive as the thought was, I decided to try the experiment. I moved my bowels and from the excrement I managed to fashion a chisel-like instrument which I left to freeze. This time I was patient, I did not want to risk breaking my new tool by using it too soon. While I waited the hole I had made filled up with fresh snow. It was soft and easy to remove, but I had to pull it down into my grave, which was slowly filling up. At last I decided to try my chisel, and it worked! Very gently and very slowly I worked at the hole. As I dug I could feel the blood trickling down my face from the scars where the beard had been torn away.

Finally I thought the hole was large enough. But if it was still too small that would be the end. I wiggled my way into the hole once more. I got my head out and finally squeezed out my right arm before I was stuck again. My chest was too large.

The heavy sled, weighing more than two hundred pounds, was on the snow above my chest. Normally I could have pushed it and turned it over, but now I had not strength enough. I exhaled all the air in my lungs to make my chest as small as possible, and I moved another inch ahead. If my lungs could move the sled I was safe. And I filled my lungs, I sucked up air, I expanded my chest to the limit—and it worked. The air did the trick. Miraculously the sled moved a fraction of an inch. Once it was moved from its frozen position, it would be only a question of time before I could get out. I continued using my ribs as levers until I had both arms free and could crawl out.

It was dark again outside. The whole day and most of another night had passed. The dogs were out of sight, but their snug little hole by the boulder was completely covered by snow, and

I knew they must be asleep under it. As soon as I had rested enough I got to my feet to get the dogs up. I fell at once and laughed at my weakness. Once more I got to my feet, and once more I fell flat on my face. I tried out my legs and discovered the left one was useless and without feeling. I had no control over it any more. I knew it was frozen, but at first I did not think about it. I had to concentrate on moving. I could not stay where I was.

I could only crawl, but I got my knife from the sled, pulled the dogs out of their cave, and cut them loose from the harness. I planned to hold to the reins and let the dogs pull me on the snow, but they did not understand. I used the whip with what little strength I had left, and suddenly they set off so fast my weak hands could not hold the reins! The dogs did not go far, but they managed to keep out of my reach as I crawled after them. I crawled for three hours before I reached the camp.

Fortunately I then did not know the ordeal was to cost me my foot.

As soon as I had been inside our igloo for a while and began to warm up, feeling returned to my frozen foot, and with it the most agonizing pains. It swelled up so quickly it was impossible to take off my kamik. Patloq, our Canadian Eskimo companion who had had a great deal of experience with such accidents, carefully cut off the kamik, and the sight he revealed was not pleasant. As the foot thawed, it had swollen to the size of a football and my toes had disappeared completely in the balloon of blue skin. The pain was concentrated above the frozen part of my foot which was still without feeling. Patloq put a needle into the flesh as far as it would go, and I never noticed it.

The only thing to do was to keep the foot frozen, Patloq insisted. Once it really thawed, the pain would make it impossible for me to go on. It was obvious that we could not stay where we were and that we had to give up the whole expedition to Baffin Land. And with my foot bare to keep it frozen, we returned slowly to Danish Island, where Knud Rasmussen was completing all preparations for his long journey to Alaska.

He was horrified when he saw what had happened to me, and he wanted to give up his trip. But I insisted I could take care of myself with the aid of our Eskimo friends, and I persuaded my companions to carry out their plans according to schedule. And after a few days Knud set off to the north with two of the Eskimos, Mathiassen to Ponds Inlet at the northeastern tip of Baffin Land, and Birket-Smith south through Canada.

I was left with Bangsted and the two Eskimo couples from Thule, who refused to leave me.

I was nursed by Patloq's wife, Apa, and I was in constant discomfort. It felt as if my foot had been tied off very tightly. The leg above was all right, but the flesh below turned blue and then black. I had to lie quietly on my back while my nurse entertained me by recounting her experiences with frozen limbs. She knew a number of people who had lost both legs, others their arms or hands, but many had been killed because they were far too much trouble to take care of. And as the flesh began falling away from my foot she tried out her special treatment. She captured lemmings—small mice—skinned them, and put the warm skin on my rotting foot with the bloody side down. Every time she changed this peculiar kind of dressing, some of my decayed flesh peeled off with it, but she insisted on this treatment until there was no more flesh left.

Gangrene is actually less painful than it is smelly. As long as I kept my foot inside the warm house the odor was unbearable, so we arranged to keep the foot outside. We made a hole in the wall by the end of my bunk, and I put my foot out into the freezing temperature whenever the odor became too overpowering. As the flesh fell away from the bones, I could not bear having anything touch the foot, and at night when I could not sleep I stared with horrible fascination at the bare bones of my toes. The sight gave me nightmares and turned my nerves raw. I felt the old man with the scythe coming closer, and sometimes we seemed to have switched roles and my bare bones to have become part of him.

One day Apa told me that I needed a woman to take my mind off my pains. She brought along a young girl, Siksik, whose husband had kindly put her at my disposal while he went off on a trip with Captain Berthie. I felt like King David, who was given young girls to keep him warm at night, but I told Siksik that I was in no condition to take advantage of the kind offer.

In the meantime it seemed as if Apa's cure was having some effect. The gangrene did not spread beyond the toes. Once the decay had bared all five toes to the roots, it did not go farther, and the flesh stopped peeling. I could not stand the sight, however, and one day I decided to do something about it. I got hold of a pair of pincers, fitted the jaws around one of my toes, and hit the handle with a heavy hammer.

The excruciating pain cut into every nerve of my body, an agony I cannot describe. Siksik had watched me and was deeply impressed. She offered to bite off the rest of the toes, and if her teeth hurt as much as the pincers, she said that I could beat her up. Ignoring her offer, I fitted the pincers around the next toe, and this time it did not hurt so much. Perhaps one could get used to cutting off toes, but there were not enough of them to get sufficient practice.

I admit that I cried when I was through with them—partly from pain, partly from self-pity. But it was a great relief to have the toe stumps off, since they had kept me from walking and putting on my kamiks. Now I could at least get on my boots and hobble around.

It was at this time that we said good-by to the two scientists. They had completed their investigations and still had a long trip before them. Knud Rasmussen also set off on his big trip along the northern coast of America. He took with him the young Kraviaq and the widow Arnalunguaq. We would not meet again until we reached Denmark.

I was left with two families: Aqioq and his wife Arnanguaq, Boatsman and his young wife. The former couple had been married for many years and now surprised us, and themselves, by having a baby, a little girl. They named her Navarana, for my late wife, which, of course, placed the responsibility for her upkeep squarely upon my shoulders.

Bangsted was to remain at our camp through the winter and go out next year by sled. Meanwhile it was his responsibility to watch out for all the boxes of valuable collections which were to be sent home next year.

We had been informed that the steamer which visited Chesterfield Inlet every summer carried a doctor, and I decided to go down there to have my foot examined. The wounds refused to heal, and I was in constant discomfort.

I took my pal Inuiyak with me. We understood each other, and he had become very helpful to me. While we waited for the steamer I dug among the ruins sufficiently to convince myself that the ancient culture was closely akin to the "Thule culture" we had encountered in all the other ruins.

After a number of days the *Nascopie*, a fine modern steamer, arrived with supplies, passengers and, what was most important for me and a number of others, a doctor.

Douglas was assistant surgeon and anesthetized me when I was put on the table. My foot was taken care of, and I was put aside in a corner of the dining room while the doctors worked over the next case. The first thing I remember upon regaining consciousness was hearing one of the young apprentices who had come up on the *Nascopie* being asked to help with the operating. He was unwilling as, he said, he would faint if he looked on at close quarters. There was no one else, and his weak objections were overruled.

He was a youngster who spent most of his time kidding his companions, and he was not too well liked. He usually carried a bag of chocolates about with him, and munched on a piece of candy. Now he was instructed to stand with his hands at the bloodiest point. He begged to be let off but was ordered to stick to the job. He grew white while the doctor amputated a number of infected fingers and, after a few seconds, fainted and dropped to the floor.

The doctor said that he really thought he should cut more off my foot but gave me the chance first to see if it would cure up as it was. I was not to walk, however, until the wound was entirely healed. In fact, he advised me to go out with the steamer in order to save my leg. I could not do this, however, as I had to take my collections and my natives back home.

During the fall the natives turned pagan again. They had been Christian for more than a year and it had done them no good—the dogs had come down with distemper just the same. The Eskimos had even gone so far as to hang tiny crosses about the dogs' necks, but it had not helped. Then a young woman remembered that once as a child she had cured a dog by binding pagan amulets around its neck. She was a cautious, clever girl, so now she fastened both a cross and a round piece of wood to several dogs' necks, and the animals recovered. Then, by a scientific system of trial and elimination, they set about to determine which had been responsible for the cure. Half the remaining sick animals were treated with crosses, the rest with the wooden amulets. The dogs wearing the pagan wood recovered. Whereupon the natives returned to the ways of their forefathers, and doubtless remained satisfied until another problem arose.

I could do nothing but sit around and wait for my foot to heal. I read and wrote a great deal and listened to Douglas, who had many tales to tell me of his recent year at home in England. He had driven about in a little car and looked up all his old friends. His descriptions sounded so alluring that a great longing for home came over me. There was an emptiness within me, a need for something, so I wrote a letter to my dear friend Magdalene and asked her to marry me. It was strange that this had never occurred to me before. The exciting part of it was that I

could not hear from her for at least a year and a half. I would
have something to look forward to.

At last Inuiyak and I left for Vansittart Island. A whaleboat
belonging to the Hudson Bay Company took us part way but
turned back when we ran into ice.

We must run and hop and leap; if we stood still too long the
ice began to tip and sink under us. On certain slabs we could
not land at all without getting our feet wet. This sort of thing
had been my greatest pleasure as a boy, but I lost the taste for it
that day and have never done it since unless absolutely forced
to do so.

My foot hurt as much as it had before the amputation. Its
throbbing almost drove me wild. I sat down and tried to yank
off my kamik, but it was too painful. Then the reaction to our
labor set in and we began to grow cold. We had to get up and
walk, yet I screamed like a madman when I put any weight on
my foot.

Inuiyak pulled my kamik off—it was full of blood. The
stitches had cut through the flesh, and the wound lay open.

This was disconcerting to look at, so I made Inuiyak take
needles and sinew and sew the ends together. I closed my eyes
and set my teeth against the pain I knew was coming—and it did
not come. I felt nothing whatever. Inuiyak was a splendid
surgeon. He said that it was dangerous to get dirt in wounds,
and to avoid it he drew the sinew through his mouth, sucking it
clean. He also rinsed needles and scissors with his tongue, and
the operation did not hurt in the least.

We turned my bloody kamik inside out, and then put it back
on; but it was impossible for me to walk until the next day.

That night I was awakened by Inuiyak screaming out in fear.
He had dreamt he was drowning. In reality we were covered by
a heavy layer of snow. We wore only our summer clothes and
were sure that we were freezing. We thought we might as well
walk on until we came to Bangsted's camp, wherever it was. We

only sat down to rest occasionally, and again found a few gulls and ptarmigans to eat. There was nothing to worry us especially, except my foot.

We spent the rest of the fall at the house at Danish Island. Practically the only break in the routine was the birth of a child to Tapartee's wife. Tapartee himself was away, and the wife had stayed with us during the summer. We were visting her tent one day for tea when she told us that perhaps we had better get out —she was giving birth to a baby. It was a girl, which was the more interesting as she had boasted to Arnanguaq that *her* child would be a boy. Arnanguaq's child was the little Navarana.

The woman dug a hole in the ground and stood boxes beside it to support her arms. I asked her if she needed any help, and she said no, she was all right. She got down on her knees between the boxes, and we returned to our house.

Shortly afterward the woman came into the house to tell us what had happened. She had, as predicted, given birth to a boy. However, every child must have its navel attended to before a word is spoken in the room, and the mother was about to perform this rite when the boy's sister had run unexpectedly into the room shouting something about her clothes. This breach of etiquette had so embarrassed the boy that he drew his genitals inside his body and promptly became a girl.

On December 26, at daybreak, we were up and ready to start.

Bangsted took the least provisions, since he could buy more at Repulse Bay. We had our three sleds loaded, and turned north.

As usual with the Eskimos, there were no farewells. We only shouted at the dogs. But when we came to the point we stopped and turned our heads for one last glimpse of the little house. Bangsted was standing quietly watching after us. He had a long trip before him too.

There were three sleds of us: Boatsman and his wife, Akratak, on one; Aqioq and Arnanguaq with the little Navarana on the second; and I alone on the third. Anaqaq and his new wife also trailed along for a time, as we took with us the last meat from the house—he said that he merely wanted to visit a number of friends along the way. The first night he arrived in camp long after the rest of us, but he bragged that it was simple for the others to make haste with their tiny women; his wife was big and fat and beautiful, and hauling her was a torture to his dogs.

Two days north of Lyon Inlet we came upon the first native settlement, where we stopped over for a while.

We also met a number of natives whom the Greenland Eskimos loved so much that they invited them to follow us home to Thule and live with us. They were, my natives told me, fine people and not "disgusting" like most of the Central natives.

Aguano was one of these men. He was now en route to Ponds Inlet, and perhaps beyond. Who could tell? He was always traveling, his object being to find his Nuliaqatie—the man with whom he shared wives. The two were especially good friends and owned two women jointly; both women were loved equally well, so they said, by both men. Neither of the women could bear children, and therefore the men had arranged to live with one woman for a year, and then shift. They had done this for several years, and all four concerned were pleased with the idea.

Qinorunna, the wife now living with Aguano, was a clever, as well as a kind, woman. She had recently bought a little baby from another woman, who had inherited it in turn from the mother. Qinorunna had paid one old frying pan for the child, but the day after the exchange loud arguments arose. The baby was sick, but, on the other hand, the frying pan was cracked. What to do!

I was called in as judge and settled the whole matter by telling the women that, since both items in the deal were inferior, they should stick by their bargains. The baby was a poor little thing whose face was almost blue, and it was impossible to make it nurse from Arnanguaq's breast. Little Navarana was more than a year and a half old now, and Arnanguaq still had plenty of milk for a second child.

At Pingerqaling I met a remarkable woman, Atakutaluk. I had heard of her before as being the foremost lady of Fury and Hecla Strait—she was important because she had once eaten her husband and three of her children.

It had been a long time ago, before the natives had either guns or wood. Wood was the principal commodity desired, and Atakutaluk and her party were driving north across Baffin Land to buy wood for their sleds.

On the way they had to travel with such implements as were at hand. They rolled hides together and soaked them in water, then let them freeze in the shape of sled runners. As crossbars they used frozen meat or salmon. We saw many similar sleds still in use at Boothia Bay, constructed from musk ox skin. Theirs had been of caribou skin.

Atakutaluk's party had numbered thirteen persons, and they set out with a load of raw goods for trading. On the way, however, a mild spell of weather descended—this is not unusual even in the Arctic—while they slept in their igloos, and they were awakened by the roofs of their dwellings caving in. The sleds had been left overnight on piles of snow (to keep them away from the dogs) but the sleds, too, had thawed out and been eaten.

It is impossible to travel during the winter without a sled, and they happened to be in a bad hunting district, so they had to kill their dogs and eat them. Then they devoured their skin clothing, and some of them died of starvation.

Those left resorted to cannibalism.

The next spring by chance our good friend Patloq, the philosopher, passed by with his wife. He saw a half-demolished igloo and drew closer to examine it. On the ledge inside he saw two horrible-looking hags—Atakutaluk and another woman. Neither could walk, and both had great difficulty in speaking.

Patloq inquired about the rest of their party.

"We don't know," the women answered, but indicated with their thumbs a snow pile back of the igloo. There Patloq discovered human bones.

"Inutorpisee? [Did you eat people?]"

"We don't know," they answered.

Patloq could tell by the appearance of the bones that they had been gnawed and split for the marrow which, I am told, is like the marrow of bear bones.

It was difficult to make the women eat anything. When a person is almost starved to death it is painful to eat. They were finally induced to try some meat, and then it was almost impossible to keep them from gorging themselves. Half a day after one has first eaten, a craving for food sets in with such intensity that only a strong-willed person can resist it. The other woman could not do so, and she died three days later in terrible agony. But Atakutaluk resisted her impulses, ate only a little at first and lived to relate the experience.

Now she was the first wife of Itusarsuk, chief of the community. She was well dressed, merry and full of jokes. She herself told me her story, but she saw that it distressed me.

"Look here, Pita," she said, "don't let your face be narrow for this. I got a new husband, and I got with him three new children. They are all named for the dead ones that only served to keep me alive so they could be reborn."

Her skin was blue around the mouth—which was said to have resulted from eating human flesh—and it was impossible to make the Eskimos admit that she had had the mole previous to the experience.

I was sorry to leave these people of Pingerqaling, who were as happy as they were remote from neighbors. However, I had to press on.

At Igdloolik I visited my friend Eqiperiang and his two wives, who were sisters. The one in favor at the moment did all the talking and joking, treating the less fortunate sister like a servant. If one happened to pass by a few days later, the former servant might be queen of the day. Eqiperiang then slept on her side of the ledge. It is up one day and down the next for Eskimo women.

We left Igdloolik behind us and set out for Baffin Land. Now we were in an entirely new country, the very seat of all the traditions of the Eskimos. It was, in a sense, sacred ground for a student of these people.

The beginning of the trip was easy, for the country rises gradually from the south. We had trouble, though, with Qinorunna's little baby. It was weak and without proper food.

One night we were very tired after finally lowering two sleds over a steep waterfall, and decided to turn in and call it a day. I usually slept in the same house as Boatsman—the other two families each had their own igloo. I was soon awakened by Aguano crying outside.

"Pita, Pita! The little baby is dead!" It had been dead when Qinorunna tried to waken it for its feeding. Both the man and the woman cried and said they were sure it must be their fate never to have children.

The little body was sewn inside of two skins, carried out through a hole in the back of the igloo and up to a depression in the cliff where there were many loose stones. Aguano built a grave and placed the baby on it, then covered the dead child with so many stones and in such a helter-skelter manner that no one would suspect it was a grave. He did this, he said, because many Eskimos must pass here between Igdloolik and Ponds Inlet and they might be frightened if they knew this was a grave. He then asked all of us who had helped him with the stones to give him our mittens. We did so, only to see him bury the mittens too. Later on, when it was permitted her to sew again, Qinorunna made us each new ones.

I tried to go on next morning, but we had to remain there for five days. Arnanguaq complained that she was ill; Akratak did not want to drive on, as we had plenty of meat and my foot needed the rest. So we stayed and mourned the customary period, and Aguano was deeply grateful.

As we drove on Aguano stopped several times, walked back, and swept out the tracks behind our sleds. He did this because the little child who had been so weak in life would, after death, have its full strength and might do violent injury to us if permitted to trail us. It was better to be careful and cover our tracks.

We followed a river with indifferent sledding into Milne Inlet. The inlet itself was hard to traverse, because the snow was deep and soft—the wind apparently never blows at the head of the fjord.

It was certainly a long fjord that the old whaler had discovered. It took us two days to reach better ice, and we had to walk along beside the sleds on skis. Aguano owned none and was handicapped because of it. Finally we came to a seal blowhole and stopped; Aqioq stood beside it and in less than an hour had killed a seal. We had eaten so much caribou on the journey that we were famished for a change in diet and sat down to a delicious meal.

We drove on toward Ponds Inlet.

The natives there had "progressed" to the use of wooden houses, but it was certainly no improvement for them. Nothing can be more hygienic than living in temporary igloos and tents, because garbage and filth cannot accumulate. But some of them were living in tiny houses there, and they had no idea how to keep them clean. It was obvious that a great many of them had already contracted tuberculosis. They may have had it before, of course, but their conditions now were far from favorable to a cure. The stench inside the houses was nauseating and the air suffocating. I noticed also that they had bought clothes from the store, and used filthy old rags for bedclothes.

Ponds Inlet is actually the sound between Bylot Island and Baffin Land. The island's high mountains are stately and impressive. Only the southwestern corner is lowland, a vast plain said to be excellent for pasturage.

Aguano and Qinorunna tagged along with us. They intended now to go as far as Lancaster Sound and hunt, while waiting for their partners to show up. They were supposed to be somewhere along the east coast of Baffin Land.

We had no particular adventures the first few days, caught a couple of seals at their blowholes and encountered beautiful weather. Then as we entered Eclipse Sound a gale struck us and we had to stop for several days in an igloo. The wind was so strong that it tore a side out of the igloo, and the snow drifted until it nearly swamped the shelter.

Next day we heard someone yelling at us far up the coast, and a native staggered toward us begging our help. His people were starving, he said; two of them were dead, and they had no dogs to drive for help. He was the only survivor who could move about, and he looked very ill. I gave him one seal and the food we had counted upon Aguano and his wife using. Then I wrote a note to the police at Ponds Inlet and hurried Aguano back with it.

Thus finally we parted company with the kind young couple, and never saw them again. The three girls cried and expressed their grief at parting in a manner entirely unlike any other Eskimos I had ever met. And at last we were alone and on our final stretch home to Greenland.

Suddenly Akratak yelled: "Look! There's open water right behind us!"

We turned and saw the open sea at our heels. It looked like a yawning mouth, the jagged edges of ice like teeth grinning at us. We yelled at the dogs and drove on with the wind at our backs.

But soon there was open water ahead of us. The ice pan on which we stood had revolved!

I was frightened now, and we decided to stand by and wait until the gale had blown itself out. The little Navarana needed to get up, so we cut some snowblocks and made a shelter for her mother, Arnanguaq. The two women sat together while we stood and talked about the situation. Suddenly we heard a scream. The ice had parted between the women; Akratak had grabbed up the child and had run with her. The mother's arms were inside her coat, and she could not get them out in time. Thus the two women were parted by open water, and I ran after Akratak and Navarana. I took the child—she had been lying on her mother's lap with no kamiks on her feet—and stuffed her inside my coat with her feet down inside my pants. She thought this was very funny and laughed hilariously, but her position prevented my jumping back to my friends, and after a few seconds the water was too broad to leap over.

The natives were frightened. We ran up and down the ice searching for a spot where we could cross to each other. Finally Boatsman shouted that he had found a place. I took off my coat, turned it inside out, and poured the child into it. Then I shouted to the father to come and help catch her, and I tossed her like a sack. They caught her, and the mother immediately stuffed her into her hood again. Akratak and I walked farther along the crack until I found a place narrow enough to jump.

Now we came to break after break in the ice. We had stopped thinking about our direction—we only sought to prolong our lives from one moment to the next.

After a while the snow stopped drifting, and the weather turned warmer. The wind still blew, but we could at least see where we were.

Eventually there seemed to be a lessening of pressure around us, and we thought we could get to a larger pan floating past. Boatsman and I made it across on my sled, and Aqioq was to follow immediately after. But the pressure began again; his dogs were frightened and pulled his sled back, so that we were separated after having been but ten feet apart.

We knew that we should wait until the time was ripe and not risk our lives in trying to get together. We were all dreadfully uncomfortable, our clothes wet from the warmth, and the ice wet too, so that our kamiks were soaked.

But worst of all was having to stand and wait, unable to do anything. We told the women to sleep if they could; they simply lay down on the sleds and were immediately dead to the world. We had been fighting the ice now for thirty hours, and they must have been exhausted.

I also snatched a nap now and then, until Aqioq's ice pan shrunk so small that his family could barely stand on it. His dogs whined in terror, and he knew he would have to try to get across now or never. He started over the ice wall at a spot where it looked fairly quiet, but it began to slip and slide when he was at the very top. The dogs fell and howled in pain. They can stand little ice pressure, because their feet were easily caught and crushed by the heavy, moving ice.

Aqioq saved his sled and six dogs, but more than half his load was irretrievably lost. Once more we pulled ourselves onto the middle of an ice pan and took stock of our reduced resources.

It seemed to me impossible to make it home to Greenland now. There were only sixteen dogs in place of the thirty-four yesterday. We had no kerosene and no Primus stove, and in all only about thirty rounds of ammunition for each of our three guns.

We were, I thought, in about the middle of the sound. With good going we could make it to either side in one sleep. If we returned to Baffin Land we could reach a settlement within a few days; if we went on to North Devon we might be forced to stay over for the summer in an unfamiliar, uninhabited country.

Thus it meant going back to the land we had just left. I would have liked to try to complete the trip if I had had my own time, but the *Soekongen* would be leaving Thule soon, and we had arranged that, if I was not there when it left, it was to pick me up at Ponds Inlet. I had, by the grace of God, saved my notebooks. It was only my good luck that I had not lost my sled and load.

Once more we divided everything between us. The two Eskimos drove the two sleds with eight dogs each, and carried the load.

Now followed two harrowing days. There was no safety for us anywhere. We could neither cook nor dry our clothes, and as it turned cold once more, we were all miserable. Arnanguaq rocked back and forth with her baby on her lap, wrapped in whatever we could provide, and moaned. After a while both child and mother fell asleep. When they woke, little Navarana took up her crying where she had left off. Arnanguaq then found several enormous lice in my shirt and accused all the white race of breeding lice that bit like wolverines. The situation was anything but merry.

Meanwhile we drifted about aimlessly in Lancaster Sound, and there was nothing to keep the women interested. Aqioq motioned me away from the women and said confidentially that Arnanguaq, after all, was a woman, and "she belongs to those who are angry when adrift on an ice pan if they have small babies." I admitted that one did not encounter the type every day and that if this was her specialty she might as well take advantage of it when she had the opportunity.

It took us many hours to reach shore, jumping across dark, treacherous stretches of water between ice pans, and shoving and pulling the ice together. I could not help admiring the two women, who were now in action for the fifth day with no more than four hours of actual sleep. They leaped about like young schoolboys, a little nervous, perhaps, but always courageous. I especially admired Arnanguaq. She was rather small and heavy, but she was as light on her feet as Boatsman's wife.

When we once more stepped on solid ground we were far to the west of the place we had left, and the two sleds were still far out on the ice. What would become of them I did not know —and the guns were on the sleds. As we watched they drifted westward, farther from us each moment.

Akratak offered to take the harpoons and try to reach the

sleds again while I cared for Arnanguaq and the baby, but I considered this a challenge, gave her my matchbox and started for the sleds. I reached them in less than three hours, but I was so exhausted by then—I had not slept in five days and I have never been able to keep awake longer—that I sank down and passed out.

When I eventually awoke I was stiff from the cold. Not only my clothes but my limbs were rigid. The temperature had dropped suddenly, and we could see the ice forming solid on the water. If we had only waited a few hours we could easily have reached shore on either side.

We drove east again to locate the women and finally heard a voice calling to us. Akratak stood at the mouth of a cave in the cliffs. They had discovered a wonderful shelter, and Arnanguaq was still asleep in it but woke when she heard our voices.

We decided to remain here until our clothes were dry and we were fit to travel again. Arnanguaq grew merry again, and we discussed our adventures on the ice as if they had been arranged for our pleasure. Eskimos are great people.

My foot started hurting once more. I had completely forgotten about it. When I examined the foot it looked like an old newspaper soaked in water, a wonderful but not very pleasant sight. The pain seemed to mount when I lay down, yet I could not bear to put any weight on the foot.

Two days' traveling brought us back to Admiralty Bay where we could see open water cut by the tides at the mouth of the deep inlet. We stayed there for three days and had nothing to eat. Boatsman and I then drove up to a bird cliff we discovered at the eastern entrance of the bay and, using our shotgun, wasted all the rounds of ammunition for it in killing a few gulls. Meanwhile the area of open water expanded at the mouth of the bay, and we knew we would have to hurry.

Aqioq, who had been here before with Mathiassen, advised us to travel far down to the head of the fjord. There, he said, was an adjacent fjord leading to the east. He had hunted caribou there and had followed a valley eastward. It was his opinion that the rivers ran eastward to Milne Inlet from there, and he thought it would be safer to take an overland route.

I thought of my ill-treated foot and hoped to God that we would not have to walk. We argued for a while and then decided to do as Aqioq had suggested. The seals became more abundant as we traveled up the bay, and the immediate danger of starvation passed.

Aqioq was the first to spot the people.

They looked strange to us, unlike any people we had ever seen before. Their faces were hollow and their eyes sunk deep in their skulls. They had no real clothes but were covered with scabrous-looking rags and filth.

They were starving.

Their voices were eerie. I have seen many shocking things in my life, but nothing like this. We thought them ghosts at first, but I talked to them. Thirteen of the tribe had died during the winter, and there was no prospect of anything but death for the rest of them.

They told us that they had been caught by a gale which lasted from one moon to the next. Their chief, the famous Tulimak (The Rib), had died first, and after that no one was able to prevent the weaker members of the tribe from eating the dogs. The starving animals had not been butchered—they had died off faster than the dog meat could be eaten. Eating the diseased and starving dogs had caused a plague among the natives, they told me. It was evident on their faces.

We gave them a seal to eat. Like very poor people, they did not want to take our food and cut off only a small portion and gave the rest back to us. There were twelve of them left, among them a few I had previously met in Igdloolik. After we had built a fire and boiled soup in their pots they seemed to revive slightly.

They told us that the corpses were left a little farther along the fjord. We could see the spot plainly, but Aqioq, who was more curious than the rest of us, begged me not to look at the bodies. Either the natives, or their dogs, had eaten some of the human flesh.

Our own plan was immediately forgotten in our desire to help these wretched humans. There were four families of them, though I learned that several of the families had been broken up by death. As soon as possible after the deaths they had repaired the missing links in the couples. Akratak learned that one of the girls had had four different men during the winter. She had accepted the men because it was believed that death is always a greater peril to a single person than to a married one.

I took a special fancy to one of the young men, Mala, who had lost his whole family. He and I stuck together, and he was in good shape again within a week. The men walked to their old camping place and brought up their property. Considerable property it was too, including two loads of narwhale tusks secured at the big killing last fall.

After a while we moved north. First we took two of the local natives with us, and each day when we went hunting we brought more. I gave them my sled to use, and they hauled up their belongings and settled down. They had plenty of needles and guns with ammunition.

Mala and I went out hunting alone for several days, driving up the fjords because he would not let me approach the spot where they had spent the winter. The place, he said, would be haunted all summer. Although the dead had been buried, one could hear their ghosts moving about; if we drove near, the ghosts might follow us and kill us.

We fed the starving people and gave them whatever we had. In return they gave us thread to mend our tents and clothing, ammunition and knives. They were not badly off, but the things they possessed could not be eaten. They were just what we needed most.

Soon afterward we moved farther up the fjord where the men could get out to sea in their kayaks and hunt.

At last I felt that it was time some of us, at least, should go to Ponds Inlet and head off Captain Pedersen. The natives agreed that it would be possible to walk across country, but we could take no sled with us, and the going would be difficult. I thought about sending some of the Baffin Landers, but we were not sure we could trust them, especially as they were afraid of facing the relatives of their dead companions in Ponds Inlet. I asked Boatsman and Akratak if they would like to go, but she was, after all, a girl and not so strong as we were; it would not look well to send a woman after help.

So I decided to go myself, and my friend Mala volunteered immediately to go along if I would pay him for the trip. He did not know at first what he wanted, but I assured him he could have any and everything he wished if we made the trip safely.

The next day was the worst of all. I shall never forget it. The clay was a slough, and we sank deep into it. We were so completely plastered with the gritty stuff that we lost interest in trying to keep clean. Whenever we stopped it was all I could do to get up. My brain felt doped, my body a dead thing. I walked ahead with the gun, and Mala plodded after with the harpoon. We dared not mention game any longer; it was too tantalizing.

If I could only lie down, I thought. To hell with everything but sleep. Every inch of my body cried out for it, but I knew what would happen if I gave in to my body. I must have slept as I walked, because suddenly I toppled over and fell face down in the disgusting stuff. I could not get my breath, yet I did not have the initiative to raise my head out of it, and only came to when Mala stood over me, shouting and yanking at my hair.

Then I thought of Mequsaq and Pipaluk. One step for Pipaluk—up with the bad leg and forward. One step for Mequsaq —the foot sank and disappeared in the hellish stuff.

One step for my mother, and my father and my sisters and

my brothers. I thought of them all, and took a step for each of them. One by one. One by one.

And then I stopped thinking of them. I knew that I might as well confess that I was going through this purgatory to get home to Magdalene. I had never had an answer from her, but I was sure I would have her someday. If it had not been for the thought of her, I could never have gone on with that red-hot piece of iron hanging at the end of my leg.

I would call the whole stretch of clay and hell Magda's Plateau. As soon as the idea came to me things seemed easier. If it were named for her I could cross it somehow—there must be something good about it.

Poor Mala had to rest. The boy was young and had been through one hell already this winter. He had watched his people die of starvation and had looked the monster in the face himself. Now he had been tricked into coming along with me only to meet the old terror once more.

I sat down beside him. We were so careless of ourselves now that we flopped into the wet clay as if it were an easy chair. I let it run through my hands as children play with sand at the beach. Mala told me about his father's death.

"Did you think you were going to die, Mala?" I asked.

"Oh, no. One never thought of that. Help was sure to come —just as it is now. We, too, could die, but we are not going to!"

His confidence was a challenge. He was right. We were not going to give up!

We jumped up together. I discovered that the barrel of the gun was full of clay, but, worst of all, the sight was gone. It had dropped off and buried itself in the clay. What use was a gun without a sight? I was in such a childish rage that I threw the gun as far as I could. It sank almost out of sight.

"Come, let's go!" I shouted, and set off. I was half-mad by now, and my fury possessed me. I walked on, punishing my foot, almost getting a thrill out of the daggers that pierced it.

Mala came along, and I waited for him where some stones

poked up through the clay. There was even one large enough to sit on. I turned around, and there was the boy carrying both gun and harpoon, and looking like a dog expecting a whipping.

"You can take this," he said, handing me the harpoon.

He was the wise one; the gun had to be carried. I had not been myself when I tossed it aside.

And then at last we reached a more friendly portion of God's good earth. We saw no living things, but we discovered a few plants, the roots of which we could chew and digest. Besides, here was year-old dung of rabbits. If one has blubber (we did not) it can be eaten easily. We collected the excrement, chewed it and got it down. It is hard to swallow, but at least gives one a sensation of having something in the stomach. We collected roots and grass and ate as much as we could. The new, juicy grass was not bad to taste, but swallowing it was something else.

We walked for short distances and then slept until we grew cold. Once Mala wakened me by laughing.

"What is so funny?" I asked.

"The idea comes to one's head," he said, "that after having had one tough time before, the same man runs into worse as soon as he has recovered from the first. One likes to be fat and comfortable, but this is a funny way of doing it."

"I want a knife, a knife of every kind," he said, and I promised them to him before we slept again. Perhaps he dreamed of all his possessions while he slept. I hope he did.

Next day we came within sight of the sea and Mala shot a rabbit. It helped some, but in order to reach the sea we had to cross a small lake by wading in it up to our bellies.

Next morning we walked out on the ice with more confidence, but when we had been walking for two hours we considered it worse than the land. But not worse than the clay—nothing could be.

There were seals on the ice, but there was also water. Mala had the first try at a seal and missed. Then I took the gun, and the seal spied me and flopped into the water.

Mala tried his luck at another seal, but it sank. I shot and wounded one, but it got away. Mala missed another, I missed another, and several dived before we could get close to them.

At last we were down to four bullets. It was my turn to crawl up to the next seal. Our bad luck had probably been due to the trumped-up sight we had attached to the gun, but now I was desperate.

The seal was no fool, and I put on such a performance as few actors have ever given an audience. I lay on my side, lifted my head and my legs like seal flippers. I rolled over and lay with my head in the wet snow on the ice—and I thought of what would happen if we died here of starvation after all our troubles. How silly we would look if we were found here on the ice . . .

Meanwhile the seal's head was up. It obviously distrusted me. Each time I crawled nearer, it grew more uncertain of my kinship. I presume I played with that seal for three hours, wallowing in the wet snow, finally realizing that I was as close to it as I ever would get. The distance between us was still formidable, but I was in a rage by now and pulled up my gun and fired. The seal flopped over dead!

We were saved. Here was a whole big seal for us, and no dogs with which to share it. We lapped up the blood streaming from the bullet hole, we stroked the skin and considered where it would be best to start eating.

It was our big day, the day that gave us back our lives. We had cared for our matches all this time, and this was the first chance to use them. We used the blubber for fuel by chewing the fat and spewing it out over some turf. We found two flat stones, placed the meat between them over the fire, and roasted it.

That is one dish I shall always remember. It was better than anything I have ever tasted in my life.

We had come down to Milne Inlet and not, as we had expected, to Eclipse Sound. We know, however, that there were inhabitants at Toqujan, and we headed straight for that community. It took us three more days, and when we finally came within sight of the village we were received with shrieks of joy and fright.

The women were fascinated at the sight of our bodies. We were so emaciated that we could have passed for freaks in a sideshow. All of them wanted to feel my ribs and made conjectures as to my probable appearance when well fed. I said I was not going to be butchered, and they thought that very, very funny, laughed uproariously, and repeated the remark over and over.

The natives were going now to Button Point on the southeastern point of Bylot Island to hunt narwhales. I was still very weak and should not have gone, but I got a lift from a man with a good team, and it proved lucky. The man had a daughter and although she was no great beauty Mala took a shine to her —and I had promised earlier to get him a wife.

We camped twice en route. Each night I used all my powers as lecturer, advocate and barker to convince the whole family that Mala was the one and only perfect man for a son-in-law. The father swayed like a reed in the wind. There was also a local widower after the girl—and he would give the girl a splendid wedding. The girl whispered this to me herself, and I told the family that if Mala married her while I was here they should have such a wedding as none of them had ever imagined. From my ship would be brought box after box of presents. The kettles I would give to all the women related to the family would be miracles of beauty, and I would present Mala with a boat which the Hudson Bay Company would sell. That gave Mala the advantage over the widower.

When we landed at Button Point, Mala was informed that he was the lucky man. He took his new wife into the tent I had given him, and I lived with them as long as we were at the point. When I finally left to walk back to Ponds Inlet, Mala said he was not yet through hunting and would come along later. He needed more meat, he said, and his feet were not yet hungry for walking. Neither were mine, but it was August, and I knew I had to hurry.

I never saw Mala again, as he did not show up before I left Baffin Land. But at the 1934 annual dinner of the Circumnavigators Club in New York my good friend Reginald Orcutt screened some pictures he had filmed at Ponds Inlet. There was Mala in all the brilliant colors of the film. It was as if I enjoyed a visit with the fine boy again, and all the old memories of our struggles and companionship came back with a rush. It is to him that I owe my life—such as it is.

FICTION

The completeness with which Peter Freuchen entered into Eskimo life is evidenced by his adroitness in writing about the feelings, thoughts and desires of the people as well as their customs, behavior and legends. All of this is reflected perhaps best in his short stories and novels.

It was not quite true that, as he once said, the loss of his foot turned him into a writer; he had published a good deal of non-fiction before that. But he did begin to write fiction after recovering from the last of the operations on his leg, and he soon became known as a successful novelist and short story writer in both Europe and America.

Most of his tales were based on stories he had heard and people he had met in the Far North. In them he was able to convey with even more depth and color than in his other works the true character of the Eskimos, the traits which endeared them to him, their heroism, simplicity, ideas of right and wrong. The selections given here are representative samples of the many Freuchen tales which reveal facets of Arctic life seldom examined seriously by other authors.

Probably no one else could develop these themes to give readers such a clear sense of Eskimo values, Eskimo justice, Eskimo attitudes. The first deals with a subject which few writers have dared approach realistically, and yet it escapes being a horror story. The second is an Arctic murder mystery in the best modern manner. The third is almost a murder story, too, and with an even more modern twist.

Hunger

One day, somewhere in Hudson Bay, I lay freezing in an igloo. There was neither food to eat nor blubber to burn, and such a storm raging outside that any immediate hunting was impossible. I lay there dreaming of food—all the delicious things that can be set forth upon a dining table appeared tantalizingly to my mind's eye, and nothing much else seemed worth thinking about. I began to tell my companions about omelets as we make them at Cape York—so daintily delicious one could swallow them in large pieces without even chewing—and many other tasty dishes.

Old Ututiak and his wife, Manik, were with me. We were on a hunt which up to now had been none too successful. We weren't too bad off, however, as we still had dogs we could eat, but it was mostly the miserable weather that bothered us.

"Tell us something, Ututiak," I said, "something about the worst hunger you have ever suffered, so I can think about something else than Cape York and the abundance of food there."

"Ah, you talk of hunger," said the old man. "You are a white man and will never know the Great Want, for since you whites have come up here, life is not nearly as hard for the Eskimos as before. Yes, I can tell about Want, for I learned to know hunger in my childhood days. My wife, too, knew hunger early in life. See how calmly my old woman sits over there, hardly thinking

225

about the two days that have gone by since we last ate. Ah, you must learn to know this land. It can be barren of everything, and yet so full of life that all the people in the world could eat their fill.

"I recall my worst experience. It is such a long, long time ago that I don't like to think of it very often, but I will tell you of the worst hunger I have ever felt.

"It was a long time before you white men lived in this land. Once in a while the whalers came and we traded with them, but they always sailed quickly away after the catch. So we people were all alone here in the Great Winter that lasted two years. All summer the ice never broke up, and snow still covered the land. That has happened only twice in my long life, and now I am a very old man.

"All summer we had gone hungry, and lived in poverty and need, and now came the darkest month—that month which is the worst for us people up here. At that time we lived at Ussu-garssuk, and most of the men wanted to chance going farther north, but my father and his partner stayed on to catch seals in the open water and through the breathing holes in the ice.

"There was nothing but hunger and want. My own mother was dead, and my father was married again—to a sister of the other man's wife. Each of these women had a child, and their old mother lived with them—now in the one house, now in the other. At that time I was just beginning to be a hunter. I had a gun—a muzzle-loader, the kind we don't use any more. Mostly, we used bows and arrows on our caribou hunts.

"Then the other man died, and his wife moved in with us, and my father and I struggled to provide for all. Besides those whom I have mentioned, my foster sister lived in our house. I mean Manik, here, whom my mother had once bought and raised to be a wife to me. She was a little younger than I was, but strong, and had begun to sew.

"Our dogs were very poor, because they didn't get any food. One day my father said he would take all the dogs and go out to the edge of the ice to look for bears, and he would remain away for several days. But he left a couple of the dogs at home, because if a bear should prowl around at night, the dogs would wake us, and then I could get out and shoot the bear.

"But my father stayed away a long time. We suffered terrible hunger. The two small children were dead, and I often saw the women, with their curved knives called *uloes,* go up toward the hill where the graves were. What they did there I will not say. For the most part, our food was a little skin, or small thongs.

"But one night as I lay pretending to be asleep, I heard the women whispering together; they pointed at my foster sister, and said that she was strong and fat. I knew that the next night they would kill her with an axe, so they could eat her. I still lay as though asleep, but I thought a lot about what we should do, and I decided to save her by running away. It seemed to me that if we *must* die, we might just as well die alone out there in the snow and ice, as to be murdered and eaten by these women.

"It's queer about women. Sometimes they are so good and kind, but in times of terrible want and need, they are always more ferocious than men. Next day I told Manik that her life was in danger, and that we must run away.

"It was impossible for her to leave at once, for her clothes weren't good enough. We had eaten the soles of her kamiks, and she would have to sew in others. So the next night I left the axe and the knives, and any other things that could kill, outside —and when we went to bed I said that unfortunately I had forgotten them, left them out where I was working, and now I didn't feel like getting up to go after them. The old woman said they must be brought in, but I pretended that I didn't understand what she meant and said: 'But what do we want with hunting knives at night?'

"Next day I told them I was going up the fjord to try to catch seals through the breathing holes. I wanted my foster sister to go along, but they didn't want to let her go. So then I said that

she would have to go around on the ice to chase the seals away
from the other breathing holes and drive them over to the one
where I would stand. For when the seals hear anyone walk on
the ice, you see, they always swim away.

"I told Manik to take a couple of sewing needles along, and
her woman's knife. I took my weapons and a little axe, and out
of the storeroom I took all my lead and powder, which luckily
the women had not seen. Also, I took my sleeping skin, and a
deer skin to lie upon. The women told us that if I didn't catch
anything that day, then Manik should come home and tell them
about it. I promised she would, but I knew they intended to
kill her when she was alone and didn't have me to help her.

"We took the biggest dog with us, to smell out the seals' blowholes, and we loaded our few possessions onto a small draw-sled.
When the women weren't looking, I also took a small pot, and
then we left.

"It was hard walking. When one is very hungry, one tires
easily, and it seemed to us such a long, long way to the head
of the fjord where we couldn't be seen from the hut. But as
soon as we were out of sight, we turned inland. If we continued
inland, we would reach other people, and our one thought was
to get away from the women.

"But we didn't make much progress, and that night I built
a tiny igloo. It was small because I didn't have enough strength
to build a bigger one, and we crawled into it and lay down to
sleep. We had nothing to eat. And next day, when we should
have been on our way again, we could hardly walk. But I was
lucky enough to see a fox quite close by. I shot it, and we ate
it at once. We gave the dog the bones, entrails and skin—all
except the tail, which Manik kept to hold over her nose, against
the cold. Manik and I ate the rest of the fox, and it was wonderful to eat fresh meat again. We felt new strength and set out
again quickly, for it doesn't take very long to eat a fox, especially one so little and thin.

"Next day we had nothing. Then I shot a pair of ptarmigan.

We divided everything between us, and made our slow way onward. We were so afraid that we hardly thought of weariness, but we became hungrier and hungrier.

"At last we walked the way we had seen white people walk when they had drunk too much rum. We staggered so that we had to support each other. I talked of eating the dog, but Manik said: 'Oh, no, wait a little and let it live as long as possible, because I'm afraid to stay alone when you go hunting. I think of the eyes of those women, when they looked at me back home in the hut.'

"But suddenly, as we walked along, we saw the dog raise his head and prick up his ears as though he had seen something or other. I could see he had the scent of something, and luckily I grabbed him by the neck, put a line around him and let him lead me in the direction where there must be *something*. Soon he lost the trail. But he found it again, and in a short while we came to a place where a bear was hibernating.

"Oh, but I was glad! Now we would eat and live. I went quietly back to where Manik was, and took all our things on the draw-sled up to the place where the bear lay. Then we began to dig away the snow around it. It lay in a hole which it had dug in the snow, and it soon began to growl at being disturbed in its sleep. I struck at it with my harpoon, and it grew angry and came rushing halfway out of the hole. But a bear that has slept a whole winter is blinded by the sun and can't see anything clearly. So I took my gun, held it up close to the bear's head, and fired; and then it was dead.

"We were so happy we couldn't say a word, but sat down, just as if we were used to having bearmeat every day. I then had strength enough to build a small igloo, for we intended to stay there a long time. We helped each other skin the bear. It was fat, since it was a female, and as we skinned it, we ate the fat that lay between the intestines. We gave the dog the entrails, and meat, too—all it wanted to eat. Manik smeared blood on her face, as a sign of thanksgiving to the bear.

"When we were through skinning the bear, I went off a little way, without saying why I went, and looked around until I found a flat stone with a hollow place in it, which we could use to make a lamp. Now we were really comfortable. We set about making a fire at once. I had my tinder box with me, and I lit the lamp and melted away some ice, so we could have water to drink. All this time we had been eating snow and ice, until our lips were full of cracks—this is very painful. But now we ate meat, and things were just wonderful!

"The next day I built a new igloo right behind the first one, which then served as a sort of entryway. And we found a couple more stones which could be used as lamps, so we warmed ourselves thoroughly and also dried out our clothes. Manik was now a regular little housewife, and she looked after my clothes and mended them, using bear sinews for thread, as we had nothing else for sewing.

"While we stayed there, a terrible blizzard blew up. We told each other that had we been out in it, and had we *not* found the bear, we would surely have died. But now we had eaten and were warm enough; our dog was with us, and we had all one could wish for. We ate all the time. The dog looked like a different creature, with a big, fat belly. We were so comfortable—in fact, I don't think I have ever been as comfortable since.

"When we had no more meat left than we could carry with us, I made coats for ourselves and a harness for the dog out of the bearskin. We also made new kamiks of bearskin, and then we continued on our way, going in the same direction—away from the women.

"We had talked about taking meat back to the women, but we couldn't carry any more than we ourselves would need to eat on the return journey. In that case we would have arrived there with only very little meat. Anyway, if my father had not returned, they must be dead by now, and so we went forward. We would never see them again.

"We traveled toward the unknown. We talked about the

people we would meet—perhaps they would be enemies, but they couldn't be worse than the women in our own home, from whom we had fled.

"Our legs seemed stiff when we began to walk, for we had lain still so long, and eaten so much. But we were so much stronger that we walked faster than before. And each night we made fire and heated water and cooked meat, which was a wonderful help.

"The last couple of days I had noticed deer tracks in the snow, all headed north. So it must be the time of year when the caribou began their northward trek. I knew that soon we would reach the places where one could always find caribou. So I began to make myself a bow from a deer horn which I had found, and a bowstring from bear sinew. But before the bow was finished, we came on the caribou.

"One morning as we lay in our igloo, just as I was awakening, I heard the dog barking outside our hut. So I listened and heard a noise outside. At first I thought it might be the rushing of a river, but that couldn't be possible at this time of the year. Then I thought it sounded like a bad storm, and then I thought it might be people. But when I went outside, I saw that there were caribou all around us—every way I looked. It was the clattering of their hooves on the ground that had wakened me.

"Oh, but there were many of them! They came and kept on coming, and there seemed no end to caribou, looking both toward the way they were going, and the way from which they came. It was well for us they weren't headed right toward our hut, for it would have been trampled down, and we ourselves crushed to death. Now I knew that we had finally reached the place where there never was hunger or need, which I had so often heard about.

"I shot only a couple of them. We ate the marrow bones and the tongues, and now we had sinew thread enough to complete my bow, for I wanted to save my ammunition. In those days one never knew when one could get more of *that*.

"Now we were saved. We thought no more of the people we had wanted to reach. We thought only of the caribou. My, but they tasted delicious! It was just like the pictures we see from your land, where you guard the herds. We traveled with them by day, and halted at night. Sometimes they gained a little on us, but we caught up to them again, and there was quite a feeling of familiarity between the deer and ourselves. We killed what we needed, and could pick and choose. We had new fur coats, and new sleeping skins, and everything we needed.

"It was a pretty hard time for Manik, though," added Ututiak. "Do you remember how we spoke of its being difficult to make all kinds of clothes—and that I, of course, should do the man's work and scrape the skins to make them soft? It wasn't so easy for me, either. Now we are old and can laugh at it, but at that time it was a serious matter.

"Sometimes we felt so alone and afraid, for of course we couldn't continue living like that. Our greatest fear was that the sewing needles should wear out. They broke often, and each time I ground them on a stone they became shorter, and we could hardly sew with them any longer.

"But finally we reached other people. They were an entirely different tribe from any we had known before, but they were friendly to us. We met up with them at a place where they lay in wait for the caribou on trek, and we told them our story and stayed with them for a long time.

"Now we were no longer children, but grown folk facing life, and you may be sure that I have never regretted that I saved my little foster sister, because, you see, in saving her, I saved a good wife for myself."

The old man smiled at his wife, who smiled back at him, and a feeling of harmony filled our little igloo, as we lay there.

Two old people, who had held fast to each other through a long life. Now he took out a piece of tobacco, scraped the ashes out of his pipe and filled it anew, and his wife turned over to settle down to sleep.

"Tomorrow," sad Ututiak, "we'll surely find a deer or something—and then you shall eat your fill, because you white people don't really know how to do without things and still be happy."

I lay a long time thinking of these two old people's adventure. And I felt poor, compared to them. They had lived a life of continual struggle and, although aged, still stood firmly on their own feet.

"But tell me, Ututiak," I said, "what happened to the women you left behind?"

"I don't care much to speak of it," he answered, "but I heard later that they had been found dead. My father never returned, and they couldn't provide food for themselves. But it was gruesome, the way they were found. The two skulls were crushed, and all the meat eaten off the bones. Only the third was whole, but she was terribly emaciated. She was the oldest of the three women; she had murdered and devoured her own daughters.

"Yes, it's just as I told you," he continued. "Women can be horrible and inhuman. I have heard of men who died together of hunger, but one always found them whole. Human nature is strange and difficult to understand."

Ignatius

The story actually begins many years ago; it begins, in fact, when Ignatius was born. His father was poor, as were most Greenlanders who lived in Godthaab, where the catch had to be divided among so many people that there was never enough for each.

When the boy was born it was decided that since they couldn't offer the new family member anything big in the way of earthly goods, at least they could give him a brilliant name. And so, after much consideration and difficult reading in thick books, of which there were but few then, the boy was christened Ignatius.

During his childhood he often overheard people say that his name didn't fit such a poor wretch as he was. He always wore cast-off clothing, his stomach was always empty, and both his father and mother were considered troublesome members of the community. They often had to apply for relief, which consisted of ryemeal and blubber. It didn't help much, even though one tried to get as much of the terrible porridge in one as possible.

No, Ignatius did not have a happy childhood. He often heard grownups insult his elegant name, which created a strong resentment in the boy. He decided to show all of them that the name would be widely known. And he was right.

The only thing for a Greenlander to do in those days was to

become a good fisherman. But his father couldn't get a small kayak for him to follow along in when they went out fishing. It was not as with little Gaba who lived next door. Gaba's father was a *storfanger* (literally—"big fisherman," a title applied to anyone who was an outstandingly successful fisherman) and built a lovely little kayak for his son, but Gaba didn't want to go rowing. He always felt tired and sick. He spat blood, and then one day he remained lying on the platform and said that he wouldn't get up.

The sick little boy got worse and worse, and one day he died and was buried in the cemetery.

The doctor crawled into the house to Gaba's parents and said that all Gaba's clothes had to be burned and that all his toys should be destroyed. That was Ignatius's good fortune, because that evening Gaba's father came over with everything. He said that he would not destroy the good things his poor son had been so happy with. He would rather give them away to Ignatius. That way he could see the nice toys being used every day. Ignatius also got the kayak and the harpoon and all the other small fishing tackle which had belonged to the dead boy.

Ignatius's father thanked the man and said that since his son had a holy name they weren't afraid to accept the gifts. God wouldn't let a boy with a holy name catch anything, even if the Danish doctor said he would. What did a Dane know against God?

And so a new existence began for Ignatius. He was, in this way, the owner of a kayak and harpoon and spear right from the time he was little. It was just as though he were a *storfanger*'s son, so he decided to prove himself worthy of owning so much.

He followed his father out, and even though the first few days it was difficult to sit still so long without bending his knees and his back grew tired, and even pained him, the other boys' envious looks when he came home were compensation enough for him. So Ignatius refused to stay home. He went out alone if his father didn't go out on the lake. At times he would sneak out and take the kayak, even though the lake was rough in toward Tysker Cape. He wasn't afraid and practiced in all kinds of weather.

The day came when he brought a young seal home with him. There was a celebration in the house then, and Gaba's parents got a large piece of meat. Ignatius decided to stop going to school in the future. The teacher came after him many times, but he was never home. He had gone out fishing, explained his mother. There was no way around it. Ignatius was told that he was behaving poorly and that he ought to go to school and learn to read the Bible and follow the psalms in church. Ignatius promised to come, but he had previously decided not to keep his promise. The next day he came home with his first real seal—a large adult male—which his mother proudly took around to friends and acquaintances. The teacher got a fine piece, which stopped his mouth for a long while.

Soon Ignatius began to shoot birds and there was no longer a lack of food in the house. Eider and auk, black guillemot and sea gulls, and now and then a seal.

Ignatius saved the sealskins for a new kayak, since he realized that he was growing and had difficulty getting into the narrow little opening in the child's kayak. When he had enough skins for the whole boat his father made him a fine large kayak. The boards and the kayak ring were bought with the savings from the boy's catches.

His younger brother got the small kayak, and Ignatius now went out with the adults, whom he often angered by not giving way to them. He got up earlier in the mornings and established himself in the shelter of those icebergs where they had thought to wait for seals. Ignatius showed but scanty respect for anyone, but no one dared say anything to him because he was developing into a *storfanger*. That was clear to everyone.

But then it happened that the minister came to the house and requested that Ignatius be confirmed. This would require participation in the religious congregation, which he would have to find time for. He went to the classroom where the confirmation lessons took place.

Then it became clear that Ignatius couldn't read. The minister got angry and told him to go to school first and then come again next year when he could read and write. But Ignatius only said that he could catch seals and fell birds with his darts, which was enough to enable him to get food and clothing for himself and his family, and if the minister wasn't happy with that, it was just too bad. Ignatius got up to go, but the minister grabbed him and the result was that the minister promised to confirm him with what knowledge he had. He should just listen very carefully and learn the psalms that way. The boy acted accordingly, and it was amazing how easily he learned.

When the Sunday of confirmation came Ignatius stood right up with the others on the church floor. The whole congregation knew, of course, what the situation was. They were all in the church and very excited about whether Ignatius would create a scandal. But everything went well. In the afternoon the newly confirmed boy gave a coffee party for the community. He also brought a piece of blue fox skin for the minister—naturally from his own catch. Never had people in Godthaab heard the like!

The years went by and Ignatius caught continually more and more. He got white whales and seals in abundance. There weren't many in the fjord, but Ignatius seemed to know where they were. He went far, far out beyond the Kuk Islands, and there found schools of harp seals—both in the spring when they were bony and coming from the south, and in the fall when they were so fat that they couldn't sink; that was when they migrated south, after having eaten themselves fat and delicious in the north. Ignatius was also lucky in that for several years in a row there was ice all the way up to Godthaab, bringing many hooded seals with it. Once he came home dragging fourteen of these delightfully big seals. Had one ever known its equal! His mother boasted of her son and complained loudly of all the work she had stripping and scraping the many skins and running around to everyone with all that meat.

"Oh, if only my son would get himself a good wife soon, so that my poor hands would get a chance to rest now and then!"

The other women raged inwardly over so much boasting, but they dared not say anything to the *storfanger*'s mother. Those who had daughters felt tempted to offer a bride for Ignatius, as was the custom, but they were afraid of being scornfully turned down.

But then a strange thing happened and Ignatius himself fell in love, but his choice was a young girl who, to everyone's surprise, would have none of him.

Had one ever heard of such a thing! Here was a *storfanger* with an enormous reputation who wanted to get married, and Kritora said, right out, "No."

She was engaged to a young man from Kangek she said, and the matter rested there.

Ignatius tried with cunning and flattery. He brought her seals' hearts and delightful blood liver. He made a laughing stock of himself by sitting on the stone outside Kritora's house. She stayed inside as long as he was there, so that he often sat out all night.

His mother brought liver to Kritora's home, and shortly thereafter people saw it being thrown to the dogs. This caused Ignatius to waylay the girl and beat her thoroughly. But this was reported to the principal, who admonished Ignatius.

"Certainly, you are a *storfanger,* but no one has the right to beat a woman to whom he's not married," said the principal. "If you had been a less important man one might have decided to fine you for that."

Such was the state of affairs in Godthaab at that time. Ignatius steadily went out fishing. And he ordered his mother to bring the best pieces to Kritora's house. Nothing helped, not even when he took two lovely frost-tanned white skins which his mother had prepared, and gave them to the girl.

She laughed right in his face and said that she was glad, because now she had what she'd been lacking to be really fine for her wedding.

Yes, the young *storfanger* had to listen to this, but the time was past, in Christian Greenland, when a man could take a wife by force. And he knew that he wasn't well liked by everyone. People thought that he was too lucky, and those whose daughters he rejected found many nasty things to say of him.

Then Kritora finally decided on the date of her wedding. It took place in Godthaab, in the large church there. Besides the minister there were many Danes present, and everything was very fancy. There was coffee for the colony's entire population. Kritora's father and the groom had both gone into debt to the colony's director in order to accomplish this. The wedding was celebrated with magnificence. Naturally, what contributed most to the excitement and significance was that Ignatius was present in the church and sang during the ceremony. Afterward he came to the coffee party and took a cup. He said nothing, but found out that the newlyweds, together with the family from Kangek, were leaving the next day to go to live with Kritora's inlaws.

The next day the bridal party left. There was a fine, large *umiak* (a large, deep boat made of one or two layers of sealskin tightened over a framework of wood or whalebone, rowed with regular oars, always only by women) and, of course, Kritora rowed in it. The bridegroom was on board, together with the various other men. They should, actually, have been in kayaks, but since this was no ordinary trip, rather a festive homecoming with a bride who was desired elsewhere, and therefore more valuable, the men also went on board the skinboat, although it was generally a women's vessel. Naturally they didn't row, but sat in the stern with folded arms and let the women pull the oars.

That was the last anyone saw of the twenty-two people who

rowed away singing. That same evening Ignatius came home and said that he had seen the boat, but that was all he said. It was only many days later that it was heard that the boat had not yet arrived at Kangek. When some kayaks were sent out to search for the boat a lot of washed-up goods were found around the islands at the mouth of Godthaabfjord and identified as belonging to Kritora and the others. Now it was clear that something terrible had happened, and a systematic search was begun. Long after, when the remains of the boat were found, it appeared that the skins had been sliced in pieces and that the boat had sunk, but had come up again later when the load had been washed out of it.

All twenty-two on board were drowned.

It wasn't long before the talk began. Ignatius had been out fishing alone on the day that Kritora and her bridal party had rowed away. No one had seen him or the boat out among the islands. Anything could have happened.

Now it must be explained to those who don't know it, that a skin boat is a dangerous vessel in which to venture far out to sea under certain circumstances. The big salt sea which flows around Greenland is cold. The high salinity means that the freezing temperature lies below that of fresh water. If the water is very still when it rains, it frequently happens that the rain forms a very thin crust of ice on top of the salt water. The rain water freezes into knife-sharp strips which can't be seen, but which can cut through the skin of a kayak or umiak. It is very dangerous.

Thus arose the old Greenland murder method of cutting the skin of an enemy's boat into pieces. No one can ever prove what has happened. No one knows anything for sure, but storytellers always add a little when they tell, on dark evenings, of the many strange things and crimes which are never reported to the Danes. These are the Greenlanders own affairs.

But this time it was too much. The unhappy parents cried, as did many others. Think—twenty-two people dead. This couldn't be kept quiet. The inspector had taken matters into his own hands by starting an investigation. Much was written on paper by the colony's director, his assistant and also the inspector.

The suspicion naturally reached these high gentlemen. First secretly and in a round about manner, but soon more and more people spoke up quite openly. And then one day Ignatius was called for questioning.

He insisted that he hadn't seen the umiak on the day that Kritora had left. He had taken care of his fishing and had come home with two seals. That would have to be sufficient for his alibi.

"Let me go home," said Ignatius. "I don't wish to hear your words any more when you speak to me that way!" But at that the inspector became annoyed and said that Ignatius could not have permission to go home. There was a danger that he would talk to witnesses and perhaps even harm those who accused him.

Ignatius was put in the inspector's washhouse and a pail was put in so that he could relieve himself, along with water to drink and bread to eat. A heavy lock was put on the door, and the windows were so small that no one could crawl through them. The next day two of the colony's workers came in with food; the inspector came along and asked if Ignatius would confess.

"No," said Ignatius.

This was repeated every day. They brought food in and the pail was emptied. Many times the inspector took him into his office and said to him, through an interpreter, that if he didn't confess he would sit in the washhouse without coming out.

This last was just something the inspector said because he was the most powerful man in Greenland. But his wife was still more powerful. She couldn't let all their clothes stay unwashed just because some Greenlander had murdered another one. She was going to wash on her washday.

There was nothing to be done but to let Ignatius out. It happened in the evening. The inspector told him he could go home, but he ought also to confess and tell the truth. Ignatius didn't answer him. He just went his way.

When he came home he spoke to no one. Of course, many people came to visit and hear the news and to tell him that they didn't believe he was a murderer. Such a *storfanger* as he, who could have all the girls he wanted, didn't have to grieve over one silly female.

But there was neither meat nor coffee. The home had grown poor because Ignatius had been arrested for so long.

Early the next morning Ignatius went out in his kayak. But people noticed that he rowed up the fjord and not down. He came home, though, with a seal and several birds besides. That evening they ate well in Ignatius' home; some meat was also given to those who had shown themselves most sympathetic.

But three days later, when the inspector's wife had finished her wash, Ignatius was arrested and imprisoned again.

He still denied everything, but as he was beginning to get annoyed with the inspector, he would no longer answer when spoken to.

The officer thought that Ignatius was beginning to break down. At any rate, he was no longer denying; now he was silent. This was the first step toward the final confession and explanation of the murders.

But the build-up was unfortunately destroyed, because another washday came around. The three free days gave Ignatius a breathing spell and his family meat, for he caught seals again. It was easy to see that he had become more brazen, the inspector said to the other Danes in the community. But what can we do? We can't walk around in dirty clothes for the sake of such a murderer.

The third time washday came around Ignatius went out hunting reindeer. And when the clothes were clean and dry, and men were sent to arrest him, Ignatius wasn't home. To his consternation the inspector heard that Ignatius had gone to

Qurnoq after reindeer. This was flight, and for five days the excitement was high. But then Ignatius came back with a large quantity of meat; he had shot eleven reindeer. This would be enough for the family to eat for a long time. When he was picked up for the new washhouse stay he brought along a large package of meat to live on in the jail. But it was taken from him by the inspector, who discovered that the prisoner's insolence had grown. He was now so impudent as to demand that the inspector bring forth evidence and more detailed specifics. Had one ever heard of such a thing! As though it weren't Ignatius who was supposed to answer the questions. No, the Greenlanders were getting worse and worse every day.

But Ignatius was never weakened. It was absolutely impossible to get anywhere with him. They finally had to let him go. He would not confess and reports had to be sent to Denmark. The inspector had pleaded with him to admit to just a small dispute with the umiak. He had also threatened Ignatius with a flogging and with short rations, but to no avail. So finally, after a half year of stubborn denial, the inspector had to let the man go. Ignatius was free.

But his parents were poverty-stricken. His father was old now and his mother had difficulty working. Besides which, none of the Danish families would employ such a woman in the house or to sew—the mother of a murderer. Ignatius found them eating ryemeal and blubber, which they got from the dole.

After three days of that diet, Ignatius took his kayak and went out fishing. He came home with lots of eider, so they had food. Blubber, however, had to be bought from the store for the time being. Then came a time when he caught seals now and then. But his mother was ailing and Ignatius had to get married in order to have his catch cleaned and scraped. There were no longer many who were willing to be his wife; there were very few parents who wanted to join the family of a man who had been held "on suspicion" for half a year. Ignatius had to make do with Kata. She was from a poor home, had few or no clothes, but she could work and made Ignatius a good wife all his life.

They had very little. It was as though Ignatius had lost his spark. Everyone noticed it, and it was whispered that he no longer ventured out to the Kuk Islands. He was afraid of the dead. Every time he came home empty-handed one could clearly see God's punishment. Why should God let seals cross Ignatius's path? He who had sent so many people to the bottom of the sea. It wouldn't be just if he caught fish as in the old days.

Then came sickness. His mother died and his father couldn't leave the house. Ignatius, who had once spoken of building a new wooden house, had to stay in the old hut. But Kata kept it clean and nice, and soon Ignatius's younger brother began to catch a little. He could fish, so they had food to eat. There were also three sisters, all younger, but they were afraid of their older brother. They had heard so much evil spoken about him. It was an unhappy home to come back to in the evenings.

Then Ignatius's father died also, so Ignatius became the master in the family. No one wanted the sisters. Sometimes they went out rowing in other women's boats and thus earned a krone a day and food en route.

It also happened that Ignatius didn't have enough crew for his boat. He liked to go far up the fjord and wander on the mountains in search of reindeer. He got some old women to row for him. Kata pulled the oars faithfully; she naturally got some little happiness out of being the *storfanger*'s wife, but that proud title was used less and less. Ignatius was now no better than so many others. It was all begrudged him.

Besides which, Kata bore him no children. Was that a surprise? asked people. It would be a shame for children to come into the world in that house.

Ignatius went in his kayak and by his side rowed Kata and five old, old women when they went up the fjord after reindeer or to gather firewood. Fortunately one of the women had a half-crazy son. He went along in the boat as navigator. It did not enhance one's reputation to come to a camping ground with such a procession. And besides, every time Ignatius and his entourage came, the other people left. If he put up his tent where there were others, they were taken down in the night and the inhabitants moved to other places.

Then one day it happened that the stupid navigator in the umiak forgot to moor the boat while Ignatius was in the mountains hunting reindeer. It lay at dock without lock or weight. All the women had gone after berries when suddenly a raging storm came up. The boat rolled over the rocks and out into the fjord. Then it blew away, while the boy watched and cried. When the women came back, they too started crying, and so Ignatius found them when he came back with a reindeer. Crying women, no boat and a long way home. This was the hunting party's fate. Ignatius rowed in his kayak; the women had to walk, and on the way two of the old women gave up. One died of overexertion and the other was taken into Kapisilik, to some people there. After that Ignatius was a beaten man.

Many years later I came to Godthaab. Young men like strong amusements and a reindeer hunt is always tempting. I wanted to take a man along and naturally I was advised against taking Ignatius. A murderer, a man who had sat imprisoned for half a year and yet had still refused to confess. His guilt was beyond doubt; they should just have been firmer with him, etc.

Of course, when I heard about Ignatius I went immediately to him. With him I would go hunting, and I anticipated an interesting trip.

I met a little man with an unsteady glance. He didn't smile, as most Greenlanders do. He did ask, though, why I had come to him.

"I want to go reindeer hunting with you. I have heard that you know the mountains up the fjord. I'd like to have you along."

Ignatius thought a while. Then he asked when we would leave, and thus our acquaintance began.

I must admit that I never got to talk with Ignatius about his life's main event. At first he was shy, but later he opened up. He wasn't used to eating with Danes; he had no practice in being a companion. His whole life he had been a loner, first too big and now too low for others' confidence.

We had a wonderful trip. We wandered around in the mountains and slept in hunting shelters at night. We gathered heather and twigs for large fires which warmed us and cooked our meat. We were carefree and not at all foresighted. Many times we shot hares, which was crazy, because our shots warned reindeer that we were right in their neighborhood.

"Wild reindeer are like women who flee," Ignatius said to me once as we watched a herd rush a great distance away. Their legs stretched out and came together, and we stood and saw them disappear over the crest of the hill.

"They're lucky, because they're able to run away," commented Ignatius. I understood that he was thinking of his long imprisonment, which must affect a Greenlander worse than many others.

But we spoke no more about that.

In the evenings we sat by the fire and talked now and then; then we were silent a while and again we would talk.

I questioned him about the fishing in Godthaabfjord. He explained the spring and fall migrations of the seals. "But I never go to Kuköerne any more," he added.

"Why not?"

"Nobody knows why," said Ignatius and looked at me so that I knew that this was not a subject to be discussed.

When we sailed down the fjord I asked him if he wouldn't like to move north to Thule where I lived.

"I don't know the land's nature and the people's minds up there," he said. "And I'm afraid of the sled dogs which we don't have in southern Greenland!"

So we parted. But I later heard that things were not too good for Ignatius. He would get a single burst of energy and go out fishing to come home with many seals. But this would be after having sat at home for long periods. He became a silent and but little liked man.

I met him now and then when I was in Godthaab for short visits, but we only exchanged a few words, and he never invited me to visit him.

Many more years passed. Ignatius was an old man; I was just "elderly." He aged faster; his life took more out of a man.

Then one day a cry went from house to house. And soon there was a procession of people to Ignatius's house. It was rumored that he was dying, and now it was clear that for many years people had been waiting for this. Would he confess on his death-bed?

His living room filled with people. The deacon stood by his platform and spoke warning words.

"Confess your soul, Ignatius. You can't die with God's forgiveness if you don't confess."

"Yes, confess, confess," repeated the old women and the gossipy neighbors who had been drawn to the center of a scandal.

Ignatius lay with a scornful smile. He was not a man to weaken just because he was going to die.

"Ignatius, do you hear me?" asked the deacon. "Ignatius, there is time to receive pardon for your heavy sins. But admit them first; let us hear about the many dead people out there by Kuköerne!"

Ignatius didn't answer. They began to sing psalms and pray to God. "Don't you hear, Ignatius? Can't you hear God's word? He will pardon every sinner who repents. Confess now; tell what happened!"

Then Ignatius died. His smile didn't desert him. He had been a silent and serious man all his life; now he smiled. But he uttered not a word. People were shocked.

One of his sisters cried at his deathbed.

"He could have confessed and received forgiveness for the family's sake," wept the sister.

Much was expected of the minister's sermon. But he spoke only about God's peace on earth and in heaven. Not a word of Ignatius or the twenty-two people dead out there in Kuköerne. He could easily have brought up that affair and given people something to talk about. . . .

Many years passed. I came and left and came again. Kata grew old, and she was very poor.

"Oh, Pita," she said. "I know you'll give me something for coffee—preferably enough so I can put in a good stock. Ignatius said that you were good to him and that you never asked him anything. Ignatius never said anything. Not even when he died. He was too strong for them!"

Now she's dead. I often wonder whether Kata knew anything, or whether there was anything to know.

Passion

Up near Granville Bay there lived two men. Each had his own hut, but in one it was quiet and uncomfortable because only a man and his son lived there. This was Ululik, who had become a widower just when he had finished building his house. That spring his wife had protested violently when it became apparent that her husband and Talilanguak would not be joined by others at their campsite for the summer. The women had decided that there would be five tents, and they had anticipated an attractive and festive community. There were salmon in the lake to the rear, many seals in the fjord and walrus close to the coast throughout the summer.

Ululik and Talilanguak had arrived earliest in order to be able to catch seals as soon as they began to come up on the ice to sleep, but the other three men had gone north bear hunting and had just never shown up. Maybe they had been cut off by the open water; one would hear about it next winter.

So there were only the two tents all summer. It was rather boring, since Ululik's wife was old and often peevish. Talilanguak, on the other hand, was an elderly man and his wife Kanajork, was young and lively. She was smart and industrious, but not really suited to Talilanguak's mature tempo. She and Ululik were the same age; they had played together as children and had remained good friends all their lives. They had often been apart a year or two at a time—fishing and marriage had carried them many places. Now, for the first time since they had played together as children, they were finally camp-mates.

Then one day Ululik's wife suddenly became ill and had terrible pains. They tried everything possible, but nothing helped. They pulled so violently at her hair on her forehead that large bunches came out, but her pain was so great that she noticed nothing: They put pieces of wood by the sickbed— wood can't feel pain—but that did nothing. Then they took frozen egg yolks, chewed them and spat them out on the places where it hurt. But nothing helped. Three days later the woman died.

Talilanguak had been so foresighted that when it became obvious that the case was hopeless, he had taken his sled and left. He went fishing and met friends from other campsites with whom he went home, so that he had amusing company and tasty meat to eat. Ululik, on the other hand, took care of his wife until she died, and then he had to observe the mourning period: for five days he was not allowed to work or to leave the campsite. He set his sled down by the beach with the front turned inland, so that it was obvious that he did not intend to disturb the peace of the dead by going fishing.

During these days Kanajork was a good and understanding friend. She brought cooking meat into Ululik's house, and she patched his son's pants, which were torn. She fed his dogs. But, like a woman, she forgot to keep track of the days, and before the fourth day was gone everything edible in the camp had been consumed.

So they had to sit and starve. Nor did they have blubber for their lamps. Ululik sat on his platform and brooded over his sorrow. He was not supposed to lie down, and he grew weak from the exertion of holding himself up. Kanajork could lie down and sleep, but angry thoughts grew in her mind about Talilanguak, who was treating himself to meat at other campsites.

"You ought to have left with your husband and avoided all this," Ululik had said to her the last time she came to visit. That touched her deeply since it showed a consideration for her which she wasn't used to. So she lay and thought now that Ululik was without a wife, whom should he get? She went over all the available women in the tribe, but some were too old and she pitied him for having to take them. There were also a couple who were slightly younger, but to these she begrudged marriage to such a young and smart fisherman. Maybe he could wait until there was a suitable widow he could take. In the meantime she could scrape his skins and sew his clothes. Yes, it would be best if he moved in with them, together with his son, now that he was single! Women always lie and think independently, as though they were men, and it is amazing that they never learn that they are not suited for making decisions!

As it happened, Talilanguak came home just when the five days of mourning were over. He let out a roar of laughter at the sight of his wife lying freezing on the platform, hungry and without light, and he thought of all the food and the splendid song and dance he had enjoyed at the camp at Netchilik. Then he brought meat inside, but there was no heat with which to thaw it. He fumbled around and managed to chop some blubber off the seal with his axe. He pounded the blubber so that it would run into the lamp. That gave enough light so that he could see to cut more blubber, and finally it grew warm enough to thaw the meat. But while he was working at all this, Talilanguak grew hungry and annoyed. He began to berate Kanajork.

"Oh, it must be wonderful to be alone with a clever, young fisherman. It's obvious that he has taken good care of you. How happy a man is to know that he can go away without his wife's suffering from want of anything!"

Kanajork didn't say anything, but she suddenly began to think that her husband was unpleasant and that Ululik would never have spoken that way to her.

The two men now began to go hunting together as before,

but the first few days Ululik caught nothing, he was so faint and weak from having sat sleepless on his platform and mourning his wife's death. His shot was therefore unsteady. Three times he shot to the side when there was a seal at the breathing hole, so that he came home with an empty sled. Talilanguak, on the other hand, caught prodigiously every time they were out.

"How wonderful it is to have a camp-mate who keeps the meat rack filled with dog food and blubber," exclamed Talilanguak when they came home. Kanajork felt the derisive remark as though it had been said about her.

She offered lots of meat to Ululik. Never before had meat which was thus offered from a successful catch been other than a token; now it was cooking meat—the only meat in the house.

Talilanguak grew steadily nastier. When Ululik came to visit and they had cooked meat, Talilanguak said that he was glad Ululik had such a good appetite and didn't refuse the catch, because it was known that in the other house the great fisherman kept delicious things which he had brought home! Ululik said nothing, but looked at Kanajork. Suddenly he realized that here was a woman who ought to be treated with kindness and made happy every day of her life.

Shortly thereafter Talilanguak visited his neighbor. Because he didn't want to outrage all good manners, Ululik cooked his last piece of meat and served it to his guest.

"Ah," said Talilanguak. "Here is a man who understands how to catch delectable animals. Let's try it; let's try it!" It was his own meat which had been given to Ululik and now Talilanguak ate all of it, although he realized that none would be left for his neighbor and son until more was caught.

That evening Ululik went to the meat rack where Talilanguak had two seals. He starting chopping one up and feeding his dogs, who were terribly hungry. Talilanguak came out and watched, but he couldn't protest and forbid the other to feed his dogs. Naturally he wanted to, but then it would spread through the whole tribe that he was stingy with his meat, and he didn't want that to happen.

Slowly Ululik regained his strength. He went fishing and began to come home with meat.

Some time passed during which nothing significant happened. But one day Talilanguak came home later than Ululik and saw Kanajork sewing soles on a pair of boots which weren't his own.

"What are you doing?" he asked, and there was anger in his look.

"Our camp-mate needs soles on his boots," she said and didn't look up from her work. At that Talilanguak grew angry. He ripped the sewing from her and stuck his knife through both boots, ripped them to pieces and threw them out the door. Then he grabbed the knife and hit her on the head with the handle and shouted, so loudly that it could be heard outside, that he thought he was married and that his wife wasn't to be used by other than he. "As though one couldn't get enough skins to keep your hands busy," he yelled. The woman couldn't answer anything, since she had sewn another man's clothes without first asking her husband.

After that day Ululik had to drive long distances to other camps where men would give their wives permission to sew for him and his little son. He never got back the fox skins he brought as payment for the sewing, and much time was wasted driving around every time he needed a pair of gloves.

Now he began to come home at irregular times, and he would visit Kanajork when she was alone. They became quite close, and a few times Kanajork said to him that she sympathized with his loneliness. She felt uncomfortable because she had no one to talk to; no woman is made to let her tongue lie idle for too long. Talilanguak amused himself by leaving her alone in the camp. His outlook grew angrier and angrier.

Sometimes when they were finished and getting ready to drive back, he would say to Ululik, "Oh well. There's no more chance of catching anything today. Let's go home and see to our women.

It's wonderful to know it's warm and cozy in the house when one gets back!"

Ululik took his young son along on the sled, partly to teach him to fish, partly because there was no one to tend the lamp for him if he stayed home. Ululik never answered Talilanguak's sarcasm, but he often went fox hunting with only his son now. His traps were in different places than Talilanguak's, and Ululik often saw to his and came home before the other one did. Then he would visit Kanajork.

They talked a lot together and Ululik confided to her that it was lonesome to be without a woman. But every time he mentioned going north to find one, Kanajork made fun of the old widows who, she was sure, sat up there and hoped that one day the strong young fisherman would come for them. However, it was obvious that he meant to get a wife for the house. This was clear because of all the foxes he caught. He took the skins off, but let them freeze in his supply room. They could be prepared by the one who would use the furs.

It was now that time of year when the light slowly begins to come back. Talilanguak noticed that Ululik and Kanajork were quite friendly with each other. And it seemed strange that the strong young man stayed single so long. Why hadn't he driven up after a woman long ago? They had just recently heard that a fisherman had died leaving a charming young wife who had immediately been taken by a silly young fisherman, a poor provider from whom Ululik would have had nothing to fear. Suspicions arose in Talilanguak's mind, and he asked his wife if Ululik was happy to be here at the campsite. But those two had agreed not to say anything to Talilanguak, in spite of the custom. Talilanguak grew more and more insulting to his campmate. He began to beat Kanajork every time Ululik came to visit. He did it just to show that he was master and could use violence on a woman if he chose.

But after a while it grew tiresome and unbearable for the

woman. She became more and more uncomfortable in her home.

"If only one were rid of that eternally beating man!" she said to Ululik one day, and thereby set his thoughts in motion. When he lay alone on his platform at night he realized that it would be pleasant always to have Kanajork with him. But Talilanguak was an elderly man with a good reputation as a fisherman, so it wouldn't do just to take his wife from him, as long as he was alive.

Then one day they stood outside, the man and his wife, with some work. Ululik came crawling out of his house. Without any explanation Talilanguak suddenly began to beat the woman. She fell down under the blows, but he continued to hit her. Kanajork grew angry and outraged and began shouting, "*Toquradlé, toquradlé!* If only death would strike you! If only death would strike you!"

That made Talilanguak stop beating her. But now the words had been said, and Ululik thought that a point of no return had been reached. He drove away without taking his son, and while he sat on the sled he decided to kill his camp-mate and take his wife.

After that day Ululik and Kanajork grew yet closer and more intimate. Many times Kanajork said sarcastically to him, "There's no reason for me to sew a new coat from the fox skins you've collected. There'll probably be another woman, certainly many others, who will be much better than I."

When she said this Ululik quietly got up and went outside, but his resolution grew stronger.

Then it was almost spring. Early one morning Talilanguak drove away, but Ululik had to do some work on his dogs' traces, so that Talilanguak was out of sight before Ululik was ready. Suddenly a longing for the woman rose in him, and he turned away from the dogs and ran into the house to Kanajork. He grabbed her and would have thrown her down on the platform, but she began to tease him and say, "You'll have to ask my husband first. After all, you're not the one who has the right to me."

Ululik let her go and went out, but he decided that today would be the day. He told his son that he needn't come along and decided that that evening there would be only one man alive in the camp.

He steered his sled over the ice packs on the beach, and as soon as he came out on the smooth ice he found the new sled tracks, sped up his dogs and set out after Talilanguak, intent on murder. The dogs were glad to run, and it wasn't long before Ululik saw his enemy standing at the edge of the ice looking eagerly across the open water. He could tell from his camp-mate's attitude that there was something around worthy of his attention. "Uk, uk, uk!" he heard Talilanguak shout. There must be walrus in the water.

There lives no Eskimo who can think of other things when the sea's powerful animal is near. Ululik quickly dug two holes in the ice, stuck his strap through them and tied up his dogs.

"I'll kill him when he stands at the edge and leans over. Then it'll be easy to stick his spear in his backside and throw him into the water," thought Ululik.

"Uk, uk, uk!" Talilanguak shouted, and at that moment two black heads came out of the water. Their white tusks shone as though they were tongues of fire. Talilanguak strained his throat and bellowed and tempted, and it seemed as though the walrus knew he was there. He leaned down and got on his knees so as not to seem too large and frighten the animals away. Instinctively Ululik did the same. It would be a waste of meat if he frightened them away just because he had private purposes which didn't concern the fishing.

The walrus went down, but when they came up again they were right next to where Ululik squatted on his knees. Immediately he threw himself down on his stomach, lifted his head up and bellowed with all the strength in his lungs, "Urr, urr, urr. . . !" Now it was obvious that the two walrus had been fooled. They thought they had come to a resting place with other walrus. They went underwater and swam slowly toward Ululik. While they were down, Talilanguak rushed over beside his camp-mate. The surface of the water broke almost under their feet. Eddies developed in the water, and with an enormous bark and snort the two walrus heads came up, so close to the men that they almost didn't have to throw their harpoons. Each thrust his weapon down into an animal. The harpoon points disappeared deep in the necks of the captured animals. This created panic in the unsuspecting walrus. They barked and threw themselves back; they churned up the sea with their tails and with uncontrollable rage tossed themselves over before they disappeared under the water. But by then the men had cast loose the loop on the harpoon line and planted an ice peg in the hard sea ice. They put their feet at the bottom and their shoulders against the top so that when the walrus had run the lines out the men felt that wonderful thrust one gets through one's body when the walrus has stretched out the leather strap. Wonderful, because one knows that he is master and can withstand it.

Now the fight began and a strange thing happened. Each man had hit his walrus, but these, in their fight to get free, had swum around each other so that the lines were all twisted together and it was impossible to haul one walrus in without the other. This necessitated great exertion, for the two walrus tugged hard, but in their bodies sat the harpoon points which burned in the sores every time they gathered their strength to swim away.

Each time the animals let up a bit, the two men pulled in the lines, and when it became clear that one wouldn't be able to manage without the other, they both looped around the same ice peg. The peg was made fast to the end of the spear, so that one of the fishermen could now free his weapon for the kill. The two walrus slowly came closer and closer in toward the edge of the ice, so that the doomed animals got less and less free line. Talilanguak held fast while Ululik thrust his spear time and again deep into the animals' bodies, when he could reach them from the ice. The walrus were both beginning to spit blood when they snorted, which was an indication that they had been hit in vital places and wouldn't be able to hold out much longer. But this just made the men more eager, and Ululik stabbed one walrus deeply between the ribs when it came up for air. He had time to twist the sharp steel in the wound. It wasn't long after that before the animal began to expire. Since water was now rushing into its lungs through the wound, it soon gave up the fight.

The other walrus was also badly wounded and didn't last long. A spear thrust hit an artery in its neck, and soon after, that one also was finished and lay heavy in the water. Now both of them were dead.

The two Eskimos shouted with glee. Two walrus killed! Huge meat supplies! If only many sleds would come visiting and the travelers need dogfood, here was something to offer them!

But there was still a tremendous amount of work to be done. They had to dig holes in the ice, make a tackle and attach the dogs to it in order to get the animals up out of the water. Finally they managed to get one out and began to pull the other one up. In the Eskimo manner they cut holes in the neck skin, pulled the line through and into holes in the ice, thereby fashioning a tackle which they let the dog team pull. They had to shift the tackle time and again, but finally both walrus lay on the ice— fat and full of blubber.

Then came the long cleaning. The two men forgot fatigue and sleep. They cut down through the thick skin, threw tremendous hunks of meat to the side, cut the flippers free, heaped the guts in piles on the ice and let their dogs treat themselves to blood and intestines. At times they would cut a hole in the stomach and press mussels out, delightful shelled mussels that tasted of the summer itself, fresh and delicate. And when they were tired of this tart taste they took hunks of the steaming liver with blubber and chewed it with relish.

That day was to be counted among the happiest! Finally, long, long after—they had no idea how long, for they had forgotten to note the sun's progress while they caught and cleaned and vigorously heaped meat in front of them, separated into huge, king-size piles—they suddenly felt tired.

They pushed the sleds together, took up their skins and lay on top of them. Soon they were sleeping amongst their good, warm clothes. Inside them, all the meat they had eaten burned. When they belched it tasted delightfully of liver and blubber so that their sleep was sweet and their dreams were pleasant.

Ululik woke up first, and all of the previous day rose in front of him when he saw the enormous piles of meat that lay on the ice. He woke his camp-mate who staggered about and remembered nothing. What fun Ululik had watching the memory return to Talilanguak as he saw where he was and what had happened.

They loaded their sleds with all the meat they could hold. As it wasn't too cold, only the bottom layer was frozen. The sleds rocked when they sat on them. It was like sitting in a kayak, and they laughed loud with delight over what had happened. Though they were headed home the dogs went very slowly, for the heavy loads allowed only the slowest speed. And one after the other the dogs had to stop and throw up everything in their stomachs. Ululik and Talilanguak laughed thinking how these dogs had eaten and eaten all they could the day before, and now it was no use. In order to pull such weight and go forward they had to empty their stomachs.

When they neared the campsite the boy spotted them, and he called through the window to Kanajork that there were sleds on the ice. Kanajork dashed out. She was certain that only one of them would come back. It was clear that Ululik had gone out to kill. Now they both came, grinning and laughing. Their clothes were covered with blood, and their faces were festively decorated with bits of liver which were rubbed across their cheeks.

She hadn't been in on the big hunt jubilation, and the men just threw the meat down on the ice, turned the dogs around and drove back to collect the rest of the enormous catch. One couldn't leave it lying out there by the edge of the ice; a storm might come up and break the ice farther in toward land.

On the way out the dogs found the thrown-up meat from the previous trip. They gulped it down again, for now they were hungry and willing to eat.

The men each took another gigantic load. What remained was left for the sea gulls and foxes. The two men had enough; they had gathered all that was worthwhile for a great fisherman to take home.

Slowly, slowly, step by step, the dogs dragged the meat home. It took a lot of time. The mountains seemed no closer each time they looked up at them. But the land lies still; no matter how slowly one goes each step brings one closer. Suddenly the dogs pricked up their ears. It was as though some new encouragement told them to try harder. They grew eager and almost managed to trot. The two men wondered about this, but they jumped on top of the loads, sat well and drove. Finally they realized that visiting sleds had come to their campsite and that strangers had gone into their houses.

Never could anything be more pleasing to a man. Here they were with as much meat as it was possible to have on a sled.

Joy, joy! But when they neared the camp and the people there realized they had returned and came rushing out to greet them with cheers, the two men sat quite still and acted as though the little bit of meat that they now came with was what they usually brought home.

"Oh, our terrible dogs!" they exclaimed. "They are miserable and didn't feel like going faster, even though they were headed home. Neither could we make them run faster, because we are such poor drivers—and that although we have nothing on our sleds!"

At that the strangers laughed and shouted that now words had been spoken which would be repeated up and down the coast about these two great fishermen who berated their own meat and spoke contemptuously of their dogs, even though they could pull more than other draft animals.

The visitors were happy young men who were going bear hunting up north. They planned to go quite a distance before the ice broke. But first they wanted to get material for pants for themselves and some old men who were too weak to go on long hunting trips.

All night long they cooked and ate the meat, until their stomachs bulged and they belched and passed wind and knew they had had enough. The strangers told about lucky catches in one place and about mistakes in another. Everything was stated with laughter. But they all said that they were happy mainly because they had eaten fresh walrus meat, the year's first catch which had been dreamed of all winter.

It was now that lovely time when it was light enough to see all day and night, so one slept until he was rested. Both men and dogs had eaten so much that the meat pile was noticeably depreciated.

When everyone had rested, Ululik decided to go along on the bear hunt. That last hunt had put his mind to work. The fight against an animal was better than sticking his spear in the backside of an old man. Now he would hunt bears together with the hunters from Cape York.

When they drove away Kanajork came out of her door and yelled after him, "I noticed that there were tears in your furs. Shouldn't they be sewn?" She was so astonished that all her modesty fled, and therefore she shouted to a man without having been first spoken to.

But Ululik laughed and said that it would take care of itself. He had heard that there were women in the north, and he was taking his fox skins along now in case there was someone up there who needed a coat and had no man to get the necessary skins for her.

Never Force An Eskimo

The Arctic world covers an enormous area, but there are not many people up north. The inhabitants are all known to each other. The names of Bradford and Street are no exception; they are known to most people in the Arctic. They were two adventurers who were killed by the Eskimos some years ago. Many stories have been told about the incident, and Canada's famous Mounted Police even sent a patrol way up north to look into the affair and, if possible, to have the guilty persons punished. They decided in the end that the Eskimos had acted in self-defense, gave them a strong warning and returned south again.

The following story has been told to me by one of the Eskimos involved. It is hard to tell whether this is the exact truth. Most people like to describe their deeds in the best possible light, and since "civilization" has come to the natives, the incident is regarded somewhat differently. And most of the people involved are dead now. In any case they assumed new names after the event, something the Eskimos often do to show that they are through with certain chapters of their lives or with certain decisive events.

Among my personal possessions is a small red notebook which is said to have belonged to Street, the most likable of the two unfortunate adventurers—a small notebook of red leather, of the kind that is given to a polar explorer by a dear, beloved friend. It is hardly ever used, but always kept as memory. Street had kept this, and it was given to me years later by one of the Eskimos.

I cannot claim that my story is the whole truth, but I write it the way it was told to me by one of my friends in the Arctic.

It was the time of year when the sun rose higher in the sky every day. The igloos were ready to collapse, and the women were busy preparing the tents. The men were hunting seals far out on the ice, but it was already getting pretty hard to get back on shore. Melting water was making ever wider cracks between the ice and the beach.

Soon the whole tribe would start the trek inland to be on hand when the great reindeer herds came north. The animals were pretty lean at this time of the year, but their furs were good and in any case they represented the only food the Eskimos would have through the summer. The tribe had no kayaks and could do their fishing only when the sea was ice-covered. Now all their thoughts turned inland. They knew they had hard days ahead, heavy burdens to carry on their backs for days, desperate fights with millions of mosquitos and miserable days in the small tents whenever they met rain on the long trek. And still they were all eager for the experience, excited about the many camps they would come across, people from faraway places to meet and, above all, flowers and sun wherever they went after the long, dark, colorless winter.

The daylight already lasted way into the night, and the children were playing outside at all hours while their parents were asleep in the igloos. But one night the grownups suddenly were awakened by the shouting of the children. The voices were shrill and excited. Something moving way out on the ice had caught their eyes; they were pointing and crying out. They did not quite dare to wake up their parents, but felt sure that somebody would hear them soon and reassure the children, who felt uneasy about the unusual sight on the ice.

Soon there was not a soul left in the igloos. They all huddled together, staring out on the ice without feeling much braver than the children. It wasn't hard to see now that the moving spot far out on the ice was a sleigh, but it was no Eskimo sleigh. As it came closer, they could see two men walking behind it, and their size and clothes showed that they were white men. They must have crossed over from Banks Land, but it was a most unusual time for such a crossing.

White men always brought excitement. They had large supplies of all the things most desired by the Eskimos, and the expectations were always great, whether the Eskimos traveled the long, long distance to the huge houses of the white men or the white men themselves came sailing in their enormous ships or, like now, traveled by dog sleigh.

The two men were approaching rapidly. Their dogs had caught the smell of other human beings, and they hurried along without having to be encouraged in spite of the heavy load. As soon as they got to the beach the Eskimos hurried down to help them while their women remained by the igloos, watching curiously. Once the sleighs were safe on dry land and polite greetings had been exchanged, Ungar, the greatest hunter among them, called the women to work. Meat must be prepared for a great meal to give the white guests the proper welcome. They all got busy, fetching the best meat they had, finding peat and lard for the fire, and soon food was steaming in all the kettles.

But still nobody knew who the two white men were. What were they doing there? Why had they come. It was impossible for them to go on from there with their heavy load now that the ice was breaking. That meant that they would have to stay there until summer when a ship could pick them up. Whatever their intentions, the visit would mean a great change in the daily life among the Eskimos, things to talk about, new faces to look at. They had good reason to be happy, and they all laughed to the guests to show them how much they were appreciated.

The two men turned out to be Americans who had spent a very long time up north. They had been in the mountains looking for the yellow metal which white men all over the world are searching for. There was plenty of copper in the region, but the Eskimos had been told that copper was too hard and dark to be desirable. They had heard the same story over and over again from white men who asked them if they had not seen the metal which was brighter yellow, heavier than gravel and softer than stone. It could be found in small lumps, but preferably large, and even the metal dust was of value. "Have you ever seen it? Please tell us where! We'll give you a pipe and a large can of tobacco if you can tell us where to find the yellow metal!"

They hardly ever found it. It was very rare to come across even a tiny bit of the right metal. And still new men turned up all the time to look harder than the ones who had been there before. They behaved like small children. In the summer they went up in the mountains, digging in the ground. Great herds of reindeer had been seen passing close by them, but the white men did not lift a finger to catch a single animal. They kept their nose to the ground, or they were washing out the river sand in their large pans.

The two men who now turned up were called Bradford and Street. It was easy to see that they had been traveling far. Their clothes were worn, their beards were long and bleached from the sun, their faces had a dark tan from long exposure to wind and light. And still they did not seem tired.

They knew a little of the Eskimo language, while Ungar and a few of the other Eskimos knew a few words of the silly language of the white men, so they had no trouble understanding each other.

"We are just two ordinary men!" Bradford told them right

away. He knew he had to reassure the Eskimos, convince them that they were not spirits bringing disease or ghosts who could chase away all animals from the district. "Just two ordinary men with nothing but good intentions."

"And we are all nothing but plain, ordinary men," Ungar answered and thus they had become friends with a duty to help each other. And the Eskimos now felt the obligation to fulfill whatever desires might be expressed by their new friends.

"A humble meal has been prepared," Ungar told them. "I regret to say that the poor meat we have has been prepared very badly by women totally unable to cook. I know you must be used to the best of food, but we would be deeply grateful if you would just taste our meat before you spit it out in disgust."

The two strangers ate with good appetite and they were very friendly, but most of the time they spoke together in their own language so fast that nobody could understand them. After the meal they both went up to the big hill behind the igloos and studied the view inland. From the way they used their arms for pointing it was clear that their thoughts went to the south. After a while they came down to the Eskimos again.

"We want to sleep," they said. "We have gone a long way and we are tired. When we wake up we want to talk to Ungar about our plans."

Well spoken, the Eskimos thought. A man should never reveal his thoughts at once, but sleep first until they are good and ready to be disclosed.

After a long nap and another meal, the strangers once more went up the hill. The first spring had come. The sleighs were left on the bare ground, since there was not enough snow left for making a platform to keep them out of the reach of the dogs. It did not matter anyhow, since it was too hot for the dogs to bother with the leather straps which kept the sleighs together. In winter the dogs loved to chew the straps to pieces.

From the top of the steep hill one could see that the river below had broken through the ice. It took a sharp curve below and around the hill and then ran straight to the sea. They could hear the loud roar of the melting water rushing out to the great, salty ocean.

The two men were in a hurry to go south. If they could only get down to the first settlement by the Copper Mine River, they would only have to wait for a short time there, get a canoe and paddle down the river until they met the steamer going south. Once they got down to the railroad, it would only be a matter of days until they got back to the States and could tell about their great discovery.

"Do you think we can make it?" Street asked, looking out over the tundra. "It seems to me the snow is even grayer today than yesterday. If it burns off while we are there, we would be helplessly lost!"

"Well, we could always walk to Fort Davis. We have enough ammunition, and the distance gets shorter with each step we walk south."

"And leave all our precious furs in the middle of the tundra? No thank you!"

"That's just why we have to hurry! We have already slept too much today. We'll take all the Eskimos with us; they can carry our load. That way we can move faster. And we'll go by night when the sun is low and it may be cool enough for the snow to carry us."

"But how are the Eskimos to get back again with their sleighs?"

"What do I care?"

"We can't take their women and children along, that would slow us down too much."

"Of course not. We leave them behind. This isn't charity. We'll promise them enough rewards to make them say yes; the rest is their headache."

"But don't you think they'll have sense enough to say no?"

"They must do it!" Bradford exclaimed. "They'll have to do it! Too much is at stake now. We have suffered through all these many months, we have found the gold mine, our fortune is made! Do you think I'll be stopped now by these worthless Eskimos? Not on your life!"

He turned around and made a sign to Ungar to join them on top of the hill. Ungar was scared. He knew that the two men were thinking of going south; he had seen it clearly. But he also knew it was too late in the year for such a trip. The white men would have to stay where they were. And a man who is longing for his own home is hard to keep happy!

"We are going south," Bradford began right away, without any polite introduction, without any modest words.

"It is not quite certain that there will not be some small difficulty in getting the snow to carry the load," Ungar answered quietly. Looking at the sky he knew that warm, sunny days were ahead of them. There was no doubt that the sun would eat away the snow and soften up the tundra below.

"If we hurry up, the snow will carry us until we reach Fort Davis," Bradford countered.

"The great white men have a heavy load. Your possessions are many and your riches will make the driving slow."

"That's why I'm asking you and your people to help us. You must take some of our load on your sleighs and make the driving faster."

"Our dogs are weak and our sleighs are poor. Our children are crying for reindeer meat," Ungar answered.

"But we'll pay you well. You must take your dogs along so you can get back quickly."

"While our wives and children are starving? We don't have supplies for such a long time. Stay with us, white men. We'll look after you until the snow will carry you again and you can drive off safely."

"But I tell you we have to be off at once."

"It is a little bit difficult for my tongue to speak against the white man. But all our thoughts go inland, and we are hungry for reindeer."

"That's none of my business! I want to take along with me all the sleighs you have. As soon as we are in Fort Davis, you'll get many rich gifts to bring back."

"But our children will starve if we are not here to provide for them."

"I don't want to hear another word from you!" Bradford shouted. He spoke for both of them while Street kept quiet. "I insist that you go with me. Do you hear what I say? Don't you understand me? Go at once to your people and tell them to get ready for immediate departure."

Ungar did not move. There was a slight smile on his face.

"White man," he said calmly. "In this country you are like a child. We know the nature of our country; that is why we cannot go with you even though it is very hard to say no to the wishes of a white man."

"Do you mean to say that you refuse," Bradford screamed, beyond himself with fury. He saw his whole plan ruined. If they left the place now, a ship might arrive from Banks Land during the summer. The Eskimos would be sure to gossip about the two white men who had been in such a hurry, and right away all the sailors would have a good hunch where Bradford and Street had struck gold. That had to be prevented at all cost. If the stupid Eskimos would not give in, they would have to be forced.

"Do you hear me, Ungar?" he shouted again.

"I have heard and I have spoken," Ungar replied, and turned around to go down the hill.

His whole attitude made it clear that no persuasion was possible, and the bare earth which was already showing through the snow proved him right. But Bradford was too consumed by his gold thirst to be reasonable. This was the one great chance which he would not give up. Bradford and Street had worked together for years, and now their final triumph was in sight. But they had to get back to civilization at once, equip an expedition and return as soon as possible. A delay of a whole year might very well mean a total loss. They had been assisted by too many Eskimos who were much too eager to talk about all they had seen. A fortune was within their grasp—and now they risked losing it all because of a stubborn Eskimo.

It was too much for Bradford—and he forgot where he was. He forgot that an Eskimo cannot be forced. They are free people, living in peace, and they do not understand the speed of the white man, nor his thirst for wealth. What cannot be done today, may be done tomorrow, or something else might happen tomorrow. Life is wonderful to the Eskimo because it is changeable, because unexpected things always happen. And the Eskimo is never in a hurry.

Bradford ran down the hill after the Eskimo, grabbed Ungar by the shoulders and shook him violently.

"For the last time!" he shouted. "Come with us, we *must* leave! We only need your help."

Ungar did not answer him. His contempt for a man who could not control himself, who lost all his dignity, was so immeasurable that Ungar only stared into his eyes while he shook his head with a slight smile.

This made Bradford lose his last bit of self-control. He pulled the small Eskimo over to the very steep side of the hill. At one point there was a sheer drop down to the river roaring below. The drop was not very high, but still a man could not possibly save his life falling down there in the strong current of the icy water.

"Will you go with us?" Bradford cried, shaking the man. The American was a powerful man and Ungar was held in a vise. "Tell me you'll order your people to leave at once!"

He held the Eskimo over the edge, and it looked as if he was going to drop him to his death.

Ungar's younger brother Pualu was looking at the scene. He understood that his brother's life was endangered and that this was one of the bad white men he had heard about, men who killed in anger and broke the peace wherever they came. Such a man is not wanted among our people, Pualu thought. Let him die in order to save my brother's life.

He quickly grabbed his spear and sent it flying straight into the shoulders of the white man. In the same moment he jumped, getting hold of Ungar before the Eskimo fell.

Bradford died in a matter of minutes, with hardly a sound. Pualu's spear had pierced the heart of the white man. The Eskimos gave him a gentle push and the corpse began rolling by itself, first slowly, then faster and faster until it hit the water. They saw the body disappear in the rushing water, and nothing more was ever seen of Bradford.

Street stood motionless as if he were paralyzed. He had always been the calmest and the kindest of the two. He never wanted to cause trouble, and he would never have dreamed of forcing anyone to go across the tundra against his will. Street had been the friend of Bradford, but it had always been his job to calm down the hot temper of the other man. Now he saw his friend being killed, but he realized that the young Eskimo had acted in self-defense, for his whole tribe.

What was Street to do now? He could not go south alone. Perhaps the natives would kill him next. They probably felt they had to cover up the first killing by getting rid of both Americans.

Street saw two men approaching him. They carried their spears in their hands, and he thought their faces looked threatening. The men were Ungar and Pualu, the two brothers. They wanted to explain to Street that they felt no anger, that they had been forced to kill Bradford in self-defense, but bore Street no ill will. He could stay with them as long as he wanted, until a ship arrived to take him home again. In the meantime he was their guest and friend.

That is what they wanted to tell him. But they did not get a chance to say anything to the stranger. Street looked into their faces and saw that they were calm and hard.

"Now it is my turn," he thought, but Street was not a man to give in without a fight; he would defend himself. He quickly ran down to the sleighs where his rifle was still lying on top of the load. As he pulled frantically the trigger got caught in one of the leather straps, long enough to show the Eskimos that the white man was going to shoot. Rifles of white men are dangerous, that was one thing they all knew. They had to stop him from revenging the death of his friend. And the Eskimos had time enough to use their old-fashioned spears.

Kutloq rushed down. He was a young and daring hunter. He wanted to spare the tribe from further bloodshed. His hand was sure; he had used his spear since he was a young boy. This time his victim was infinitely more important than bear or walrus. Kutloq took careful aim, the spear flew out of his hand—and Street fell dead to the ground.

The body was right away carried far out on the ice. The Eskimos tied some heavy stones to his legs and let Street sink down in the water at the spot where they thought the body of the other white man would have been carried out by the river. They wanted the two Americans to be united in death, to keep each other company on the long journey. Later they killed the dogs as well. Let the white men have a dog team in the other world, Ungar said, and they let the dogs sink down in the water to join their masters.

Ungar took charge of the dead men's belongings. The sleighs were carefully unloaded, the many precious fox and ermine furs conscientiously counted. The white men had had a fortune in furs with them; now the Eskimos had to dry them and prepare them well. It would have been to the eternal shame of the tribe if anything had gone wrong with great wealth of the dead.

The work kept them busy by the coast the greater part of the summer. They had to wait and see whether a ship would arrive, since it was their duty to turn over the property of the Americans to the captain. And one day late in summer a ship finally turned up, a sealer which had run into heavy storms for

months and had had a very poor catch. The captain had been
forced to take his vessel far off the beaten track to search for
seals. He was desperate to get enough of a catch to pay his
expenses at least.

The captain was pleasantly surprised when he discovered the
Eskimo camp on the beach, certain that they would get some
valuable furs for a cheap price at last. A lifeboat was launched,
and the captain went on shore where he was greeted by Ungar,
the head of the tribe. And Ungar spoke enough English to
make the captain understand him:

"Two white men were here with their sleighs, but they
drowned." Ungar pointed to the sea and the captain understood him. He became interested and wanted to hear more.

"We have kept the wealth of the white men. Will you give
it to their families?" Ungar asked him.

"What sort of wealth?" the captain asked carefully. Strange
things happen in the Arctic; nobody wants to get deeply involved in anything.

"A great many furs. Fox. Ermine. One would be grateful if
they could be taken along to the white man's land."

"That's possible," the captain told him. "They will be turned
over to the right people."

"There are other things as well. A most valuable iron pot.
A very good sleigh, knives, axes. We would be grateful to keep
those things if we may pay for them with furs."

"Well, how much could you give in return?" the captain
asked. "Show me what you have."

In the end the Eskimos filled his ship with precious furs.

"We have one thing to confess," Ungar told him. "We don't
want you to carry with you a bad impression of our people. We
have already taken from the dead man's possession two sewing
needles which we needed badly. It was a wrong thing to do,
but I have a very large and beautiful bear skin which I can
give you as payment. If it is not enough, tell me and we will
return the needles."

"Oh, I suppose that will be all right," said the captain, trying to suppress his sly grin. "I do not blame you. Give me the bear skin and we'll think no more of this irregularity."

"Take the guns with you," Ungar said. "And here are some pieces of the thin, white skin which the white men draw lines on. We cannot use them, perhaps thoughts have been written down meant for the people in the white men's home."

"You are an honest man," the captain reassured him as he left with his load. He looked through the papers Bradford and Street had left behind, and as soon as they were out of sight of the camp, he dropped both the guns and the papers in the sea. Looking at the furs both from the Eskimos and from Bradford and Street, he smiled to his first mate:

"It turned out to be quite a good season after all."

The Eskimos were happy with all their wonderful pots and knives and other things which they had honestly paid for. And they knew they had no cause to fear the revenge of the spirits, since they had returned to the white man's land all the belongings of the two dead strangers. For a long time to come they talked about the two white men who had visited them that spring. And for many years Ungar kept a small notebook of red leather as a memory of the two strangers who had died because they had not had the sense to know that an Eskimo cannot be forced.

Ptarmigan

Nobody could deny that Ilatuk was a marvellous wife. Her lamps always sent out the light without any soot or smoke, because they were always well taken care of. She could scrape and chew all her husband's skins better than anybody else; when she made his footwear, it looked like the sole and the leather had grown together. Everything would have been absolute happiness, if it had not been for the ill fate that had caught up with her and Awa: she only gave birth to daughters.

This had an explanation, but what good did that do? Awa had no sons, and he could only look to a sorrow-filled old age, nobody to hunt for him when he himself grew weak, nobody to carry his kin further. And this was sorrow.

Awa had a couple of times traded her away and taken a young woman instead. He was the greatest hunter in the tribe, and nobody dared to disobey him when he told one of the younger men that he wanted his woman. He at once got what he wanted. But it did not take long before everybody could see that Ilatuk's new husband had become very prosperous. He went out hunting before anybody else, he returned always with much meat and many skins, his clothes were finer and warmer than anybody else's. His fox skins were better taken care of, so they fetched better prices in the store, and his house was clean and well looked after.

275

Awa, on the other hand, sat home and strained his eyes by working at his hunting gear in very bad light, because of miserably trimmed lamps. His clothes were never dried or mended in the right way; his boots were not waterproof. He tried several times to beat her up, but the new woman of his in fact could not do the chores.

So after two experiments, where he had to throw out the new woman and take Ilatuk back, he now was living happily at home with his old wife, but four daughters were playing around his house.

The reason for all this was something that happened the first time Ilatuk gave birth to a child; she was disturbed in the middle of the delivery by many white men, who came shouting and laughing into her tent. In fact the child, who was on its way out of the mother's womb, was a boy, but he grew so angry and embarrassed that he sucked his sexual organs into his body and became a girl. And since then, no boy dared to take place inside Ilatuk, so she now was a mother of four girls in spite of everything she had done to make up for her misfortune. She had followed all the rules the medicine man had ordered. And now she was pregnant again.

Awa decided to move far away from other people who might frighten the spirits of delivery away. He drove far inland to the caribou country with his entire family, but as he was a clever and industrious hunter, it was no problem for him to provide food enough for all of them while they were waiting for the boy to be born to the family.

Ilatuk had not touched the slightest piece of meat from a female animal from the time she felt that she was carrying a new child. She had never drunk water from the same cup as any of the small girls, and if they had to drink from a brook, she always had been careful to be above any other woman before she laid down to satisfy her thirst. If they came to a lake she never would drink water with anybody else.

But alas! One day Awa returned from hunting and found

that a new little girl had come to the world in his tent. Ilatuk sat upright without tears or words, she just gazed and gazed at the little new child lying there screaming without knowing how little welcome she was.

"No name can be mentioned!" was all Awa said. Everybody knew what that meant: the child was not to live, therefore it was essential to be cautious and not give it a name. Then no spirit could take revenge for manslaughter. When it had no name it was not a human being and was thus without protection. Ilatuk saw her husband pick her little newborn daughter up by the left leg and walk out.

Awa walked fast in his sad thoughts. Would it never be possible for him to have a son? The child had stopped crying, and he had put it in under his coat. He knew very well that if he looked at the child he could not help feeling pity with it, so it would be impossible for him to kill it.

He walked toward a mountain some distance away, where he intended to place the child under some stones and leave it, but suddenly he heard dogs howling, and looked up and there came three sledges in great speed toward him.

What are these people here for? He had hoped to get away from all other people, so that nobody could embarrass his child; but nevertheless no son has been born, so now, of course, it did not matter. At any rate, here he was, taking a little newborn girl out to die. It certainly was with mixed feelings that he looked at the sledges coming his way.

The dogs had seen Awa, and hurried up to him; it was difficult for the drivers to stop them before they reached the man. None of the three men saluted him, none of them left their sledge. Just the opposite, they sat down turning away from him, and did not express any delight in seeing him; nor did they allow their shouting to tell him that they were happy to meet him.

It was evident to Awa that somebody was dead, and nobody

wanted to be the messenger before he was forced to tell the truth.

After a while, the usual ceremonies came to an end. Awa had seen that one of the sledges was driven by a young boy. And, of course, he recognized the dogs at once; so he understood that his very good friend Ptarmigan was dead. Soon he heard that three men and a boy had been hunting caribou for many days, and the day before yesterday, Ptarmigan had been killed by some falling rocks while he tried to mount a hill. The three survivors, therefore, had taken a long detour, so that the dead man could not follow them if he was a ghost; nobody could really know that. They had driven over rocks and barren ground in order to avoid leaving tracks, and they had to throw away all their meat, as the dogs could not drag it over the cliffs. Now here they saw a man, which delighted them very much, as they needed dog food and something to eat for themselves.

There stood Awa, who forgot entirely what he had had in mind to do when he went out. Just in this moment the little girl inside his coat started crying again. The three strangers heard it, and even if no Eskimo ought to put questions forward about unexpected events, they could not help looking surprised. The boy who was driving the late Ptarmigan's sledge was so young that he could not give his thoughts faster speed than his words, so he said:

"One hears a child crying. Perhaps Ptarmigan is reborn. Oh, if only Ptarmigan's name was attached to somebody a great hunter would be with us again!"

There stood Awa with a little girl under his coat. The name was mentioned: the child was Ptarmigan, and Awa was without power to kill it, even if she only was a girl.

He returned to his tent and placed the newborn girl next to Ilatuk. "Ptarmigan has come to us. It has happened that a great hunter's name belongs to a girl!" After that he went outside and fed the dogs of his guests as much as they could eat, and the three visitors were taken inside and served many kinds of meat; Awa had never shown himself meatless when visitors came to his tent.

After Ilatuk gave birth to her fifth daughter she never had any more children. The four older girls were very clever in everything a woman has to do. Before they were many winters old they could sew mittens, which is the easiest thing for a woman to do. Later on they were made to learn to do many other things with their mother as a teacher. They chewed the skins from birds and foxes free of fat, so the factor in the store praised the skins Awa brought him and paid the best prices for them.

But the youngest girl, whose name was Akriserk (Ptarmigan) had no inclination at all for women's work. As she showed great desire for dog driving, the father decided someday to take her along seal hunting at blowholes. It is very helpful to have someone driving round some distance from the blowhole one is standing by. The seals from other places will then be frightened and sooner come to where the hunter stands waiting for them. Soon Ptarmigan also learned other parts of the hunting. She was very cunning in sneaking close up to the seals when they were sleeping at the ice. Her movements were so clever in imitation of the seals that they let themselves be fooled; she came so close to them that she threw herself right across their blowholes, so it was impossible for them to go down to the water. It happened several times that the seal bit her rather badly to get down, but Ptarmigan only laughed. And soon she caught just as many seals as her father.

But, of course, when other hunters were present, she kept herself quiet on the sledge, and never did she dare speak up; neither did she eat with the men at the hunting places— always alone.

Because of this, it was very useful that the family take land away from other people, so they might take advantage of her ability as a hunter without feeling shame.

As the winter came, Ptarmigan showed herself able to catch

foxes equally with any man. Her sisters complained badly that they lived so isolated. They never had any of the pleasures men can provide women with, but Awa refused to change his place and stay closer to other people, except when they all went to the trading posts to get what was needed for the house and the hunt.

Then it happened someday on a bearhunt that his gun did not go off: the bear attacked him and bit him something awful in his leg. Ptarmigan was not right at the place, but she hurried to her father and saved his life by a fast shot that hit right between the eyes of the bear.

Awa could not walk for long long time, but nobody suffered for that. Ptarmigan's catch was enough; in fact she brought more meat home than Awa ever had done. But the four sisters did not show the same politeness to her as they had been compelled to do to the father as long as he was the provider. They directed Ptarmigan to drive closer to other people every time they had to move to another place.

Awa was still weak in his leg. Thus he only drove one sledge with two of the women and very little load. Ptarmigan took the rest of them and all of their belongings on her sledge and drove in front of her father.

One day they saw old sled tracks, which showed them that they were nearer to people.

"Now it will be seen by many that here comes a man whose meat is to be brought home by a mere woman," said Awa.

Therefore it was decided that man's dress was to be made for Ptarmigan, so nobody could know that she was a girl. Awa would have been red in his face by shame if some visitors found out that they were treated with a woman's catch.

Before long, they were rather near to other people's settlement, but it was an entirely strange tribe, and nobody there knew anything about their secrecy.

People came visiting them, and soon they knew the faces and the names of their new neighbors.

One young man was named Angut. He was the greatest hunter and brought more game home than the rest of the men together, and he saw to it that nobody was in need at the settlement. Besides he had great caches, many places where he had killed and cut game up unseen by others. He and Ptarmigan often met with each other out on the hunting field, and soon the two of them competed with each other as to who was the greater hunter. But neither of them was second to the other; they were equal in bringing game home to the tents. Often they went out together, and they always returned with the same amount of kills.

Angut's mother was Semigak, and she did not like that anybody else should be as good a provider as her famous son.

One day Angut's mother visited Ilatuk together with two other women. They came unseen close to the tent, and then they heard Ilatuk shout to somebody; it was easy to hear that it was somebody who talked to her daughter. Great was their surprise therefore as they saw that it was Ptarmigan, who had gone after water for the mother, as if she were a mere girl.

Semigak grew suspicious that Ptarmigan perhaps really was a girl; she had often had the idea that her way of walking looked feminine, but she never dared say it to anybody. Now she whispered to her two companions, and the three of them decided to find out what secrecy was combined with this.

If Ptarmigan proved to be a girl, it certainly would be a great shame on the entire settlement, as everybody would have often eaten woman-caught seals, and who could know whether the great Nerivik, the huge woman who sits at the bottom of the sea and commands all the hunted animals, would not feel insulted by this and then keep every seal and walrus away from the people afterward?

But the three women were too clever to let anything out at once. They decided only to find out the truth, so they later on could create the sensation much better and stronger, when many people were present.

Ptarmigan and Angut kept on getting an incredible amount of game; all that the rest of the hunters brought home was almost nothing compared with these two.

When the fall came, the situation allowed smooth-ice hunting some place a little away, and everybody went out to take part before snow would fall and spoil the chances. Smooth-ice hunting brings more seals to people than any other way of catching them.

Semigak went along, and they all had to build an igloo to sleep there at night; it was too far to drive back to the settlement, as the days were very short now. They made a huge snowhouse, and all of them slept in there.

"Now it will be easy, when everybody undresses, to see what sex Ptarmigan really belongs to," said Semigak to the others.

But when night came, it was seen that Ptarmigan slept with all her clothes on.

Said the old woman: "How comes it somebody does not undress? The lice are going to hurt such ones who sleep in the coat and pants!"

"It happens that such a regulation rules in my tribe," said Ptarmigan, "that he who has caught a seal does not undress until he has the next seal on his meatrack. After that he undresses entirely and sleeps naked and searches all his clothes for lice, until the next seal is harpooned. This system seems to give good hunting luck in my tribe!"

Nobody could say anything against this, and everybody went to sleep. The next morning they woke up to see that much snow had fallen during the night, the smooth ice was destroyed, and all the hunters went home.

Old Semigak was not defeated yet: "Let a great party be prepared," she said. "In a bowl berries pickled in blubber will be served. The other bowl will send out its delicious steam and smell of fat boiled meat, so the house will be filled with it. The girls will at once hurry to the berries, that have been oil-soaked since last fall. Girls all the time have a sweet tooth. Men prefer meat to give strength. Let it been seen what Ptarmigan takes at first!"

As the guests entered the house, Ptarmigan at once grabbed a handful of berries. Semigak saw it, and she could not help winking with one eye to her fellow conspirators.

Ptarmigan saw it, and she understood right away that she had given herself away:

"A handful of berries was taken to be given to that little poor girl at the entrance; she does not dare take for herself. And now, one wants to look for some strength-giving meat to eat!"

Nothing was found out that evening either.

Later on, the fox trapping had given a great many skins to Angut and Ptarmigan. Each of them had the sledge entirely loaded with fox skins when it was decided to travel to the trading post and buy some of what the shop had to offer.

Again Semigak caught an idea. Said she: "Here it will be easy to find out what one wants to know. If a girl comes to a trader, she always wants colored ribbons and nice clothes and needles and scissors; also mirrors are in woman's desires. Men go for ammunition and tools and knives for their hunting!"

Ptarmigan and Angut went inside with their many fox skins. They could not carry them in all at the same time. Angut at once asked for guns and boards for a new sledge.

Ptarmigan steered her feet across the room to some shelves where some red flannel and blue ribbons were placed, some of them made of silk.

Again old Semigak triumphed too early; she made signs through the window to her fellows who were outside. Ptarmigan saw it and realized. Said she:

"Now it happened that somebody has spent just half of the skins for the benefit of the sisters at home, so they will feel that somebody has been at the trading post. Now it will take place, as half of the foxes are left for real trading, that one will take a look at the guns and the ammunition!"

It was seen that Ptarmigan bought two guns and many tools good for men to have on hunting trips.

As the spring returned to people, and the sun as well, Angut and Ptarmigan went away after bears. Each of them killed four bears and drove home with the skins. Their dogs were heavy with much food, and the sledges loaded down with meat.

A huge gluttonous party was arranged and much eating delight was created by fat marrow bones boiled in the soup; they also had delicious bear meat. While new pots were hung across the lamps to provide a new course in the meal, they all tugged at the ribs while storytellers entertained the guests during the waiting time.

Now Semigak said: "It would be most unlikely if the cunning of the bears just killed had not affected the hunters. Some questions might show whoever is the wisest, since it seems impossible to find out which one of the two is the greatest hunter!"

Now Ptarmigan turned around to the old woman and started to talk:

"The chance will just have it that some words are to be said! Nobody is wise in this settlement except Angut and myself! You, Semigak, are not very clever. Three times you have tried to find out about my sex. But you failed all three times because all kinds of wisdom keep away from your head. The one who is wise is Angut, because he found out that I am a girl. And that is why he will get me as his wife. But also I am a wise one, because I knew how to get the best hunter for a husband!"

And this is the end of the story about Ptarmigan.

The Law of Larion

One day in 1934 in the Yukon, where Freuchen's plane had to make a forced landing, he fell into talk with an elderly Indian who showed him two well kept graves. They were the resting places of two European officers, one English, the other Russian, and the date of death on both was February 16, 1851. This is also the date of what in the history of Alaska has been called the Massacre of Nulato.

Freuchen's guide that day was the grandson of a man who had played a leading part in this grim event, a triumph for a great, almost legendary Indian chieftain named Larion. The Indian told the old story with obvious relish, and Peter was sufficiently interested to do some further research. The result was an historical novel published years later, "The Law of Larion."

The legend of this chief was elaborated and the story of his greatness told in the famous Freuchen fashion. The background of the selection given here is this:

Shortly before the middle of the 19th Century, the rivalry between the Russians in Alaska and the English in the Hudson Bay Company for mastery of the fur trade was keen. Larion sided with the Russians and for many years was loyal to them. In the end, feeling himself betrayed by them, he took his terrible revenge.

The scene of this concluding part of the novel opens with Larion, accompanied by his wife, setting out to kill singlehanded two Englishmen whom he holds responsible for the death of his son, Dislen. Actually they had sold the young man a gun in exchange for his furs. When Dislen and his bride proudly brought it back to his tribe, his father, in his ignorance of such weapons, discharged it and killed the youth. So by his code, the men responsible must die, too.

The sun was higher in the sky. First came the sparrows, then more and more small birds.

They were nearing the end of the difficult journey. Now it would soon be spring, and the ice would break. Revenge knows no time of year, and Larion was used to traveling at all seasons. If he could not reach his objective over the ice, he would have to wait until he found a canoe. Then he would either kill its occupants or steal it from them while they slept. He could not say which.

After some days he and Inaluk halted. They rested, slept and dried their clothes, and Larion caught some birds and a hare. Then, at last, they approached the place they were making for.

They saw smoke rising, which showed that people were at home, and they saw some Indians leave the house with a sledge. A woman was dragging it, and three men walked in front. Two white men then came out of the house and stood down by the river, looking after the Indians as they went.

The water from the melting snow and ice had now begun to flow down from the land to the river, forcing itself in under the ice. Larion realized that there would only be a few days before the ice began to break up with an uproar. Perhaps this would help him when he went to parley with the white men, before the fight began. He decided to ask them whether they remembered Dislen, after which he would tell them that they were destined to follow Dislen to the place from which no one returns.

When the two white men had been inside for a long time, and no more smoke came from the chimney, Larion decided that they were sleeping and that he and Inaluk could now cross the river without being seen. For safety's sake, however, they crossed higher up. The going was difficult, for the snow had melted and the ground had thawed on the surface. They slid about on the slippery, mossy soil, and their progress was slow. Finally, Larion packed all their possessions into a bundle and took them on his back, and Inaluk carried the sledge.

When they crossed the Yukon, they used the sledge again, but it was hard to drag it in the wet snow. They felt the ice tremble under their feet. When at last they got across, they found that the ice had receded, and the melted water was rushing down from the shore. After they had searched for a time, they found a place where they could get up the bank. Larion said he thought the ice would break at any moment. It would, therefore, be impossible to get home before the thaw had destroyed both ice and snow.

They went far into the forest, and after they had eaten, Larion went out to explore the surrounding country. First of all, it was necessary to find out in which direction the white men's house lay. That was easy. Then he had to discover where they went to fetch their fuel. He saw that they had been foolish enough to cut down the trees close to the house so that there was a small open space around it.

Next day, he made a long tour of the district. He soon ascertained that the ice on the Kopak River would be safe for some time, but he could not depend on the Yukon itself. He even thought he heard a distant crack; perhaps the ice was already beginning to break up.

Every evening he returned to Inaluk, who looked at him but asked no questions. Larion did not speak to her. He was always absorbed in his own thoughts. He could scarcely bring himself to eat, but she put food before him and then retired a little way off and pretended to be busy with other things. By the time she came back, he had eaten his fill. Inaluk always found something to give him, and he himself often brought home small animals, a bird or a hare.

One day when they were about to drink some warm soup in which birds had been boiled, Larion stopped in the act of lifting the pot to his mouth. He had heard something. Yes, there it was again. A hollow sound, a sort of thunder. The ice on the Yukon was breaking up.

He sprang to his feet and shouted to Inaluk that she was to get ready and come with him. They must take their knives with them, all three knives. They must also take their axes, her small one and his big one. Inaluk must also carry Larion's bow and arrows, those with the steel points. She quickly loosened the strap that bound the arrows together. They were now ready for use, and Larion and his woman were armed for battle.

He could not help wishing they had been near an ochre mountain so that he could have painted his face and made himself frightful to look at. Larion had examined the neighborhood. He had eaten fat meat which gave him strength and lightness of body. Inaluk's slowness irritated him as she prepared to follow him. They threw wet moss over the fire. Then they were ready to start.

At first they walked quickly, but after a time more carefully. Suddenly they stood still and listened. Yes, Larion was right; it was the Yukon. No other sound in the world can be confused with it when one is near enough.

They went on. They were glad that it no longer grew really dark, for even the dim light was useful in their slow, careful approach. They soon reached the open space where the white men had cut down the trees because they were too lazy to go further afield.

Larion signaled to Inaluk to halt. She sank down behind a tree and did not move, but her eyes were alive, and nothing escaped her.

Larion crept round the house. There were two sheds in which the white men appeared to keep their salmon and other things they did not want inside the house. The sheds were carelessly placed and afforded Larion good cover as he moved toward the house where the men slept. First one shed and then the other hid him from the windows, and it did not take him long to get quite close to the house. Then he lay still, waiting. No one came out of the house, and he crawled up close to the porch where the windows were covered with thin skins with holes in them. The windows faced the Yukon.

As he stood there, the door opened and the white men came out. For a moment, Larion felt as if he had drunk a great daught of firewater in one gulp, and was quite dazed. If they had caught sight of him there, they could easily have over-powered him. But the strange feeling lasted only for a moment. Larion's head cleared, and he remembered that Dislen's mur-derers stood before him, men who must not be allowed to live now that he had found them.

The white men did not see Larion. They had eyes only for the breaking ice, and at that moment it happened just below the house. There was a heavy clap as of thunder, then a mighty heave, and the whole surface of the ice moved several man-lengths downriver. One of the men began to laugh and shout.

This was the signal for Larion. When his enemy mocked even the Yukon, he deserved death. Larion stopped in front of them. At once they knew, from the expression on his face, that the man was dangerous. Although not tall, Larion was always an impressive figure, and now he was afire with deadly purpose.

For a time, the noise of the breaking ice prevented speech. Then they spoke.

"Who are you and what do you want? This is not a trading time, and we do not want guests."

Larion stayed where he was. The white men spoke Indian language badly, like small children, but he could understand it.

"Do you remember Dislen? He came here with Gana and bought a gun," Larion at length asked.

The cheerful one of the two began to smile.

"Yes, we remember him well. And now you also want a gun? But have you skins enough to buy one? They cost many skins, you know."

"That gun cost a great deal, for it cost him his life. Now you shall die because you gave Dislen a gun that was faulty. It killed him. I am Larion, Dislen's father. I am here to avenge my son."

One of the men had a gun in his hand. Now he lifted it and quickly pulled out the ramrod in the hollow part. Then he raised it, and his right hand moved to the little tap which, Larion knew, controlled the thunder. He also laid his cheek against the weapon, and Larion saw that it pointed straight at him.

Larion turned his heavy spear and gripped it just below the point, for the shaft was heavy. Larion's great reputation was largely based on his ability to throw a heavier spear than any other man, and now he whirled it with tremendous force. It hit the barrel of the gun before the man's finger had time to give the death signal. A shot rang out and there was a whining in the air just above Larion. Death flew past him, as did the gun itself. Larion had struck it with such force that it had flown right out of the white man's hand, who now stood there quite defenseless.

The other man ran toward the house and shouted something to his companion, who answered in a language that Larion could not understand. Nor was Larion in a mood to listen. He gripped his spear with both hands and turned it over, for now he was going to use the point.

All this took only an instant, but Inaluk heard the shot and had time to realize that the struggle had begun and that the men with the thunder weapons were two against one. When she had heard the shot, she had believed Larion dead. Her first thought, however, was not that she was now a widow and life was over. No, Larion had taught her to fight to the end, and she rushed forward.

She soon saw that no one was dead, and a warm feeling of pleasure streamed through her. Larion stood erect, his arm circling round to swing his spear. Before him was the white man who must soon die, for Larion never missed.

The spear flew out of Larion's hand and pierced the white

man's body. Inaluk was right. She saw the man fall with the spear sticking right through his back. He groaned, and Larion rushed over and pulled the spear out again. Now Larion was shouting wildly, and his war cries echoed round the house.

Inaluk saw his eyes grow red with fury. When this happened, none must go near him until his blood lust had been satisfied. At such times, Larion knew neither friend nor foe, but slaughtered any who came near.

For a moment, the other white man stood as if paralyzed. Then the door of the house opened and two Indian girls came out. It was easy to see that they were very frightened. One of them had a gun, and as the white man rushed toward the house, she ran and handed it to him. This gave him confidence, and he shouted something to Larion, a challenge perhaps. Inaluk could not tell.

She saw that the man was still making for the house, and she sensed that it would be dangerous to let him reach it. Inside were many guns which would enable him to send death out through the windows before they could get away.

She had not time to think how she could actually prevent this, but she ran toward the house to bar his way. If he attacked her, she was sure Larion would come to her aid and would thus have the chance of getting close to the man, unopposed. Only the two women were in sight and they were huddling against a pile of wood. The chieftain of Kuyukuk would not consider them of any account as a foe.

As the white man turned to rush into the house, he saw Inaluk. He shouted. In his panic he probably thought that the house was surrounded. In any case, she stood in his way, so he raised his gun. He did not stop to see who it was, nor did he aim. His finger simply pulled the trigger and death flew out. There was a loud explosion which was the prelude to an even louder one; for at that very moment the ice gave way again and seemed to echo the voice of the thunder weapon. Inaluk fell and lay motionless where she fell. Inaluk was dead, and Larion knew this. He threw his spear, but the man jumped aside and it hit the ground by the house.

Larion sprang forward to cut off the man's retreat in the same way as Inaluk had done. The white man seized the barrel of his gun to defend himself with the butt. He tried to hit Larion, but the latter jumped back, and the gun hit a stone which broke in two. The gun itself was cracked when the white man lifted it up again, and a cracked bludgeon is no weapon for killing. The next time, the gun hit Larion but it did not hurt him. The whole weapon went to pieces in the man's hand, and Larion saw that he had not had time to put in the black powder which fed the thunder.

The white man shouted to the girls, but they did not answer. Larion realized that he wanted something fetched from the house. The girls ran to the back. There must be a door there, Larion thought. That did not matter now, because he had reached his spear and had time to bend down and pick it up.

Now Larion felt sure of himself. He heard a shout and looked round. It was the girl running from behind the house, and she had one of the dangerous thunder weapons in her hand. The man shouted to her.

"Throw it, throw it!" The words were easy to understand.

The man himself stood behind a pile of firewood, hiding himself from Larion's spear. The girl came nearer, and Larion turned toward her. She gave a shriek and ran away. Then Larion turned his attention to the white man. He tried to get round the pile of firewood. The man rushed to the other end, and there stood the girl ready to fling him the gun so that he might send death into Larion.

Larion ran back to the opposite end of the pile, but the man moved according to Larion's position so that he was always as far as possible from him. Suddenly, Larion realized that the pile was, after all, only wood, piled up by men so that a man could as easily take it down again. He began to throw the wood from side to side. Soon, he would be able to jump over the wood and stand close up to the qaneken. Then Dislen would be avenged. This, also, was the man who had mocked the Yukon and who had spoken in angry and commanding tones to Larion when he first saw him.

The qaneken cried out in fear. He shrieked to the girl to throw him the gun across the wood so that he could defend himself. Larion understood this, for now he was quite calm. How could she do this? He kept his eye on her so that he was always aware how far away she was. At the same time, he went on throwing the wood from side to side so that he might finally be able to jump over it. Then, the white man left his cover, rushed away from the woodpile and shouted to the girl.

"Senahiana! Senahiana! Throw me the gun."

She threw it.

Larion was as quick as the other man and nearer the gun. He rushed forward and got between the white man and the place where the gun had fallen. Now, he was between the white man and the woodpile, so that his prey could no longer seek shelter behind it.

Then the man ran. Fear possessed his body, and his only thought seemed to be to get away from the place. Down toward the Yukon he ran, the mighty river which a short time ago he had mocked and laughed at.

Larion ran after him, howling his war cries. Ha, ha! The white man was a slow runner. Did he really believe that he could escape Larion who had been through all the countries on this side of the great salt sea?

Larion enjoyed keeping just behind him, shouting his war cries. Whenever he heard an extra loud shout, the white man made a spurt, but he could not keep it up for long.

Finally, he turned in the direction of the ice. He was not far from the river, and Larion decided to kill him on the river bank. Suddenly, Larion missed his footing on a slippery slope and slid. As Larion stumbled, the white man got a small lead.

He used it to rush out onto the ice. His idea was to get across, and it seemed as if he were making better progress out there. Perhaps it was only that the ice was carrying him along, it was hard to say, for at that very moment the Yukon moved forward again and the ice piled itself up like rocks on a mountain. The thunder of the ice was so loud that Larion had to stop his war song, for it was impossible to outshout the Yukon.

The white man sprang from ice block to ice block. He looked like an insect trying to save itself. At one time he would try to run straight across, but that was impossible. Then when he forgot that Larion also meant death, he tried to get back, hoping to reach firm land. But ice floe followed ice floe. He jumped from one to another toward the shore.

All at once, a strong eddy turned the whole thing round, and the man was slung right up into the ar. He looked like a baby bird who is thrown out of the nest to teach him to fly. He fell but quickly rose again. He ran but discovered that he was running the wrong way. When he turned he came to water. He gave a long jump to reach another block of ice but fell with his legs in the water and only his arms clinging onto the ice.

Then, there was something that pulled him away. It took hold of him from below and would not let him save himself. He swam a little way, for the water was quiet for a while, and then he managed to crawl up onto the ice again. He was even able to stand up. He turned toward Larion and began to swing his arms. No one could hear what he shouted; the crash and the roar of the ice drowned all other sounds. Then something below him flung him into the water again. He clambered up again but the ice massed itself round where he stood and heaved violently. He tried to walk, but suddenly it seemed as if the Yukon thought that this game had been going on long enough. The river had been icebound all the winter and was starved for human prey.

Larion only knew that down there in the depths lived Tjox-wullik and many others, and now the Yukon longed for white flesh.

The ice blocks began to drift. There had been a pause in the movement, but now the journey began afresh. The white man grew smaller and smaller, just a tiny insect in a whirl of ice. He was visible for a moment and then he disappeared again. Back he came, his arms waving, and then he disappeared for good. The Yukon does not take long to make up her mind as to the fate of a human being.

Larion stood looking after him. Soon, the piece of ice on which the man had stood was no longer recognizable among all the others. It had twisted and turned, and now it was quickly drifting downstream. The noise and the speed confused the senses, but Larion resented that he had not been able to carry out his revenge. He had not needed the Yukon's help.

Suddenly, Larion remembered that Inaluk was also dead. One more of his family had been killed by the thunder weapon, and they were not fully avenged. Larion, looking back, saw the two girls. They were quite quiet. They only stood and looked at him. He walked quickly up the slope leading to the house.

Suddenly, one of the girls shrieked and ran away. Her cries were heard because the thunder of the ice had died down and there was now only the sound of water.

Larion was angry. The desire to kill had not yet died within him. He had always found it difficult to subdue his anger after a fight, and now he decided to follow the girl. She did not run very quickly, but she shrieked, and that irritated him. He took his heavy spear and weighed it in his hand while he ran. He was renowned for the fact that he could throw a spear while running. He saw the point of the spear find its way into her shoulder. She fell forward, and the spear stood upright as if it were growing out of the ground.

Larion the fierce. He killed and killed yet never felt any joy from his killings. This girl's death gained him nothing. There was no honor attached to killing a woman in flight. All that should be done was to catch her and violate her if a man felt

so inclined. If there was no possibility that help would come to
her, no honor had been won in the killing.

He thought of this. Tjoxwullik had once spoken thus to him
when he had regained his calmness after a fit of anger. Now he
remembered it. He dragged the spear out of the woman's body
and stood still for a time.

He was alone again as he had so often been before. He suddenly longed for the company of other human beings. For this
reason, Larion remembered that there was one more girl. He
would take her. He turned and, to his surprise, saw that she
was standing quite close to him watching him. When he came
up to her she did not try to run away. She lay down on her back
and tried to entice him to her. She even smiled and whispered
something he could not understand.

Larion took hold of her hand, which she held up to him, and
pulled her up onto her feet.

"Are you not afraid?" he asked in an almost friendly voice.

"Yes," she said. "I am very frightened of you!"

"Why did you not run away then?"

"I had seen enough to know that I could not escape death
if you wished to kill me!" She smiled again as she said this,
and again tried to lie down in front of him.

Larion dragged her with him, and they walked on a little
way. He thought that this girl was not like every other girl.

"How many of you are there here?"

"There are only two of us here, yourself and miserable, silly
me!"

"Where do you come from?"

"From far, far away. My father brought me here and gave
me to the two qanekens. The girl you killed also belonged to
my tribe, but I did not like her. Now she is dead!"

Larion sat down on a tree stump and began to think.

"Is there no one else in the house?" he asked at length.

"All that were here are dead now."

He went on in front of her into the house. On the way, he

saw the bodies of Inaluk and the white man he had killed, but he said nothing, and went on into the house.

There were remarkable things in this house. In the back room he found a number of skins. "Durabbin will be pleased with them for they are the Tzar's property," Larion thought to himself.

Afterward, he sat down and told the girl that he meant to stay here for a time. First of all, he wanted to eat. When he saw that there was meat in the place, he ordered her to cook it. There was wood enough in the house, and they made up the fire in the fireplace, blowing the embers until they glowed. They cooked beneath a smoke hole that went straight up through the roof.

Larion suddenly realized he was tired. His attacks of rage were always followed by great exhaustion, but Larion did not give way, and ate a great deal. They consumed large pieces of well-cooked meat. The girl also had a good appetite.

"Are you still afraid?" he asked.

"Yes, I am very frightened of you!"

When he had satisfied his hunger, he lay down to sleep, but before he slept he thought over his future plans. He noticed that the girl washed the flat pieces of wood from which they had eaten the meat during their meal. Then she put them back in the place from which she had taken them and threw the bones out to a dog, which was tied up at the back of the house. Larion had not noticed the dog. It ought to have barked and warned its masters, but no doubt the noise of the Yukon had frightened it.

He slept and rested well. When he woke again the girl, who lay on the other bank, was watching him. He desired her and called her to him.

"My name is Senahiana!" she said and smiled. She let him do what he wished with her until they were both tired and fell asleep.

When they woke, Larion went outside. The Yukon was now much calmer but still running swiftly, and ice blocks were drifting downstream. Sometimes the river seemed to be choked with ice, but always it moved on. The Yukon wished to get down to the salt ocean. It had been quiet long enough.

Outside the house lay Inaluk and the white man and, a little farther away, the murdered girl. Larion could not bear to think about this girl. Why had he killed her? Why had he killed Thimsian, too? Larion did not know, himself, but he was a chieftain and would not allow himself to be cowed, even by his own thoughts.

The girl, Senahiana, made up the fire inside the house. Larion returned to ask her if she had seen many white men.

"Yes, more than I can remember by name." She came over to him and laid both hands round his head. "And I have learned to make love in the manner of white men. Come, and I will show you!" she said, half shutting her eyes.

Larion pushed her away from him. She seemed to think he was a child, and yet, her touch affected him strangely. So he rose quickly and said that he would eat as soon as she had cooked their meal.

He went into the room where skins and goods were stored. A bundle of straps lay in one corner. He took them and fastened most of the skins together in two big bundles. He left out one or two wolverine skins, for he intended those for Inaluk.

He knew the type of skin Durabbin liked best. As he sorted them he found those that Dislen had brought. Larion recognized them instantly because they had been stretched differently from the ones used up here.

He stood for a moment wondering whether he should take them, but then he remembered that Dislen had used them as decoys on a spying trip and, therefore, he was entitled to them. The rest was pure booty.

He opened one or two boxes and found axes and knives and other trading goods. He took two axes, many knives, needles and five pairs of scissors. He filled a little skin bag with thread and other useful things and set them aside.

The meal was not yet ready so he went out. He had already noticed a good canoe in one of the sheds, and he let his hand glide over the calking. Yes, the bark stitching was good. He also saw a vessel in the hut containing tallow and tar, which would be useful for mending leaks.

He went in and ate. The girl served him. She also gave him bread baked from white powder, but that he pushed away from him.

"Do you not eat white men's food?" she asked. "I should long for bread if I were forced to do without it for long."

"That is of no importance," answered the Indian. "Longings must always be overcome."

Larion said no more. He was a silent man, she thought, and she tried to sulk a little and pretend to be angry. Larion paid no attention to her.

Senahiana did not even know his name.

"What is your name, and where do you come from? You are so strong and victorious."

"Others will tell you my name. My land lies along the banks of the Yukon."

"No one can cross the river now. It will not be navigable for a long time yet. But there is plenty of food in the house for both of us," Senahiana said.

"There was a time when women dictated my actions," said Larion, "but that was only during the first three years of my life. Since then, I have made my own decisions."

He went out and walked in the direction from whence he had come with Inaluk. He went to collect their little pots and sleeping blanket, and a few other things they had brought with them. They were all lying cozy and dry under the rock, and he noticed how well Inaluk had packed up everything together. Inside the bundle lay dry moccasins which he now put on.

It was evening when he returned. The girl was not there. He

went out and looked round carefully. No one else had been near the house. She could scarcely have gone for help to avenge the dead qanekens, for it was far to the nearest village. Inaluk had told him this and had also said that there were two rivers to cross.

Larion went to work. First he carried out all the skins he had collected into two big bundles and put them in the canoe. He covered them all with reindeer skins with the hair turned outward so that they might be protected against wetness. Then he carried down a little box filled with those objects which he had decided to take away as war booty.

When everything was packed into the canoe, Larion carried Inaluk into the house. He laid her down in the white man's bunk and covered her over with the skins he had kept aside. In the other bunk he laid the white man and the Indian woman whom Senahiana disliked.

It was now dusk. It never grew quite dark, as the spring was far advanced. Larion felt sleepy and, taking his sleeping blanket, he lay down a little distance from the house. He found the place that he had already used as shelter when he was keeping an eye on the house, and there he slept, for he knew there was no danger. The girl had taken the dog with her, and that told him that she had not crossed the river to the village which lay so far away. It would take her several nights to get there at this time of the year.

Her shrieks woke him. He lifted his head a little and then went back to sleep. The girl came rushing out of the house. He had slept a few moments until he was again waked by her shrieking and cries for help. "I am frightened!" she cried. He turned over and slept again.

The next morning, she came running to meet Larion when he approached the house.

"Where have you been?" Senahiana cried. "I have been very, very frightened, for there are corpses in the house. I came back and thought that you were lying waiting for me, but it was the dead woman. I am very angry with you."

Nobody had ever spoken to Larion like that before. He, therefore, spoke kindly and softly to her and asked her where she had been yesterday.

"I ran away. I was afraid to be alone!" Senahiana answered. "The dead outside the house frightened me. Why did you not tell me that you were going away? You must tell me when you go away, and you must take the corpses away at once. I want my tea; it is morning."

Larion gave her a good beating. To begin with, she shrieked; later on, she fainted. Then he left her where she lay and began working again. He carried all the fuel into the house. He laid it round Inaluk's bunk and beneath the bunk on which the other two lay. He carried in armful after armful and, at the same time, kept the embers on the hearth well alive.

After Larion had walked in and out of the house several times, Senahiana woke but did not stir.

"Get up and make a fire and cook our meal, but do so down by the river!" Larion said to her.

Senahiana remained where she was. Larion continued going in and out, still carrying the wood.

"I told you what you were to do and I am accustomed to being obeyed!" Larion said, his voice confirming his words. Senahiana got up and said that she could not make a fire for she had no flint. Then Larion did something quite unusual for him. He went with her to the place where he wanted the fire made and helped her to arrange it properly. He knelt down, started the fire, and then fetched water from the river. He hung a pot over the fire on a branch, which he bent over together with another one so they made a bow across the fire.

The girl sat down and looked at him. She understood that he was angry with her, for he had beaten her, but she did not intend to give in. She could not imagine why he wanted a fire down there. She still felt pain from the beating and burst into tears. Larion did not say a word.

"You'll never sleep with me again!" the girl panted. "I'd rather lie alone. Get the bodies out quickly. I could not sleep all night I was so frightened. Hurry up, I tell you! Hurry up!

Larion went up to the house and in through the door. She stopped crying as soon as he was out of earshot. Senahiana was very angry and began to realize that it would be difficult to influence this coarse, strange man who did not know or care about the best way of living. She was determined to win, however. Senahiana had known many men and had been passed from one to the other. She deeply despised the Indians and wanted to live with white men. She determined to keep this Indian here until her friends came back and killed him. Then a new day would dawn with much tobacco, tea and whisky.

Larion went into the house and saw that all was ready. He took out the meat hanging there, laid it on a stump of a tree and returned to the house. He laid large pieces of fuel in the fireplace, and when they were alight, he placed them about in the room so that the floor and the wood he had piled should catch fire. Then, the girl's face appeared in the window which he had smashed.

"Are you mad? Are you going to burn down the house? You'll destroy the whole thing. My food, my tobacco, and my whisky— my whisky! I know where the whisky is!"

Larion did not know what that was. He went calmly back and forth, arranging his pyre. The fire began to blaze up beneath Inaluk's bunk. The other one was also well alight, and now it was time Larion got out.

When Larion reached the door, Senahiana was standing there blocking his way. She was quite wild. She clawed at his face with her nails. She smacked his cheeks with the flat of her hand, and she threw herself against him in an effort to push him back into the house.

He took hold of her and lifted her up, smacked her bottom

once or twice and put her outside the door. She fell down in the wet, thawed mud and shrieked violently. Larion shut the door and felt the warmth of the smoke against his face. Then he sprang up onto a tree stump and began to sing of his own great deeds. He remembered all Gissa-Usch's songs, and he made up new songs as he went along, about Dislen and about his revenge. Now he was burning a house full of great treasure. All the things that the Indians of the district most longed to possess were here, quickly turning into ashes. He stood holding the iron poker from the fireplace in one hand, and swinging his fearful spear with the other, and the more it burned the redder his face grew.

He sang about Inaluk, he howled his war cries, and he quite forgot that there was no one to hear him. This was his triumph, the consummation of his revenge. Larion was doing what no one else had ever dreamed of doing. He was burning un-dreamed-of treasure, which would have made him a rich man, in honor of his son, both his wives and his daughter-in-law. He had killed the owners of this treasure who had tried to defend it. He could, with unstained honor, have taken it all, but he had chosen to burn it in honor of those he had lost and who could now live in freedom in the world of the dead. They had been avenged in a more terrible manner than anyone ever before.

The girl lay where he had thrown her, looking at him as if he were a madman. She could not understand what was happening. Senahiana had come from a tribe who had lived long with white men. They had given up war and made their living by bringing goods in canoes from trading post to trading post during the summer, and in the winter on sledges drawn by dogs. She was a stranger to the old free life, and Larion had never known anything else.

He went on singing, and his eyes shone. He felt as light and above the earth as when he had drunk firewater. Now he could be happy again. Those he missed were happier than they had been here on earth. They had been avenged, not only by the death of their enemy, but also by the destruction of the pile of costly articles he had given them as funeral gifts. Inaluk had been entirely covered with wolverine skins. This would help her to be as successful in the other world as this much-feared animal was successful in this.

The flames rose higher and higher, and the smoke poured forth in black clouds. If there had been other human beings anywhere near, they would surely have appeared, for the glare could be seen from very far away. To this, Larion was indifferent. He had shown that no one could stand against him.

Larion's song ceased. Suddenly the roof fell in, the fire flared up, and he saw Inaluk's spirit escape in the flames. It hovered over the treetops and then went quickly toward the place where the two of them had slept and where she had packed up his moccasins for him. It excited him wildly, and he began to bellow again so that he was heard even above the sound of the Yukon.

The fire died down again until the house was just a smoldering, blackened heap. Then Larion felt so tired that he could scarcely move.

Larion sat resting for a long time. At last he rose, cut off great chunks of meat and threw them into the pot over the fire which the girl had kept burning. Then there was nothing to do but wait until the meat was cooked. Larion sat gazing into the fire. Senahiana was not hungry, but he gave her a piece of meat and told her that he wished her to eat it. In the end, she ate first one bit and then another while Larion emptied the pot. She told him that she was used to having tea after meat and that they used to have bread with every meal.

"One can have many habits, and just as many can be laid aside," Larion said.

Larion did not know how long he had slept. He woke because the dog at his side began to bark.

Then, he saw Senahiana coming toward him with a knife in her hand. He did not move, but lay watching her. She hesitated a little, and then she came nearer, walking on tiptoe. She looked absurd, thought Larion, and almost smiled. The dog knew her well but barked, nonetheless. She did not seem to hear it, for she was so taken up with wondering whether she would kill this man or endure his treatment of her. She thought she would probably manage all right without him.

"You had better kill the dog first," Larion said calmly. Senahiana started. So he was not asleep. He had seen her coming and it was useless to deny it? She ran away shrieking, in pure terror. Larion rolled over and went to sleep again. Then there was peace for a long time.

When he woke it was morning. Small blocks of ice were still floating down the river. Probably they came from the various rivers that fed the Yukon, but the main point was that, although the river was flowing as quickly as before, its level was considerably lower than the day before.

Larion stood watching it for some time and then walked round the burned-down house. Yesterday he had put aside the musket that Senahiana had tried to throw to the white man, the gun with which he had hoped to kill Larion.

It stood leaning against the tree where he had left it, and he had put the black powder, which was used to release the thunder, into the little box. He had also some of that which was put on top of the powder so as to shut it off so that all might be in order. Then he remembered that the girl had lived so long with white men that she must know how to shoot. He would, therefore, take her with him for safety's sake.

Larion said that she must help him to get the canoe into the water.

"Into the water!" she cried, staring at him; but she realized that she could expect no mercy. She worked as if in a trance and had no idea what she was doing. She simply did what he told her. She only remembered that she exerted herself a great deal and that she lifted heavy things. Afterward, she regretted this deeply, for if she had not worked like this he might not have been able to get the canoe into the water. Finally there it lay, gurgling in a little bend in the bank behind a tree that had been knocked over in the flood.

Larion picked up the big bundles of skins and placed them in the middle of the canoe. His little box and his sleeping blanket he put in the stern. Then he went up and fetched the gun which he had left behind the house. He took all the meat he could find: two haunches, two big shoulders and some rib meat. There was so much of it that he had to go back and forth three times. The girl sat there apathetically, doing nothing. Finally he ordered her into the canoe. This brought her to.

"No," she screamed. "I will not go with you. You have murdered my friends! I am frightened! I will not go with you. Go away yourself, but leave me here! Take the meat, take everything, but leave me!" She screamed again, and her face was contorted with fear.

The thought flashed through his brain that she would be useless on the journey, so perhaps it might be better to leave her behind; but he picked her up in his arms and lifted her into the canoe like a dead goose. He called the dog, who immediately sprang aboard and wagged his tail for his new master.

The canoe darted out. The dog barked with joy, the girl screamed with fear, and the current took hold of them all.

Larion had paddled canoes all his life, but he had never before experienced anything like this! He had thought that this canoe was large when he first pushed it into the water. The white men had had a little canoe, as well, but Larion did not dare to take that in the swift water, and, besides, it would not have held the whole of his cargo. So he had cut up the small canoe and peeled off the birch bark in those places where it came off easily in large flakes. These he now had with him on board in case he needed them for repairs.

The river was very rough, the waves high. At first the canoe turned round and round several times, but finally he righted it and was able to keep it in the right direction. They whirled along. They often came on ice blocks. Then, Larion tried to paddle along behind them so that the ice took the force of the waves. Suddenly, he discovered that there was water in the canoe. It had been very dry and this was the first time it had been in the water. Simultaneously, the water grew a little calmer, and he did not hesitate to make use of this. This was a good spot for landing. He increased his speed and reached dry land.

The girl jumped ashore. He called to her to help him. At first she did not wish to do so, but there was no possibility for flight, so she ran forward, caught hold of the canoe and held it.

They had to take out all the baggage. Happily, the two bundles of furs were only wet outside, for the reindeer skin round them had kept them dry, but the little box in which he had kept all the treasures he had taken was full of water and had to be emptied. Fortunately, the flint was dry, so that it was possible to make a fire. Larion cooked the meat and threw a certain amount of green moss into the soup.

"Don't do that," said the girl. Larion forbade her then to speak unless spoken to.

He turned the canoe upside down and soon found the leak. This he patched. The water level had risen now, and there was practically no current. The ice must be blocking it somewhere lower down the river. They would be forced to wait. Later in the evening the water rose higher still, and there seemed to be no current at all.

They lay down to sleep, and Senahiana crept up close to the man. He received her without friendliness or even a smile, but he wrapped the sleeping blanket round them both, and they were both so tired that they fell asleep at once.

At daybreak, Larion woke and looked round him. The river was still rising, so there was no hope of going on at present.

Preparations for departure were therefore useless. The day passed with various occupations.

Late in the afternoon they both heard padding steps in the forest. In a short while, a large brown bear appeared from among the undergrowth and went down to the river to drink. It stood still, lifting its nose into the air, scenting something. It had, of course, just emerged from its winter sleep and would have no inclination to fight.

Larion's heart began to thump. He had often killed bears in close combat with bows and arrows, but now he would show that he was the man who could send death from far away. The thunder would resound and death would fly into the brown king of the forest. He took the gun and had a feeling almost of affection for Senahiana who was sitting beside him. She would witness his triumph. The thunder weapon had cost him a great deal, it had kept him awake during many a night, but now, at last, all his dreams were to be fulfilled. He was like a little boy who was about to kill his first fox in his own trap.

He took the gun and pulled out the ramrod as he had seen the white men do. Then he held it exactly as Durabbin held it and pulled the little steel pin in the middle of the gun. Nothing happened.

Oh, he felt inclined to laugh. He had forgotten to cock the gun. Once again! This time the trigger worked, but the thunder did not come out of the hollow stick, and the bear stood there glowering at him.

Larion took the gun down and looked at it. Finally he was obliged to humble himself in front of the woman. Perhaps she knew about guns. He whispered to her asking for advice.

"The black powder must be poured in," she said, looking very wise.

"Of course, I quite forgot the most important thing!" Carefully he crawled back to his box, took the black powder out of a wooden horn and poured it in. Then came the muzzle-loading. He packed it in as he had seen others do it, and then put in two bullets, loading again. And now he was sure of himself. The bear was still there. Good. Here came death!

Larion pressed the trigger again. Again the hammer came down on the piston, but no thunder, no death. The bear turned scornfully round and stood turned toward the forest. As if to scorn Larion properly, he stood there for some time with his backside exposed and his head in the undergrowth. Anyone could have hit him, and certainly Larion, but he obstinately refused to use a spear after all this. His defeat was too great and Larion realized it. He sat there holding the costly gun which was valueless to him. Only white men understood how to use it.

"You can't shoot!" said the girl quietly. "Your black powder is wet; I saw it was so when you put it in. I have seen whole boatloads of powder thrown away because they were wet and could not be used!"

He did not answer. She knew so much; he was only a child now. Then he began to ask questions.

"Cannot it be dried so that it can be used?"

"Qanekens said no! When once it is wet its power has disappeared! A very powerful white man said that."

Larion was silent. He did not act in a violent manner, he did not throw away the gun fiercely, he just tossed it down the cliff into the water. The Yukon could have it; Larion could get on all right without it. For now, this dream also had gone from him like so many others. He got up and examined the patches he had put on the canoe. Yes, they were firm enough. The canoe would be all right in the morning if it were possible to continue their journey then.

Two days later they heard a terrific noise from lower down the Yukon River; no thunder of guns could rival this. The river had cleared its throat and got rid of its ice masses.

They were now traversing country well known to Larion. The Yukon was not yet really navigable, but Larion knew all the dangerous crosscurrents a little farther down. He kept close in to the steep banks on the right side where the water beat up against the clay walls. There were certain belts outside the coast where the waves from both sides canceled each other, and in these belts the canoe floated calmly enough. Later on he would have to get across to the left bank which was low, where the water had risen far into the forest.

Now Senahiana was longing for food and would have been only too glad to eat anything. They passed the mouth of the Kuyukuk River and the water grew calmer. Just behind the point which had been formed by the meeting of the two rivers, they saw three tents made of white sailcloth, the kind Senahiana knew so well from the Hudson's Bay's summer camps.

It was Durabbin out hunting. The wild geese which were flying up the Yukon had enticed him away from home. He had come up by land and was camping here, shooting and shooting. It was evening now, and it was the turn of the wild ducks who were flying past safely. The Russian officer was at his post when he caught sight of the canoe.

He recognized Larion and saw that his friend had a woman who was not Inaluk with him. The Indian let his canoe drift close in to land and shouted to Durabbin. Senahiana could not understand what was said but she saw the white men. There were four others besides the leader, and the sight filled her with joy.

What was this? It looked as if Larion were going on farther. He spoke in a friendly tone, and the men on shore laughed and shouted gay remarks to him. One of them held up a bottle and laughed. She longed to go ashore. But Larion did not land. He went on.

Senahiana turned to him questioningly.

"Aren't we going to land? Can't you see that they are white men?"

"What of it?" said the chieftain, although he ought not to have answered a woman. She forgot what she was going to say. She became hysterical and screamed:

"I want to land! I won't stay with you a day longer! I want

to go to the white men, and I'll accuse you of having killed
the Hudson's Bay men up there. You'll be hanged and I'll stand
looking on, and I shall laugh and laugh when your jaws fall
open and your life slips out of your mouth!"

Larion steered the canoe a little farther out into the river.

"Can't you hear?" Senahiana cried. "I want to land and go
to the white men. It is there I belong. I despise an Indian's life
and house. You must let me land, and then you can go on
where it pleases you."

Larion stopped paddling. They drifted down until the tents
were only small points in the distance.

Senahiana grabbed an axe lying at the bottom of the canoe
and drove it through the thin bark of the little vessel so that the
water poured in.

Then suddenly, she was frightened at what she had done, but
it was done now and she screamed at Larion.

"It was your own fault! Get ashore quickly and do not dare
touch me. The white qanekens can still see us. You don't dare
hit me; they will punish you if you do."

Larion put his foot over the leak, thus stopping the water to
a certain extent. Then he took the axe out of her hand. She was
hugging it to her, overwhelmed with terror and misery.

Then he gave her a box on her ear with the handle of the
axe. She screamed and held out her hands in front of her to
protect herself. Larion gave her a thrust in the stomach making
her bring down both her hands to defend herself there, leaving
her head unprotected. Then he hit her again with the axe so
hard that she fell overboard.

Quickly, Larion took his steering oar and paddled rapidly
away so that she should not catch hold of the canoe. She only
made a feeble attempt, and then the current took her. Larion
had already turned his back on her and was busy dealing with
the leak so that the canoe should not sink and the cargo should
be kept dry.

He had to turn the canoe right round, stern first; and it

was like this that he reached Nulato, where he drove the vessel ashore. He did this so violently that it became a total wreck immediately.

What did it matter? Larion was at home among his friends at last, his revenge accomplished. No longer were there any white men on the upper reaches of the Yukon trading in the furs and skins that belonged by right to his friend, the Tzar.

Durabbin came home to greet Larion and hear all about his journey and experiences. It had taken him two days to cover the soft ground through the forest. When he arrived, he found Larion with Kidjuk. Doa was there, too, and Tawl, whose name was now Ivan Komygin since the man who spoke about the white man's god had washed Tawl's head and made a pact of friendship with him.

Durabbin was not pleased to find his room turned into an Indian dwelling place, but the sight of a huge bundle of skins, which had been unpacked and arranged in good order, helped him to speak pleasantly. He sat down at the table and ordered firewater with which to celebrate Larion's return.

They drank, and with each cupful he drank, Larion grew happier and happier. In the end, Durabbin and the man who spoke about God knew all the details of Inaluk's death and the murder of the two white men, which Larion considered to be the greatest deed of his life.

"I thought you had a woman with you in the canoe!" said Durabbin.

"If she was there she left it. I cannot remember!" Larion had so much to tell and so much to be proud of that a wretched woman more or less was of no consequence.

Durabbin grew more and more silent as Larion talked, and he had to drink a great deal of vodka to keep himself in a good temper.

Finally he got up, saying he was tired and wished to sleep. He also desired to be alone with Kidjuk. Suddenly, Kidjuk wished to show her father the power she had over this white man.

"My father is a chieftain and my sister a young unmarried girl. They must both sleep in the best place in the house."

"Your sister can stay with me and you go away yourself if you like. It is all the same to me."

Doa pricked up her ears. It was the first time Durabbin had noticed her, but she thought it would be best to appear offended. She rose and asked Tawl to take her to her friends who lived a little way outside the fort.

Kidjuk sulked over her defeat. Larion, on the other hand, felt happy that the vodka had enabled him to speak many words that he would not otherwise have spoken. He said that now he also must go, as he wished to visit his brother-in-law and give him details for the poem to be sung at the *potlasch* he intended to hold in honor of Inaluk. She had gone away with him but had not returned. Her part in the matter had been great; she was to be honored in the same way as a man.

Kidjuk told her sister that she, too, had better go immediately. Doa was offended, she might have had a great experience if her sister had not been afraid of being set aside.

Next day, Durabbin sent a messenger to Larion to say that the Russian chieftain would be honored by a visit from him. At the same time, he sent him a charming tinder box and asked for forgiveness that he had not had a present of welcome ready for him the day before.

Larion did not answer a word when he received this invitation. He took the gift and threw it aside so as to show his scorn.

"What rubbish!" was all he said, and the messenger returned, well pleased with his reception.

A little later, Larion went to the fort.

The guard at the fort was expecting his arrival and opened the gate wide, put his gun in front of him and lifted it from the ground with both hands. He did not speak, and fear kept him immovable while Larion passed him. This put the Indian in a very good humor, and he forgot that he had not been asked to stay the evening before.

Durabbin had called several together to honor Larion. The man who spoke about God was there, but there was no smile on his face. The others stood a little way behind Durabbin.

Durabbin began by saying that he would like to hear again how Larion had managed to obtain the many skins that he had brought to the fort the day before.

Larion glanced at the skins and saw immediately that there were far less than he had brought yesterday.

"I brought a number of skins for my friend the Tzar as gifts. Some of them are there, but you must have taken the rest to your storehouse!"

"What do you mean by 'the rest'?"

"I know exactly how many skins I brought. There were a great many skins in the large bundle. They were for you and your master. You have taken a number of them, perhaps for him and perhaps for yourself. I do not know. One thing I know, all the skins are not here."

"Have you come here to start a quarrel?" asked Durabbin.

"I was asked to come and visit you to speak about trading. That is far from quarreling!" Larion was surprised at Durabbin's tone.

"Larion, you told me yesterday that you had killed two white men up at Kopak. Do you confirm this statement?"

"Naturally I confirm it. They both died in revenge for my son, and here is part of the booty I took after the victory. The rest you yourself saw last night, but today they have been removed."

"Nothing has been moved from here, and you cannot say how many skins there were," Durabbin answered sternly.

"Few men have contradicted me and lived for long afterward, but you are in friendship and alliance with me. The same applies to your master the Tzar. Therefore, you can speak freely."

"You forget that you are in my fort where it is I who am

master. Besides, you tell me that you have killed two white men. They were, it is true, from another land, but they were protected by the Tzar and therefore you gain no honor. You must be punished, and we cannot accept your skins. They will remain here until the men from that other country have been informed that no Russian had any part in this infamous murder. We did not call upon you to go to war. We cannot have you as our guest here. We will keep the skins which rightly belong to the white men who are dead."

Larion quickly recovered from his surprise.

"Oh, is that how it stands with the Tzar? Is he afraid to answer for the actions of his men? I heard here that the qane-kens who lived beside the Kopak were the Tzar's enemies. I sent my son to spy on them to see if they sold firewater and thunder weapons to the Indians. My son obtained proof that they did so, but it cost him his life. Therefore, I went up there and killed them. If you have changed your mind, see to it that all the skins I brought are returned to this bundle again. Many of them are missing. Write down in your papers how many there are. Anything can be forgotten except that which is written on paper."

Durabbin stood up. He was furious. He shouted to Larion that he must not come near him until next winter, when he would send messengers for him. If he remained here or came into the neighborhod during the course of the summer, he would do so at the risk of his life and his freedom. White men avenge white men.

Larion went. He did not run, he walked calmly. The guard at the gate grected him in the same way as when he had arrived.

When the passage of the birds was over and the spring reindeer had gone north, Larion called his tribe round him and informed them that he intended to send a messenger to his friends in Nulato. He had chosen Gissa-Usch to be the one who should take Larion's words to Durabbin.

This way of sending proposals was consistent with his dignity.

A poet would speak the words in such a way that they would fall softly on the ears of the listeners. He sent finely dressed skins and fresh eggs with the messenger, goose eggs and duck eggs such as white men liked.

He equipped a beautifully painted canoe, and Gissa-Usch sat in the stern while others paddled him. He was a messenger; his word was Larion's word: to insult him would be to insult Larion.

The canoe approached Nulato with great dignity, and the Russian soldiers with their wives stood on the shore and received it, swinging their arms and shouting their welcome.

Durabbin himself came out, and with him were both Doa and Kidjuk. Both of them now lived in his house. Gissa-Usch had orders to bring Doa home with him. Larion had not yet taken another woman, so that his sister and brother-in-law had moved into his hut and cooked his food and prepared his skins. Larion needed a woman to run his home in a manner befitting a chieftain.

Durabbin greeted Gissa-Usch handsomely, and Gissa-Usch returned his greeting in the same way.

"I come from Larion. I have words to speak to you that are of importance."

"I thank you for the message. I shall be glad to listen to his words!"

Durabbin was now given the gifts. In Russian manner he did not pour scorn upon them. He thanked and showed delight.

"Let us go in," he said, but they had not gone far before they heard a shout from the lookout man on the point. Ships were coming up the Yukon. They were coming from the sea with messages and letters from home. All else was set aside.

A year had passed since the last ships came. Two or three times during the summer months the wooden boats had come up the Yukon with goods, instructions and letters from home for the soldiers. Two of these large ships were now approaching, rowed by white men and Eskimos together. In the stern of each boat sat a chieftain, passing his commands on to a junior officer, who stood upright in the stern with his hand on the tiller and shouted the rowing rhythm to the crew.

The ships approached, one behind the other as was usual with white men's ships. All ten oars in each boat struck the water simultaneously and with a regular rhythm. In this way the rowers felt less fatigue.

There was a great commotion in the fort. Friends shouted words of welcome to each other. The commanders had great difficulty in getting their orders carried out. They wanted all the goods unloaded immediately so that they could then begin to eat and drink.

Only when all the goods were safely stored did they sit down to the meal prepared by the cook while the others were unloading. The chieftains went into the big house where Durabbin had arranged seats for all. Gissa-Usch came, too, for Durabbin had told his colleagues that the Indian had come as a messenger from Larion; and now it must be settled whether honor should be accorded Larion or whether his deeds should be overlooked and forgotten. They decided to give Gissa-Usch firewater to drink so that he would speak freely.

They asked him why Larion had not come himself. He answered that his brother-in-law had felt less friendliness in his mind than usual since his last visit to the fort. Therefore, he wished to invite Durabbin to come to him. He would hold a great potlasch. He was preparing for it already by collecting the best food that could be found in Alaska. If the other chieftains who lived in Nulato wished to come as well, the joy of the host would be all the greater.

They drank and consulted together. Then they said that perhaps it would be a good thing if they all went up there together so as to obtain full information about the Kopak matter.

Then Gissa-Usch began to boast on Larion's behalf of his attack on the white men. He also spoke of the war booty Larion had brought and delivered here within the Tzar's jurisdiction.

Ah ha, the foreign qanekens thought that they could cheat the Tzar. They had used their own means of payment to buy the skins from the Indians, and then Larion had come and taken it all without giving payment and had brought it to the Tzar's friend and helper here in this place.

There was a little pause. Somebody cleared his throat. Durabbin said that certainly Larion had brought one or two skins with him, but all that he had brought had been quite unimportant and worthless because it had been spoiled by damp during his canoe journey.

The others understood this, they said, but Gissa-Usch thought that it was his business to contradict it. He knew enough Russian to realize that Durabbin wanted to honor his friend by depreciating the value of the booty as the least that might be expected from such a warrior. Gissa-Usch, therefore, said that although it showed Durabbin's friendship and his care for Larion's honor, the truth was that the skins he had brought had filled a whole canoe right up to the railing. There had been two big bundles. Kidjuk, sitting there, and Doa, her sister, had seen the skins and they had the right to say what was true, although women's praise or censure was of no importance, Gissa-Usch added disdainfully.

Again a little pause, and then the foreign chieftain who seemed to be the older asked how many skins there were and where they were now.

Again a silence. Then Durabbin stood up and said that when his guests woke next morning they would find presents of skins beside each man's bed, and now they must drink. His cook had brewed glorious kvass which, when mixed with vodka, produced joyful thoughts and deadened speculations about the number and quality of skins. The others laughed loudly and it seemed as if they had almost forgotten that Gissa-Usch was among them and that the same show of honor was due to him as to Larion himself, seeing that he had brought direct words from his chief. Kidjuk saw to it that his cup was kept filled, and both she and Doa drank like the men. Gissa-Usch noticed that Doa sat on the laps of several of them and that one of them had the habit of putting his face close to hers.

Later, there was a great deal of noise; all spoke and laughed at once and no one seemed to want to listen to Gissa-Usch's song, which had been carefully prepared and was full of many words.

Good. He knew that out in the yard they were also feasting. It was the soldiers' mealtime and they also had been served with firewater. Gissa-Usch went out there. They asked him to sing and handed him a great cup of firewater. Out here among the common people they enjoyed singing a great deal more than did the chieftains in the house.

Next morning, Gissa-Usch was called in to Durabbin, who told him that as he came to speak on Larion's behalf he must also hear the answer to his brother-in law's message.

Larion had transgressed against the white man's law. He had killed white men, and white men always kept together. Larion must not come to Nulato until he was invited with assurances of peace. Until white men from the foreign country had visited Durabbin's fort, it was impossible to receive Larion as a friend, for it would mean that Durabbin would be regarded as accessory to an action which, in reality, he detested.

Gissa-Usch knew that this answer would anger Larion, and he forsaw war. He thought that it would be best that neither of Larion's daughters should remain in the Russian camp after this, and he said as much to Durabbin.

"Neither of the two girls can go home. I will keep them as hostages. Let Larion send for them later. At present they give great pleasure to me and my friends."

Gissa-Usch realized at once that it was essential for Tawl to remain in the fort. Tawl would be a good spy. Tawl, now called Ivan Komygin, was highly trusted. He had his own gun and went out shooting with Durabbin. He was present when skins were packed, and he knew exactly where all Larion's skins had been hidden. He had seen that a number of them had been given to the chieftains from the coast, and it surprised him to see that they put them inside the linings of their cloaks. A strange place to hide skins, he thought.

Durabbin sent the rest of Larion's skins down the Yukon in a very special way. Tawl was to take the package. The man who usually put certain strokes on a piece of paper so as to remember the number of skins must not see them; neither must Tawl tell the Russian soldiers anything about them. There was a great deal of secrecy about Larion's skins. Tawl realized that the white men who had been killed were dangerous, although they were no longer alive.

Gissa-Usch went home. As a feeling of hostility had arisen, the reason for which no one could understand, he thought it best to go away at night when there was no one to see him go. It was easy for him to get in and out of the gate, for the guards knew him. It woke no attention when he dragged his canoe up onto the land in the middle of the day to dry it.

His warrior companions crept around him late in the evening and they set off immediately, while the Russian guard was eating and drinking with the other soldiers.

They were soon up in the Kuyukuk River, and then they paddled slowly, thinking over all that they had seen and heard during those days when they had had the luck to meet people from the big port situated where the Yukon flowed out into the sea.

Larion received his brother-in-law with dignity and listened to his story with great interest. For a long time he sat thinking over what Gissa-Usch had said, and it seemed as if he did not know exactly what had better be done. A council meeting was called for the next day, and then Gissa-Usch told the story of his mission.

It was quite clear that Larion's great war booty had been sent to the Tzar, his friend. It was therefore impossible to arrange an immediate attack, which, otherwise, would have been Larion's best tactic. Attacking the enemy when they least expected it had always brought victory with it. Larion understood that Durabbin was not acting for himself but for his friend and master. Therefore he must wait.

The council of the elders decided that the Kuyukuk tribe must keep away from Nulato until they were again invited to visit it. The invitation, when it came, should be accepted, and the acceptance should be accompanied by such a gift as might reasonably be considered payment for all the skins that Larion had taken from the qanekens at Kopak. Meanwhile, they had no intention of going without the comforts that the white men had brought to the land and which made life so easy and pleasant. It could be arranged for young men and women to go on trading journeys to Nulato, but they would be dressed in different clothes from those usually worn by the Kuyukuk Indians. On his many warlike journeys Larion had brought back clothes from many other tribes, so it would be an easy thing to deceive the Russians. Even if Kidjuk and Doa saw them, a secret wink would be enough, and they could also reckon on help from Tawl. Help from the Kuyukuk women married to Russians could also be depended upon as soon as they knew the tribe desired information and cooperation.

War was not declared immediately, and that pleased everybody. No one had ever tried fighting against fire weapons except Larion, and no one dared count on his luck and skill.

While all this was going on, the Russian boats were on their way down the Yukon, their two commanders well content with their journey. In Nulato they had obtained a great deal of information which they could send home to the Russian Fur Company and which would show them to be capable and outstanding men when it came to making decisions. Added to this, they had all had their share of the haul of skins from Kopak. They had agreed together that this little incident should not be mentioned to the company, and so as to ensure silence, they had given several extremely valuable skins to any of their underlings who might talk or who exercised authority over the crew.

If Larion's skin robbery became known, the Russians would be obliged in view of their relationship with England to seek him out and hang him as a thief; but since Larion had been of great service to the Tzar and since his cooperation had been invaluable in producing peaceful conditions among the natives in Alaska, Durabbin was very unwilling to do this. Politically, also, any action of this kind would create great difficulties, for Larion was the well-known leader of a famous tribe and had a great reputation. Durabbin, therefore, in consultation with the two visiting officers of the company had decided that they should keep the skins themselves and in this way hush the whole affair and protect his friend and ally.

That summer an unusually large number of ships arrived at Mikhailovsk. Consequently, the commandant received a correspondingly large number of visitors. First of all, came Russian frigates which the governor of Sitka had sent up to demonstrate the power of the Tzar in these waters. English corvettes also appeared, bringing a protest from the English government who contended that the agreement which had been solemnly signed in 1825, giving England the right to carry skins and other products on the Russian rivers of Alaska, had been infringed. The complaint had come from the Hudson's Bay Company, stating that their men had been exposed to violence and even murder, and it was hinted that this had happened with Russian consent.

The commander in chief at Mikhailovsk was very polite and showed a hospitality which had never been equaled in these latitudes: with regard to the complaint, he could do nothing but offer countercomplaints. The Hudson's Bay Company had sold fire weapons and brandy to the natives; this was absolutely forbidden. The Russians had done nothing worse than expel the disobedient traders and confiscate their goods.

One day a strange vessel came in. It was flying the British flag and was commanded by Captain Collinson on his way to the

Bering Straits. It was an Arctic expedition on its way north and east in an attempt to locate, or at any rate, throw light on, the Franklin Expedition. This latter expedition with about fifty men in the two ships *Erebus* and *Terror* had been away for five years and was no doubt in need of help. Collinson's ship was called the *Enterprise* and was well equipped. He himself was capable and energetic. Now he had come to St. Michael's—as the English always called Mikhailovsk—to fill up with water and get any news available.

One day, one of the underofficers on board the *Enterprise* said that he had something to report. He told the captain that he had been present at the feast that had been held for the crew from the British frigate the evening before. There had been plenty of drink and dancing, and both Eskimoes and half-castes had been present. He, with the help of the interpreter, Orlof, who spoke English as well as most of the native dialects, had heard that up in the forests near the Yukon lived a mighty Indian chief. There were many stories about him, and his fame in war was great. There was apparently a story going round that this Indian chief had lately killed over forty white men in the interior. He did not know who they were, but he imagined that if they were, as he was told, people who came from the east or the north, they must have been Her Majesty's subjects. If so, it was important to show the world, and particularly these damned Russians, that revenge would be demanded.

The next day Captain Collinson went to see the commandant of the fort. He arrived in full uniform and surrounded by his staff. Since he had been announced beforehand, the Russian officers were also in their finest uniforms.

Captain Collinson spoke of the current rumor and said that it had been confirmed by several conversations with the interpreter, Orlof. Orlof was then called, and explained that he himself had said nothing but had only repeated conversations he had had with certain Eskimos who had been up the Yukon.

These Eskimos were now sent for. They were shy and unwilling to answer. They remembered nothing, for they feared they would be sent up the Yukon again. They said that their tongues must have run away with them. They had drunk fire-water and that always gave them the desire to speak big words.

Then Kutlok, who was among them, spoke up. He said that his sister had belonged to Larion, who had been good to her and had beaten her into shape until she was able to behave as the wife of a great chieftain. Unfortunately, she had been killed during the fight with the white men. If he consented to speak, he hoped that these great men would give him protection and, in addition, a present which would show that he had only spoken under duress.

Rich gifts were promised and, by degrees, Kutlok was induced to speak. He repeated Gissa-Usch's song and said that it only mentioned two white men as having been killed, but there might, of course, have been more.

The Russian commander said that he felt sure that this was simply a case of Indian boasting and their desire to flatter each other in song.

"If there had been anything in it, I feel sure that Commandant Durabbin would have mentioned it in his report, but there is not a word about it."

A messenger was sent up to the nearest post on the Yukon, and the reply came back that they had certainly heard about the matter, but that, according to rumor, there were fifty white men who had come from the north. Larion had killed them all and had taken their possessions.

This was not the first time that Larion had given rise to fantastic stories. Anything could be believed where he was concerned.

Captain Collinson stayed on in Mikhailovsk for over a week to find out the rights of the case if possible. Then he felt that he was not entitled to spend any more time over it.

Lieutenant Bernard came forward and asked for permission to stay behind and examine the matter closely. If British subjects had been killed, reparation must be made. Perhaps it might be possible to find in this matter points of complaint against the Russian government, which the government in England, as all knew, would be only too glad to have at hand. Bernard volunteered to remain behind if another man, or two men, would stay with him so that he would not be alone among uncivilized people.

The second doctor on board, Dr. Adams, immediately volunteered to stay with Bernard. They were close friends, and Dr. Adams, a keen student of native conditions, was anxious to stay on in St. Michael's. One of the crew, Thomas Cousins, also volunteered, as he had his eye on a Russian-Indian girl. He was an efficient fellow, and it would be a great help to have him as a batman.

Then the *Enterprise* proceeded northward.

Durabbin sat in Nulato feeling very bored. His hunting had not been so successful this year, and his relationship with the Indians had deteriorated appreciably. Larion had not appeared at the fort, and when he stayed away there was very little excitement about. No-Unnegu had had his innings with Durabbin. He had delivered a good number of skins, to be sure, and he had induced many Indians to come and trade, but his personality was not attractive. His constant attempts to make difficulties for the two sisters had also very much annoyed Durabbin.

The truth was that Durabbin had created for himself a decidedly awkward situation by keeping them both in the fortress. They both lived together in his house, but there was very bad feeling between them, which was not to be wondered at, as Durabbin could not make up his mind which of them he preferred. One of them at a time was enough to comfort his loneliness. Kidjuk, the elder, to whom he was accustomed, who knew his habits and was always obedient and willing, was not the burning flame that Doa was. There was fire in Doa; there was in her a passion and a madness that preyed upon his peace of mind and, at the same time, made him so wild that he often swore that he would turn her out of the house immediately. If he went on a hunting expedition and took Doa with him he often forgot the game and the beauty of the country around him, for she was enough to engage all his senses, even while she teased and tortured him.

But Kidjuk, also, could be very difficult. She knew that Tawl was waiting faithfully for her. Ivan, as he was known down here, looked at her with his great faithful eyes, only waiting for the day when he was certain she would tire of her life as Durabbin's mistress and would go with him out into the forest.

One day the watchman's signal was heard again. "Boats from the coast!"

Durabbin was delighted. Change and a break in his monotonous existence. New people to speak to, news from the outer world.

Durabbin was on the landing stage to receive the visitors. A noncommissioned officer was in command of the Russian boat, so, obviously, it was not a case of investigation or inspection. That, at any rate, was a relief. A letter? Yes, that could, of course, mean anything, but it might also be just an ordinary official communication. Please come up to the fort! Let the crew come on land and make themselves at home while I read the letter. Surely you need not return immediately?

The officer went with Durabbin. The latter was the commandant, it was true, but he belonged to the civil administration so that he could, without any loss of dignity, invite sublieutenants to come as his private guests.

He read the letter. It dealt with the question of Larion and his supposed murder of forty men up in the north. Durabbin had never heard of so many and he immediately asked Kidjuk. He often found that he could talk to her about matters of importance as she knew a great deal and had a good brain.

Durabbin read about the supposed murder of the Franklin Expedition by Larion. If he thought there was a grain of truth in it Durabbin was ordered to make an official report; if he thought it was only empty talk and Indian boasting, he was to write to Bernard saying that he himself did not dare investigate the matter but would be glad if the English lieutenant would come up to Nulato with the winter post and make an investigation on the spot. In this letter, Durabbin was ordered to make the whole matter appear most mysterious. In this way, it was hoped that the young man could be induced to leave Mikhailovsk at once, so the Russians would be able to keep their Christmas in peace.

Durabbin felt that he had suddenly become important in affairs of state. He felt himself a factor to be reckoned with in the great game of politics. He sat down and wrote a masterly letter to the commandant in Mikhailovsk in which he invited John G. Bernard, himself, to come to Nulato. Larion, he said, was not actually in the fort but could be found somewhere in the surrounding district. The truth could be obtained from his statement alone.

The post was quick, which helped matters. The boat only remained in Nulato for two days, and on its return trip it covered the hundred sea miles to Mikhailovsk in record time.

When Bernard received the letter, he expressed surprise and delight at the efficiency and speed of the post. It did not take a month to receive answers to important questions.

Unfortunately, the winter had set in very early this year. It would not be possible to send the Englishmen up the river on a boat. The commander of Mikhailovsk, who had never set foot in the forests, gave a detailed account of life in the interior.

Time passed surprisingly quickly and soon it was Christmas. Since it was kept in the Russian manner, it took time to get over the huge amount of food and drink that was consumed. Therefore, it was not until early in the new year of 1851 that Bernard set out for Nulato in a sledge.

There were not many dog teams in Mikhailovsk, for there was not a great deal of food to spare for animals. Therefore, only one dog team could be found for Bernard, so Dr. Adams and Cousins had to be left behind. Neither of them objected. They had learned to like the Russian way of passing an Arctic winter. Lieutenant Bernard set off with the interpreter Orlof and a driver.

A journey by dog sledge is pleasant enough for the first three hours. If the passenger is cold, he just gets out and runs a little way until his feet are warm again. By degrees it becomes rather monotonous. Surely, thought Bernard, we must soon reach some sort of human habitation. He had heard that there was a station "not far away." They drove quickly forward. The driver of the dogs was a half-caste, a Russian-speaking man. The interpreter Orlof drove his own sledge.

The journey developed on the usual lines. It began to be tiring, then almost unpleasant. A few hours later, Bernard had pains all over his body, and his thoughts turned back to the fleshpots of Mikhailovsk. Bernard said nothing, however; he was a sailor and an Englishman. It never entered his head to complain.

At about this time, a message came to Durabbin from Larion that he wanted certain articles and that one of his daughters must come home. Larion left it to the Russian to decide which of the two he wanted to keep.

Durabbin was pleased when he received this message. It showed that there was no longer enmity between the Kuyukuk Indians and the Russians. But when it came to deciding which of the two daughters he wanted to keep, he felt hopelessly uncertain. He was stupid enough to speak to them about this message. Neither of them wished to leave him. They had both absorbed the atmosphere of the fort and were both longing to see the new man who was coming. Perhaps he would bring them lovely presents. Not until he had arrived would they decide which of them was to return to their father.

Durabbin explained that he needed one of them to help him with the trading and to help him in his conversation with the natives. Kidjuk was his wife, given to him by her father. Under the influence of Ivan Komygin's longing eyes, she had often longed to get away; but when she thought of the plentiful, well-cooked food and her easy life, she decided that she did not want to leave.

Doa said openly that she wished to see the foreign man. She had acquired a taste for white men's lovemaking and had learned to return it. She sent Larion a mocking reply: when it suited her she would come; when no one wanted her she would pick up her cloak and leave at once.

Larion was given the answer that one of his daughters would return to him, but not just at present.

Never had anyone sent him a message like that before. The messenger was almost afraid to speak the words, and after he had delivered it, he immediately went out and left the chieftain with Gissa-Usch and his sister.

Larion felt very lonely. His son was dead and his daughters lived with white men. It was about time that Durabbin was taught that all Larion's wishes must be obeyed. War was, of course, the most obvious means, but his alliance with the Tzar was still in force. His honor told him that this alliance must be openly canceled before anything was done. Strangely enough, Larion hesitated to call the council together and ask them to give him their opinion after he had put forward his own point of view.

As a beginning, Larion sent three young men down to Nulato with fox skins to sell. They were instructed to prolong the trading time so as to spy out what was happening. They were to go in relays, each relieving the other so that there were always Kuyukuks in Nulato who could receive information from Tawl about those things which were of importance to Larion.

One fine day Bernard arrived. It was high time, for every morning when they broke camp he felt a tiredness that he had never felt on board ship. Every morning his one desire was to remain in bed, and every morning he fought the desire to stay on for another day in the camp. He could give the excuse that he was ill. He longed only to be allowed to sleep and sleep, but up to the present he had been able to fight this longing for sleep, though it increased every day.

Now, he saw the houses of Nulato standing high on the river bank. The moment that Bernard saw the wooden houses and the people, his fatigue was forgotten, his feet became lighter, and his head was no longer as heavy as lead. He answered Durabbin's greeting joyously and warmly pressed the Russian's hand. He had reached his goal. Now he would be able to begin his investigations.

As usual, there was a mighty meal with streams of vodka and fine sweet wine served with the food. There were large bits of fresh meat in the soup, and the well-cooked cabbage leaves crunched deliciously between the teeth. There were sweets and cakes. Lieutenant Bernard felt a great friendship toward the Russian commandant as if they had known each other for a long time and had been through many experiences together. There were not many at the feast, but yet it was a great feast and the joy was loud and spontaneous.

When bedtime came, Bernard was shown to a smaller house which was used only for honored guests. It had been thoroughly heated, and he saw a huge bed with soft pillows. Nothing was missing, not even Doa, who came with him when he went to his room. From the first moment that she had set eyes on the young Englishman with his fair hair and charming blue eyes, Doa had made her choice. She found no difficulty in making the lieutenant understand that up here in the forests men lived a natural life and a woman belonged to a man. Doa had lived so long among white people that she had learned to value cleanliness and good clothes. They slept long and sweetly, and it was not until late the next day that they were seen again. Then, the feasting began again. Lieutenant Bernard enjoyed eating and drinking and the company of all these pleasant people. He had forgotten his errand for the moment.

Kidjuk, also, was pleased with the turn of events. She thought their visitor splendid and admired his fair hair, but she was not sorry that Doa had made her choice and that now she had Durabbin to herself. Now they were two couples, and every day would be happy and festive.

In this way, several days passed, and then Bernard woke to action. He explained to Durabbin through Orlof why he had come.

Durabbin had received his instructions. It is not difficult for a Russian officer to feel personal friendship toward a certain person and yet remain faithful to the interests of his Tzar and country. In this case it was fortunate that, for the present, he was able to keep strictly to the truth, for he had never heard of the forty white men whom they said had been killed in the north. He was certain that if there had been forty and these forty were now dead, Larion would have told him of it. It was Lieutenant Bernard's task to clear up the matter. Durabbin would passively allow him to set his inquiries afoot. His own instructions had not told him to be overzealous in helping the Englishman. The idea was that the time should be passed until the summer came and the Yukon River was open to river traffic. By that time, the young Englishman would have tired of the whole inquiry, but the impression must be given that he had received all the help that was possible. It would be a small thing for Durabbin to wander about with him in the forest and give him a taste of the mosquito plague and work off most of his energy on the tundras. Durabbin felt that there was really no need here for a conflict unless something quite unforeseen happened.

Bernard was told everything that was known. Ivan Komygin was called, and he gave the story of Larion's splendid feat, but he said that only two white men had been killed. Dislen, also, had mentioned only two qanekens who were unlawfully trading in the Tzar's land. Ivan added, however, that it would not be at all impossible for Larion to defeat as many as fifty foreigners. Ivan Komygin was Tawl, who was proud of his chieftain.

Two days later Lieutenant Bernard came to Durabbin and asked if his interpreter and two others, one to be Ivan Komygin, if possible, might be sent as messengers to Larion. He thought that if Larion could come to Nulato he would tell them the whole story, and they could then decide what more should be done.

Durabbin was a little taken aback at this. Larion was his friend, although they had lately had differences of opinion. A message of this type was quite different from those which were usually exchanged between Larion and the commandant at Nulato.

He explained to Bernard that it was scarcely the right kind of message to send to the Indian chief, but the young Englishman had already written a letter which was to be read to Larion by Orlof. There was a copy of it in his diary so that it must not be altered.

"Perhaps you mean that I ought to offer him a free pass so that he may be sure of returning, even if he is guilty?" Bernard asked. "I could never do that. If British subjects are killed for no reason, I shall demand your Tzar's help in arresting the murderers. They must be made an example."

Durabbin said nothing, for he was amused at this way of behaving in a foreign country. At the same time, he could not but admire the man. Englishmen think they are masters all over the world!

"You must, at any rate, send some presents with your messengers. That is the custom here in Alaska, and it is an outward sign of friendship. The gifts will be repaid and Larion will feel safe. Larion is accustomed to very careful treatment."

"Larion is an Indian. I do not know anything about Russian methods with natives, but England has had many hundreds of years' experience in the treatment of natives, and we do not need to be told how to behave. I must ask you to give me equipment for my interpreter and two more men."

In the end, Ivan Komygin went with Orlof and one of the Russian soldiers.

Ivan had heard full details of the white men's conversation from Kidjuk, and Ivan became Tawl the moment he stepped outside the stockade.

They reached Nowikakat and found Larion at home. The proud chieftain received them with dignity and immediately asked them to eat with him. Larion always had delicacies ready to offer to strangers. He did not look at Ivan, nor did he address a word to him; neither of them gave any indication that they had ever met before.

The two Russians were tired after their long journey and grew quickly sleepy after they had eaten. They were taken to a hut where there were soft skins on which they could lie. They were soon asleep and forgot that they were messengers who came to order Larion to return with them to Nulato to answer for the evil deeds of which he was accused.

While they slept deeply, Tawl and Larion talked together for a long time. Larion was given to understand that his reputation had greatly increased and that he was considered dangerous; and this is pleasant news for any man. In addition, he was told that the new foreign chieftain down there was sleeping with his youngest daughter so that neither of his daughters was prepared to return home. Larion promised himself to avenge this.

The next morning Larion got up early, went to the hut where the strangers were sleeping, and threw a large piece of wood through the door. This woke them, and as they could not understand why this had been done, they asked Ivan for an explanation.

"Larion demands his gifts so that he may be in a position to repay them."

"Greeting gifts? We have none. We come with words and that is the aim of our journey."

A little later they were told to come into Larion's hut. There, a meal had been prepared for them, fat soup in which swam large pieces of reindeer marrow. There was no talk of gifts, but when they had eaten, Larion asked Orlof whether he was going on farther or whether he was going to honor the village longer with his presence.

This gave Orlof an opportunity to deliver his message and to show that they were not his own words but those of his chief. He pulled out the paper on which the message was written. In a loud voice, he read what Lieutenant Bernard of the British Navy had written to Larion.

There was a moment's silence. Then Larion asked what Orlof meant to do when he had delivered his message.

"We are to return and hope that you will come with us," said Orlof.

"You know the way yourselves; if not, follow your own trail and you will certainly reach your destination!"

"Are you not coming with us?"

"You know the way, as I have said, so that you have no need of a guide."

There was silence for a time and then Orlof stood up and prepared to return. He had come by dog sledge and Larion had fed the dogs well. Ivan and the Russians were on snowshoes.

"Tell Durabbin that he must send one of my daughters back to her father," said Larion as they parted. "He can only keep one to pleasure himself with. I need the other to look after my house. As I receive distinguished guests, I must be in a position to look after them well. Their friendly gifts are of no use to me, alone, when I have no one with whom to share them."

Lieutenant Bernard was very angry when Orlof came back without Larion. "Why didn't you arrest the chap?" he asked.

"He is a chieftain and how could I arrest him? I had only two men with me."

"You should have shown him your credentials as a Russian official. My God! Is Russia's authority really so weak that her subjects dare to disobey an order and mock the Tzar's representative?"

He went straight to Durabbin and demanded that he should send soldiers to fetch Larion. Durabbin did not directly oppose him, but the days passed and nothing was done. Durabbin said that he must receive authority from Mikhailovsk before he dared to send soldiers away from the fort. The Indians might attack them at any moment. "We will send a message to the coast. The answer will be back within a month," he promised.

"Yes, but by that time the murderer may have escaped."

"Larion is not a murderer fleeing from justice. Larion is a great warrior and an honorable man!"

"The greater the warrior the more important it is to make an example of him. He must be hanged if he is found guilty. I shall demand this of the Tzar on behalf of the Queen of England," Bernard said stiffly.

Durabbin, however, relied on the joys of the palate. They drank sweet wine, warmed and spiced, and vodka flowed like water. They both became very drunk, and so did the girls.

It took over a week to get over all this feasting. Then there was a Russian church festival day, and no work could be done, so Durabbin had a further respite. But Lieutenant Bernard could not be soothed into inaction forever. He again began his efforts to discover what had happened to the Franklin Expedition. If a crime had been committed, he was determined to ask for satisfaction on behalf of the British crown.

Durabbin began to realize that his English guest was more troublesome than he had expected, but at the same time he was a very pleasant person and interesting to talk to. Durabbin spoke a little French and Bernard also knew that language. Furthermore, they were both very happy with their girls. They used to take them for walks and amuse themselves by treating them like great ladies of the outside world.

Later on, another message was sent to Larion. This time, the interpreter, Orlof, managed to get out of going. He said that he had twisted his ankle and was therefore unable to undertake a long journey. In reality, he had been impressed by Larion's personality and realized that he was not a man who could be treated like an ordinary criminal and summoned to a court of law. He should be treated as a man of good standing, and Orlof was certain that this second message, which again demanded Larion's presence in Nulato, would be as useless as the first. There was no question of greeting presents.

It was finally decided that one of the Russian soldiers, who was married to a Kuyukuk woman, should be sent to Larion with the lieutenant's orders, and a half-caste from the coast went with him so that there might be two of them in case of difficulties.

They met Larion up the Yukon at Nowikakat.

"I had expected that one of my daughters would be with you!" he said as a beginning.

"They both remained behind. Durabbin needs a woman, as does also the foreign chieftain. Each of them has one of your daughters!" The messenger had learned enough of the Kuyukuk language to be able to make himself understood, but he did not know enough to fashion his words into a polite sentence.

Larion pretended that he had not heard; he stood on the shore and let them land before he spoke again.

"Give me my greeting gifts so that I may choose suitable return gifts of the same value. Then we can talk together more easily if you come with messages from my friend Durabbin."

"I have no gifts for you, nor do I come from Durabbin. The words I bring you are from a foreign man whose name is Bernard. He says that he is surprised and angry because you did not come back with the interpreter Orlof when he came to fetch you. Now he has asked me to say that you must wait no longer than it takes you to put on your traveling clothes. Then you must return with us and we will see that you arrive safe and unharmed down in Nulato where the foreigner wishes to hear your defense. His countrymen are angry because you have killed a number of men from the same part of the world from which he comes."

"Are those the only words you have been ordered to say to me?" asked Larion in a calm voice.

"Yes, and that is enough. You can say more when you all meet together at Nulato. You must hurry. We have orders not to eat in your house nor to receive gifts from you until you have spoken to the foreign chieftain so that your alliance of friendship may, if possible, be restored. Perhaps there is hostility between your tribes."

Then Larion laughed loudly and told the two men that they had better return quickly to their countrymen and to any strange men there might be down there, and tell them that Larion would certainly come; but just at the moment he could not leave his village. His miserable clothes were unmended and were not in a fit state to keep him warm on a journey, for he had no woman in his house to sew or keep his clothes in order.

"If you will not come with us voluntarily we have orders to bring you by force," the messenger answered.

Larion gave a signal, something like a whistle. From behind each tree a warrior in full warrior dress sprang forth and began running toward the Russian. The man's courage failed him, and he said wildly that they were not his own words that he had spoken; he was only an underling who did not want to offend the great Larion. If Larion did not wish to come with him today, that was his affair entirely and the Russian would never attempt to force him.

"Now I think you know what I came to say. Farewell! I will return to Nulato!"

Larion called a war council. He was really angry and made a vociferous war speech. His face showed all the anger that he had hidden so carefully while the Russian was near. He now gave full vent to it and began to sing about the salmon in the Yukon that would taste the foreign man's blood before they reached the salt ocean.

The council had not yet had a chance to speak, but when Larion ceased his chanting, one of the oldest members said that he had felt for a long time that the foreigners should be taught that they were welcome guests only as long as the country's own sons approved of their conduct. They were mistaken if they thought they were the masters here. It was high time that they understood who gave the orders here and who upheld old customs between the tribes.

Several others said that the old man had spoken well. Larion repeated his oath that the salmon should drink white men's blood before they reached the sea. Blood, perhaps, of a different taste from that to which they were accustomed, but, at any rate, blood.

They set out before it even began to get dark. Soon they saw far in the distance the Russian and his companion. They were not traveling quickly, so that it was not difficult for the Indians to leave the river and go into the forest so that they were in front of them when they camped for the night. The two messengers had no idea that they were surrounded by spies while they slept and that the next morning many eyes watched them while they ate their breakfast and broke camp.

Slowly, the two white men wandered down the Kuyukuk. They were not clever with their snowshoes, and it was evident that the sledge they were dragging gave them a great deal of trouble. They had continually to straighten it, for they were following yesterday's track where the furrows had frozen, making the single-runner, narrow toboggan overturn often in the many depressions in the snow.

By midday they were tired and decided to stop and make tea and have a little rest. The Russian sent off his companion to see whether he could find some water for the tea. There is often water from springs, even in the coldest weather, and he thought there might be such a spring in the neighborhood. If so, it would be easier to make tea with spring water than to melt snow or ice. Besides, the sun was shining so brightly that it was not unpleasant to sit and wait while his companion was away.

The poor Russian did not hear the bushes rustle behind him. He did not know that his last hour had come. He heard, perhaps, a rushing sound in the air and then nothing more. A club had broken his skull and his brain gushed out. He was dead.

The man returning with the kettle of water was struck dumb with terror. Larion went up to him, took a bit of the murdered man's liver and a piece of his heart and told the weeping wretch to eat them. He began to bawl loudly. He wanted to go to heaven when he died, he said. Once more, Larion told him to eat, and once more he refused. That was enough. He was struck down from behind.

Messengers were sent to other villages belonging to the tribe, and soon Larion was surrounded by no less than a hundred warriors, all burning with ardor to avenge the insult offered to their tribe through their chieftain.

They traveled by night only. No trails were left on the ice of the river and they traveled very slowly. Their final halt was made at a point scarcely half a day's journey from Nulato, and now it was decided that they would send ahead some women and old men to allay any doubts in the fort and among the surrounding Indians. Larion knew that although the Russians were easy to fool it would be more difficult to trick No-Unnegu's people. No-Unnegu himself was always prying around and was a past master in the art of detecting tracks and finding spies. Therefore they lay low for two days.

When the women came, followed by the old men, they were ordered to go on to Nulato. The old men felt proud of again being of use in war. They realized that they were to be sacrificed for the common good, but they would be proud to die in such a way that their descendants would speak of them as brave and courageous.

They were to go to the fort and trade with Durabbin. At the same time, Tawl was to be informed, but nothing was to be said to Larion's two daughters. Their relationship with the white chieftains might cause them to warn the men. No one could foresee the mind of a woman.

First, they all went to the Indians' houses. They were received by No-Unnegu, who mocked them on their arrival.

"Here come the best men of the Kuyukuk tribe to trade with the white men! The young and inexperienced must stay at home because of their great fear of the white men and the white men's friends. It is reasonable, of course, but their time will come! When their faces are wrinkled and their knees crooked from age, they will no doubt have enough courage to come and beg for knives and tobacco. Then no one will insult them. Until then, it is surely better to remain at home and see to the hunt."

The expression on the old men's face did not change. They felt sure that the mockery that had been uttered would be the last that would come from No-Unnegu's mouth. His tongue had sown much evil throughout the years. Nevertheless, the old men could not refrain from paying him back in his own coin.

"Can your wife help me to mend my moccasins?" asked one of them. "I cannot see her."

During the night, a young spy got so close to the fort that he was able to lie down on top of a woodpile. He lay there quite motionless. By chance, Tawl came next morning to look for a dog that had strayed. The spy did not dare to move, for a soldier was on guard outside the gate, but a faint screech from an owl could not possibly arouse suspicion. Tawl pretended he had heard nothing but remained in the vicinity. Even his sharp eyes could not detect anything that could possibly have given that screech, but he knew that at this time of year owls did not screech. His kinsman had to signal twice before he discovered him on top of the woodpile. He lay there covered with snow, just like another log of wood, and it was impossible to approach him without arousing suspicion. It was not until after dark that Tawl came out again and the young spy was able to crawl down. By that time he was so stiff with cold that he could not walk, and Tawl had to put the boy's feet inside his own jacket to thaw them with the warmth of his own body. Later on, all his toes fell off, but he had been able to warn Larion's spy inside the fort and thereby assure victory to the Indians.

That evening, the two officers sat up late, talking about Larion's behavior and drinking heavily. Lieutenant Bernard knew that the chieftain was Doa's father, but he did not mince his words in spite of the fact that she was present. In his pride, he did not suspect any danger from her side. Finally, Durabbin wanted the fire made up and shouted for Ivan Komygin. No answer. Ivan was not there. That was strange, for if there was anyone who could be depended upon it was Ivan. He could not be found. Doa said that perhaps he had gone to the Indians' houses, as there was a girl in one of the huts he was rather fond of. Why she said this she did not know herself, but no doubt she thought that this excuse would be the most acceptable and innocent.

Durabbin cursed and swore that Ivan should be beaten. He was in Russian service and subject to discipline. Lieutenant Bernard agreed with him and said that the natives needed to feel the whip. He flattered himself that he had done much to put Durabbin on the right track as regards the treatment of natives. This annoyed Durabbin and they began to quarrel. They drank a great deal and each stuck to his point. At last, Bernard also grew angry and got up to go to bed.

He went over to his sleeping quarters, and as he went, he shouted to Durabbin that he was counting the days until Larion came so that he might finish the job and show the Russians how England dispensed justice in foreign countries. Then, he would be able to get away. They were both very drunk.

Bernard called Doa, who was glad to get away from all this

quarreling and longed for bed. Peace descended on the fort. All the men in the garrison house were asleep, and the night-watchmen, knowing that the commandant was drunk, settled down in a little room where they could sleep with their clothes on. Tawl, on the other hand, had ceased to be Ivan Komygin, for he was with Larion. The last orders had been given, and the fight might begin at any moment.

Quietly, they advanced to the Indians' houses. There, the sleepy lamps burned low in the three largest houses.

An owl screeched, and soon afterward the women felt the call of nature and went outside. There were three women and they took the children with them. They said that it would be counted to their shame if the children wet their bunks, "So out you come, whether you want to or not!" The children cried and protested, but no notice was taken of this, and their mothers took them out.

A little later, one of the old men rose and said he could not understand what had happened to the women. He went out after them, and then there were only three Kuyukuks left in any of the houses.

Later, the smell of smoke became noticeable, and several woke and said that the lamps must be smoking. In one of the houses, a Kuyukuk said that he would go out and see if there were anything burning. They saw that he had not put on his cloak and expected him back in a minute, as no one could stay out long in that cold without his clothes on.

No one in the house knew, of course, that the old man had gone out to meet his kinsmen who were preparing death for all who remained inside the houses. They realized it all too soon. The smoke suddenly became so thick that no one could doubt that it came from the entrance. Several of the Indians rushed toward the door but they found it blocked by burning branches. The enemy was outside; they were all caught in a trap.

There was a Kuyukuk man in No-Unnegu's house, too. He realized what was happening and tried to push his way out through the fire but did not succeed. No-Unnegu, the old fox, had always reckoned with two exits, now there was only one. He knew with whom he had to deal and felt sure that Larion would win this time.

The old Kuyukuk Indian resigned himself to his fate. He crossed his arms and began to mock the Kayar Indians who before dawn would be no more. He derided their stupidity and mocked their apathy.

This was more than No-Unnegu could stand. The old man's scorn irritated him so much that he forgot the peril in which he himself stood. He caught hold of his opponent and threw him to the ground. Then he took a knife and cut off the man's left ear. At the same time he let out a voluptuous howl. A silence followed in which the men listened to the crackling of the fire and began to realize that the smoke now made breathing difficult.

No one thought of anything but saving himself. Some of the young people tried to break out through the burning entrance, but if they got through they were speared to death outside.

The old Kuyukuk Indian's song died away. Perhaps he was killed, perhaps he was suffocated. No one ever knew. When the Kuyukuks finally managed to get in, there was no one alive inside the house. They found a corpse which they thought might be No-Unnegu. He had crawled in under a bunk so as to hide away and save himself if possible. This was the epitaph of the last Kayar chieftain: dead under a bunk without attempting to defend himself.

Larion and his men stood quietly waiting. The spies had gone forward to the fort to see whether Tawl had everything in order. When they came back and announced that the signal had been given, Larion divided his men into four divisions. He now had under him the largest number of men he had ever commanded, but, of course, this was the most important engagement he had ever organized. He stood silent for a moment. Surely everything was in such order that any possibility of a mistake had been eliminated.

No one could have believed it possible for a hundred men to come close up to the fort without being noticed. The snow lay white on the ground, and there was a guard. But the sky was overcast, and the guard had been asleep for some time when Larion reached the gates. Tawl had arranged places where the pointed stockade could be crossed. He had raised two tree trunks inside the fort, and Larion had raised two corresponding ones outside. Thus, the men were able to climb the trees outside and cross over to the ones inside. Nothing easier.

When Larion and five others had got in, he crept over to other places where the same tree ladders were used. Men climbed over the stockade, and all of them felt joy at tricking the white men who thought themselves so safe because they had put points onto the ends of dead wood.

Tawl forced open the door leading into the church built in the center of the stockade. There was a passageway through the church by which to escape if it became necessary.

Larion knew exactly where everyone slept and what should be done. The white people had strange customs. Instead of giving up the habit of stealing, they put locks on their doors so as to make it impossible to force them open. A man was obliged to have a certain instrument before he could go in and out of any door that the owner wished to keep shut. Tawl knew this, too, and there was such an instrument stuck into the door of the house where the soldiers slept with their women. Larion had decided that these women should not be told of the projected attack, for possibly some woman might wish to protect her husband so that her children would not be left fatherless. The matter of the Kuyukuk women must be left to chance. Larion's attack was directed first and foremost against the chieftains. They were his equals, and when once they had been rendered harmless, it would not be difficult to finish off the underlings who were accustomed to depend on their chiefs for orders.

A light shone from Durabbin's window. It was not covered with skin but with firm, transparent, icelike slabs of a material which would not melt. The door was half-ajar so that it was easy to push it open. It was quite a small room, but it opened into another that was bigger, where Durabbin slept in a big bed with Kidjuk. The light was burning feebly and Durabbin was asleep. He had drunk much and his head was heavy; he did not, therefore, notice the slight noise when the handle was slowly turned and a man came in. It was Larion. Kidjuk was an Indian woman and she slept lightly. She woke when a board creaked under her father's step. She sat up in bed and saw him. Durabbin stirred and noticed that the blankets had slipped to one side, exposing his naked body to the cold.

"Keep still, I'm cold," he said without opening his eyes or regaining full consciousness. He turned over and fell asleep again with his mouth open.

Tawl came in, and then Kidjuk understood. She herself had also been drinking and smoking heavily, but she saw that they were armed, and she had heard Durabbin utter threats against Ivan Komygin; he was to be whipped as she had seen some of the Russian soldiers whipped. They had not afterward drowned themselves from shame or sought a bloody revenge, but Tawl was different. Kidjuk knew that. She realized now that this was death entering the door and she screamed. Durabbin woke.

He opened his eyes but was not wide awake at once. He had to rub his eyes and pull himself together a little. At last he began to speak. First of all, he tried to be angry and told the Indians to go away and leave him in peace. Then, at last, he realized that it was no good speaking to them like that. He laughed a little and held out his hand to Larion, told him how pleased he was to see him and that they must drink firewater together.

The Indian said nothing. Kidjuk screamed again because she

wanted to warn Durabbin. He turned toward her and told her
to be quiet, for, he said, this was not the time for women's nonsense. "Let us men speak together without interference."

Still no word from Larion. The situation was uncanny, and
the Russian, whose brain was still befogged and slow, began to
feel as if Larion were threatening him. He forgot what little
Indian dialect he knew, but this always happened when he was
drunk.

He did, however, manage to make Larion understand that it
was the Englishman who had sent for him and not he himself.
"Tomorrow we will talk together, and I will tell Bernard that
you have done nothing wrong. Let me get up, and we will go
off and drink together."

Larion was silent. Durabbin felt more and more uncomfortable, but he did not know what to do next. Suddenly, Kidjuk
understood her father's silence. For the first time she noticed
the war paint on his face; all the ochre colors in the mountains
seemed to be collected on his cheeks and forehead. She realized
that she was just lying there in the middle of a war and she
screamed again.

Her scream brought about a diversion in the heavy silence.
Durabbin found a vent for his disquiet. He turned to the girl.
Here was somebody to whom he could speak harshly.

"Keep quiet, woman! Men are speaking here," he said.

Those were the last words Durabbin spoke on this earth, for
the spear point that never failed penetrated between his shoulder blades. Larion knew the place where death most easily
entered a man, and Durabbin fell over in the bed, gurgled a
little and lay still.

"Now you can have your woman to yourself, Tawl," was all
Larion said. Kidjuk sat there sobbing.

Larion stood silent for a moment, wondering whether he
should take his booty at once or wait. Then he realized that this
was only the beginning. He had been a little too much set on
this man's death. He had been his friend, but he had failed him

and, therefore, he deserved his death. Also, he was the one who gave orders in the fort. It was Durabbin who had the power to open the door to the storehouse where all the treasures were kept. To defeat Durabbin was the same as defeating all foreign white men. But he had fallen without defending himself, and little honor was attached to his death. No one would sing of Larion's great deeds in this case. Larion could have wished for a more difficult ending to his relationship with Durabbin. Neither he nor No-Unnegu, both of them chieftains, had shown themselves brave or honorable to the end.

Lieutenant Bernard slept in another house. He had not heard anything that was going on in the fort, as his room was never very quiet at the best of times. Both he and Doa had drunk a great deal, and her turbulent mind boiled up over the smallest thing when she was drunk. She was born in a land among people whose senses were pure and whose brains were clear, and where, therefore, every little disturbance had more effect than among Europeans, whose tradition of drinking had given them the power to keep their balance.

Doa was angry about a gift that Kidjuk had received and for which she herself had no match. The fact that the two men had spoken slightingly of her father had also enraged her. It was long since she had seen him, and when she asked whether they were going to visit his village or send messengers inviting him to the fort, she was given a scornful answer. Bernard said that when Larion came he would wish himself away as quickly as possible. Such things should not be said about a chieftain, least of all about her father.

Doa took hold of Bernard's shoulder and shook it, trying to force him to listen to her. That was too much for him, and he slapped her hand. She had not meant to irritate him to the point of beating her, for she had often boasted to Kidjuk that her lover belonged to a race who never beat women. She had always insisted that this was to their honor, for it showed that they were strong and sure of victory.

Bernard allowed her to continue to talk and scold him; then he took up a book and began to read. Doa's speech soon died away to a murmur of words. Offended and sulky, she sat up in bed and tried in vain to attract his attention.

Then the door opened. This time it was not opened stealthily, for Larion had heard Doa's voice from outside, and he realized that the two of them were awake. Therefore, he came in quickly.

The young officer did not hesitate for a moment. He sprang out of bed and stood facing Larion in an attitude of defense.

At the side of his bed stood his military rifle, a double-barreled gun of heavy caliber such as was used on ships. All he had to do was seize it, but Larion was nearer to it than he. Bernard was instantly aware of the fact that here was an enemy who was dangerous and that his only chance lay in quick attack.

In addition to his spear in his right hand, Larion had his battle club in his left. This had never been known to fail its mark, and now he lifted it to attack his enemy; but before he could do so the Englishman was close upon him, and Larion received the greatest surprise of his life. Here was a boxer who knew his craft. Bernard got in a good left hand drive against Larion's chin which knocked him off his balance. He fell backward but felt no pain. He did not know that he had been hit but only that he could not remain standing. The thought ran through his mind that here was a new, supernatural way of fighting, known only to the white men.

Then Bernard made a mistake. He did not know the impression he had made on Larion. If he had followed up his blow he could have knocked the Indian senseless to the ground, but he turned instead to seize his gun, thus giving Larion a chance to get up on his feet again. The latter rushed forward, and in the same moment that Bernard lifted his right hand to the trigger, Larion swung his club from below and knocked the barrel of the gun upward so that the bullet tore a great gash in one of the rafters. Bernard took a moment to rally. He had still one side of his musket intact, and he brought the weapon back into position in another endeavor to shoot his enemy. By now, more people were in the room. Bernard recognized Ivan Komygin when he came in, but he did not know whether he was friend or foe. Therefore, he hesitated a moment. Then he saw, or thought he saw, that Ivan was helping the Indians. Anyhow, there were enemies enough, whoever came to his help, and Larion seemed to be their leader. Therefore, Bernard aimed his gun again at Larion, but now it was Ivan Komygin who knocked it up into the air, so that the shot again penetrated the roof. Bernard was left completely defenseless. He tried to turn round to grab his sword so as to defend himself to the last, but now Larion's opportunity had come. Everything had moved so quickly that it had been impossible to think out the best thing to do. The terrible spear which had never been known to fail was now to be thrown and it would go straight through the Englishman's body.

Then something happened that Larion never understood. Doa, his own little daughter, surprised her father and gave an entirely different turn to the struggle. Doa's mind had always been incalculable. Like a cat, she sprang at her father and twined her arms and legs round him, hampering his movements. She screamed something about nobody killing her Bernard. He was her man and she could fight as well as anybody. She would show them!

Doa's hand was groping about just beside her father's body. She was feeling for a knife which she knew lay on a table just beside him. The room was now full of Indians, and one of them, who saw her strong little hand catch hold of the knife, managed just in time to catch her arm and frustrate her plan. Larion fell to one side and that saved his life.

Bernard had managed to seize his gun by the muzzle, and al-. though he could not lift it very high because of the low ceiling, he was still able to get a good swing. He aimed at Larion's head with all his strength. It was just at that moment that the Indian chief lost his balance, and the butt end of the rifle hit the floor and broke in two. Bernard was again defenseless.

Doa realized that she had saved her father. She thought that, in any case, Bernard would go under; there were too many against him.

Just as suddenly and unexpectedly as she had clung to her father, Doa now sprang over to the young English officer. She threw herself against him, pressed herself up against him, but with what different feelings. The woman was uppermost in her now. It was the last thing she did, for rage seized Larion. He no longer thought of her as his daughter. His spear flew out of his hand, aimed less carefully than usual, and it hit the lovely little Doa in her side, making a fearful gash before it penetrated Bernard's abdomen, slitting it up so that the intestines welled out. The Englishman fell back as if dead, but Larion wasted no time in examining what had happened. He caught up Doa in his arms and ran out with her. Those in the room were filled with terror. Their chief had killed his own daughter; that meant disaster. They must no longer fight in this house.

They went out one by one, but Tawl remained in the room looking around him. Now he had finished with Ivan Komygin, now he was Tawl again, but he longed to possess something that would remind him of his time at the fort. He saw two pistols with white bone handles that shone like walrus tusks. Tawl had often seen Bernard shooting with them. They were in an open case. He took them.

Outside in the yard, Larion walked up and down with Doa in his arms. He said nothing and no one dared speak to him.

The fort was awake. All now had heard the shots in Bernard's house, and the soldiers had gone to their posts, but no words of command were given and no commander appeared, so what could a well-trained soldier do? A Russian always remains where he is unless he is ordered to move. Attack or retreat—that is the business of the commander. No one moved because Durab-bin did not come. Only the interpreter Orlof fled as soon as he could get his clothes on. A few of the women also ran out, for no Kuyukuk Indian would harm them; they were only married women who had either been given to the white men or been taken by them. If their husbands were killed they would be able to get home again. That, Larion would decide.

The other Russians barricaded themselves in. They were heard moving heavy beams against the doors.

The Indians outside waited and waited. Larion walked up and down the yard with Doa in his arms. He did not trouble to seek cover. Perhaps he wished thereby to show his scorn; perhaps he longed to be killed. Now that he had accomplished his revenge, he could die with honor.

Then the thunder broke loose from the windows of the soldiers' house. They fired in unison, and three of the Indians fell without a sound. The others heard the bullets whining around them. That was death flying past them, penetrating the timbers of the opposite house. All who were in the open space hurried to get away. Those who have grown up in the woods and have learned the art of making themselves invisible among the trees do not generally care for open spaces. So they just disappeared, and Larion was left walking back and forth alone. Perhaps he did not even know that firing was going on.

Then Gissa-Usch rushed across the yard and spoke to Larion. At first the chieftain refused to listen, only shaking his head, but Gissa-Usch took hold of his brother-in-law by the arm and pulled him to one side. They had scarcely got out of range of the windows when there was a new burst of firing. This time no one was in the open, so no one was hit.

Some of the Indians had collected together again and were anxious to go on with the attack. They had their bows and arrows with them and sent a shower of arrows over the big house in which many of the Russians and some of the women were sheltered. But what can an arrow do against a house? There was firing from inside the house, and a few more arrows whined through the air, some sticking in the wooden walls of the house. Others fell short of the target, and the Indians could not fetch them for fear of being shot at. Tawl thought how fortunate it was that the arrows were such weak projectiles, for they could be shot slantwise into the air from behind a woodpile; but a bullet, owing to its great speed, had to be aimed straight at the object and could not fall upon it from above. If only one could send fire arrows they would be even more efficacious than thunder weapons. He reflected that it was a pity that Larion had not thought of sending flames down over the wooden houses by means of burning arrows. It could have been done if they had had whale oil with them or burning tufts of grass. Now it was too late, for the day was about to break. When it grew light and those inside the houses had had time to organize themselves, they would be the stronger, even if they were fewer in number.

When Larion had gone, there was no one to lead the Kuyu-kuks. Tawl knew all about the arrangements in the fort, and he could show them the way out through the house that belonged to the white men's god, but he was young and had no authority to command. Some of the others disagreed about what should be done. Then, suddenly, mixed with the sound of shooting from the Russians who were barricaded in, shots came from Lieutenant Bernard's house. It was Orlof, who had by now loaded his own pistols and was firing through the window, so that the Indians had to take cover from attack from two sides.

At that moment a shout came from some Indians who had rammed open the door into the storeroom where all the trading goods were kept. They saw before them the possibility of rich booty and thought that it would be best to get away as quickly as possible with as much spoil as they could carry. Both the foreign chieftains were dead, and great honor had been won by them all. Larion had gone, and his departure had shown that his sorrow over his daughter's death was so great that he would abstain from further revenge. Therefore, it seemed to be against his wish for them to remain.

The sun was about to rise giving the white men a clearer view of the whole situation. It would be best to withdraw. Away, away! Much had been won, and they had all taken part in the greatest victory of all times. No-Unnegu was dead, the Kayar tribe as good as wiped out. Why stay? Take the booty and go. The whites had locked themselves in, and, anyhow, they were friendly men who never wished anyone harm. The Russians were born with smiles on their faces. It was, without doubt, the new foreign chieftain who had aroused the evil in Durabbin which had caused his death. Let us get away!

Orlof was shooting no longer. He was busy looking after his friend, Lieutenant Bernard, whom the Indians had left for dead. Bernard was still alive, and the first thing Orlof did was to shut the door and lock it. He put down his pistol and began to see what he could do for this badly wounded man. But what was there that he could do? Bernard was lying on the floor, in great agony, his intestines already full of dirt and dust from the floor; but he was still conscious.

"Orlof," he groaned, "it was Larion who did this to me. Get me up onto the bed. I must get well. Larion will pay for this. Help me, Orlof! Where is Durabbin?"

"The Russian commander has not appeared. I don't know where he is. The natives have taken the yard. I only just managed to get over here!"

"Then Durabbin must be dead," said Bernard. "I will take command of the garrison. He was a brave man. I liked him. Orlof, I'm in great pain, and I shall not get through this by myself. Why did we leave Adams behind in St. Michael's? We must have Adams up here. He would soon get me on my feet."

Orlof said yes, but he knew that when the intestines have come out of a man the end is not far off. Inflammation will start within a few hours and then he will die. That is well known among soldiers.

A little later, Bernard woke up again from a doze. He asked for writing materials and Orlof gave him paper and a goose-feather pen. With an almost superhuman effort, Bernard began to write.

"16th February, 1851, Nulato," he wrote, for Lieutenant Bernard was a very tidy-minded man and wanted to show that, although he was in great pain, he had not forgotten the date. Then came another attack of pain, and he was only able to write a few indistinct words in English saying he was wounded and needed help. He was able to sign his name.

"Send that to Dr. Adams and tell him to hurry."

Bernard fainted again, and Orlof did not know what he ought to do.

He again heard shots outside and thought that a violent struggle was going on. It was only the Russian soldiers shooting blindly. The sun had not yet risen, for the year was young and the sun's path very low, but it was quite light, which gave the soldiers more courage. They liked showing off their superiority, and therefore they fired their guns to frighten the Indians, if for nothing else.

The Indians had taken their dead with them and had disappeared. Whether they had gone to their homes or whether the attack would be resumed next evening it was impossible to guess. Two spies were sent out. They came back and reported that the houses of the Kayar Indians had been burned down. They had managed to get quite close to the encampment where they saw people moving about who were not Kayar Indians and must be enemies. They reported that the ruins were still smoking and that the roofs of all the houses had fallen in. That much they could see.

Orlof took command for a time. He was not a military man, but he had been the middleman between Durabbin and Bernard and he knew something of the two officers' plans. Finally, they decided to send a messenger down to Mikhailovsk to fetch the doctor and, if possible, reinforcements. There was need for

great haste, for Bernard was very ill. His intestines still lay outside his body and were by now gangrenous. He breathed heavily
and was delirious. The doctor must hurry.

A half-caste Indian in the fort named Ivan Bulegin had here-
tofore lived with the Russians down near Sitka. He had a great
reputation as a runner and had won all the prizes the com-
mandants had offered for letter runners who were both quick
of foot and resourceful. This man was chosen to take Bernard's
letter to the doctor. Orlof also wrote a note, and this letter was
entrusted to another man named Pauloff, who was to travel by
Bernard's sledge which was still in the fort.

Both the messengers started at the same time, but they had
not got far before they were both captured by Kuyukuk Indians.
The Kuyukuks had supposed rightly that messages would be
sent for help, and they argued that if Larion had decided to
kill everybody in the fort it would be best to stop the messengers.

Up to the present, Larion had not spoken. He sat with little
Doa on his knee. She was cold and stiff now. Very slim she was
and delicately built. Now she was dead, killed partly by her own
passionate nature and partly because of her father's pleasure in
war. Kidjuk sat beside him and dared to speak to her father now
and again, but she got no answer. He heard nothing outside
himself. Strangely enough, he ate when food was handed to
him, he drank the soup and held out the bowl for more, but
this was done mechanically.

Gissa-Usch became the leader, although he was no warrior
and his thoughts were engaged, above all, in composing a la-
ment for little Doa, in which she and all the others who had
been killed that night were praised and glorified. It must never
be possible to wound or mock Larion as a man who had fought
against women, so the wording was very difficult.

Pauloff sat on his sledge, shouting encouragement to his dogs.
Suddenly four Indians stood on the trail in front of him. Pauloff
was not brave. He had begged and prayed to be excused from

this task, but no one had listened to him. Now, his only hope was to win the friendship of these dreadful men by means of humble submission. He stopped the dogs and explained that he was going to fetch a medicine man who would heal the English chieftain. By this means the Indians learned that Bernard was not dead, that a medicine man could help him and that there was not such a one in the fort. If they could stop help coming, he would die and Doa would be revenged.

Pauloff was pulled off his sledge, and they were just beginning to examine his clothes when shouts were heard from the river. Evidently something was happening out there on the ice. Some Kuyukuks had seen Ivan Bulegin. He was fleeter than most runners. Like an arrow, he shot past the Indians who were try-ing to stop him, his snowshoes flapping up and down like the wings of a flying spirit. The snow stood out like a cloud behind him, and it seemed as if it would be impossible to catch him. Then Tawl felt intuitively that it was essential for Ivan to be caught. They had both been called "Ivan" in the fort and had often competed against each other, and it had always annoyed Tawl that he had been obliged to exert himself to the utmost to defeat Bulegin in various tests of strength. Now it looked as if Bulegin was in luck and would reach the coast and tell them about Larion.

That thought, alone, was enough for Tawl. He had Dislen in mind and he knew that his dead companion would never have given up the chase even if he had to run into the jaws of the enemy before he reached his object.

Tawl shouted to his friends that Ivan Bulegin was the most important, and they all set off after him. Tawl quickly outstripped the others, and it seemed to him that the distance between himself and Ivan Bulegin was slowly lessening. They ran on and on, and neither of them thought for a moment of giving up. Ivan Bulegin knew that he could hold out longer than anybody else, but he had not the best terrain and the snow-shoes he was wearing were a little different in shape from his usual ones. Here, Tawl had the advantage. On top of all this, Bulegin felt the straps on his left foot begin to come loose. He looked down and discovered to his horror that the knots were coming undone and that the ends of the straps were flapping behind him. When he had not seen this it made no difference to him, but now that he knew about it, he bent his head down again and again to see if it was getting any worse. Bulegin realized that he had lost the race, but that did not mean giving in, for all that.

Suddenly he swung right around, facing Tawl. This put Tawl off his balance, but nevertheless he swung his club and it fell on Bulegin, although not with any great force. Bulegin was not killed, but he bent over double in pain, for the club had hit his shoulder. He caught up his long knife to try to defend himself, but now Tawl was ready. He dodged Ivan, lunge by lunge, and managed to get his own knife into the ribs of his opponent. This ended the struggle.

Not a word had been spoken, but now Ivan Bulegin sank down onto the snow groaning heavily. Tawl said nothing. All he wanted was to get hold of the paper asking for a doctor to be sent. He pulled off the little box that Ivan Bulegin had fastened onto his back with a strap and examined it. In it he found tobacco, a pipe and some food for the journey. Then he came on what he had been hunting for, a piece of paper. Tawl knew that he had here before him something that he had brooded over for hours—the problem of how the white men sent living words from one man to another. This message would never reach the medicine man. The examination was over. Tawl had defeated the man who lay there bleeding on the snow and who was obviously just about dead. He turned and went back to his companions.

Ivan Bulegin was not dead yet. First of all, he knew that Tawl had not found the letter to the medicine man in Mikhailovsk, for it was in one of his moccasins, stuffed in between the straw and the sole. Secondly, he had seen that the dogs harnessed to the sledge had not followed the Indians. They had deserted Pauloff, whom the Indians had with them. If Ivan could only get hold of them, there was the possibility that he could drive into Mikhailovsk and deliver his message.

In the meantime, Tawl had returned to the Kuyukuks. He pointed out that they must all hurry back to the fort, for it was possible that other messengers would be sent to Mikhailovsk for safety's sake. They must all be caught. Pauloff was taken to Larion; Ivan Bulegin lay dying. Tawl had the letter safely in his own possession. All seemed in order.

So they all turned and went back to Nulato. In the waning day, Larion's strange conduct made them all feel uneasy and undecided. The dogs remained behind, and Ivan was to all appearances dead and frozen stiff in the snow. The sledge dogs lay down in the snow. Ivan was awake and as soon as the Indians were out of earshot he began to crawl toward the sledge. He pushed his way through the deep soft snow surrounding him and eventually reached the dogs. He did not dare stand up to his full height, but bent almost double, he was able to get their harness into order and crawl up onto the sledge. Then he gave the starting signal and away they went. Ivan Bulegin had to drive farther than any one else had driven before without stopping, but his mind was set on saving Bernard, and he knew that it all depended on whether he got to Mikhailovsk in time.

That drive cost him all that remained of his strength. The dogs also suffered badly, but Ivan never thought of resting or of sparing either himself or the dogs. He knew that it would be almost a miracle if he were able to hold out, but his state of mind was now such that he felt he must carry out his mission if he were to die in peace.

The dogs set off at a great rate, they ran feeling that they had no driver behind them. Ivan did not stop them and get off now and again to run beside the sledge to keep warm as was usually done. He sat there, strangely still. A short distance from Unalak-leet, he met a dog driver who was out seeing to his traps. The man was terrified to see a living person in such a condition. Ivan's feet were swollen and his nose was white from frostbite; he could scarcely speak but was able to whisper to the man, who was a half-caste Russian like himself, that he must get to Mikhailovsk, as it was a matter of great urgency. The man thought there must have been some kind of tragedy. He gathered this from the look in Ivan Bulegin's eyes, and his wounds. Ivan could say nothing about the disaster at the fort, for it had cost him too much strength even to say as much as he had.

The man got him to Unalakleet as quickly as possible and there no time was wasted. They sent Ivan on, wrapped in blankets and with fresh dogs, the fastest they had.

There was a great turmoil in the fort at Mikhailovsk when at last he arrived there. With great difficulty, as he could by now scarcely speak or move, Ivan was able to make them understand that the letter lay hidden in one of his moccasins. It was quickly extracted and read.

Dr. Adams, at once, asked for a sledge and the necessary escort and equipment. The letter had said nothing except that Bernard was wounded; and they could not ask Ivan Bulegin about conditions at Nulato, for he had now lapsed into unconsciousness. He had been taken into the fort at once, but the doctors who examined him realized that they could not save him, for the frost had attacked both his feet, and his nose crumbled away as soon as it began to thaw.

It was clear that Dr. Adams must go at once, but how many men ought he to take with him? The commandant hastily called a meeting but argued that it must most certainly have been an accident. If there had been a quarrel between Bernard and the Russians there would have been a report from Durabbin. Lieutenant Bernard needed help, that was evident, but he had written the letter himself so that clearly he was not very badly wounded.

Dr. Adams went. The men from Unalakleet went back with

him as far as their home; from that point, fast sledges were sent all the long way up to Nulato.

When the doctor arrived, Lieutenant Bernard was dead. He had suffered a great deal before he died. The fort had no officer in charge and panic reigned. A noncommissioned officer had used his authority to commandeer all the vodka there was. He explained to Dr. Adams that he had drunk to deaden his sorrow over his friends' deaths.

Under these conditions it would have been easy for Larion to surprise the fort and kill all the garrison, but he had gone home. It was never known where he buried his daughter. Never again did he make war against either white men or natives in Alaska.

His daughter Kidjuk, who married Tawl, often came to Nulato later on, but Larion was never seen in the place again.

Gissa-Usch's song about Larion's war against the Russians was not as grandiose as his former songs had been. It was as if altogether too much had happened to fit into a poem. Larion's honor as a warrior would never die; his reputation was so immense that the white men never attempted to avenge their chieftains.

Once, when Tawl was down at Nulato, he was told that the Tzar had defended Larion's action to Bernard's king. The two countries were now at war far away from Alaska, and it was partly due to Larion's exploits that the rulers of these two countries had not been able to live at peace together.

Deep in Alaska's forests, Larion lived on and became an old man. His word was still law because he had accomplished so much. His reputation was so great that never again need he achieve anything great in order to be honored and obeyed. But no one ever saw him laugh, for his mind was heavy. He had lost all those whom he loved most in life.

RUSSIA
AND
SIBERIA

Toward the end of 1936, Freuchen, who had just completed a successful lecture tour in the United States, found in his mail an official invitation to him, his wife, Magda, and his daughter, Pipaluk to visit the Soviet Union as the guest of the government. There was talk of his joining a Russian aviator in a flight over the North Pole to San Francisco.

When he arrived in Russia, he was pleasantly surprised to receive piles of rubles for expenses, other piles in payment for royalties on books which had been published in that country and on which, after the common Soviet practice, no payments to the author had been made. But when he went to inquire about plans for the flight, he learned that the official who had issued his invitation had disappeared.

The vanished one's successor eventually revealed the fact that the aviator had changed his plans and was lost shortly after he passed over the Pole. It was suggested that Freuchen might substitute a trip through Siberia. Supplied with maps and travel aides, Peter outlined a journey up the Lena River, which would take him to where he might be useful in any expedition fitted out to rescue the missing aviator. But he had to wait for weeks while red tape was unwound and one after another three successive escorts were assigned to him. The one with whom he actually set forth, a man accomplished in both English and German, was Nicholas Beguitcheff, and he told Peter he was an admiral.

The Soviet Way

The famous Trans-Siberian Railroad was very comfortable—at least for me. As a privileged visitor I was given a luxurious compartment with a private shower bath. I also had a private telephone, which did me little good since I could not speak Russian and had nobody to talk to. Beguitcheff was a very pleasant traveling companion but he would never talk about himself.

The second day out of Moscow I was visited by an American fellow passenger, Alice Shek, a schoolteacher on a trip around the world. She had seen me at the station in Moscow, surrounded by serious-looking men in uniforms, and she had not dared approach me. She had heard me lecture in Brooklyn and recognized me at once. She was a very agreeable young woman with sense enough to travel third class on her limited funds.

She shared a sleeping compartment for four, and as the difference between the sexes was officially disregarded in the Soviet Union she had to share it with two male American students and a Japanese professor. The heat was insufferable crossing the plains, and as I had a private shower I asked her to use it. She did so for several days until finally Beguitcheff intervened. He had noticed that this young lady visited me rather often, he told me.

"Just to get a shower when the heat is too intolerable," I told him truthfully.

"Impossible," he declared. "This cannot go on!"

I did not know whether he wanted to protect her or me, but he was obviously upset and I tried to calm him down. "I am an old married man and would not dream of molesting the girl, much as I like her," I assured him.

Beguitcheff looked surprised.

"What you do with the girl is your private affair. I was objecting because she is a third-class passenger while you travel first class. We should not associate with passengers from other classes!"

Equality and brotherhood! The Russians are a strange people, indeed. They have class distinction not to be found in any other place. In Denmark we are satisfied with two classes on the train; in Russia there were four. In the dining car the first-class passengers ate in a reserved section with enormous soft chairs, upholstered in red velvet. We had to be careful not to mix with the second-class group who ate on smaller chairs covered in some plain gray material. They in turn were particular about contact with the third class at the other end of the car. This last group sat on bare wooden chairs.

There was also a fourth class for people in no hurry and for large families. The fourth-class carriages were often disconnected and left on a side track until another train could take them another stretch. They were freight cars without equipment. The passengers furnished their own mattresses or straw pallets. They made camp next to railroad stations, and while they waited the women put up laundry lines from one car to another, their gaily colored clothes blowing in the wind.

There were other cars of a more sinister character—the prisoner transports. We met them every day going in both directions. Whenever we stopped at a station, which we did every other hour, we often saw these cars surrounded by armed guards, the miserable prisoners peering out at us through small vents. I asked Beguitcheff about these transports and his invariable answer was that they were all Trotskyists. I asked for permission to give them some cigarettes which was denied me. And when I criticized the inhuman way of transporting people he was indignant.

"You should have seen the transports on which I had to travel during the war. We suffered worse hardships in those days when we were fighting for what we enjoy in Russia today. And the fighting went on much longer than the world knows. In those days I would have considered myself lucky if I could have traveled as these prisoners do. When they get to their destination they'll be well cared for. We do not punish people in Russia, we just see that they do not again threaten our society."

We crossed the Volga on a beautiful moonlight night and went on and on through Siberia. People are the same all over the world. In Kungur we were surrounded by men and women selling hideous souvenirs. Carved bears and ashtrays with the inscription: "Souvenir from Ural." We stopped for only twenty minutes at Kungur, and I could see no reason for buying souvenirs of this remote spot. The conductor told me, however, that most of the passengers left these ugly objects on the train and that they were collected by the crew and sold at half price to the next suckers.

My American friend Miss Shek was agog with excitement whenever we made a stop. She always dashed into the village or town, catching the train again at the last moment. But once she did not catch it at all. I did not know she had been left behind until the two American students came running through the train to tell me. She had left her passport and all her money on the train. They were afraid she would be arrested and would disappear in Siberia forever.

I went to my admiral who took the situation calmly. "No one is ever lost in this country," he assured me. "No one disappears, we have the best police in the world, don't excite yourself." He picked up my private telephone and in a moment had the connection.

The two students were still frantic and I was uneasy. But three stops and several hours later the girl rejoined the train, proudly relating her experience. When she was left behind she was in despair. Some uniformed guards took her to the stationmaster, who was furious and talked a blue streak to her in Russian. She listened to a long telephone conversation in which she recognized only the word *Amerikanska*. In the end she was served tea, cookies and cigarettes, and she realized she probably was not going to be imprisoned after all. When she had finished her tea a car drove up with two smart officers who took her to the local airport, where she was served more tea before boarding a small plane. She was wondering whether she was being taken to Moscow when the officers pointed out something on the ground. She looked down and saw a black worm crawling across the steppe below—her train! In a few minutes they landed, and she was escorted back to the train. Admiral Beguitcheff looked at me with a superior smile. "The Soviet way!" he said.

I had always realized that Siberia is vast, but I had never been prepared for the beauty of it—wide rich fields, lush green pastures, magnificent forests. We crossed majestic rivers choked with timber, we met freight trains with flat cars filled with gay holiday crowds dressed in colorful national costumes. The soil was glistening black and fertile like my own wonderful Danish soil.

We passed a huge penitentiary with a number of large brick barracks—the single exception to the wooden houses we saw everywhere. We passed coal mines and huge railroad yards.

Before we left the train at Irkutsk our American friends gave us a farewell party. They had been provided in Moscow with a surplus of food tickets to take care of the normal Russian appetite which no outsider can match.

In Irkutsk we settled down at the Central Hotel which had very little to recommend it. Our first stop was the passport control where our papers were checked and where for unknown reasons my baggage was reduced to the barest minimum. Some of my clothes and even part of my Arctic equipment had to be returned to Moscow. And I was not allowed to take along my reserve wooden leg. My main interest in Irkutsk was to make the trip to Baikal Lake. Through my friend Professor Otto Juliewitch Schmidt in Moscow I had been given an official permit to kill six of the Baikal seals for scientific study.

That evening Beguitcheff asked me to abandon the plan. I would never be allowed to go to Baikal, he explained. When I asked him why, he simply shrugged. If I did not want to spend the rest of my life in Irkutsk, I had better forget Baikal and the seals.

Reluctantly I agreed and probably to compensate me Beguitcheff promised me a plane trip to Yakutsk. The famous Russian pilot Gallicheff was going to take us there—a real honor. Since his last year's rescue of one hundred and fourteen people from a shipwrecked steamer, he did not fly just anyone.

We had to go and find the great Gallicheff—a search impeded by the housing shortage in Irkutsk, as in all Russian cities. The tiniest apartments were shared by people who never quite knew who the other tenants were. At last we found him in a drunken stupor. He had apparently been sent to central Siberia because of his addiction to alcohol.

I spent the rest of the day with some Danish compatriots. They were employed by the Great Nordic Cable Company, and I invited them to dinner. Beguitcheff advised me to entertain my guests in our hotel room and I, of course, complied. During the evening he drank enough to become confidential. He said he had been sent with me to report on everything I did. There were others, in turn, watching and reporting on him. For that reason he had not wanted to be seen in the public restaurant in the company of more people "of my sort."

I wandered around Irkutsk while we waited for Gallicheff to sober up. The old part of the town was practically impassable.

There was no pavement of any kind. They proudly pointed out the spot where Admiral Kolchak had been shot by his troops. If he had only been on the right side he would have gone very far, they said.

The third day Gallicheff was able to function again. He had been drinking, he told me, while waiting for a new engine for his plane. He would be very happy to take us to Yakutsk, and his lengthy flight would give him a chance to test his new engine. I suggested timidly that it would be wise for him to make the test before he took passengers aloft but to no avail.

We flew above enormous forests and endless green fields, always following the course of the Angara River which runs from Lake Baikal to the Yenisei. Something went wrong with the new engine very soon, and Gallicheff was forced to land near a small town called Balagansk—an idyllic place much like a Danish village. The river was calm and gentle with a quaint old-fashioned ferry running across it. There was a farm close by and I saw an old woman coming out in the yard with bread crumbs for her chickens. The men were out in the fields bringing in the hay. I could hear them laughing and singing. I would clearly have to revise my ideas of Siberia as a land of terror.

We soon took to the air again, but in a matter of minutes it was apparent things were not as they should be. Our wobbly flight barely missed the treetops, it seemed to me, as I looked down on the gigantic slim spruces. A plane falling down in this forest would never be found again, and I was relieved when we returned to idyllic Balagansk. After an hour we were in the air again, reasonably safe and steady.

We left the Angara and flew north toward the Lena River across forests that stretched as far as the eye could see. Once in a while I could distinguish a group of white birch among the heavy dark spruce. And we flew over a number of forest fires. Nothing was ever done about them, Beguitcheff told me. The forests were so vast, they increased every year no matter what was cut, and the Russian forestry service was still in its infancy. Anyway fires always burned out by themselves.

We came to Ust-kutshuk, an ancient center where trade routes crossed in prehistoric times. Tartar chieftains had made camps here with their armies, waiting to attack the rich and peaceful caravans; great battles had been fought here between rival princes. Now the place was peaceful enough. Gallicheff brought the plane down on the Lena River, and I had some trouble getting on shore. Beguitcheff and I were told to inflate a small canvas raft, which the mechanic handed us, and row across the river. We managed to launch the craft and Beguitcheff got into it. I handed him the two oars and got ready to jump into the boat, but he was already drifting away. When I told him to use his oars he just laughed. He had no idea how to row!

I have met many strange people in my life but an admiral who could not row seemed a fantastic phenomenon. He explained to me later that he was not really a naval officer by profession. He was a chemist! He had made some invention which had been useful to the Red Fleet and as a reward had been given admiral's rank.

We were taken to the local inn which was clean, warm and friendly. I felt as if I had stepped right into a nineteenth-century Russian novel. A gigantic oven dominated the room. It was made of brick, and on all sides there were shelves, large and small, strange protuberances, nooks and crannies. Some of the shelves were used for beds at night—practical and warm. In this old-world room we were served a meal which seemed equally old-fashioned in its abundance.

Outside on the river huge shiny log rafts were drifting by. Some cabins had been built on the rafts to house the loggers and their families. These people live deep in the forests through the winter, getting the timber down and out to the ice-covered rivers which all flow into the Lena and down to the sea. After the lumber is delivered the families return in small boats which may take them months. Usually they are back in time to go hunting for their winter meat supply, and the process of lumbering begins all over again. Throughout Siberia these people lead a strange remote life, dominated by fear of God, faith in Stalin and a fierce patriotism.

Beguitcheff told me a story about a group of three hundred people who recently had been discovered living deep in the forest. They were officers and men from the army of Admiral Kolchak. When their hero was killed in Irkutsk they escaped with their families into the forests where they settled by the river banks, eking out an existence from fishing and hunting. The men kept their faith in the old order, and from time to time they set out on long expeditions to sabotage the new regime, blowing up bridges, dams and railroads. They had cached large supplies of ammunition and explosives. When, finally, primitive life proved too hard on their women they sent a letter to Moscow asking for government assistance. They wanted fishing nets and other equipment that would help them to live. A fishery expert was sent from Moscow to help them, and a political commissar came to teach them the blessings of the Soviet system. But eventually the connection between the mysterious acts of sabotage throughout the country and the long absences of the men was related. And the men were executed and the women and children scattered to all corners of the country.

We were on our way again the following day after waiting for hours for the head wind needed to raise Gallicheff's plane off the ground. We followed the Lena River low enough to see the sidewheelers moving slowly with their barges in tow. But we had to go down at Kirensk for more engine repairs. Beguitcheff and I spent our time with the local youths in parachute jumping from the tall parachute tower. I was told that Stalin had ordered every city to make young people air-minded.

Our wobbly flight continued, but we did not get farther than Peleiduy, where we spent the night and where I experienced the haunting enchantment of Russian folk music. In the evening the young men went strolling in the sunset through the forest with their girl friends.

Our old German Junker completed the last leg of the journey the following day. We barely made it—the plane was too small for the four of us, the engine too heavy for the plane, and the head wind not strong enough for easy flight. We skimmed over trees, farmhouses, fields, an enormous prison camp, and came down that night in Yakutsk in a terrible rain storm.

There was no one to meet us. From the air strip we had to wade through ankle-deep clay in the pouring rain up a steep hill to a little bench outside a shack, the only visible structure. Two sad-looking girls within the shack did not invite us inside, and we had to wait on the bench in the rain. The pilot found a phone inside the house and called for a car, which arrived after half an hour. But it came for Gallicheff and the mechanic, not for the two of us, and they walked out of our life, leaving us waiting in the rain.

Every fifteen minutes or so Beguitcheff went inside the shack to use the telephone. He shouted at the top of his voice and used my name frequently. When his fury was spent he joined me on the bench outside with angelic patience. The rain never ceased, the girls never asked us to go inside, and it was three hours before we were rescued. An open truck appeared at last, driven by a young woman who had her boy friend with her. She told us to jump up in the back with our luggage, and off we tore through the mud and the rain.

Finally some houses appeared, the wide road narrowed down to a semblance of a street, and we turned sharply into a driveway. The truck stopped outside the impressive entrance to Glasewmorput, the Arctic Transportation Trust Company, and we found our way to the head man of the local office, Julius Liss. He was the big boss of the district, and Beguitcheff warned me that our future depended on this fellow. Liss spoke English and German, he was obviously well educated, and he realized at once that our concern then was to find decent living quarters. There were no hotels in Yakutsk, but he gave us an official requisition and we returned to the truck.

The woman at the wheel took an angry look at the paper and drove off madly. Suddenly she turned into another driveway and stopped in the back yard of a house that looked far from promising. Our entrance was the signal for a general uproar. Beguitcheff waved his requisition in front of us, but they would not let us in. A glimpse at the rooms convinced us they were right. We saw double layers of cots everywhere, inches apart, people were even sleeping on the bare floor.

Back to the truck again, another reckless drive to the Trust Office and Julius Liss. A new requisition sent us tearing off in the opposite direction, but at this new address we were not even allowed inside the house. There were already three cars in the yard and a number of people with requisitions fighting to get in. I stayed in the car while Beguitcheff investigated. In this lodging house people slept in eight-hour shifts, the beds were in use twenty-four hours a day. We returned once more to Mr. Liss.

When we reached his office Liss was beaming. Things had changed for the better in our absence. The editor of the local paper had just been arrested, and we were given a requisition to take over his apartment. We ran back to the truck and told the girl she could go home if she got us to the editor's place before it was occupied. But we were bitterly disappointed when we got there—two cars were already waiting. Closer inspection gave us hope. The two cars contained only three people, which meant they were important persons, and the two rooms of the editor would be ample for the five of us.

We settled down in luxury—the three strangers in one room, we two in the other. A wonderful maid, Sjura, turned up from nowhere to look after us. I was offered the editor's bed, and as it still seemed warm I proved myself a real bourgeois by asking for clean sheets. The others followed my example. Sjura disap-

peared and surprised us all by returning with snow-white bed
linen.

The most prominent of our fellow lodgers was the head of the
local political police, an interesting and highly intelligent man
by the name of Lamarkin. Our conversation was necessarily
limited since he could speak only Russian, but he played chess
like an angel and the harmonica like a god.

The second man was in charge of all the fur trade on the
Lena River. He spoke English fluently; had lived in St. Louis,
Missouri, and Leipzig; knew a great deal about foreign countries but preferred the Soviet Union. His main difficulty was to
see that people spent their time in farming rather than in hunting and trapping. The free life of a hunter was more appealing
and he got more furs that way, but his main concern was to
make the state of Yakutsk agriculturally self-sufficient. There
were also thousands of prospectors spending their time washing
gold in the rivers of the Aldan district instead of farming, he
said.

The third lodger was a quiet man of high rank. These three
important people tacked an official paper on our front door to
keep out unwelcome guests. Sjura brought us bread, tea, sugar
and candy, and we settled down for the night.

In the morning I had to go to the Yakutsk police to have my
passport checked and to receive my official permit to stay in the
district, normally a procedure that was quite an ordeal. Beguitcheff had no difficulty, of course, but my strange passport was
suspect. The examining officer sent for the chief of police who
saw at once that my passport was issued in San Francisco. Why?

I explained to him that I had been in Hollywood a few years
ago, and while I was there my passport had expired. It had to be
renewed and the Danish consulate general was located in San
Francisco.

"Yes, of course, but then why was it issued in San Francisco?"

I repeated my explanation and the good chief of police said
he understood what had happened. A few minutes later he

asked me why on earth my passport was issued in San Francisco. This time I explained in detail. But he decided these complicated geographical problems could not be solved without the aid of a map. An enormous map of the world was produced and hung on the wall.

"Where is this Denmark?" I pointed it out, and they noted with satisfaction that so far my explanation was correct.

"But where is San Francisco then?" Once more I pointed at the map. The officers examined it carefully and agreed happily that I was still a man of truth. San Francisco was just where I said it was.

The chief expressed his surprise that Denmark was such a vast country. Modestly I explained that there was quite a bit of water between Denmark and San Francisco.

"San Francisco is in other words a Danish colony?" Well, not exactly a colony, I told the police. We permit other people to live there.

After a few minutes of Russian consultation the chief of police returned to the starting point: "But why was your passport issued in San Francisco?" I gave up.

In the end it was decided to refer the intricate problem to an investigating committee. In case Beguitcheff should turn out to be my "accomplice," the chief of police kept his passport as well as mine and gave us a restricted permit for a temporary stay. The main drawback was that we could not eat in the official canteen without our passports. This was the only place where we could get substantial food—meat soup, delicious Russian bread, quantities of pancakes and tea in enormous samovars, served with cookies and candies. Beguitcheff sent a wire to Moscow, and the following day he received his passport which enabled him to take me along to the canteen.

We had expected to get a plane immediately in Yakutsk to continue north to Tiksi on the Arctic Ocean, but we had to be patient. Julius Liss advised us to get our supplies and fur clothes in Yakutsk while we waited for the plane he promised us. Just wait till tomorrow was his constant refrain. No plane appeared. Wait till tomorrow and tomorrow and tomorrow.

In the meantime we went sight-seeing in Yakutsk. We saw the historical museum with various devices used to torture the peasants in old days when they could not pay their taxes. I visited the palace of the old tzarist governors, luxuriously furnished with treasures that often had to be carried across Siberia on human backs. Grand pianos, precious paintings, gobelin tapestries and exquisite furniture. And I saw the new "Culture Park" with the omnipresent parachute tower. I was much amused to watch the expressions of the Mongol men and women as they jumped in their parachutes—never a smile on their wooden faces.

I saw a Shakespeare performance in Yakutsk, an unforgettable experience. Although I could not understand a word I thought it was the most moving presentation of *Othello* I had ever seen. The cast consisted of local Yakutsk players and some Russian guests. The theater was packed and the audience was entranced. I was amazed that the Soviet regime should be so enthusiastic about Shakespeare, who did not exactly praise the virtues of the common man. Beguitcheff explained that the education of the people began with the classics. The Soviet people, he insisted, are mature enough not to be influenced by a capitalist dramatist who wrote hundreds of years ago.

Something went wrong with my artificial leg in Yakutsk, and I sorely missed the one the authorities in Irkutsk had forced me to return to Moscow, but Sjura, our marvelous maid, knew what to do. She took me to a shoemaker who did my repar work while his customers waited. We stayed there for hours while he fixed my leg, but Sjura brought me food and kept me company until my mobility was fully restored. Afterward she took me to the flea market.

Everything was for sale in this place. Beguitcheff told me that a great many people had sold their belongings to the flea market, not because they were badly off but because too much wealth did not "look good."

The days went by and Julius Liss had still no plane for us. Beguitcheff wired Janssen, head of the Arctic Trust in Moscow, without result. One evening we heard the sound of marching soldiers outside the house. A squad under the direction of a smart officer stopped outside our windows, and my name was called. I must confess that I was rather nervous as I walked out to answer the summons. But I was greatly relieved when I found the military parade had a peaceful purpose, which was to bring me my passport. It had finally been found genuine by the special investigating committee, and I was a free man for the time being.

The following morning we received an urgent call from Julius Liss. He handed us a telegram with the news that the two young pilots, who had been sent out to Yakutsk for our sake, had crashed the day before and been killed instantly. I was shocked and disappointed that it would now be impossible for me to go to the New Siberian Islands and take part in the search for Levanevski. To find another plane was out of the question, Liss explained to us, but a "caravan" was going north the next day and he suggested we go with it.

The caravan turned out to be a group of river boats—in our case four—with a long line of barges in tow. We were taken out to a side-wheeler and given a comfortable cabin.

I was not allowed to go on the dock without Beguitcheff, and we were both forbidden to leave the ship after seven o'clock in the evening. And when I tried to walk along the dock an armed guard stopped me. I wanted to exercise, I explained, but he found my behavior suspicious and ordered me back on board.

Our captain was a pleasant old sailor, but the first mate was a handsome woman who maintained strict discipline. Our ship carried no cargo; it was only a towboat. Each of the four boats towed three barges. All in all there were six hundred and twenty-five people in the caravan, four hundred of them passengers. Most of them stayed on the barges, where they lived as they did on shore. I was impressed by the huge brick baking ovens. All the towboats were side-wheelers, and a constant look-out had to be kept because of the danger from driftwood.

There was nothing hurried about our long trip down the river, due to the chance of running aground on the constantly shifting sand and clay. Getting stuck in the river might well be considered an act of sabotage, and the captain preferred to stay put overnight. Every evening at sunset we dropped anchor, usually in some quiet cove close by the forest. We were allowed to go ashore, and some of the men went hunting all night long.

One of the barges carried a group of young geologists, eight young scientists and engineers who had come from an expedition to Pamir to inspect the gold mines. They told me that one of the mines produced between ten and fifteen tons of gold a day. They would not tell me, however, where they were bound for. They met me with the same secretive silence I encountered everywhere in the Soviet. People would suddenly break off a pleasant conversation when they suspected my innocent questioning. They showed me their instruments, and I was pleased to see that they used the same kind of Hildebrand theodolites I had used for years. I visited them often for a few days, but I was suddenly told one morning to keep away from their barges. No reason was given.

The majestic Lena flows straight north, sometimes for days through enormous forests, sometimes between steep banks and towering cliffs. We passed large coal deposits where I could see the black veins on the cliffside. The Russians are said to be clever, but they are certainly lucky as well. Here the coal was ready and waiting to be pushed straight into the waiting barges. We stopped at one of the mines, which I inspected. The miners were mostly young powerful men, but there were some women. About half of the miners were convicts, and I was not allowed to talk to them. I was told that all the miners lived together, received the same wages and the same treatment. The only difference was that the convicts were forced laborers and got no vacation. Once in a while they would try to escape, which meant certain death. Without the proper papers one was helpless, could not buy food or clothes or use any public transportation.

Slowly the scenery changed, and it was soon apparent we were approaching Arctic regions. Reindeer were grazing by the riverside, and the tundra stretched out on both sides as far as the eye could see. We left cliffs and mountains behind, but one day we were surprised by the sight of a man-made mountain. It consisted of food and supplies of every conceivable variety—bales and crates, barrels and cartons, lumber and textiles, canned goods, cereals! It had all rotted and was slowly disintegrating. Nobody knew why this mountain of supplies had come into being. Beguitcheff was told that once a fleet of barges had come to the spot, unloaded and sailed off.

It must have been sent by someone in authority for some specific purpose, and all the treasures, tempting beyond measure, were left untouched by man. What self-control in the Arctic wilderness, to ignore this mass of desirable goods. "One does not steal in the Soviet Union!" Beguitcheff stated drily. It was all due to some confusion in the central administration during the revolution, he thought, or more likely to the deliberate acts of Trotskyists! Or the barge captains might have gone up the wrong river. The Soviet Union is so large, a few shiploads look fabulous in the tundra, but they are easily forgotten in a government office.

At last we reached the Lena delta, covering a vast area of which our small range of vision on board gave only the merest hint. Everything was flat until I suddenly saw an enormous wooden cross looming on the horizon. It was raised on the island of Stolpe in memory of the American polar explorer, Lieutenant George Washington De Long, whose tragic expedition in the *Jeannette* ended here. De Long had died on Stolpe, presumably on October 30, 1881, the last date of entry in his diary which he kept until the end.

His expedition had caused a world-wide sensation, partly because of its tragic end and partly because it made an important contribution to polar research and hydrography. It was an involuntary and unexpected contribution. Everything left behind by the *Jeannette* expedition was found on the Greenland coast after drifting for five years across the polar basin. De Long had made the same error which had cost so many other Arctic travelers their lives. He had hauled with him a large wooden boat that had cost them precious time and robbed them of their strength. It was still not realized that the ice itself is a much better and simpler means of transportation than open water.

A strong easterly gale forced us to anchor off Stolpe for a few days, and I wanted to go ashore to pay my respects and also to look for further signs of the De Long Expedition. The captain had no objection, and a boat was made ready for me when a signal was flashed from one of the other side-wheelers to "report" at once. Such a report meant that our captain had to go and see the political commissar, and in his absence we were not allowed to leave the ship. He returned in an hour with the terse order to stay away from Stolpe Island. No explanation.

We cleared the delta, reached the Arctic Ocean and sailed east to Tiksi, an excellent modern harbor. At first I was not allowed ashore, for no apparent reason again. We received visitors, some of them marvelous chess players, and Beguitcheff went ashore several times, but I was kept on board for a few days, presumably in order to be "cleared."

Finally the commander of the Arctic Station on Tiksi sent his boat for me, and I was received as an honored guest. I was given a wonderful room with a bed in which I could stretch out crosswise with all my six foot three, and I was assured that Tiksi was the only place in the Soviet Union where there were no bedbugs. The boast proved to be correct.

The Arctic Station in Tiksi was large, consisting of forty-two young, gifted and eager scientists; it was extremely well equipped and had apparently unlimited funds. It was one of sixty-six such stations all along the coast of the Arctic Ocean. Their main task is to carry on the most detailed study of all natural conditions in the Arctic, temperature changes, living conditions and particularly the possibilities of passage north of the Asian Continent for ice breakers and regular commercial vessels. There was a widely held opinion that the sea was open and passable for four months of the year, which would mean a considerable strengthening of the Soviet military potential. It would be of tremendous advantage to the navy, but also supplies of every variety could be transported by this northern route to the easternmost parts of Russia.

The ice was under constant scrutiny by air and sea. Pilots landed on the ice and left behind intricate instruments which sent back automatic radio messages concerning temperature, barometric pressure, wind strength and direction, even the drift of the ice and the depth of the sea. Whenever the instrument was running out of energy this also was reported automatically and it was immediately replaced. A great many experiments were carried out with devices like windmills, which supplied electricity, and with Arctic plants.

I was taken along on a trip across the tundra which stretched all the way out to the coast in this region. From the tundra it was usually impossible to reach the water because a wide belt along the shore was covered with piles of old tree trunks. But landing beaches had been cleared by burning a way through the old logs. There was no sand, only a soft mush of sawdust from the constant rubbing of the tree trunks.

In a flat-bottomed boat with an outboard motor we sailed up one of the countless broad smooth rivers crossing the tundra. We were looking for a place described by some hunters who thought they had come across coal deposits during the winter. We reached our goal and beheld an open coal vein, a yard or two across, stretching back as far as we could see. We took samples back with us to Tiksi, and a cable was sent asking for an expert to come at once and examine our specimen.

He arrived by plane the next day and turned out to be one of the young geologists I had met on the way down the Lena River.

He was satisfied that the coal was of high grade, and the discovery was celebrated by an enormous dinner party. A few of the men drank only wine, but most of them guzzled down the ever present vodka and some got very drunk.

Beguitcheff had enough vodka to confide in me once more that he was still sending off reports about me every day, but so far he had sent off only favorable ones. He was worried about his long absence from Moscow, he told me. There was always a danger of intrigues being carried on behind his back. But he was very proud his two sons were not going to be manual laborers! They were going to be officers or high government officials. When I asked him how he could be so sure, he whispered to me the great secret—his wife had once danced with Voroshiloff! At a party in Moscow they had danced a fox-trot together! After such an encounter one's sons did not become plain laborers!

One of the more voluble participants in the party was the local baker. As a native of Estonia he spoke German fluently, and he told me his life story. He was a former bank robber and murderer. If he had carried on his particular trade in any other country he would have been hanged or decapitated years ago. But in the Soviet Union—and he beat his enormous, hairy chest—in the Soviet Union he had spent time at a reformatory school and now he was the best baker in Siberia! He was a useful member of society. "And such a man the capitalists would have executed!" he roared indignantly as final proof of the wisdom of the good Stalin.

The fate of Levanevski was still my major concern, and I tried to get some news. Sir Hubert Wilkins, my old friend, had already arrived at Prince Patrick Island and was searching in vain for the lost Russian plane. In Tiksi there was a geodetic expedition, equipped with planes, under the leadership of a startlingly beautiful twenty-five-year-old woman. She gave me permission to join the flights of her cartographers who were mapping the Lena delta from the air by stereophotography. We flew over the whole wide delta and far out at sea. And I persuaded them to take me to the New Siberian Islands. While we were waiting for permission from the commander there, a new visitor arrived in Tiksi, a young engineer by the name of Warchavsky. He had saved up a year's vacation to spend in the Arctic, and he had come with a plane that the government had put at his disposal. He was eager to go across to the islands and promised to take me along.

An inspection trip to Moostah Island was arranged before we left, and I went along to this substation of the Arctic outpost. I met the three scientists who spent the summer on this little island consisting mainly of clay, and they showed me the enormous thigh bone of a mammoth sticking out of a clay hill. They claimed that it was at least one hundred thousand years old.

There were some seals near the island and I shot one. I could not make the Russians taste its meat, but one of them gratefully received its fur. I wanted to cook some of the meat, and when I found a red axe hanging on a wall I used it to cut up the animal. The next moment the man in charge of the substation jumped on me. In very correct German he explained that I had committed an appalling crime. The axe was intended for use only in case of fire, as its color should have told me. My guilt was beyond doubt and I would be prosecuted and punished. Beguitcheff came to my defense before my violation of the Soviet law had serious consequences, and I was let off with a fine of ten rubles.

The following day we flew out to the New Siberian Islands in two airplanes, but we did not stay long. We were given a warm welcome by the poor woman who was in charge of the local "hotel" where there had been no guests for more than a year. She lived alone with a grandchild, and she was in seventh heaven because she finally had a chance to prove her skill as a cook. She proved it to excess. She served us hors d'oeuvre of tremendous proportions, followed by several varieties of soup and meat, cakes, pies and *kvass*—the Russian beer that is always a specialty of the house.

Kvass in the Soviet Union is just like baked beans in northern Canada and Alaska. Everyone has his own way of cooking them. We drank a great deal of this beer, which was very good. And we were joined in the meal by the local radio operators who told me they had been in radio contact with Levanevski for several hours after he had left Rudolph Island. He had let them know about the icing of the wings before his signals had suddenly ceased. They insisted he would never be found, and so far they are right. And as I sat there enjoying the tremendous meal I could not help remembering how hard I had tried to join Levanevski in his final flight.

We returned to Tiksi where we were told that Dr. Shimanovski, the head of the Arctic Station, had been appointed professor at a major university, and this promotion was again celebrated by a lavish dinner.

The following day a convoy of ships entered the harbor, among them the *Molotov,* and the captain informed me that he had orders to take Beguitcheff and me back to Archangel, whence I could go home by way of Leningrad.

The *Molotov* was a large and dirty steamer. Beguitcheff and I were given the sick bay to share, and as soon as we were settled the captain asked me for a conference. He had been advised that the ice was very heavy in the Wilkitsky Sound, which we had to go through on our way west along the Siberian coast to Archangel. The captain had received a cable informing him that I was experienced in ice navigation, and he asked me to act as his ice pilot on the long trip ahead of us. Naturally, I was flattered and I promised to help him in any way I could.

Before going into the Wilkitsky Sound we had orders to go to Nordvik with two heavy barges loaded with lumber. Large salt deposits had been discovered in Nordvik, and they were now to be exploited, as they were most important to the Soviet fisheries in the Pacific. The salt, which was necessary for the preservation of the enormous catches of fish, had so far been sent by boat from the Black Sea through the Suez Canal, south of India and up to Kamchatka, or by rail from the Caspian Sea on the long route through Siberia. These new salt deposits in Nordvik on the Arctic Ocean were much closer than the old mines, and the sea lane along the Siberian coast and through Bering Strait was much shorter.

Our departure was constantly delayed because we had to get a convoy together. Time was obviously running short; we were already in the first week of September, and heavy snow had set in. When we were ready to go at last we were told to take on another two hundred tons of coal. Then the next day it was discovered that the *Molotov* had forgotten to take on water. The eighth of September was finally decided upon as the day of departure, and a great farewell party was staged. The next day there was no sign of our leaving, and Beguitcheff and I spent the day in a violent campaign against the bedbugs.

On September 11 we finally went to sea with the barges in tow. In the meantime some fantastic order had resulted in the removal of the rudders from the barges. I protested against attempting passage through heavy ice without rudders. The captain admitted it did seem rather extraordinary, but he had received orders from Moscow and could not discuss them with a foreigner. So with these two helpless barges in tow we finally sailed.

We met ice the very first day. It was not heavy in the bay, and we made our way through it without any trouble. The *Molotov* proved to be a sturdy vessel, taking the bumps and blows in her stride. The barges were worse off. We shortened the two lines as much as we could, but their bows continued to collide violently with the ice. We made our way through it carefully, slowing down when heavy snow began again, and soon we were at a standstill. The *Molotov* had run into a sand bar and could not get off without help.

We unloaded eight hundred tons of ballast and waited for high tide, but it was no use. We had to wait for an oceangoing tug that arrived the following day and pulled us off. We had not suffered any damage and were ready to go on, but we had to wait because both snow and ice got worse. Finally the heavy ice breaker *Malygin* turned up with another steamer from our convoy, the *Vanzetti,* and one barge in tow—all the barges had suffered heavy damage, and we moved slowly in the wake of the *Malygin.*

The ice was softer than I was used to in Greenland and there were no icebergs, but it was still heavy going. The weather turned colder and after two days we had to stop again. There was no possibility of proceeding farther. The *Malygin,* which carried seventy passengers and a crew of one hundred twenty, turned a hose on the ice to make a skating rink. And soon the ice was black with people in a gay holiday spirit in spite of the trouble we were in. And in the evening we were all invited to the movies on board the *Malygin.* One night a young girl settled down on my lap during the film—the sixteen-year-old Sascha, a waitress on one of the barges. The other people from the barges were not allowed on board the *Malygin*—I could not discover why.

The next day we inched our way through the ice and joined the third ship from the convoy, the *Bellamore Kanal.* Further progress was next to impossible, and a conference was called by the political commissar on board the *Vanzetti.* It was decided to abandon all attempts to go west through the ice and to go northeast instead, in order to reach the open sea. By this time all the barges had large holes in the bows, and though they were in no danger since they were loaded with lumber, they slowed us down considerably. I have never suffered a more nightmarish ice voyage. In two days we were north of the ice and turned west once more toward Wilkitsky Sound. But in a few hours we met more ice!

The *Malygin* received a radio message that the whole sound

north of Chelyuskin was choked with ice and completely impassable. A fleet of vessels was waiting there, unable to move. It was obviously useless for us to try to go on, and the commissar called another conference. Cables were dispatched in all directions and replies were anxiously awaited. I was not invited to the conference, but I was asked for advice. I did not try to hide my conviction that it was both ridiculous and contemptible, in a dangerous situation far at sea, to have to ask for orders from Moscow or Yakutsk. In the end it was decided to keep north of the ice, go due east again and try to return to Tiksi with the barges that were partly submerged by now. In Nordvik they were waiting eagerly for the building material we were supposed to bring them, and our return to Tiksi must have upset all the ambitious plans to exploit the salt deposits at once, but we had no choice. I had to sign affidavits and declarations to that effect before we could go east.

It was very pleasant to feel the swell of the open sea again, but probably most uncomfortable for the poor people on the barges. Good-sized cabins had been erected on the decks, but the barges were now so deep in water that every swell washed over the decks. During the night the light wind became very strong and soon developed into a gale. The barges were in a precarious situation. We had to let out the two lines as far as they would go. The violent pitching and heaving were a heavy strain on the lines, and in the dark night we did not dare go on.

In the end the sea proved too heavy for the tow lines. I was on the bridge in the middle of the night when the second mate reported that both of them had broken. We turned about and began an immediate search but it was useless in the dark. To make matters worse it began snowing heavily and we could not use our searchlights. In the morning visibility was still limited, and the snow did not let up until afternoon. When it cleared there was nothing to be seen but a very heavy sea. We searched for hours, and finally we caught sight of the larger of the two barges. It was a miserable sight.

The cabin on deck had partly collapsed and there was nobody to be seen at first. The deck was awash and the waves were crashing over the roof of the cabin. We used our steam whistle and got some action at last. The cabin door opened and we could see a number of people huddled inside the frail shelter. Some of them rushed out at once, but the deck was covered with solid ice, and they could not keep their balance. Four people were washed overboard at once. We tried to rescue them but the sea was too heavy. We lowered a boat, but it was smashed to pieces against the side of our ship. We were forced to give them up and concentrate on the people on the barge. The captain took the *Molotov* up against the wind and stopped the engines, as soon as we had the helpless barge to leeward, and we drifted down to it. The barge passengers apparently thought their troubles were over and rushed onto deck. Again some of them were washed overboard. We heaved our lines to them, but none of them reappeared.

When we were close to the barge we let down the ship's ladder and some Jacob's ladders. The people rushed to grab them and again some fell overboard. There was no panic, they just did not know what to do. They had never been to sea before. The whole crowd on the barge consisted of lumbermen and carpenters, with their families, who had been chosen to go to Nordvik for the construction work.

Three of us from the *Molotov* finally were lowered down by ropes to the deck of the barge; otherwise we would have had no chance of saving anybody. I forgot that I was no longer twenty years old and had a wooden leg. While I was trying to keep my balance on the icy deck of the barge I saw a sight I shall never forget.

A young man was waiting to get hold of the Jacob's ladder hanging down the side of the *Molotov*. The steamer was rolling heavily and the barge was pitching up and down. The only way to get up was, of course, to grab the ladder while the barge was on the crest of a wave and climb up as fast as possible. The young man did not understand the method. He grabbed the ladder while the barge was way down and crawled slowly up the ship's side. He had climbed only a step or two when to my horror I saw the barge lifted up and tossed against the side of the *Molotov,* catching the young man in the middle. His chest, arms and head were above the deck of the barge, the lower part of his body was caught below. I was close by him, and I could have sworn that he was laughing as I saw his mouth stretch in a wide grin.

The wave receded, the barge sank once more, and we stared at the monstrous sight—he was still clinging to the ladder, but the lower part of the body was not there! The barge had cut him in two. Slowly his hands slipped from the ladder, and the upper half of his body disappeared in the sea.

We continued the rescue work at frantic speed. Most of the people were disciplined and knew enough to jump for the ladder at the right moment. An old woman, who did not have the strength to climb the ladder, got a rope around her middle and was hauled on board like a squealing pig. The few that were left did not have the strength or the nerve to leave the cabin and had to be led out, one by one. The last to appear was my little friend Sascha. Her home was deep in the Siberian forest; this was her first trip to sea, and she was paralyzed by fear. I called out to her, but before I could reach her, she had scuttled back to the safety of the cabin. Her stupidity made me so furious I forgot that a wooden leg does not have toes and cannot get a grip on ice. I slipped and fell, but I had sense enough to hold onto the rope I had in my hands.

Suddenly Sascha appeared in the cabin door again. She had returned to pick up her most prized possession—a horrible pink celluloid comb! She carried it in her hands with a triumphant smile.

We held on to each other and slowly made our way across the deck. In the meantime the ship's ladder had broken in two and was useless. I tied the last of the lines hanging down from the *Molotov* around Sascha and watched her being slowly hauled on board.

I was now the only man left on the barge, and I was slowly drifting away from the ship. Three times a line was thrown to me before I was quick enough to get hold of it. At last I caught it, tied it around me, and jumped into the icy water. As I was slowly being pulled to safety I was afraid the barge would catch me as it had that poor young man.

The following morning we finally caught sight of the second barge. It was barely afloat; the deck was submerged and the cabin was gone. All that remained above water was the remnant of a pump. Four men were clinging to it—the only survivors. And we could hardly believe our eyes when we saw that one of the four was stark naked! His body was red as a lobster from the intense cold. The other three were sheltering him as best they could in their weak condition. They were all exhausted from cold, hunger and the struggle to hang on to the pump. They did not have strength enough to catch the lines we threw them, and another man and I climbed down to assist them.

There had been eleven men on the barge. The other seven were lost—some of them had been washed overboard, the others had jumped off, either because they could not stand it or to make it possible for the last few to survive, for only four could hold on to the pump.

Those four had witnessed the terrible struggle of the last man to commit suicide. He had said good-by to his friends and slid off the barge, but he had on heavy sheepskin pants and jackets that kept him from sinking.

In the end one of the four decided to give up the struggle, too. He could not stand the cold any longer and had lost all hope of being rescued. But he wanted to make sure he would sink at once so he had carefully removed his sheepskin jackets and pants, thrown all his clothing into the sea, and was ready to jump when he saw the *Molotov* on the horizon. He quickly changed his mind about dying. Fortunately he was a solid man, well protected by a layer of fat, but his skin was covered by a layer of ice. His arms and legs were not frozen, but they had gone quite numb. He recovered quickly, once we had made him warm and comfortable and had fed him a solid meal. He slept most of the way back to Tiksi.

All the survivors did well, but twenty-seven men lost their lives, and we had a gloomy return trip to Tiksi.

As soon as we arrived in port we were told that Julius Liss had been arrested for Trotskyism and had been taken to Moscow. All our hardships, the loss of life and property were due to his deliberate sabotage, the authorities assured us. Dr. Shimanovski told me that the waters north of Cape Chelyuskin were closed by ice for the winter. Several ships were ice locked and the crews had to be rescued by air, so there would be no more trips to the west until spring.

The stormy weather continued and a number of ships entered the harbor, among them the ice breaker *Sako* with a scientific laboratory on board. The man in charge was an old friend of mine from the Leningrad Congress in 1928, Professor Sajmojlowitch and his colleague Professor Wise.

It had been decided that the *Molotov* should go east around the whole Siberian coast, but before leaving I had to say good-by to my miserable friend Sascha. She had been told to stay in Tiksi during the winter, as there was no way of her getting back to her inland forest home. She did not want to stay among strangers in Tiksi and begged me to take her with me on the *Molotov*. When the voyage was over she could go with me to Moscow, the greatest ambition of her life.

She was bitterly disappointed when I explained that it was impossible. But she was willing to do as I told her and returned to her cabin. She came back with something in her hand. It was a little piece of glittering quartz—from all those whose lives I had saved. She said it was not very valuable, but then the lives I had saved weren't worth much. I still have the little piece of quartz in my possession.

By the end of September we went out to sea again. We were joined by the *Kinigsep* and the *Vanzetti* with one political commissar for the three vessels. This inevitable commissar seemed more necessary than the captain. The weather had changed again—clear nights with northern lights. Over our heads wild geese flew in great numbers, going from north to southeast.

We had only two hundred fifty tons of coal on board. There had been no more in Tiksi due to the sabotage of my old friend Liss, I was told. We moved east with a speed of eight miles an hour, since the three ships had to stay together and the slowest set the pace. We had only two inches of water under the keel, but the captain was not worried about running aground again. The bottom was soft all along the coast, padded with hundreds of thousands of years of sawdust.

The slow voyage was monotonous, and I spent my days studying conditions on board our ship. I was amazed to see the oilers and the firemen drop in on the captain in the chart room to discuss our progress. The morale on board was very good, a pronounced spirit of friendship and cooperation, but the officers and the crew had separate quarters and ate in separate messes. The commissar switched from one mess to the other. The men were all cordial to me, but there were always many things they did not talk about.

There were many good chess players on board. In our ward room the doctor was the champion, and in the crew's quarters one of the firemen was a master at the game. He was a very intelligent man who spoke English, French and German. But I could not make him tell me anything about his past. We had a stewardess, however, who was most eager to tell all about her life. Her name was Maria Abrahamnovna and she had been a concert singer in Moscow. She had been exiled to this Siberian freighter as a punishment for some crime. She did not care to talk about it, but as soon as her term was up she planned to return to her career.

We went into the harbor at Cape Chelagsky where we got

more coal and where the large ice breaker *Krassin* was waiting for us. This huge vessel could break through any ice in the Arctic and had just come from Alaska. I visited the captain who lived in very luxurious quarters. He spoke English fluently, told me the latest news from Alaska and gave me as a gift a full year's supply of the *Cosmopolitan* magazine, which was very useful on the *Molotov* where I had no reading matter. He sent a greeting for me to Charles Brewer at Point Barrow and to Sir Hubert Wilkins on Prince Patrick Island, and he told me of the current rumor in Alaska that Levanevski had been heard from. He was supposed to be somewhere near eighty-three degrees north, one hundred and seventy-three degrees west—a report that turned out to be unfounded.

Once again we were on our way, plowing through hundreds and hundreds of miles of Arctic Ocean until we reached Wrangel Island, where the political commissars for the region had a big conference. I took the opportunity to visit some scientists who were on an expedition to excavate a number of mammoths. I saw no less than nine partly excavated giant animals. One of the men gave me a bit of hair from the skin. But the moment I touched it, it became a dot of black powder in my hand. These relics were all to be preserved by a secret process and taken back to Moscow by air.

We left Wrangel Island behind, changed our course to the south and entered Bering Strait. Once more I set foot on Diomede Island—this time Great Diomede and not Little Diomede which I had visited without permission many years ago. And thus I had traveled around the world. The circle was small, true enough, since it had always been so far to the north, and the total distance was probably only half of the length my friends in the Circumnavigators' Club in New York had traveled. But still I had gone around the world and was qualified for membership in this exclusive club.

We passed the international date line and made it an occasion for great celebrations. The captain proved to be an expert Cossack dancer, but our stewardess Maria Abrahamnovna had no difficulty in outshining the amateur performers. We had a chess tournament which the mysterious fireman easily won.

A stormy passage through the strait took us eventually past East Cape. Soon we rounded Cape Chapman and arrived in Provigeniya—to me the most attractive spot in all of Siberia because the only Eskimos under Soviet rule lived there. They had settled on one side of the fjord with the Arctic Station on the other. The arrival of a white man who spoke Eskimo had been announced, and I was met by a deputation of four Eskimo women who rowed me across. A meeting in my honor had been called in the schoolhouse. I was delighted to find that I could easily understand their language. They had many of the same names as the people in Greenland and Hudson Bay.

All in all there were two thousand Eskimos living in the area; twenty families were living on Wrangel Island. The Soviet government granted free transport to any Eskimo who wanted to go to Wrangel, provided he remained there for a minimum of two years. And every year the Provigeniya colony had contact with the St. Lawrence Island Eskimos who were American subjects. They traveled across the strait by boats in summer and dog sleds in winter.

The Soviet rule had abolished all churches, and the clergymen were without jobs. Some of them had left, others had settled down with the Eskimos, a few had married them. As soon as the churches were closed the Eskimos returned to their old religion, which had been dormant during two hundred and fifty years of Christianity. The Eskimos had been baptized Christians for generations, but the old pagan cult had been kept alive without the knowledge of the white rulers. The *angakok*—the native witch doctor—was ready to take over where the minister left off, spoke the sacred angakok language and was apparently familiar with the old ritual.

Before we continued south the *Molotov* got a new chief engineer—a charming girl—and we took on a number of passengers.

The political commissar moved to the *Vanzetti,* presumably because his political influence was more necessary there than on the *Molotov,* and we were ready to be on our way once more. The Eskimos showered me with gifts when I said good-by—tools and household goods to show to my friends in Greenland. They were all packed in a crate, the contents carefully written down, and Beguitcheff promised I would get the crate in Moscow. I never saw it again.

Two days out of Provigeniya we received orders to proceed to Korf in northern Kamchatka to load salted fish for Vladivostok, and after another stormy passage we entered Korf Bay, one of the most valuable fishing centers in Eastern Siberia.

I was interested in inspecting this organized fishery. There were three bases in Korf leased to the Japanese, all closed to foreigners. At first I was not allowed to visit the Russian stations either, but as soon as Moscow cleared me by cable I was allowed to go everywhere. And I visited the native Koryaks, who though they resemble the Eskimos speak a different language. Some of them fortunately spoke a little English and some Russian. I inspected their particular wooden houses and collected some hunting tools, an open kayak and some harpoons of an ingenious design. I got together a very valuable collection which the authorities promised to forward to the Ethnographic Museum in Copenhagen. I never saw it again.

There were fifteen hundred people employed in Korf Bay, all of them Russians and many of them women who dressed just like the men. A group of sixty, half of them women, boarded the *Molotov* to take care of the loading. Sampans came alongside with loads of salmon and herring, but we had a great deal of trouble before we were fully loaded.

The *Molotov* was in bad repair, the boilers were being repaired constantly, and in Korf something had to be done to them again. The water had to be changed and we had to cross the bay to another base for water. Trusting providence, the engine crew emptied the boilers, but before we could fill them up with fresh water a terrible gale threatened to drive us ashore. The anchors barely stood the strain of the terrific wind which lasted for forty-eight hours. The second mate, who had been ashore when the gale began, could not get back on board, and the loading crew of sixty men and women could not get back to shore. They slept in the coal bunker, which amused them greatly, but they insisted that the *Molotov* pay their cleaning bills.

I went ashore to visit the enormous barracks where the people worked and lived. The women appeared clumsy and oversized in their padded clothes, but they showed me snapshots taken during vacations in which they looked quite different. Their hard work entitled them to four months' vacation every year, and most of them went back to Russia. During the summer several of them lived in Crimean palaces of former princes. The pictures showed them in snappy bathing suits or playing tennis dressed in white-flannel slacks or spotless shirts—a curious existence. They earned a lot of money, but they had to work hard for it.

Something was wrong with the boilers again, and the engineer could get no steam for the winches until he filled up with fresh water again. We were all put to work, crew and passengers. There was a call for volunteers to work the pumps in the water boat, and I was stupid enough to respond—partly because I wanted to watch one of the volunteers, a Valkyrie by the name of Marja. She was mild and friendly in spite of her terrific strength, and the two of us joined forces in the boat, where the pump had to be worked by hand. I had been looking forward to this chance of talking to her, but the pumping took every ounce of my strength.

We had to take some passengers along from Korf to Petropavlovsk, but before leaving we had to get more coal, which meant going across the bay to the coal pier. In the meantime the weather turned bad again and the anchorage by the coal pier was dangerous. So we decided to load coal from another ship in the harbor, which proved just as hard in the heaving sea. Before we gave up the job one man had broken a leg, another man had been crushed to pieces.

Two days later we managed to load eighty tons of coal. We needed four hundred tons, but we had no chance of getting it and put out to sea with what we had. The voyage down to Petropavlovsk was miserable as the Pacific showed its most unpleasant side. We had engine trouble constantly, but the Valkyrie who was our chief engineer looked more striking than ever when she appeared covered with oil and dirt. Thanks to my hard work, however, we had enough fresh water on board for showers, and she was spotless when she appeared at meals. Beguitcheff gave talks every evening, some of them slightly surprising. Once when describing the horrors of American capitalist society, he happened to pick on the Ford plants in Detroit. The automobile workers were slaves, he told his audience; they were so exhausted when they left the job at night, they could hardly stand on their feet. And on Sundays they slept twenty-four hours, they aged early and died young.

For once I had to protest vigorously. I had been in Detroit, I told him, and I had seen the town and visited the plants. I had seen what Ford had done for his workers—the churches he had built, the schools, the hospitals, the athletic fields and movies. I told him that every worker had his own car. I told him about the city Ford had built for the workers on his rubber plantation in South America.

Beguitcheff was deeply impressed—particularly by the fact that the American workers owned their own cars. He asked me again and again if it was true. The following day I was called by the political commissar who asked the same questions.

As we sailed down the Kamchatka coast I was looking forward to our visit to the Kommandorskie Islands where my great countryman Vitrus Behring was buried. I went ashore with the captain and Beguitcheff, and we were well received by the commandant, who served us tea and fresh cake but refused our request for more coal. And I was allowed to visit Behring's grave. A rusty chain roped off his final resting place, and there were a few old cannon balls in each corner. I told the commandant that we were preparing to celebrate the two hundredth anniversary of Behring in Denmark and asked if I might take four of those cannon balls home. He promised to send them to me in Copenhagen at once. They never got there.

The next stop was Petropavlovsk where a harbor pilot took us into its excellent port. The first day nobody was allowed on shore, all passports were checked, every person on board was cross-examined. The examiners were unable to understand why I was on board, and the fact that I expressed a desire to go ashore was considered highly suspicious. In the end I managed to get a landing permit, and I went ashore with the beautiful first engineer. We had hardly entered the town before she met a friend and deserted me. I walked on alone through the streets and stopped by the windows of a bookstore to inspect its literature.

Then I walked on to look at the city, but I soon returned to the bookstore, which seemed more interesting, and was immediately approached by a policeman who carried a carbine equipped with a murderous-looking bayonet. He arrested me on the spot. When I protested he asked for my passport which I promptly showed him, but he waved it aside and took me to the police station. An officer who knew some English asked me all sorts of questions. I answered rather angrily that I was in the Soviet Union as the guest of the government in Moscow, and I considered the arrest an outrageous insult.

"Kindly explain your lengthy stay by the bookstore," he returned, quite unimpressed by my words. "Why did you stay there for so long a time when you had already examined the store?"

So I had been followed all the way! I told him that I was an author and, consequently, inclined to be interested in books. This explanation was quite unacceptable, and after some hurried consultation I was returned to the ship under guard and forbidden to go on shore again.

The following day was November 7, the twentieth anniversary of the revolution—a great celebration for everybody except me. Beguitcheff told me happily that I had been invited to watch the parade from the specially erected stand of the district commissar, but I refused. I had been forbidden to go ashore and I would not leave ship unless I received an official apology. Beguitcheff left and soon the captain turned up with a policeman to advise me that my landing permit had been restored.

"I am not interested," I told him. "I'll remain on board and I shall report the incident when I return to Moscow."

They left, rather disturbed, and in another hour I received my recompense. An aide from the office of the commissar arrived with a personal invitation for me to view the parade as his official guest. I gave in and saw a most impressive performance of the many troops in Kamchatka. The public was in ecstasy, particularly when the Partisans came riding by on their small sturdy horses. I was told that the Partisans had liberated Kamchatka from the Japanese and were the idols of the populace. The celebrations lasted all day and most of the night, and when it was all over I was free to wander about Petropavlovsk —for a while at least.

I visited the palace of the former governor, which was now "Propaganda House." The magnificent rooms had been kept intact with all their original lavish furnishings. I visited an exhibition of old torture instruments and was invited to speak to the Club of Former Convicts, a very exclusive organization of those who had been sentenced to hard labor and deported to Siberia under the Tzar. They had been compelled to walk from Russia to Kamchatka, the soldiers had whipped them on during the forced marches from prison camp to prison camp through heat and cold across the Siberian plains.

A regiment of soldiers had supposedly marched the same long

way from Moscow, as a result of a practical joke played on them by Tzar Nicholas I. After a six-hour drill on the parade grounds of the Kremlin he had opened the gates and given them the order "March to Kamchatka!" No one could countermand the imperial order, and the soldiers that survived kept on marching until they reached the Pacific Coast.

Our stay in Petropavlovsk stretched out to nearly two weeks because our boilers were in urgent need of repairs, which could not be arranged without official permission from Moscow. We were finally moved from our pier to the naval yard, which had recently been completed, but there had been no time yet to build houses for the workers and their families, more than five thousand in all. They lived mostly in tents where they must have suffered terribly in the cold, which was already intense in November. The workers and the officers were friendly people, but as suspicious in Kamchatka as everywhere else in the Soviet Union.

I used to have lunch in a restaurant in the company of a young naval officer whose ship was lying next to the *Molotov*. As an old sailor I naturally discussed the sea—and our ships— with him. One day I asked him how large his ship was, but his answer was very vague. A few days later I happened to ask the speed of his ship. The next day I inquired about the size of his crew.

Suddenly the pleasant young officer jumped from his chair. "You are pumping me!" he screamed. "You are trying to pry out of me the size of my ship, the crew, the engines, everything. I could have you arrested for espionage and deported at once." He would let me go on one condition, he said. I had to remain on board ship during the rest of our stay in Petropavlovsk, and should I be seen alone in town again he would put me behind bars, no matter who had invited me to visit the holy land of Stalin!

Once more I was detained on board and saw little of Petropavlovsk after that. In the meantime winter had set in, the inner harbor was covered with ice, and we moved to the outer basin, which was kept open by an ice breaker. At last the coal steamer from Vladivostok arrived, and with a limited supply of fuel on board we were ready to move south. A farewell party was given in the clubhouse on shore, and I was invited to give a talk on Greenland. Beguitcheff acted as my interpreter, but I was doubtful about his translation, particularly when I heard the name of Stalin frequently mentioned.

On a beautiful winter morning we left the smoking volcanoes of Kamchatka behind us and slowly plowed our way through the Pacific at a speed of six miles an hour. We passed Cape Lopatka, the southern tip of Kamchatka, and ran into one of the worst storms I have ever experienced as we met the full fury of the Sea of Okhotsk. We had planned to go inside the Kurile Islands, but one of our boilers went out of commission again and we had to seek shelter by going east of the island chain. By now our speed was reduced to less than four miles an hour.

December 1, when we sighted the lighthouse on the tip of Hokkaido Island, the northern end of Japan, we were getting critically low in coal. The following day we entered the Sangarski Straits between Hokkaido and Honshu, and the captain radioed to Vladivostok for permission to enter a Japanese harbor to get more coal. We were ordered to proceed without a delay. Our coal should last until we were in the middle of the Sea of Japan where a tug would meet us. The Russian authorities expected war to break out at any moment and did not want to risk leaving any Russian vessel in Japanese waters.

We had a strong tail wind which, combined with the current, saw us safely through the strait. But once we were in the Sea of Japan all hell broke loose. We ran into heavy gales, one boiler was still out of commission, and the other had so many leaks we could hear the whistle of escaping steam all over the ship. The screw did not turn enough to steer the ship, and we had run out of fresh water!

We had been adrift in the Sea of Japan for a few days when

the *Anadir* finally came out to tow us to Vladivostok. After standing by for twenty-four hours she tried to get close enough to heave a line over, but the art of seamanship was apparently lacking on the *Anadir* and the two boats collided! Fortunately the *Molotov* suffered no hurt. The other vessel had been damaged above the waterline, but was able to proceed toward Vladivostok with us in tow. We had been guaranteed a speed of eight miles, but we never managed to better a mile and a half an hour. The engines were dead, the pumps had stopped, and we had to man them twenty-four hours a day. But all our troubles were forgotten when we finally entered the harbor of Vladivostok on December 8.

I went straight to the wonderful Hotel Chelyuskin and dined with Beguitcheff on soup, roast goose and ice cream—an unforgettable meal after all our weeks at sea. The customary visit to the passport office was next on our agenda, and as soon as we had our necessary papers, Beguitcheff announced proudly that he had secured our passage to Moscow on the Trans-Siberian Railroad that very night. Our train was two hours late in starting, but we were finally well installed in a comfortable compartment and were on our way back to Moscow.

Two hours out of Vladivostok we were awakened by a terrible crash. Our train had run head on into another one; the two locomotives were derailed and the first four cars of our train were broken to bits. We were in the fifth!

We were told that no one was killed, but we were not allowed to leave our car to inspect the wreck. We had to stay in our compartment until morning when we were slowly pulled back to Vladivostok. We were not allowed to return to our hotel and had to wait in the railroad station until a new train was set up late at night. But we were well taken care of in the officers' clubroom, and in the evening we were installed once more in a comfortable compartment.

The passengers, however, were not so agreeable as those who had kept me company going east from Moscow. One man seemed to dominate the crowd, a "gold king" from the Koljma district in Eastern Siberia. He boasted to me about the fights on the barricades with Lenin during the revolution and about his power in Koljma. Forty thousand people in his district had to obey his slightest command! He seemed to me a most objectionable type—no less a tyrant than the Tartar princes he had replaced. He insisted on drinking with me, and when I refused he was furious.

Beguitcheff explained that I never touched alcohol, which did not make matters better. He expressed his profound contempt for me to the whole train. I told him to behave like a civilized person and to leave me alone. There were several passengers present and they were all horrified. One could not speak like that to the District Commissar of Koljma, Beguitcheff warned me, but we never saw the man in our compartment again.

The first day out of Vladivostok we passed Khabarovsk, a city in the middle of the vast plains. It was snowing heavily, but when I looked out I could still see rows of airplanes in all directions. I did not think there could be that many airplanes in the world, let alone in one district of Siberia, but some officers on the train told me calmly that the Soviet was, of course, arming for revenge against the Japanese.

I settled down to go through the old numbers of *Politiken* that had been forwarded to me in Vladivostok, and when I came across a picture of Trotsky I showed it to Beguitcheff. He was breathless with excitement, carefully wrote down a translation of the caption under the portrait and asked for permission to show it to some friends in the train. I never saw the picture again. Some time later we began once more our endless discussion about Stalin. The difference between the Western European and the Russian press, Beguitcheff said, was that Stalin in his infinite wisdom first read everything, weeded out all the lies and distortions and finally gave the people the unvarnished truth. In Scandinavia the readers were, of course, filled with nonsense and lies.

I asked him whether a Russian newspaper would be allowed to print a cartoon of Stalin. Beguitcheff was amazed at the mere idea. How could one! There was nothing about Stalin one could possibly ridicule. When I showed him a copy of *Politiken* with an amusing cartoon of our Danish king he was dumbfounded. Once more he asked to borrow the paper, and I never saw it again.

December 12 was election day, a festive day eagerly awaited on board "the train that speeds from east to west through the greatest country in the world." Several "election meetings" had been arranged with countless speakers "discussing" the election issues, in other words competing in their praise of Stalin. The train stopped at a polling place en route, and we all went out in the bright winter day with a temperature of forty-five degrees below zero. It did not seem very cold since it was dry and sunny. All the propaganda and all the election posters were superfluous to me since there was only one legal ballot!

One by one the passengers were shuffled into the private booth—even I! As a proof of Russian hospitality foreigners were welcome to vote, Beguitcheff explained to me. As we went on our way again the atmosphere in the train was tense until the election outcome was announced—one hundred percent of the passengers and crew on the train had voted for Stalin!

We stopped for hours in Petrovski-Savotsk where the Decabrists had been sent into exile, and we saw an endless train with convicts pass by, men and women in freight cars peering at us through the narrow barred slits. Armed soldiers guarded them, looking like giants in their heavy winter clothes, but the prisoners did not carry much protection against the cold. An appalling sight! The next day we stopped for five hours in Illanskaja, and more prison trains passed us, all of them going east, farther into Siberia.

In a heavy snowstorm we crossed Yenisei. Soon the great River Ob was behind us and we were approaching Europe. The bare steppes now were covered with beautiful white birches, and we rode through forests once more. But when we were approaching Moscow I had my revenge on the arrogant "gold king" from Koljma. The train was suddenly stopped and a number of policemen entered all the compartments. This was something more serious than the usual passport checking. I was ordered to remain in my compartment, but Beguitcheff disappeared. He told me later that the master of all Koljma was the man the police were after. He was picked up with two girl friends, arrested and handcuffed and removed from the train. I saw the prisoners being marched off and I have never seen a man's back express such despair. No one dared give him a greeting, tell him good-by or wish him well.

That night I arrived back in Moscow after a round trip of nine months. Magda and Pipaluk had returned to Denmark shortly after I had left for Siberia, but my friend Michailov from the Arctic Trust was on hand and escorted me to the Hotel Moskva. I had a hard time getting into the hotel because my passport had expired and it was, consequently, against the rule to give me a room. Michailov arranged it on condition that I stay in my room until he returned the next day, and I settled down in this wonderfully luxurious new hotel.

In the morning Beguitcheff turned up with a very grave fact. My passport did not carry the required visas. It had been insufficiently stamped in Vladivostok.

"It looks as if we shall have to return to Vladivostok for the right stamps!"

I was really worried. The trip had been wonderful, I insisted, I was very grateful for what he had done for me and for the Russian hospitality, but a return trip to Vladivostok? No, definitely no.

Beguitcheff promised to do his best, and we began a wild chase through various government offices to get my papers in order. Glasewmorput was the first stop. Beguitcheff disappeared and I went to see my friend Janssen, the director. The same young secretary sat outside his office, but she told me that Janssen was not in.

"Hasn't he arrived yet?" I asked.

"No, he has not arrived."

"When will he be here?"

"I am not sure he will be here today."

"Is he on vacation?"

"No, not vacation."

"Was he here yesterday?"

Apparently not and he was not expected the next day. Nobody was quite sure when he would be in.

Beguitcheff called for me and took me to see my old friend Professor Otto Juliewitch Schmidt, whom I told about my experiences. We agreed to meet again the following day, and Beguitcheff and I started off again. As we left I told my friend that I had not been able to see Janssen, and Beguitcheff was quite horrified.

"Don't you know that Janssen has been removed? He was found to be a Trotskyist of the worst sort, a dangerous enemy of the state!"

It was a stroke of luck that he had been captured before he could do more damage than he had already done, according to Beguitcheff. Julius Liss had obviously been one of his accomplices, and Janssen was, no doubt, responsible for all our mishaps and troubles.

In the end the Danish embassy cleared my passport for me, but I was not allowed to leave. There were no plane reservations available. And the limousine which had been put at my disposal suddenly disappeared. I began to notice a distinctly cool atmosphere. I had invited a number of friends to a farewell dinner, but most of them were suddenly prevented from coming. I don't know what happened, but the few people who did turn up were all quite worried because they had not been warned in time to decline my invitation.

In my hotel that night I received a letter from an English

journalist, Tom Bell, who asked me to come and see him at the Hotel Savoy the moment I got his note. The mysterious letter sounded promising and I took the elevator downstairs at once. I was quite convinced that I was being shadowed everywhere in Moscow, and to be on the safe side I walked around a few blocks, ducked into a dark alley and had the satisfaction of seeing my shadow pass by and disappear.

Tom Bell turned out to be an English communist writer who had lived in the Soviet Union for several months. He told me he could not get out, and he did not know why—or so he said. He asked me if I had my exit permit. And when he heard that I had my passport he urged me to come and see him immediately before my departure, as he had something important to tell me. I was not eager to carry any secret messages from him or to be party to any kind of conspiracy, and I failed to see why he had asked me to go to his hotel at this late hour. But as he had roused my curiosity I promised to do as he asked.

Before I was finally cleared the next day and had my passport back again, I was called before a three-man board at the central police station. They had a great many questions to ask me— probably the reason for the cool atmosphere I had noticed on my return to Moscow. A magistrate was in charge of the cross-examination, but he was polite and cordial and began by bringing me a personal greeting from a friend of mine, the former Soviet minister in Copenhagen, Timeneff.

Their questions dealt exclusively with the tragedy in the Arctic Ocean when I had been aboard the *Molotov*. They wanted to know what had led to the great loss of lives and who was responsible, and I told them my honest opinion about the way things had been handled, particularly the stupid instructions to remove the rudders from our barges. In the end I was offered tea and wonderful candy, they thanked me for my cooperation, and I was free to leave.

I hurried back to my hotel to finish my packing and tried to get rid of my constant shadow, a woman interpreter. She was not going to leave me until I was safely installed in my train, she assured me, and only very reluctantly did she let me take a bath without her personal participation. By telling her that I needed a nap I finally evaded her and sneaked out to the Hotel Savoy and Tom Bell. The poor man told me again that he was not allowed to leave Russia. He asked me to take along a letter from him and mail it as soon as I was back in Denmark. It was only a note to his wife, he insisted, and although I did not quite believe him I agreed to take the letter. To be on the safe side I put it inside my hollow wooden leg.

Beguitcheff saw me off in the evening, accompanied by his oldest son, who was most eager to have me tell him about the disaster in the Arctic Sea. His father was not willing to admit that things had not gone strictly according to the plans of the infallible Soviet authorities, and he begged me not to disillusion his son. Beguitcheff introduced me to some Red Army officers who shared my compartment and who played chess with me most of the way to Leningrad.

A representative of VOKS met me to take me to the Arctic Institute to meet some Siberian Eskimos and to get all the photographs of my long voyage. I had been allowed to use my camera everywhere—on condition that my films be developed in Leningrad. And the Russian hospitality was magnificent until the very last. Before boarding my train for Finland, I went to a department store to buy gifts for my family and friends. With my keen sense of economy my purchases were very modest, and I was very angry when I found out that I could have bought out the whole store, since VOKS would not let me pay for a thing. I was a guest and it was all part of their hospitality.

In Helsinki I left behind all my clothes and got a complete new wardrobe and at last I was free of bugs. The hotel management was used to travelers from the Soviet Union; all my clothes and even my suitcases were disinfected. I was ready to board my ship on Christmas Eve. We celebrated Christmas on the Baltic Sea, and two days later I was back in Copenhagen where Magda was waiting at the station with a crowd of reporters who kept me from letting my own newspaper have a scoop about my nine months adventure in Siberia.

WORLD WAR II

Underground

After his return from Russia, Freuchen lived for a time with his family at a farm he had bought years before on the Danish island of Enehoie. They were engaged in getting in the harvest with the help of the maturing Pipaluk's admirers when World War II broke out. There was no question of where the by now famous writer-explorer's sympathies lay; the farm had been a haven for German refugees from Nazism, and five of them were still there on April 8, 1940. That evening Peter saw a great fleet of ships steaming North, then clouds of war planes flying toward what he presumed was a massive attack on England. Only the next morning did he learn that Denmark itself had been the objective of the invaders.

His first concern was to get the refugees to safety, then to wonder how a man in his fifties with one leg could best fight the Germans. He had to sell the farm, partly because his wife's health had been poor there, and she had taken a small apartment in Copenhagen where she had spent half her time anyway.

He was obviously disappointed that there was no chance for a real armed Danish resistance to the invaders. In fact, he said later, life during the early days of the occupation went on pretty much as before with very few Germans in evidence. But when, in the selection which follows, he speaks of the change in his life, it was not of this that he thought. The chapter that closed was the chapter of his life as a farmer on Enehoie; in leaving that place he felt that he had lost his roots as he had after he left his home in Thule. But the problems of the war quickly submerged for him all personal considerations.

411

One chapter of my life was at an end. A new and stormy one was about to open. After a few weeks spent in our apartment in Copenhagen, we moved with Pipaluk into a house we had bought a short distance outside the city—a beautiful old house in the suburb of Birkeröd. While I was still in Copenhagen I had a visitor, an old acquaintance, who told me a little of what was going on below the surface. He was a cautious man, a characteristic I had yet to acquire, and he asked me many vague general questions. How long did I think the German occupation would last? What did I think of the Hitler-Stalin alliance? Did I expect Germany to win the war? I did not know much about politics, and I was quite outspoken in my replies. No matter what happened the Allies would win the war, I assured him. And I told him without hesitation that life in a Nazi Denmark was not worth living.

When he left he warned me not to be so outspoken. How could I be so sure he was not a German agent? True enough, I said, but I did not care who knew my opinions. I had chosen my side and I did not want to keep it secret. Patiently the man explained that such an attitude might be praiseworthy, but it impaired my usefulness in the struggle ahead. I got the impression I had been tested by one of the many patriotic groups that were being organized in those early days, and I was eager to hear from him again.

While I waited in our new house in Birkeröd I had visitors of a less pleasant kind. I was looking out my window one morning, boiling at the sight of German soldiers maching by, when the doorbell rang and three strangers with grave faces entered my room. They mentioned their names and produced some legal papers. Two of them were attorneys, the third a magistrate. They had heard that I had recently purchased this new house and they had come to disposses me! I told them that the house belonged to my wife and that the deed had been made out to her. In reply they read aloud a document which advised me that bankruptcy proceedings had been instituted against me in the magistrate's court, where I must appear at once.

I could barely control my indignation when I perceived, through all the legal double talk, that the firm which was now suing me carried the family name, Freuchen & Company, and was still operated by two of my cousins, the same men who had swindled me when I bought Enehoie fourteen years before. I still owed them twenty thousand kroner, they claimed, for which sum they wanted to ruin me.

I went at once to my attorney in Copenhagen, who told me not to worry about such a trifle. There would be no bankruptcy once he was through with my relatives. He talked to them and warned them that they would suffer from the publicity as soon as it was known they had sued their own cousin, the grandson of the founder of their business. They called off their legal action, and as soon as my publishers began paying me royalties the matter was settled.

The triumphant advance of the Nazi hordes concerned us deeply that early summer. Our mood was grim, shortages became acute, rationing and restrictions of every kind ruled our lives. Many food items were already unobtainable, and fuel would obviously be very short during the winter. Those of us who had gardens with big trees were well off in that respect. One day three young men called to suggest that I cut down some of the larger trees. They would do the job in return for some wood. I liked their language and their bearing, so I accepted the offer and joined them when they went to work.

We got to talking and I learned that woodcutting was just a pretext. Their main job was to find out if I could be trusted. They were looking for hideouts for British agents who were being dropped by parachutes. Would I join them and put my place at their disposal?

They did not put it as bluntly as that, of course. Approaching new men was always a risky business, and there was a great deal of double talk before we finally got to the point. I naturally agreed and the whole matter was soon settled. Their leader left immediately, but the other two finished their job before going on to the neighbors to offer their services. They had to play their part to the last detail.

The first English parachutist to be entrusted to me arrived a few days later; he had landed in the fields a short distance from my house. I was impressed by his equipment. He brought his own food, a bicycle, even a shovel with which to bury his parachute as soon as he landed. He was soon followed by many such agents, and it was my job to provide a safe hiding place, to keep curious people away when the parachutists dropped, and to cover up their tracks—as I had to do one morning when a neighbor saw that someone had been digging in his garden. He discovered the parachute, and his wife was eager to use the strong silk to make clothes for their two children. I had to persuade them to keep the clothes hidden for the duration, since parachute silk was easily identifiable.

Late one evening I had a dramatic visitor—a young man who told me, after the usual beating about the bush, that he was a member of a sabotage group whose task it was to blow up bridges and railroads. The members consisted mainly of young patriots who were in need of a more experienced man as their leader. He asked if I would take the job.

I could not talk to him in my house, I said. We must go into the garden. He praised my precaution and urged me to help him and his friends in their patriotic work. But I had learned to be careful by then, and I said I was opposed to all this lawless underground business. I intended to abide by the instructions of the Danish authorities, and he had better tell his friends to forget me.

Two days later I met a colleague in our underground work and we compared notes. He had been visited by the same man and urged to become the leader of the same "sabotage group." The fellow obviously was a German agent. We had to be constantly on the alert.

I was asked if I could find a good hiding place for the arms and ammunition that were to be delivered by parachutes, and I found a large old garden shed which had long been in disuse. Once in a while I was asked to pick up the material that had been dropped at night. I remember the first time I was asked to pick up some machine guns which had been concealed in the Grip forest. We had no car at our disposal, and we could not use a horse and wagon at night. The first move was to take the arms from their temporary hiding place to a house by the edge of the forest. Since I never had had a machine gun in my hands before and did not want to meet the Germans without being able to use the weapon, I urged one of my friends, a lieutenant in the army, to join us.

He organized the expedition very efficiently, and we agreed to approach the forest from different sides at three o'clock in the morning and to move toward the hiding place we had been shown on the map. There were eight of us on the job, half would carry the arms, the other half would distract pursuers. We had to cover quite a distance by bicycle before we divided and approached the forest from the appointed directions. Seven of us were on hand, the missing man was suspected of being unreliable. But when we met at the hiding place in the forest we found the arms were gone. There were signs of recent digging, nothing else. We were afraid of betrayal and parted at once. I got home safely, although I was expecting a bullet in my back at any moment.

Later on we found out that another underground group had moved the arms, but we had no idea who they were or what happened to the weapons. Each unit was kept an entity in order to reduce to a minimum the danger of implicating others in case of arrest and torture.

I got my wind up one morning when I saw two sinister-looking men coming out of my garden shed where I kept revolvers, time bombs and other interesting material. I ran out to investigate, but they just said they were hard up and had taken shelter in my garden overnight. They asked for cigarettes and matches and disappeared. Later on I found out they were my superiors in the underground movement. They had come to check up on me and the supplies.

Our work was interrupted temporarily when one British parachutist was killed in his fall. His neck was broken when we found him. The parachute had failed to open. A few days later one small group was betrayed to the Germans by a member. They were all arrested except the traitor, who was killed by the underground and dropped in a lake with heavy stones tied to the body. Unfortunately the body was discovered by the Germans, and we were all ordered to lie low for a while.

My lectures gave me a good excuse to travel around the country, and I was often used as a courier. Most of my lectures were fictitious, but for appearance's sake I made a few engagements and I saw to it that I was paid in the presence of the right kind of witnesses. I went about the country without much interference, and I took with me illegal papers and often dangerous stuff—weapons and explosives.

In due time we resumed activities in my district, and our first objective was a nearby factory working full time for the enemy. We decided to blow up the whole plant, but all the details must be arranged before we could operate. We knew we must have a doctor in case a saboteur got hurt. We could not risk taking an injured person to an unknown doctor or to a hospital. I approached a young man in Copenhagen who was eager to help us. Unfortunately two days before we were due to carry out our plans he could not resist the temptation to boast at a party of his great secret. He was a member of the underground, he said, and he was going to take care of the wounded after a big explosion that would come off in a few days.

We were told about his stupid talk that night, and we had to cancel our plans. Some of our men were so incensed they wanted to "execute the traitor at once." The next time he boasted he might reveal the name of his contact—in this case myself—and thus endanger the entire group. I managed to prevent any such drastic action, but once more we had to go into hiding. Some time later another group blew the factory to bits, and it was never rebuilt during the occupation.

All my life I had been used to speaking my mind without any serious thought of consequences, but this habit of not guarding my tongue was a great handicap during the war. I learned to be careful, but sometimes I was sorely tempted. In my own suburb of Birkeröd the Danish Nazis organized a camp for its youth movement, and we were constantly exposed to the sight of these traitors marching and singing all over the neighborhood. It was less depressing than we expected, since the recruits were mostly the mentally retarded or the juvenile delinquent. But their presence was most objectionable—particularly on commuters' trains. They were loud-voiced and abusive, and I seemed to be their favorite target.

I managed to keep my self-control, but I was unable to resist the challenge of a broadcast over the Danish State Radio. A well-known lawyer had been giving a series of talks on the greatness of Der Fuehrer and the blessings of Nazism. He finished by condemning all sabotage as indefensible stupidity. Every day brought more evidence of the growing strength of the underground, and this fellow traveler was trying to persuade his countrymen to take no part in these "criminal acts." His main argument was that so far not one reliable Dane had dared to raise his voice in defense of these bolshevik acts of terror. Finally he offered to guarantee no retaliation if anyone would appear with him and speak over the radio in favor of sabotage.

I could not resist this offer. I wrote him at once accepting the proposal. He repeated his guarantee, and a date was set for our radio appearance. I prepared my script carefully, but the day before I was due to go on the air I was warned to stay away. A representative from the underground came from Copenhagen to tell me that the Nazis planned to shoot me a few blocks from the broadcasting house. I was ordered to cancel my appearance, and I heard no more of the affair.

The underground movement was slowly being better organized; the early confusion and overlapping were eliminated. Each unit was kept separate, and we learned to take better precautions. For the first time in my life I had to discontinue my habit of keeping a diary. I have no longer a clear picture of the course of events, but a few episodes do stand out in my mind.

There was lawlessness everywhere. Irresponsible persons conducted their own private kind of warfare in a most irregular way. I still remember the day when two of my group went off to Odense one morning on a private errand. They left at eight o'clock, arrived in Odense at noon, and went straight from the station to a small grocery store. The owner was alone behind the counter, and without a word they shot and killed him and returned to the station. They were met by their local contact who told them that the storekeeper was loyal. It was his son they were supposed to kill. All right, there was still time enough for a small matter of murder before they had to catch their train back home. They returned to the store, killed the son and caught their train.

The underground gradually developed into an efficient machine that never gave the Germans a moment's peace. When Hitler fell out with the Soviet Union the communists joined wholeheartedly in our movement, and it seemed to me that the men on the extreme left and the extreme right did the best work.

Some of the tasks we were given seemed incomprehensible. I spent some nights in ditches close by a railway, covered with grass and dead leaves. My job was to count the number of trains passing by, presumably to check on troop movements. The Germans were said to be pulling out some units from Norway for use farther south. The railroads were carefully guarded, but we still managed to pull off a few derailments. The resulting accidents often claimed a large number of victims among the Ger-

man troops and held up further transport for days and sometimes weeks. German construction of airfields and fortifications
was sabotaged by putting sugar in the cement with the result
that it never settled properly. A quantity of precious sugar was
sacrificed for this purpose.

German soldiers and Danish collaborators were killed every
other day, but retaliation proved too costly. The Danish traitors
did not matter much. In their case the Germans only demanded
a tooth for a tooth. But in the case of the German soldier the
enemy killed ten hostages for each dead German. And they
began ordering Danish passengers to sit in the front end of all
trains—to be blown to bits in case of sabotage.

The morale among the underground workers was excellent in
spite of many reverses. I asked all these young men why they
had joined us when they knew it meant risking their lives every
day. Some said it was because the Germans had taken their girl
friends, some because their friends had gone underground and
they wanted to follow the example. Some said they could not go
about doing nothing, others that it "wouldn't be decent not to
join." None said straight out that he was willing to give his life
for his country and for freedom. We Danes are always afraid
of appearing sentimental.

Pipaluk had moved away from Birkeröd. Magda had insisted
that the time had come for her to meet other people, and I tried
to find her a job where she could learn something of journalism,
her main interest at the time. She lived in a different part of the
country from us, but I fear she learned more about sabotage
than journalism.

She became involved in some demonstrations against the local
"field mattresses"—the name given the Danish girls who went
to bed with the Germans. Pipaluk and some of her friends got
hold of a few of these girls, undressed them in public, cut their
beautiful blonde hair to a crew cut, and made them walk naked
through the streets. The Germans were furious at this treatment
of their girl friends, and when Pipaluk got mixed up in more

underground activity I decided to bring her home to help me in my work.

Few things could make a Dane more indignant than the sight of a "field mattress." But when the young men voiced their fury at such betrayal I could not help wondering what would have happened if suddenly seventy thousand Germans girls had settled in Denmark. There were no more "field mattresses" in Denmark than in other occupied countries, but they caused us a lot of trouble. Venereal disease was spreading rapidly. A great percentage of the enemy troops in Denmark came from Rumania, Greece, North Africa and the Eastern Front. And Denmark was considered a vacation spot for the exhausted soldiers who were sent out to relieve the occupation forces in Scandinavia instead of being given home leave.

My natural enthusiasm got me into trouble on many occasions —once I was saved only by the fact that I was a journalist. One day in town I was annoyed by the sound of singing voices, but the singers turned out to be Danish students not enemy merrymakers. They were staging a demonstration against Denmark's forcible adherence to the Anti-Comintern Pact, and the leader of the demonstrators, the young son of the prime minister, told me they had already "protested" in front of the royal castle. The guards had turned them back, and they were now on their way to the state department building.

I joined them at once, but after a few blocks we were stopped by the police. They blocked our passage across the main bridge, but the students fooled them by sneaking around another way. The police were still placidly blocking the bridge when they heard the singing voices of the students behind them on the other side of the bridge. I tried to climb up on the statute of King Frederick VII outside the palace to make a speech, but the police arrived in time to haul me down, and the result was a free-for-all fight.

Suddenly a German staff car arrived. I stumbled and fell in all the confusion, and a number of demonstrators stepped on my arms and hands, but in the end the police persuaded the students to stage their demonstration in a park outside the city limits. On their way through the streets they broke windows and turned over Nazi cars. Some of the boys were arrested, among them the young son of my old friend Niels Bohr, the physicist.

In the morning I was called to the central police station and cross-examined by a Danish officer.

"You are on the staff of *Politiken,* aren't you, Mr. Freuchen?" he asked.

I had to admit that I was.

"Well, that settles it. In your capacity of reporter it was your duty to mix in the crowd and find out what was going on. You may go."

I was lucky to escape so easily, but the tension was increasing week by week. My telephone line was tapped, and our friends often got us into trouble. The son of the minister in Birkeröd, an ardent patriot, organized a private club in the neighborhood. With his friends he burned German cars, ruined German supplies and harassed the enemy in every way. The work was unorganized and often senseless. One day he cut the tires of all the bicycles belonging to the Danish Nazi youth in Birkeröd, but he did not cover his tracks and had to be smuggled out of the country to Sweden in a fishing boat.

The young man wanted to reassure his parents that he was safe and he sent them a postcard. He signed his own name and asked his parents to extend his thanks to the good people who had helped him, including the fisherman. And he did not omit a single name! Fortunately the Germans never thought of looking for useful information on open postcards.

There were spies and enemy agents everywhere, and we had to be very careful with our speech in public places. The most despised group of enemy agents were the "Vienna Children." They were Austrians, and during the terrible famine in Vienna after the First World War these Viennese youngsters had been brought to Denmark and Norway and cared for in the homes of hospitable citizens. Thousands of these children had been fed and clothed for several years before they were returned to Austria. They had learned to speak the language of their foster country fluently—and were now being sent back as spies. Many a good Danish patriot was arrested because of these visitors. A peculiar way of returning hospitality!

Due to the limited food supply and the strict rationing, there was a lot of hoarding and black market operations. We kept track of some of these cases and paid these "patriots" surprise visits.

"It has been reported to us," we would say, "that you good people have stored food for your suffering fellow citizens who have been forced to go underground. We appreciate your loyal spirit, but we do not want you to be embarrassed by having this food around, so we are here to relieve you of it."

There was nothing much these recalcitrants could do without self-incrimination.

The long-expected concerted action against the Jews of Denmark was suddenly put into effect one day. In Denmark there were nine thousand citizens of Jewish origin and in addition all the Jewish refugees who had entered the country in the years before the war. Seven thousand of them were now smuggled across the sound to Sweden, where our good neighbor's humanity and generosity can never be fully repaid by Norway and Denmark.

For a few weeks the salvation of the Jews absorbed the energy, the time and the resources of the underground. Some of the Jewish people were saved by being put temporarily in Danish prisons where the Germans never thought of looking for them. Others were entered in hospitals under false names. Sick people who could be returned to their homes without endangering their lives were replaced by Jews who took not only their beds but also their names for the time being. Some Jews ostensibly committed suicide; death notices appeared and funerals were staged while they went underground and waited for passage to Sweden. One wealthy Jew paid a fortune to the underground to refund all the fishermen who took his people across the sound.

On their way to their exile in Sweden some Jews passed through my house where there was always a strange collection of guests. One of them was a well-known bank robber who had been taken from prison in order to make forcible entry into factories that were to be sabotaged. He was an interesting fellow and we became good friends. He was just antisocial.

My "lecture tours" brought me into contact with a great variety of people—some of them decidedly unpleasant. Crossing on the ferry to Jutland one day I ran into a man I had known at the airport in Copenhagen in his pilot days. Now he was dressed in German uniform and sat in the restaurant in the company of two German officers. He called out a greeting as I passed, but I pretended not to hear him. He ran out on deck after me.

"So you don't know me any more, is that it?" he shouted. "I am not good enough for you."

"No, you are certainly not!" I assured him.

"I'll make you change your mind," he warned me. "I shall see to it—you are well known already!"

"Yes, but fortunately not for the same reason that you are," I retorted and added a few words which made him rush back to his officer friends to have me arrested as a saboteur.

I ran down to the car deck and tried to hide among the vehicles. They had not discovered me before we landed, so I explained my situation to one of the car owners. He took me in his car, let me lie on the floor and covered me with a blanket. As we left the ferry his wife and daughter sat in the back seat with their feet on my broad back, and nobody bothered us. The response was always the same whenever I asked for outside assistance.

Keeping the underground press in operation and distributing

the banned newspapers was a job that called for ingenuity and a great deal of hard and dangerous work. I took care of much of the distribution and had to devise new methods constantly. One of the more original ways of sending the papers from one of the Danish islands to another was to smuggle them into a suitcase belonging to a German officer. We had a great many resourceful and self-sacrificing assistants.

I remember with gratitude my good friend Tove Bang, a great actress. She appeared on the stage every night, and when she got home from the theater she spent practically every minute until dawn working at a printing machine in her cellar. When she was through in the morning she disassembled the machine, put some parts in the attic, some in the cellar and some under the back stairs. After breakfast she set out on her bicycle to deliver her papers. She finally got home and managed to sleep a few hours before she had to appear for rehearsal, followed by a strenuous performance in the evening. She was magnificent, and when she was arrested I was deeply concerned —and equally relieved when she turned up a few weeks later in Sweden.

My good friend Franziska von Rosen worked as a hospital nurse and had her own apartment in the city. Consequently she had a permit to ride her bicycle back and forth from her job. She acted as a courier and allowed her apartment to be used as a hideout.

I was only a small pawn in the large game. But I spent hours waiting for parachutists, and I went about the country safely because of my "lectures." When some American pilots crashed on one of our islands I was sent down to look into the matter. Of a crew of eight, one had been killed, seven had bailed out. Two of them were seriously injured and had to be taken to the local hospital where they were discovered by the Germans. The other five had to be secretly cared for—a difficult job on an island with a population of only twelve hundred. The farmers took them in and moved them from place to place as the Germans searched the countryside.

The airmen could not escape from the island, and when the Nazis could not find them they resorted to their usual cruel procedure. They arrested the minister as hostage and announced that a certain number of farmers would be shot unless the Americans were handed over by daybreak. With the typical American sense of humor the aviators had settled down in the cellar of the hotel which served as headquarters for the German staff. But they were finally captured and taken to prison camps in Germany.

We were determined to rescue the two remaining officers who were still in the hospital. I arrived at Samsö late at night and was let into the hospital by the back entrance. I saw the officers and had a talk with the surgeon who was willing to do all he could to help us. He could not release the patients yet; their injuries were too serious. But he promised to stall the Germans for two weeks more when I agreed to return for the men. Unfortunately I could not keep my promise.

I was at home in Birkeröd, preparing to leave for Samsö, when my telephone rang early one morning, and a friend warned me that the Gestapo was on its way to arrest me. My telephone was still being tapped and his message was picked up. Within a few minutes the Gestapo arrested him.

I thought at once of escape, but I saw through my windows that the house was guarded. I made sure I had no incriminating material in my desk and sat down to wait for the Gestapo. Two officers arrived shortly, one of them a native of Schleswig who spoke Danish fluently. He told me I was under arrest and would be shot if I attempted escape. He also advised me to take enough food with me to last at least twenty-four hours.

Magda and the maid quickly made me some sandwiches. I took along three hundred kroner in cash and we were off. On the way we stopped at several houses to arrest more Danish patriots, but most of them had been warned, so only a few joined me in the truck.

We were driven to the Hoevelt Camp which the Germans had taken over from the Danish army. We were ordered to stand at attention on the parade ground outside the barracks, but when we had stood for two hours I got tired and sat down. A soldier ordered me to remain at attention, and after two more hours we were finally taken inside. But not before the local letter carrier had passed by and let me understand he would tell Magda where I was.

Inside we were put behind bars, the fourteen of us being divided between two small cells. One of my fellow prisoners was a friend from my university days, Professor Edgar Rubin, whose only crime was that he was a Jew. In the early days of the occupation his name had been picked at random as one of a group of Jews to be shot as a hostage, but he had not been at home when the Gestapo called and they murdered someone else instead. But now they had finally caught up with him.

The prison food was terrible, but one of the guards made a profitable business selling the officers' rations to the prisoners. A wealthy businessman among us produced the necessary cash, and we were all fed a fair diet as long as we remained in camp.

From our window we had a good view of the German airfield close by. The Nazis were short of pilots; many of the regular Luftwaffe officers had been killed, and an intensive training program was under way. The usual time was cut in two and there was, consequently, hardly a day without a crash. When these crashes occurred outside our windows we were highly amused to see German soldiers rush out with paint pots to paint British markings on the plane.

The Nazi lack of logic was even more apparent inside the prison than out. We were seven men together in the cell, without any restrictions. But when we were taken out for our daily airing we were severely punished if we were caught talking to one another.

British bombers came over regularly on their way back from raids over Hamburg, Stettin and Berlin. Very often they had a bomb or two left which they dropped on military targets in Denmark. Our camp was an easy target. The Germans were petrified when the bombers came over and hurried to the shelters in the basement, leaving us alone above ground. This fear turned out to be our salvation.

While we waited for something to happen we passed the time giving lectures. I had my old repertoire, my friend the professor gave us a course in psychology, and our wealthy benefactor enlightened us about his business—glassware and window-panes.

Practically every night we heard the air-raid alarm, and we felt the bombs coming closer and closer. More than anything else I hated the feeling of being caged, of waiting helplessly for the bomb to strike.

One night a few minutes after the alarm had sounded we heard a terrific crash, and the barrack walls began to tumble down. I hardly knew what happened I was so deafened by the explosion. But I must have seen somebody summoning me outside. In any case I scrambled through a hole in the wall, ran across the fields and threw myself into a ditch.

Helping hands were there to receive me and to show me the way to a parked bicycle and a hiding place.

The whole rescue operation had been well thought out. False air-raid alarms had been sounded night after night to frighten the Germans, and finally dynamite had been placed where it would blow out the barrack walls. It sounds simple enough now, but it was a difficult operation and cost some Danish lives and many German.

I was taken to a safe hideout and began a hateful existence underground. I never could get reconciled to the secrecy, the elaborate precautions, the enforced inactivity, but I had to lie low for weeks. At first I stayed with a good friend who was a dentist, and in whose torture chamber the Gestapo was not likely to look for me. It was decided that my long gray beard made me easy to spot and I had it cut off. A barber did his tonsorial duty as I sat in the dentist's chair. I was sorry to see it go —particularly as it had a certain cash value. A Danish razorblade manufacturer had offered me five thousand kroner for my picture shaving off my beard with his brand of razor. The obvious course, when offered five thousand, is to demand twenty thousand, which I had done, and I was still considering a counteroffer of ten thousand when I had to go underground. The result was that I not only got nothing for my beard but had to pay the barber to shear it off, and for the first time in twenty years I looked at my hairless face.

With my smooth countenance and artificial leg, instead of my wooden peg, I was allowed outside at last. In fact, I was ordered out when my hideout was considered unsafe. I was told to go to a neighborhood café where I was to be met and escorted to another hideaway. The moment I entered the place I ran into an old friend, a champion bicyclist, who recognized me in spite of my lack of beard. I gave him a sign to ignore me and he remained seated over his coffee. But when two Gestapo soldiers came to the door he got up, passed by me and whispered that I was to go out through the back and stay there!

I don't know if the Gestapo had come to look for me, but I was relieved to have the back door between us. Fortunately there was no guard at the back, and I remained there until my friend arrived with a truck in which he drove me to his place. He had a bicycle shop with a workshop in the rear equipped for unexpected guests. He had bedclothes and food stored away, and many underground workers had lived there before me. In due time I received further instructions from another contact man —an inconspicuous Esperanto teacher who looked like a Mr. Milquetoast. He brought me a revolver and told me about my family. The underground had kept an eye on Pipaluk who had been involved in extensive illegal work. When our men heard from Gestapo headquarters that she was to be arrested they picked her up, and she joined me in the underground.

An extraordinary period of night activity followed. Even without my beard I was too easily recognizable to be let out in daytime, as was Pipaluk who resembled her mother Navarana. We could still be used at times for night work, however, and from the workshop of the bicycle champion we moved to the small apartment of a prison guard who had only two rooms which were often occupied by underground workers. The generosity, the courage and self-sacrifice of people in modest circumstances never failed to impress me. This man had a six-year-old boy who was used to playing in the back garden, but when Pipaluk and I moved in he was told to stay indoors. Small children had sometimes told their friends about strange people arriving in the night and, inadvertently, had been the cause of many arrests.

The prison guard was a useful man to the underground. But in order to be above suspicion he would often report some minor offense of his prisoners. Pipaluk and I stayed with him for a few weeks while we were looking for permanent quarters. I was active at night, moving about in the blackout without any serious risk. Some of the meetings I had to attend seemed useless, but I was able to prevent a few of our most ardent but thoughtless colleagues from passing out death sentences without proper investigation.

At one such meeting I was told that a certain professor at the University of Copenhagen was in cahoots with the enemy. His home was under observation, and he was receiving German guests daily.

"We have to finish him off at once!" one of the zealous youngsters insisted. But we managed to postpone this drastic action until the man had been thoroughly investigated. And I soon found out that the professor, the head of the map division of the general staff, had the printing press for our most important illegal newspaper in his cellar. He could give warning of unwelcome visitors by pressing his knee against a button under his desk. In order to be above suspicion he had to cultivate the German officers. There were many similar cases.

Naturally there was confusion, lack of coordination and over-lapping of functions, which were not eliminated until the "Free-dom Council," the high command of the underground, was organized. When I arrived in the United States toward the end of the war I found that it was this organized resistance which gave Denmark a place in the ranks of the Allies. At the time we had no sense of the consequence of our particular fight, we saw only a small part of the whole picture. But we realized that our constant needle-pricking had its effect on the Germans, who got more tense, more nervous and also more hateful. Every Dane arrested was considered a hardened criminal and was treated like one, no matter what his offense. And I felt it when I was recap-tured by the Gestapo.

There was nothing dramatic about my recapture, I simply walked into the arms of the police. I had been out on a "safe" assignment and was on my way back when I was suddenly faced with armed Germans and no chance to escape. I had undoubt-edly been betrayed by someone who knew all my movements.

The following days were not those I want to remember. I was cross-examined for hours, I was beaten, and my artificial leg was taken away. The officers fired questions at me and slapped me constantly across my face with wet towels. They were enraged when they got nothing out of me, and the silliest trifles made them wild. I began by pretending not to understand German. At first they believed me, since they had not yet found out who I was. Once my identity was established, they screamed that I had lectured in German all over *Das Vaterland* and could speak the language all right. I replied that I had forgotten it and was rewarded with another beating.

The Gestapo told me gleefully over and over that I could not possibly avoid execution for all my evil acts. What amazed me was that my escape from the Hoevelt Camp was never mentioned among my many misdeeds. Some of the German guards had been killed that night, and a death sentence was the invariable result of such a prison break. Apparently the Gestapo had no record in Copenhagen of my previous arrest—their intelligence service was always inefficient.

I was finally put into a cell with many others, and I must confess that I was scared. Every morning we heard the echo of German boots approaching our cell, every morning someone was taken out to be shot, and those who remained had a hard time getting conversation going again. Once the sound of the boots had ceased we knew we had at least a twenty-four-hour respite.

One day we were all removed from the cell, and we thought our last hour had come when, to our intense relief, we were put into a great truck and driven off. Such a transport was likely to end in a concentration camp in Germany, but we were too relieved to care. After a long drive we found ourselves in a transient camp for prisoners on their way to Germany. While waiting for a larger transport to be organized we were locked up in an old schoolhouse and kept under constant guard. But our guardians were not very impressive—most of them young boys who had just finished a three months' training course for the Danish Nazi youth.

More prisoners poured into our camp every day. Some of the newcomers surprised me because they were not the kind of people I had expected to find in the underground. And I was inspired to see all differences disappear, personal likes and dislikes, class distinctions, political convictions—all were subordinated, we were only Danes. And still we were careful about talking together or exchanging information. There was always the feeling that the prisoner next to you might be a stool pigeon. We all kept quiet about the things that really mattered, and I felt I was back in the Soviet Union once more, surrounded by suspicion and silence.

The Germans were not satisfied with me as a prisoner, I was lacking in subordination and discipline. As a punishment I was ordered to do K.P. With my friend, Otto Bülow, I was put in charge of the dishwashing in the disgusting kitchen where food not fit for dogs was prepared for us. I was an old hand in the kitchen, of course, from my many years of expeditionary life. Bülow had spent most of his life traveling around the world in one capacity or another. He had earned his living as a dishwasher many a time, and we were both quite grateful for this punishment. Bülow was one of the most courageous men I have ever met and we were both charter members of the Danish chapter of the Adventurers' Club, which I had organized. In the kitchen we also had the advantage of meeting the women who came in by the day to do some of the cooking and cleaning. They worked as "couriers" and brought us news from the outside. We were all up to date on developments.

All prisoners were taken out for a short walk once a day, and the yard was divided from a dirt road by only a barbed-wire fence. People passing by were not allowed to stop, but they managed to get news to us. It was from one of these passers-by that I learned of the capture of Mussolini and the surrender of Italy. There was a great celebration in camp that night—the Germans obviously knew what it was all about. They were nervous and depressed, but they did not bother us that evening.

Before any arrangements had been made for our transport to the south, I received a serious warning from the outside. My case was coming up for a final trial, and there was no doubt of my fate. I had to escape. My friends made the necessary preparations from the outside while I chose the simplest way out. Leaving the barracks at night, crossing the yard and climbing a fence proved unexpectedly easy. The Germans were demoralized and the guards were obviously relaxed. My friends waited for me at the appointed spot on the other side of the fence and took me down to a Copenhagen harbor where a fishing boat, bound for Sweden, was waiting.

Shortly after my escape several of my fellow prisoners were released, but in most cases the German magnanimity proved to be a deliberate fraud. They let loose a number of people against whom they had no evidence, but once outside prison they were shot "while resisting arrest." My friend Bülow met his death that way. He was released and returned to his home in Elsinore. When he had been at home for a few days the doorbell rang early one morning. His wife opened the door and screamed when she saw the Gestapo outside. Bülow ran to the door to investigate, the Germans shot and killed him instantly. A friend of ours from the same camp was warned in time that he was to be shot, but he could not escape. He got into a kayak to row across to Sweden, but was discovered by a German coast-guard vessel and shot through the head.

During this same period one of our national heroes, the minister and dramatist Kaj Munk, was murdered. His dead body was found one morning in a ditch by the highway. From our excellent intelligence service I was told that the Germans had made elaborate plans to murder me in like manner. I have the greatest admiration for the men who made up our intelligence service— loyal Danes who must have had courage and nerves of a rare kind. A great many of them worked in German offices, and they not only risked discovery and execution, but they also suffered the hatred of their countrymen who did not know the true nature of their work.

After a short run to Sweden I returned to Denmark with newsprint for our illegal press. Bad weather but good seamanship made the crossing something of a routine in those days. And the Germans were, of course, demoralized by then and willing to accept bribes. A pound of butter for a family in Germany did wonders.

On my return to Copenhagen Pipaluk and I were once more united, and we moved into a small apartment belonging to a quiet and, to all appearances, an innocent university student. We were more crowded than in a German prison cell, and in due time the two of us were moved to the house of my good friend Franziska von Rosen, the nurse at the Municipal Hospital who had a permit to ride her bicycle at night and thus was very useful. We stayed in her apartment day and night for a few weeks. We were so well known by now that our usefulness in Denmark was at an end, but we had to wait until our passage to Sweden was arranged. Our contacts in the underground came to see us while we were there, and we had momentous meetings lasting until the early hours of the morning, deciding the future of our country. We summarily dismissed the majority of the civil servants in these discussions, and we turned thumbs down on most members of parliament. These great debates soothed my restlessness during the long days. Fortunately I had no idea how far our plans were from the actual course of events.

Finally my old friend the Esperanto teacher came with the word that our passage to Sweden was arranged. Pipaluk made one last risky expedition to the office of *Politiken* to get money from my editor, and when she returned we were ready. A truck called for us, waiting in a street two blocks away. We were let down into the basement, crossed through a labyrinth of subterranean passages, and finally crawled into the truck which took us down to the harbor. We had no trouble getting onto the pier and into the warehouse where we were both hidden in a coal bin. We looked a sight, particularly Pipaluk who was dressed in a white sheepskin coat, but we considered ourselves lucky to have got so far.

Hours seemed to go by while we waited for the all-clear signal to go on board. We never got it. Instead, we were told we must leave the pier. The Germans had apparently been tipped off and guards were everywhere. Getting off the pier was harder than getting onto it. We obviously could not walk past the police and had to await some means of transportation, hiding in the coal bin while a cold rain made its way through the roof and dripped down on us. After some hours a truck arrived, loaded some heavy crates, and we were put in one of them. Thus concealed, we were driven back to the apartment of Franziska von Rosen, where we scared the wits out of a neighbor who happened to open her front door as we entered the apartment. She recognized us through our coal dust, however, and managed to swallow her screams.

In a few days our friends were back again—this time with a warning to be careful even when we were in Sweden, to lie low and not talk about our experiences. A few days previously a prominent Danish author had spoken on a Swedish radio program and told a dramatic story about his escape, mentioning a few details. The next load of Danes, escaping by the same route, were caught and killed.

Once more we entered the harbor unchallenged. The constant flow of refugees arriving in Sweden had made the Germans double the guards along the docks, but we never saw them this time. Perhaps they had received their pound of butter, perhaps a knife in the back. We never knew and did not ask. We were taken aboard a small freighter and led down to the dark hold. There were seven of us, men and women, old and young. We were all too nervous to talk. We had done what we could in the common fight against the enemy, and now we must escape to save our lives. But we did not dare to say a word to each other. One never knew in those days.

At dawn some of the crew came down and ordered us to crawl into the crates left for that purpose. The boat might be inspected by the Germans, and we had to look like legitimate freight. Next to me was an elderly woman who was a telegrapher. In a large crate on the other side of me Pipaluk was put in with a member of the King's Guard. The wooden boards were replaced on top of us and fastened with nails.

The engines started up. A German inspector entered the hold and checked the cargo. I am sure we all held our breath while he moved around the dark room, but the smell of fish and engine oil was probably enough to ensure a cursory examination. He gave his official o.k., and after a while the movement of the ship told us we were under way. The terrible nervous tension made me forget my cramped position in the confined space. Once the captain entered the hold to tell us he could not let us out for a while, as German coast-guard vessels were swarming around him and he might be boarded any moment while in Danish waters. The captain was a taciturn grumpy man who gave one an impression of unreliability. Yet he had saved the lives of hundreds of strangers at the risk of his own life and his vessel.

I had no way of telling how long I waited. A few times I dozed off, or maybe fainted from lack of oxygen, but I had sense enough to repeat to myself over and over again—make no sound whatever happens. My leg was bent in an extremely painful position, and one nail had gone through my shoe. One could hardly be worse off, I thought, and I wondered how my fellow passengers felt in their "prisons." There was no sound. No inspector could possibly detect our presence unless he opened the crates.

I shall never forget the wonderful fresh air I gulped in when we were finally released. And as I left my crate I was ashamed of my own self-pity. The elderly woman next to me had torn her legs against the rusty crate nails and they were bleeding, but she had made no sound.

We were in Swedish waters where no German vessel dared follow us. The freighter was bound for Oslo, but due to "the high seas" the captain went first to the little island of Hven, lowered a boat, and set us all ashore in the peaceful haven of Sweden.

LETTERS
AND
MISCELLANY

For all his activity and adventure, Freuchen seems almost to have lived with pen in hand. Besides his published books and stories, there is a formidable mass of newspaper articles, radio broadcasts and, above all, letters. In them the man revealed himself even more clearly than in his more formal writings. The ones presented here are from various periods of his life and touch on a variety of subjects, by no means confined to the Arctic.

In the very first, one sees his budding interest in Northern exploration stemming from an already well developed yearning for adventure, preferably far from home. Then we encounter his reaction to the Nazi prison camp in which he was confined for a time after the occupation of Denmark and over which he passed so lightly in his published account of his underground activities.

In other selections he speaks frankly and with feeling about his views on many issues, great and small—on Nazi dictatorship, Negroes and their treatment in America, the Irish in New York, the economy of the Louisiana bayou country. In still others he writes for children, and the reader can understand why they were so fond of him.

And finally there is the last letter he ever wrote. It was penned during the second day of that Arctic air journey which he was undertaking with old friends, as told in the preface to this book. He died the next day.

January 20, 1903

Dear Uncle Christen,

Today I'm 17 years old and, as you know, I'm still going to school here in Nykøbing.

You have so often told me that I must finish school, and when I'm with my friends I too feel that I ought to pass my "student exam" [roughly equivalent to graduating from high school] and go to Copenhagen to study [at the university]. But then I think that when you were my age you were getting ready to go to Australia to look for gold and it seems rather empty to plan on bandaging sick people. I'd much rather go to sea at once and live as my grandfather did, having adventures like his. But my mother keeps telling me that one gets more from travels and experiences if one is, for example, a doctor; so I'm going to try to pass that exam.

I would definitely like school and the work much more if we had some better teachers. We have a wonderful teacher for mathematics and physics; his name is Oluf Kragh. He's very interested in politics and I think that someday he'll be something as a politician. When I hear him talk I often wish that I could have a part in deciding the development of the country and the people. But when I've been to visit you and you tell about a gold-digger's life in Australia, I think that you must have had a more worthwhile life. Everything here at home is so certain and planned out that there's no chance for any risk or excitement.

Often when I'm out sailing my boat I dream that it's going over unknown waters. But I dare not say this to friends at school, because they'd just laugh at me and I can't really explain what it is I want. Many times I have a feeling that they would like to come along when Tom and I go sailing and stay out at night, but because they can't come they just make fun of us. Then it's hard for me to find the right words to answer with.

But when I'm with you at Krageskov [Christen's farm] I wish I were a farmer. It must be delightful to spend one's whole life on a farm. Mostly, I would like to work with animals and watch them grow up. But we've spoken of this so often.

So next year I'll be a student [at the university]. I'll make it, even though I think that the ones in my class who spend all day studying have less fun than I have when I go fishing. I also earn a lot of money selling fish. Sometimes I come late to school in the morning when we've had our lines too far away. The teacher is furious when I tell him I'm late because I've been out on the sound.

I read in the papers that a [university] student named Knud Rasmussen is on an expedition to Greenland with Mylius-Erichsen. It gives me something to think about; so one can go along even though one's only a student.

I hope to come visit you when my vacation begins, so I can forget school for a while. If I could only be free from the plaguing teachers for a few days I think it would be easier to breathe. It's very strange that old people, over fifty say, are always so nasty and irritable; they must have been young once, but now it seems that all they want to do is persecute us others because we haven't yet become as musty as they are.

As you can imagine, I'm sick of school, and it's probably because you told me about your youth—and mom's stories about her father. But it seems a little cowardly to leave home and go to sea; so I won't.

Goodbye and greetings for now. I think it helped a little to write to you. You mustn't think that I go around so depressed every day, just sometimes it comes over me. Say hello to everyone.

Love,

Copenhagen   March 10, 1934

To the President of the Nakskov Rotary Club:
I hereby inform you, and my friends in Nakskov, of a very sad fact, that conditions have forced me to resign from the Rotary.

From America I have undertaken to investigate what the feeling is towards the German Rotary Clubs after Jews were expelled from these clubs. At the last meeting in Copenhagen I learned, in answer to an inquiry, that the main office in Zurich felt that "the Rotary was going excellently in Germany" (as quoted by President Gustav Lunn). Since I know that Jews are being forced to leave the clubs just because they are Jews, that they have suffered incredibly without receiving the slightest support or defense from the Rotary, I can no longer be a member.

I demand that the German clubs be expelled from the Rotary International until things are better.

This necessary step for me is also a deep regret. I have such good memories of the Rotary, both here and many places abroad. I have friends and sanctuaries in America; I have gotten to know people who have done me an enormous good. It is past, and I am sorry about it—but it is not advisable to act against one's convictions. Thank you for all that was good, for friendship and for education.

With many greetings,
Peter Freuchen

Sept. 4, 1943

Dear Mother,

We are allowed to write on open postcards, and I can tell you that we are all right here and can receive visits from relatives. I am with some very nice people. Unfortunately none of them plays chess. We are only ten here. There is a good view of North Zeeland and we get plenty of fresh air.

Don't worry about me.

Best wishes to Pipaluk and the sisters
from your
Pef

Sept. 7, 1943

Dear Mother,

We have just learned that we are being moved today. We don't know where to, but at least it is a change, and there are bound to be new experiences. I will write to you whenever I can and I am as always all right until you hear otherwise. You and I have learned never to lose our good spirits.

Best to Pipaluk and the sisters
from your
Pef

Overgaards Barracks
Sept. 12, 1943

Dear Mother,

I just got hold of some paper and can get a letter smuggled out by one of the women who do the housecleaning here. Today is Sunday and four have been released. It is done quite haphazardly. None of us has been informed as to why we were arrested. No trial or anything. And they were let out without formalities of any kind. We have heard that a statement has been submitted to some, which they were to sign. Most of them refused to sign, as they would then be obliged not to harm Germany, either in writing or speech. But they were released all the same.

We have got that new office in the State Department, which is supposed to look after us. They haven't been out here yet to see us, and two weeks have gone by. This is absolutely outrageous, and we are very upset about it.

We are all right here, though. There are many different kinds of people here, and we are not allowed visitors, but we have a way of getting around that, as we are permitted to "receive packages" and then we can talk with the person who brings them. But we must be sure nobody is here when the inspection comes; we are very careful about that. The guards are very young fellows, who are bribed with cigarettes.

We get good food. Yesterday and today we had ice cream, and just now a confectioner arrived with two big layer cakes. People send us a lot of food; we are almost drowning in fruits and candy. It is all over our rooms.

We sleep ten together in each room. One of my roommates is a member of Folketinget [Danish Parliament]. His name is Victor Larsen, who knows Polly and Regitze and asks to be remembered to them.

Everybody is dying to get out. I am proofreading my new book, which is not going to be bad at all.

Oh-, someone is coming, I can't write any more now.

Your Pef

Anyhow, I went downstairs for coffee, although I have decided not to take more than 3 meals a day. There was that layercake, sent to us from a great pastry-cook. Then walking back and forth again in front of the house. Our yard, which is quite small, faces the street and has a steel grating around it. So we take our walks in full view of anybody passing by. Nevertheless we are not allowed to write our address on postcards. We don't know why. It is just an order.

Hard candy keeps pouring in. I got a box from Pipaluk yesterday. It was sweet. I am longing so much to see her. It would be nice for Magdalene too, to have her at home again for a while. Magdalene has my secretary until October. The one none of us like. She does her work well, but is not pleasant to have in the house. She drives out every evening, and doesn't return until morning. She thinks that is all right as long as she keeps to her working hours. But Magdalene is afraid of being alone at night.

We, of course, have no radio here, but people tell us through the grating about what is happening and what they hear on the radio from England. We get newspapers every day.

I have gotten to know many people here. Living under these conditions, one sees many sides of their characters, which otherwise would be unnoticeable, and then discovers that fundamentally they are all nice.

And that is a good discovery.

Best wishes to all of you

from

Pef

Stockholm, Sweden, March 30th   44

Mrs Farrar & Rinehart
    Madison Avenue
      New York City
My Dear Bosses.
I am out of jail and out of Denmark, which at the time being is the same.

I happen to get away and jump over to Sweden, where I am happy to be and where I hope to stay only as long as I can write my new book ready, which is going to be something real.

Well you never knew the last one. I only had five chapters to send across when those damned murderers and bandits run into our little Denmark and there we were.

I have had quite a bad time, but what of it. I did my very best to make it disagreeable for the thieves too. And I was arrested and was done several things with. I also lost my dear little island, but what of it? The good sense of humor doesn't stay only there. I had quite a succes with my book "White Man" in Denmark. That is what is called CIVILISATION in English. You may have had it, what little came to U.S.A.

I sold it now for Sweden and for Germany to come, when Hitler and his gang is handled a bit. A publisher already prepares for a new time down there and he seems to be rather intelligent as he buys option on the right books (mine).

How are you? I am over here in Sweden with my daughter Pipaluk, but Magdalene unfortunately was fallen sick and could not join us on our rather adventureous trip. But she is all right taken care of. I hope to come to U.S.A. soon. That is we all are looking forward for the invasion to come and wash out our old countries. Did you do anything with my book "Siberian Adventure"? Or what are you doing?

Well this is only to let you know, that I am outside the reach of Hr Hitler, and that is a fine feeling.

I wonder how many of you folks still remember me. But I am trying and get in contact with Harold Matson so he may try and get something out of you.

If possible I shall try and go to Greenland via U.S.A. If I am lucky enough we will meet. But we all have to be ready to jump back again when it is needed. It is a strange feeling to have ones country occupied and all of us working against the usurpators. Now somebody thinks that I can do good, if I can reach Greenland that might make a book to.

I am working on a new novel, and I have so much other things to do just now, as I am just arrived, that I have no means of do half of what is requested from little me.

In any way this is to notify you, that I am alive and still going strong.

So is Magdalene though she is left behind. She will catch up.

And remember me to everybody who seems to care. Special the two ladies and Harold Matson.

My very best greetings to both of you

most sincerely
PETER
Peter Freuchen
(man alive)

[*To Jim Tully, the American novelist known as a "tramp writer"*]

April 15th, 1945

Dear Jimmy.

Again I had a lovely letter from Myrtle and again I answer *you*. We men are like that.

I am back from Mexico and now I am doing the South. That is a hell of a country. Hot and filled with disgusting people. The way they treat the Negroes tells better than anything else how they feel themselves disgraced. I have seen so much of that now, that it for me is unbearable, and then think of those who have witnessed it for years. I got yesterday a great example of the situation.

I came in a bus, and the Negroes were put way back in the car. The white ones had plenty of room. But the poor Negroes were squeezed in and sat on top of each other, and the rest of them stood up in the middle of the car. It was hot and terrible to look at. I tried to persuade the driver to let them spread over the bus. But no! I then told him, that I would give my place to an old Negress. But no! Then I told him a few things, and I said to him that I understood it was not himself but the country and the spirit and the inferiority complex. Then he told me, that he was going to put me out of the car, if I did not shut up.

I am a coward so I did not hop off the bus, because I had an engagement to fullfill. But I know I could write a great story about a Negro soldier coming home and refusing to submit to these conditions again after having fought for his country and all of us. That could be something great, and the day will come that the white ones will lose.

Some white people to whom I talked could not see my point at all. Two so-called highclass idiots told me that they had a great friend—a Negro rector at a University for Negroes. They went fishing with him. But at mealtime they took turns to cook the food, and he took his plate and sat himself outside the tent and ate there. They talked to each other through the canvas. And nobody felt bad about it. Can you imagine? At night the Negro took his sleeping bag and put it into a special little tent he had—just so the white people would not be hurt by sleeping near him. They really believed they were friends.

I did not bother to tell them what I thought of the way they behaved. They are incurable. But I think the Negro professor had a good laugh out of them; he certainly shows himself above them in culture and tact.

But I have no time to write you. I am working! I hope to be able to send you my new book soon, Jimmy, and I am doing another.

Al and Millie might have told you that I am going to re-marry, you know how it is with men and women.

But for the time being I am rumbling round and lecturing. People—I am afraid—only hope the old times will come back. They will not, and we have to prepare for that.

And Myrtle did not get any letter. Just the same tell her some nice thing from yours as ever

Peter

Napoleonville Louisiana   Feb 24th   46

Dear Jimmy and Myrtle.

Now I am almost the old man again. I wrote you, that I got a heart attack and that kept me down for a while. But now I am reading day in and day out in the papers how people die round in the world by heart attacks, so it is just as well to feel that I can stand it. So, after that trip here to the south, I am leaving for New York in a few days, and there I will start over again.

Down here we found a real nice place and I have seen a little of the sugar cane business, but most of all I have had an opportunity to look a tiny bit into the Negro problem, and I can see clearly that it is much more a problem of the white ones who are quite out of their time and don't understand the age in which they are living.

We have been round looking at all the old ruins you can think about. Here used to live French planters whose life was based on the slaves and they had money to burn and send for fine architects from Europe—mostly French—to build them beautiful houses. They now are falling to pieces, which certainly is a pity. I can't understand why this state or the federal government does not make up a law to prevent all these valuable buildings from decaying. Just think of how much they are needed as hospitals, recreation homes, veterans stations and so on.

It is a token of the industrialists, that they never keep up what can not be turned into money. Most of the plantations are run by big concerns who put some engineer in charge, and that accounts for some smaller—and more practical bungalows—and the old castles can stay.

Well, it is always hard to see somebody that does not care for the past, it never does add to their reputation.

But the white people here really are to pity. I asked one of the better ones why they did not allow the Negroes to vote.

—They don't want to vote, he said. He is unable to understand how much nicer it would be to live in a country where they all were alike. And U S A is the foremost nation in U N O, that is, the people who cry aloud in the papers never think of their own home. But maybe we all are made that way.

We are to go into New Orleans for a couple of days to take a look at this famous city. We were lucky to get hotel reservations until Thursday evening, when our plane goes to New York, where we will be the next morning.

We have been out with a funny mailcarrier in a powerboat that runs on the lakes and in the swamps. Have you ever been there? Those French people that stay there are undoubtedly descendents from criminals or deserters—people who liked to be let in peace. If not, why should people choose to live such places. But now they got used to it, and several young men and women that had been in the army or navy were just as happy as possible to be home again. They are collecting moss from the trees and they trap a little and they fish some. Never more than they have to, and what in hell should they do that for. The mailboat runs a whole day three times a week, after first having had a car ride for half an hour. It must cost uncle Sam quite a lot of money, because the people got very few letters—thirty that day in all. It may some time go as high as 100 letters all of them written in pencil on the envelopes. None of them get newspapers, and the amount of stamps are not two dollars each day. So the post service does not make much. But they were all clean to look at, they were healthy in spite of drinking that poison water of the swamp that is said to kill everybody. They get all their belongings from Montgomery Ward and they have enough of money, only they do not believe in fancy houses nor any luxuries at all.

Is that happiness? Against them I see the Negroes, who are not allowed in the movies, nor in the churches of the white ones. The day will come, and it is not far away where it will be different, and the war has brought it closer. I hear that between the two wars two million Negroes have moved north and now they are missing them terribly down here in the south, only they have invented some machinery both as far as the sugar cane goes and also for cotton. There they have a machine that can do for sixty hands. It is just in time for the colored ones to educate themselves for something else.

But as soon as I am back in New York I shall jump to work again. This has been a vacation of four months—and that is just a little more than I can afford and stand.

And so you just sit down and take it easy. Now I am to toil and get something off my hands.

Best greetings also to Al when you see him.

Dagmar sends her best wishes yours as ever

New York   17th of March   46

Dear Jimmy.

My best thanks for your letter. Yesterday I sure was thinking of you, as I stood more than three hours and looked at the Irish Parade through Fifth Avenue. Not less than 75,000 Irishmen walked through New York. Some sight, I tell you. I was most impressed by the veterans. You sure could see that they had been fighters. They marched straight, and their breasts were covered with ribbons and medals, nice boys. And also it looked like the entire population of Eire had come here as policecops and firemen. The said departments kept on and kept on turning up. And people cheered them, they are very popular. It looked funny, that almost every unit had several Catholic priests walking and watching them.

But some of the longshoremen were real Irishmen like I know them from Dublin and other places. They were for a big part already drunk in honor of the saint. It was more than three o'clock before they came to the place where I stood, so you will not be surprised. And they had to walk on, until they reached old man O'Dwyer, the mayor who was born in Ireland. There also were the rich ones. Many young girls on horseback. One of them could not manage her animal, and the horse ran away with her, as she evidently had rented the mare and it was at the southside of Central Park, where the renting stables are. The horse would rather go home, and she was unable to prevent it. But one of the riding policemen took hand on the horse and her and led both of them back to the parade and calmed both of them down. He knew how to handle both of them.

But what a multitude of Irish girls in colleges. They streamed and streamed. Lots of them belonged to the college of Immaculate Conception. They looked very nice. But to a Dane it looked strange to see the different churches having their bands with all kinds of uniforms and gay leaders and small kids dressed like generals and what else they could invent. Some young girls with very little clothes on their thighs and legs walked with dancing steps up the street and kept the rhythm for the music. It must be of some torture for the many priests to look at them and think of it all as forbidden stuff.

There also were very old dignified ladies with their university hats on and robes. One of them, evidently a special honored one, walked all alone in the middle of the street between two bodies of Irishmen. She was just as proud as she could be, until some boy standing beside me yelled out on top of all sound: —Hey Grandma! and everybody laughed, the policemen as well, and the poor lady got mad, she turned red all over her face.

But it sure was a grand view. I assure you, Jimmy, that realizing, that all the Irish people came over here because they had a hell of a time at home, and poor you all were and had nothing but your spirit, one can not help remembering that now no man can run for mayor in this city without the Irish, and the police are Irishmen and so many of the longshoremen. And hard fighters you are all of you, that tells us that the only thing in the world really is to go on and work hard for what you want. I presume that the next generation will see so many wealthy Irishmen, and that will be the end of their tribes. Because they will give their children an education that will pull the souls out of them and make them soft and weak and mixing up with the "better" people, which are the worst. I just had an argument with a Dane belonging to the rich ones here in New York today. I told him that it was amazing to see how few of the wealthy people at home had fought hard against the Germans. They could not afford it, because they had too much to lose. Well I shall write you soon, now only I am impressed by the 75,000 Irishmen.

Greetings to Myrtle from yours

Peter

Radio Broadcast 1948

Who knows after all much about starvation, who can tell how it feels to be without means of getting clothes to cover ones body? Are there any of my listeners who have been in the situation, where they did not know where to lay down and sleep?

Yes, I know there are many who think they have tried some of that I speak about. They have been hungry—often very hungry, they have frozen terribly and many of them had been without sleep. I have tried some of all of it myself, but as far as I was concerned, there was never any idea of giving up the hope— always did I have some thing to fight for and hope for. The fact that I am sitting here, after a good breakfast, warmly dressed and having had a good night's rest, is a token of the happy end of all my adventures, some of which I some times regarded as horrible and cruel.

Now I feel nothing but shame because I pitied myself time and again, when I thought it was tough. It was nothing but playwork compared with, what millions—yes 30 millions children—are up against to day. Children born like the rest of us, children who never asked to be born, but were put into a world, that our generation made a hell for them far far worse than the one we learned about in the school.

The hell of despair—nothing can be more cruel. I must admire those children because they still are alive. There is in them still a faint hope of better days, there is a willpower to fight and resist, and try and get possibility to live just a few days more—even if nothing—nothing at all—has been offered them thru many many years.

The UN Appeal for Children comes now and wants your help.

You will at once answer, that you are met with collection after collection and you have already shown your charity in many ways. But this is not charity. It is selfdefense against the terrible accusation, those children who will survive can hurl against this generation.

"You allowed the world to stay cruel and helpless and cold, in spite of the fact that it would have been possible to make us happy and support us to a better life, if wisdom had ruled among those, who have enough in these days. There is food enough in the world, there are clothes and fuel sufficient to all, why can't we have our share?"

Thus the children can speak to day—all these millions of children, who run around like the most miserable animals and always facing death—how many of them will survive?

Or think of those, who finally fight themselves forward to keep going. They will have to do this by fighting the weak ones among themselves. The next generation will see immense amount of people, who know nothing but crime and vices—they were forced into it from the very beginning. It is an insurance against this, we now will try and save us self and the world from.

Note from America to *Politiken*   1950

Harry Truman and the music critic.

It cannot be denied that the most talked about topic here these days is the unrestrained letter of Mr. Truman, President of the United States, to a music critic, who in his unfavorable review questioned Miss Margaret Truman's abilities as a concert singer and used terms which made her father furious.

President Truman's affection for his daughter is well known. He is said to have made the statement, that the only sleepless night he remembers ever to have had was the night before her first concert. And after all, he has been through a great many things both in wartime and in peacetime.

The letter which the President sent to the music critic must be quite extraordinary, violent expressions, threat of corporal punishment if the two men ever should meet, it is—to put it mildly—surprising.

It was said on the radio yesterday that the original letter was estimated by collectors to be worth $30,000.00, and that the critic is inclined to sell it for charitable purposes.

However, this is not the only opinion in the case. I have been out lecturing and heard people say: "Well, there is a man who is not afraid of saying what he means!" Somewhere they told me that President Truman doesn't use diplomatic language, he uses a language that can be understood, and it is every man's right to defend his home. And he speaks a language which comes to him naturally when he gets real angry. "That's what we like him for" and so on, and so on.

And the Speaker of the House of Representatives himself stood up and said: "If we had many fathers who would defend their daughters like this, we would be better off here in the United States!"

It would be erroneous to assume that this did any harm to Mr. Truman's popularity. People in America are often hardboiled, but they like somebody who is able to get excited for a cause. They also like that a father defends his daughter; it tastes of good old days.

There were probably not many here who considered the journalist, whose right it is to write his opinion without being molested for it.

[*To Navarana and Lärke*]

Noank, June 25, 1950

My dear little girls,

In my last letter I told you about the amusing birds which live nearby. Now they have built their nest deep inside a steep sand hill which nobody can climb. But mother bird has been doing most of the digging. Father bird flies over to a small lake close by and goes fishing. He is lazier than the wife, and when he has filled his belly with fish he remembers her and flies home to her to tell her that now he is full. Then it is her turn to fly over and get something to eat. Meanwhile he will do the digging. So the bird wife flies to get fish and I see only the husband at work. But he does not work as fast as the wife. He only takes out a little at a time. They carry sand in their beak and claws and simply drop it outside the entrance hole.

When he has worked at that for a short while, he will fly back to the lake where he finds his wife. She, too, needs something to eat. But he just tells her that now she has had enough, and it is better that she go back and work some more.

Then a few days ago they had finished digging. The wife was sitting outside preening herself. Her feathers had become somewhat worn and ruffled from crawling back and forth in the narrow corridor, so now they needed a little going-over.

Next step was to line the nest for the time they were to lay their

eggs, for the eggs have to be placed in a soft and warm spot or they
will get cold, and then no young ones will come of them. But the
wife understands this a lot better. The husband would just bring
some trash. He would bring old fishbones. Those he just vomits,
because he swallows the entire fish which then lies in his stomach
to be digested. However, the bones are too hard for him, and of
course he has no teeth. So he will just have to throw them up again
and then eat some more.

He probably thought it was a shame to let them go to waste, for
he kept bringing fishbones to put in the nest. But this was too much
for the wife. She could use some bones and fish scales to place all
the way down at the bottom of the nest, but when she had had
enough of that she got mad and started jabbing at her husband.
Then she crawled in and out several times and threw out a good
deal of his fishbones which he had thrown up. Naturally they
would not look very nice in a dainty nest for dainty eggs.

Therefore she began flying about to look for some fine, thin
twigs, and on top of them she put dried leaves of grass, and to top
it off she gathered down and bits of cotton fluff which she found.
He flew over to the lake and began fishing, but never brought back
anything for his wife. She would have to fly to the lake herself if
she wanted something to eat. And so she did, but nevertheless she
managed to finish the nest one day. Now she has laid her eggs. I
never see her anymore, for she is inside sitting on her eggs.

Now I am wondering how long it will take before the young
ones are hatched. Then I will write and tell you how they are
getting along.

And now lots of regards for your mother and father from your old

(unsigned)

Noank, April 8, 1951

Dear little Navarana,

Now the snow is gone and the sun is shining. We are getting a
suntan and the flowers have come out. Our snowdrops are all gone,
they are only here very early in the year, and they are beautiful to
look at before any other flowers are out. But then come the yellow
and red and blue flowers and one does not care about the snowdrops any longer, so they just crawl back into the earth and are

offended. That is because nobody is paying any attention to them. But they will be back next year.

Today I was out to weed and I picked up a lot of roofing felt which flew off the roof during the winter when we had such a terrible gale. I thought there would just be earth underneath, but then I saw something strange lying there. It was a whole lot of tiny little snakes. They were no longer than one of your arms, but much, much thinner of course. Because snakes always are. They had been out in the sun yesterday and had fun. But towards evening when it got cold they just crawled under that piece of roofing felt. They probably thought we would have sunshine again today. During the winter they had lived deep down in the earth in a mouse hole. They had crawled down there in the fall and eaten the mice so that there would be nobody to bother them. But the sun lured them out into the open, and there was a whole lot of them. We just put the roofing felt back to cover them and left them like that.

At first I thought these were not live animals at all for they did not move. Last year a little boy lived here in this house. He had a lot of rubber snakes and rubber mice and that sort of things. He had put them among my books in order to frighten me when I discovered them. But now that there were some real live snakes I at first did not know what it was. However, they are good snakes, they do not bite, and they eat beetles and larvae and other animals that are not so nice to look at.

Soon I shall be going up to Greenland. Then I can not write to you every week, but whenever there is a homebound ship I shall send you a letter and tell you what it is like up there.

Perhaps your mother has told you that there are huge mountains of pure ice sailing around in the water. But they will drift southwards to the warm countries. They themselves think they are the largest things in the whole world. And so they want to go and see what it is like in other places than Greenland. It would have been wiser for them to stay up there, because when they are caught by the current and start drifting southwards, the water will get warmer and warmer, for down south it is summer. And the icebergs have no weapon against that. They start melting, and that does not take very long once it has started.

At first a little bit of them will melt away, then they get quite annoyed that they can not fight back. Suddenly they will turn upside down to try and see if it works better this way. But the warm water will continue melting them and melting them, and so the iceberg will twist and turn. They are very, very large and they create big waves at all sides when they turn around, but—as I said —it is of no use. Finally they get so mad that out of plain ill temper they will crack into thousands of tiny pieces. They, too, will melt so it does not take many days before the whole thing is over. Often there are gravel and pebbles inside the ice. When it melts, they will simply sink to the bottom and nobody will be able to see that a lot of icebergs have been sailing around here.

Now give my best regards to your father and mother from

Your Morfar (Grandfather)

On board *Gyda*—May 11, 1951

Dear little Lärke,

Here is a little, old letter I wrote you about a year ago. But it was never sent, which shows how forgetful your old godfather has become. Now that I'm leaving I found it while putting my papers in order.

Here it is:

At the moment I am on a large steamship sailing to Greenland. We are sailing out from a big city called Philadelphia where three million people live. It is quite a way out to the open sea, down a big river called the Delaware which is so dirty that you can't possibly imagine it. This is because all the cities' sewers run into the river, and there are lots of factories that empty their dirty wash water into it. Otherwise, everything's fine on board; I have a stateroom to myself and my own shower, but I won't use it until we're out on the Atlantic because it draws salt water from outside and I'd get very dirty if I took a shower now.

As you can well imagine, all ships that come to Philadelphia have to be completely repainted when they leave. The white paint always turns yellow in the sea here. Some say it's the air that is poisonous, but I think it's the water which has some chemical in it that evaporates and destroys the white paint.

They have tried to make people stop throwing their messy waste into the river where the ships sail, but it would cost so much to build sewers out to the ocean that the factories say they would have to move away. But the mayor doesn't like that very much because then the grocers and bakers would have no one to sell to and so they wouldn't be able to stay in business. It's very difficult.

But in six hours I won't care, because then I'll be out on the open sea and there the water is refreshing and salty and delightful. Fortunately, there are no other passengers on board, so there's no one to disturb me and I can sit and write and be comfortable alone. There's a pilot on board now who's going to show the captain the way down the river; he can take this letter back to you.

I have 40 pigeons in two cages which I'm taking care of because I'm taking them along to Greenland. We are going to try to catch falcons with them, because falcons like pigeons more than any other kind of bird. We send a pigeon out with a band on its leg. The falcons go after the pigeons and kill them at once by breaking their necks, so they don't feel anything. But we put a web with many loops of nylon thread on the pigeon, so the falcon is caught and we can put a band on its leg. Then we let it go. Then, if it's shot some day, we can see where it has been and that way we can find out where falcons fly in the winter. No one knows that now.

You and your little sister can go out in the woods and see the green trees, and you don't think about the fact that up in Greenland there are no trees. Those who live up there have never seen a tree and when one asks them what in the world they would most like to see, the children say that they would most like to see a tree that is so big that it's as big as a house. And they think it must be a lot of fun to look at such a tree. That's because they don't know what trees look like—except in pictures.

But we're sailing now, so I'll say goodbye, and please don't be angry because I forgot to send the other letter until now.

Say hello to Vibe and your father and mother, from your old
Godfather
And thanks for all your letters.

Tovkussak—June 17, 1951

Dear little Navarana,

I have two ravens which I got from a Greenlander. But they're not very old now so they can't fly. I can't decide what to name them but I'd like it if you would write and tell me some good names for them. I'll try to teach them to talk and to say "Navarana." If I'm successful they'll call you when we come to Copenhagen in the fall. Then you'll know who I am if you can't recognize me.

Naturally I'll be able to recognize you because I have two pictures of you which I've put up in my window here in Tovkussak. That's the place where I'm living now. There's a little girl here your age; her name is Birte.

I've shown her your picture and she always wants to hear about you. She thinks you must be very brave because you're not afraid to let the pigeons in Rådhuspladsen [Copenhagen] eat from your hand. She says she wouldn't dare do that. She has just come up here with her father and mother and big brother, whose name is John. They can take the boat out rowing when the weather is good. But we've just had a terrible storm, and last night it snowed, but today the snow has all melted.

I was far out in a deep fjord where we caught a whole lot of codfish. There were also some small children out there, but they were very hungry and also very dirty, because their father had no money to buy soap. We lived in a tent and ate outside and cooked our food over a fire. When it was windy it was impossible to get the fire to burn. But I've lived in Greenland so much in the past that I could teach the others to make a fireplace where we could build a fire of heather and twigs which we gathered in the mountains. While we ate, the little Greenland children always came and stood watching us. After we'd eaten they always got food—as much as they could eat. They also got eggs, and as they'd never tasted eggs before they were very happy.

One girl was called Linda Lisa. That's a very fine name I think. Her brother's name was Malakias, also a nice name.

But there were so many mosquitos up there in the fjord that we were glad to be finished there and to go home. Where I live now it is always a little windy and so the mosquitos stay away.

I've just been down to feed my two ravens. They sit and scream when anyone goes by because they always want food. We give them codfish and other fish which we cut into big hunks and toss down their throats. The birds have no teeth so they can't chew; they swallow the whole piece at once. But it's good for them.

I've ordered a sheep and two small lambs and five hens and a rooster. They'll be here in a few days and I'll write and let you know how they are.

Keep well and say hello to your father and mother from your

Grandfather.

Tovkussak—July 1, 1951

My dear little girls,
You can imagine that when one sits up here in Greenland one often longs to see a tree with green branches. Because all there are here are some small willows—twigs—that crawl around among the stones because they're afraid to stick their branches up into the air, since during the winter the snow drifts would chase them away. And it is often so windy that it is better for them to stay down in the shelter of the stones.

But otherwise it's delightful to be here. We catch many fish, and that's why we're here. There's a little girl here who comes to see me every day. Her name is Birte and she is six years old. Her father is a fisherman and he has just now come back with his boat. He doesn't have a very big boat, but he caught 700 codfish and 150 cat-fish and 8 large halibut. Birte ran down to the bridge he ties up to and called to him. She found out that he caught 700 codfish, and then ran up to ask me to teach her to count to 700, because she doesn't know how. Her mother teaches her because there are no other children here, just she and her brother, who is 10 years old. But in another house, a little too far away, is an 11-year old girl who comes to play on Sundays.

She also helps me feed my ducks; they get bread from the cook. We have three cooks. There are lots of people here and we all eat together in a large dining room. We eat three times a day, but whenever fishermen come back with fish they get food—anytime of the day or night. So we have to have three cooks so that there's always one who isn't sleeping. It doesn't matter whether it's night here because now it's light all the time. But, on the other hand, it gets very dark in winter. But we're not here then because there's too much ice to go out and fish with the boats.

I have three ravens which I feed every day. One of them has been very sick because there were some dogs after it which bit it terribly. It can't even lift one wing and it doesn't look very nice because the dogs pulled out lots of its feathers. But it's very tame and at night it sits in a box in my room. During the day I put it outside and feed all three of them with fish and meat I get from the cook. They would rather have fish, though, because they never drink anything so they can't eat food that's too dry. But fish they like very much because it's mostly water.

Soon we're going out to catch whales. There have been some in here but they weren't big enough to make it worth while going after them. We will just catch one big whale, since that will be enough meat for everyone here for the winter. Because we have a freezing plant which keeps meat frozen so that it will keep many months if you don't eat it. We use it to freeze fish that is being sent away. Then it is packed in fancy boxes and sent to America in a ship which also has a freezer in its hold. Even when it's summer people wear woolen gloves and heavy clothes because it's so cold in there. But they have to do that so the fish won't spoil before it comes to America, then no one would pay for it. That's easy to understand.

A couple of eagles frequently fly by here. They're very big and the Greenlanders are afraid that they'll take their children, but that's just a superstition. No one has ever seen an eagle fly away with a child. But it doesn't matter if they take care of their children; that never hurts.

Say hello to your father and mother and stay well until we see each other in the fall when I come home.

Your loving
Grandfather-Godfather

Tovkussak, August 10, 1951

Dear Lärke,
It's a long time since we have written to each other for I am far up in Greenland where we very rarely have mail service. It's a little cold here, but we put on warm clothes so it really does not bother us.

Most of the time I wear oilskins, for every day it storms and rains, and we have had quite a bad summer. And I do a lot of sailing around in motorboats to check the fisheries. But that is coming to an end now for there are no more salmon. They are delightful fish which gather every year below the rivers in order to swim up through them and lay their eggs in the lakes above.

They are so clever that they can find their way to those very same rivers down which they came when they were little. Up in the lakes there are no large fish that will eat them while they are small and can not swim very fast, that is why they go up there. But it is quite cumbersome for them to travel up against the rapid current. Often there are waterfalls, but then they jump high into the air to get past the falls and on, all the way up to the lakes where they want to lay their eggs.

But salmon are such peculiar fish. When they have tired from swimming against the current they will stand completely still at the bottom of the rivers, and though the current will be rushing past them it will not carry them along. I do not think anybody knows why this is so.

We catch them in nets. But they are very large-meshed nets so that the small ones can pass through because we are only interested in the big ones. Then we take them home, rinse them nicely and place them in a deep freezer where they are frozen to a temperature of minus 30 degrees centigrade ($-22°$F). When they are thoroughly frozen they are put in our store room where the temperature is minus 10 degrees centigrade ($14°$F). They remain there until a ship comes to pick them up. It too has frosty weather in its holds. The salmon will be shipped to France, so you can understand that they have to travel a long way to be eaten.

There is a girl here by the name of Asuba. Right now she came to me to have her fingers bandaged. She had been down at the pier and put them into a machine. Now, that was a foolish thing to do, and she will lose the nails on both fingers, and she also cried a lot. But the other day something worse happened. For down at the bridge we have a crane which we use for hoisting. Suddenly they found a finger sitting in one of the hooks. Then they came running up to me where I was working and asked me if I had seen a boy who had a bandaged or bleeding hand. No, I had not, but then we found him. He had gone into hiding for it is strictly prohibited to go near that crane. So he lost his finger. But he did not cry very much and said it did not matter too much for he had enough fingers as it was. But this will show you what happens to such foolish boys.

My three ravens are doing well. Two of them are able to fly now, but as soon as I step outside they rush up to me, sit on my head and make noise. When I am standing at my work and someone else approaches they get angry and start jabbing and pecking at his boots, or they jump up and peck at his hands. They would also like to eat all day long. Then when they are full, they fly off, but a few hours later they return and start screeching and then they want more.

Almost every day a strong wind is blowing so we do not catch very many cod or halibut or catfish which we are very unhappy about.

But I hope you are all well, and every day you can enjoy the forest. There are no trees here at all. Give my best regards to your mother and father and Vibe.

Your Gudfar (Godfather)

[To his son, Mequsaq]

June 15, 1954   New York

Dear Mik,

I just got a letter from your sister and Aunt Polly, who wrote that they'd been over to visit you and that you were very good at dancing. They were very happy with the visit, and they were glad to have had good food and cigarettes and much more.

Now they write that you'll be going to the zoo soon in Nykøbing with your friends. Then Pipaluk and Aunt Polly will go to Vesterskov and meet you there. I am therefore enclosing some money so that you can get them a cup of coffee, or whatever they want, when you see them. They'll be happy with that.

You can ask your good foster father to help you a little with the money. Perhaps he can also take care of it so that you don't lose it before you go there.

The trip would be fun and you'll get to see all the strange animals. It's very warm here now. I hear that it hasn't rained much at home; it's very bad at Enehøje [P.F.'s farm in Denmark] because there isn't much grass for the sheep. So it's good you don't have to take care of them any more, because they're terrible about running in the fields when there's not enough grass in the meadow. You can surely remember that.

Stay well and say hello to your good foster father. Have fun when you take your trip.

Many greetings from,
Dad

1 check.

April 11, 1955

Mrs. Karen Blixen [Isak Dinesen]
Denmark

Dear Madam:

I realize that you must be, at present, receiving many greetings and congratulations, since we Danes are generally shy and need the excuse of anniversaries and special occasions in order to be a little ceremonious without feeling embarrassed.

But now it's your birthday and so I have the courage to say some of all that I would have liked to have said for so many years. Unfortunately I'm only a poor writer and don't know the right words. But it's felt and true just the same.

Arctic explorers are big actors. They walk around and play at exploring the Arctic and think that everything turns about the ability to freeze and to drive dogs and to show muscles and energy and a beard and latitudes. But if one has *Out of Africa* sent up to ice and snow and cold, one needn't be embarrassed, since there is no one to see it. And then one realizes how completely differently the spirit of a primitive people can be understood, and the mystique of an environment condensed, by a weak little woman who has her whole nervous system and all her capabilities with which to get at the essentials.

Americans are also actors. Gold teeth and chewing gum and "ninety miles an hour." But if, in the middle of the prairies where evening after evening one lectures in poetry-forsaken small towns to women's clubs and Rotarians, one gets a copy of *Seven Gothic Tales* in one's hand, then one forgets that people can be insipid and silly and motor-driven. Then one lies at night and can't think, just feel. Then it grows clear that there is a gospel one never even opened.

I am completely unknown to you, and my books are as far from yours as possible. That stupid expression about "each has his own field" is a lie! It's just that delicate instrument called a soul that we others lack. And when we meet it no envy is possible; it's unconditional surrender. But in the recognition of this lies happiness. The happiness of having experienced your books, the happiness of knowing that the world had possibilities for understanding all that we others barely sense—never could express.

Yes, in these days distinguished critics will write clever things about you. Inspired speakers will praise your art. What do I care? I am just one of the many, many little men who became so very, very small because in a little weak and beautiful woman he met the completely big, which he could not cope with himself with his muscles and bravado.

Which is why I can't express what I want to. I'm just so distressed at not being able to write something wholly correct and wholly beautiful to you.

Your sincere admirer,
Peter Freuchen

Noank, Connecticut   Dec. 26, 1955

Dear Mik,

Many thanks for the letter; it was nice of you to write to me. Now Christmas is past and its cold here today, but yesterday it was very warm. It changes quickly. There are many, many people out driving cars on Christmas here and several accidents occur. Many people get killed.

There's no ice on the water here yet. Perhaps there is on Nakskov Fjord. Do you remember when we had to walk over the ice to get the mail and you rode on your little black horse called Black Flower? It's better to be where you are now. You can have many more friends. It was a little lonely on Enehøje when you were alone with the sheep all day and had no one to talk to.

There was a fire in the neighborhood the other day. Everyone got out, but there was one woman who wanted to go back after her cat. When she ran in the roof fell on top of her and she was burned to death. She should have let the cat be; it came out by itself.

Soon it will be bad again with tobacco. I'm enclosing some money so you can buy it yourself as I understand you'd rather have tobacco which you buy yourself. Then you can get what tastes best. I'm also sending some stamps which you can give to your good foster father because they can't be bought in Denmark. They're from the United Nations. A whole lot of people wanted to buy them, but they didn't make very many so we couldn't buy more than five each. So people just went out the door and came in again and bought five more. But I couldn't get more because they know me.

But now I'll wish you a happy new year. Say hello to your foster father and have fun with your friends.

Many greetings from,
Dad

1 check.

April 4th - 56

Mr. Kenneth F. Sandbach
609 Jefferson Street
Gary
Indiana.

Dear Mr. Sandbach:

As you are working on a paper on psychology, you unfortunately struck a wrong person by addressing me. I know very little about psychology and on top of that I am a Dane who speaks very poorly English. So I am not entirely aware if I understand the exactly meaning of the word "maturity" in my own sense.

"Maturity" as far as bodily growth is concerned of course can have nothing to do with a psychological idea. Just the same, I have in my experience met with several people whose maturity in certain lines was positively outside any discussion. Now, I am an Arctic man, and I have seen several cases where just lack of physical maturity inflicted upon them, so they were not able to keep up to the limit of fellowship and unselfish helpfulness required on an Arctic expedition as they were undertaken in former days.

I have seen Eskimoes who according to white mens standard were regarded as "primitive" and underdeveloped, but in many cases showed themselves "mature" beyond their white "masters."

I also know several great scientists—certainly "mature" in their own line, but they are so naive and helpless as soon as they step outside their own borders. It is—I guess—the case with all of us in our days. "Maturity" is something un-obtainable for any single man.

If whole people or nations may show themselves "mature," is to be considered a great question. Very often in history certain people have tried to form their nation (or state) according to own wishes, only later to find, that they failed because the followers were not "mature."

"Maturity" according to my idea is not desirable for anybody.

Because what could such a man or woman have to wish for? or dream about?

To me "maturity" is to have reached ones goal and thereby be able to solve every problem in life.

Nobody can obtain this. I have seen politicians who came into power and after that found themselves completely immature to act as statesmen, because they met with entirely unexpected problems. They were not mature.

I have seen great countries who suddenly found themselves on top of the world, and soon neither their government nor their press nor the people themselves were "mature" to cope with the situation.

No, Sir, I can not answer your question: I do not know enough English to express what I mean by "maturity". Along certain lines: yes, but not as far as the entire conception is concerned.

Maybe: ability to be able to face all kinds of situations and not feel ashamed for admitting a defeat or lack of Knowledge.

But please, go to people, who know more about these things than your most respectfull

Peter Freuchen

Note from America to Politiken

NO MORE BARBED WIRE

April 26, 1957

NOTE: There had been talk for some time of putting up some sort or fence along parts of the armistice demarcation line to help the U.N. Emergency Force in its policing activities.

At the latest press conference, which *Dag Hammerskjold* held at the U.N., the correspondent of *Politiken* put the following question to Mr. Hammerskjold:

—Mr. Secretary General, since there is now talk about a fence to mark the border between Gaza and Israel, I would just ask about that fence. Would you use your great influence to take care that they do not use barbed wire for that fence? There would be awful suffering for animals and people, and it would be of no use, as it is just a demarcation line. These days there is plenty of good mesh wire, so if you would just ask them not to use barbed wire you would do a very good thing for humanity and it would be very dignified for the United Nations!

Secretary General Hammerskjold answered: On the other hand, the wire has to be sufficiently unpleasant for people not to play with it. I think that your argument, Mr. Freuchen, is one of those arguments which makes it wise not to use barbed wire beyond what is considered technically necessary by the military experts.

Let me address myself to associations concerned with humanity. I will ask The Society for Prevention of Cruelty to Animals to join. I also request businessmen of, for instance, the leather trade to unite with all who consider barbed wire abominable, disgraceful to mankind.

Barbed wire can cause terrible sufferings, that we all know. In a desert with sandstorms people can get lost, and if they get into barbed wire their fate is torture and often painful death. It has been seen too often, how animals have been chased into barbed wire and die a pitiful death. It is also a fact that the financial value of hide, for inst. in Denmark, is reduced 50% for more than half of our domesticated animals, because scars from barbed wire makes the leather useless for a great many things.

If Dag Hammarskjold agrees, that barbed wire is only a military obstacle, then the first step is done. A call from mankind should then be submitted for the U.N. to urge all nations, who wish to be known as humane and civilized, to abolish barbed wire. Any in existence now can be left till it rusts, but should not be replaced by new barbed wire.

Unfortunately, we have little or no influence on the threat this terrible fence is to the young men who become soldiers. But everyone should agree, that other methods can be found, more effective and economical in the long run, to fence in fields and mark borders than these treacherous and terrifying little rusty poisonous spikes, waiting for an opportunity to inflict pain and infection to any living creature who comes near.

Public opinion ought to be stirred against barbed wire. When the Secretary General of the United Nations—the man whose voice matters most in the world today—goes in for doing away with barbed wire, then it's time to act.

We all know, that a crowded lot of miserable refugees live in the Gaza Strip. They are doomed to idleness, and every day they get more and more unfit to work as people, who earn a living. It is easy to understand, that these poor devils are not so easy to manage. But this is just the reason the U.N. has sent soldiers from other countries down there to keep peace and guide it all to lasting decent conditions.

There are guards everywhere, because naturally there is an urge for all kinds of excursions. Therefore there must be a clearly marked boundary line. And as most of the area is desert sand which drifts in storms, trenches or ramparts won't do. Something more recognisable is needed. But it ought not be barbed wire.

It shouldn't be that, although those wretched refugees violate the ban on leaving their camp at night, they would end up in the barbed wire with all the suffering that goes with it.

It is unworthy for the U.N., the organizer of peace, it is unnecessary, and it will create sorrow and bitterness. And think of the poor wild animals running up into the fence. Don't forget runaway sheep and other kinds of stray domestic animals.

It would be a fine project for Denmark—Scandinavia—to start a real campaign against barbed wire.

Peter Freuchen.

[To a distant cousin in Denmark]

New York   June 19, 1957

Dear Ellen Siesbye:
Are you still lying out at Rosenvænget and playing sick? Or are you home and laughing at the various people who offer their sympathy? Either one has its advantages. To lie in a hospital is really a vacation to many people. I have a cousin on Lolland who's been a hard worker all his life. He had a small farm and he and his wife worked like slaves on that farm getting only "the joy of work" from it. That's of course worth something, but it makes people tired in the evening when they come in from the fields. Then there's just bolting supper and into bed, in order to get up early enough in the morning.

Now his wife is in Maribo Hospital and is going to be operated on. I haven't heard from Elly for some time, so I don't know how it went. But, as you can imagine, it's a kind of vacation for her poor body to lie down and let others prepare food for her. No washing up, no milking to do, etc. These farm women are exhausted before their time.

But it's the same with us. We ought to be a little less energetic. But Dagmar, my wife, went to bed at 5 o'clock this morning; she sketched all night to finish something for her magazine. And the first models came at 10 this morning; the last left at 5. That's too much. But the assignment is—for Dagmar, I mean—that she will sketch tonight until she no longer can. Then she'll deliver the sketches tomorrow morning and we can drive out to the country this evening—Thursday. Ahh, how we will sleep and rest and lie in the sun and swim in the cold water!

These days everything that's cold is appealing. It's swelteringly hot and abominably sultry here. But it WILL not rain. This morning there were some clouds, and we rejoiced, but the sun came out soon after and it was just as hot again.

. . . I interrupted the letter to go in and watch the world championship light-weight boxing match in Colorado. Can you imagine anything more idiotic than using an evening to watch a boxing match? But it's the heat that does it. Joe Brown won. But how little it matters which of the two men can wallop the other the best! Dagmar went to bed. She couldn't do any more, so now I sit here and shall just finish this letter. Then I too will go into the lovely cool. We have a bedroom with a new machine to cool the air. How cold it is I don't know; it's just so delightful to come into from the other rooms. My tropical fish are almost cooked and our cat just lies and stretches itself trying to put on as much extra surface as possible to cool off. It scarcely eats a thing in this heat. Neither do we. For lunch today we had some jellied soup with an egg in it. Then a quarter of a melon and lunch was finished. Dagmar has invented a devilish drink which consists of instant coffee stirred in cold water, then some skim-milk and a few drops of sucharyl—that's the same as saccharin. She drinks it with apparent relish. But she can't tempt me with it.

I had lunch with Dag Hammarskjöld today. Neither of us ate very much. But we've been invited to the Japanese Prime Minister's at the Waldorf Astoria. We'll have to make sure to eat as much as possible there in order to make it worthwhile having gotten dressed and gone there.

Today I found out that I'm going to defend my "masterpiece" on The Seven Seas again; it will be against Allan Villiers, the man who has just sailed the *Mayflower II* across the Atlantic. He's very popular so it won't matter so much if I lose to him. It will be to a good man.

But my anticipated trip to Greenland has been put off until September. I regret it now. It would be nice to be up in the cold these days. Short and to the point, I meant to write a nice letter to you. But you'll have to take a raincheck on it, because I can't now. It's too warm to collect any thoughts. So you will just have to be satisfied with a greeting to yourself and those of the family who come out to say hello to you.

Sincerely,
Peter Freuchen

Mc Chord Air Force Base, Tacoma, Wash.
Sept. 1, 1957

Dear Dagmar,

We are now at the first stop of the journey. It's been splendid so far. I was picked up in a smart Cadillac, in which Bernt Balchen and MacMillan were seated. We drove to the airport where we met Lowell Thomas and the production manager, whose first name is Gilbert, the last name something like Ronston, I didn't quite hear it. A very civilized man—he gave us each a bundle of notes for incidental expenses.

I sat next to Hubert Wilkins on the plane; he is my special friend. He told me that his wife has taken up painting and is doing portraits. They had been to a party the night before, and she got two new portrait commissions there. So she does something too. He said that she greatly admires your drawings in Vogue. Wilkins himself is going to the South Pole on September 24th and will be away 6 months. He is to inspect the various stations which were put there for the geophysical year. They are having some difficulties with the people who replace the ones who were there before. Many of them bring new instruments and want to carry out observations in different ways, etc. He also says many of them get bored and homesick.

As a matter of fact the main topic of conversation so far, between us old men, has been that the young people nowadays don't want to get out. They can't get movie photographers either, who will take risks. They always say, it is "rather dangerous" and they "don't dare

to do that" and they don't care for climbing. Wilkins and Bernt
Balchen have had the same experience, etc.

Well, we got to Chicago, but the temperature there was 92, so we
were glad we didn't have to stay there very long. We were photographed there. I am a little embarrassed, because both there and
here in Tacoma people come and want my autograph, while the
others stand there looking somewhat puzzled. Most people recognize
Lowell Thomas, too, but rarely the others. Bernt Balchen, who was
the first to fly the Atlantic at the north, seems almost unknown.
MacMillan is still addressed "Admiral," he is somewhat reserved,
but hale and hearty as ever. A remarkable man for his age. We are
all having a good time together. We are quartered in two barracks.
Bernt Balchen, Gilbert and I live in one, and the others in the
other. Nice rooms. We had had dinner on the plane, but Balchen
was still hungry when we arrived here last night, so the three of us
went over to the officers' mess and had a slice of roast beef. I cut
the fat off and didn't eat potatoes. I really must try to avoid fattening dishes.

We haven't seen the other three this morning. We came upon a
gang of prisoners who were out cleaning the camp. Then we went
to the officers' mess for coffee. But it was with a "Danish" bun.
Breakfast is not until 10 o'clock. We fly from here tomorrow to
Alaska, where we will start shooting the film in Anchorage. I am
delighted to be here.

It is beginning to get hot. I am wearing the grey suit, which is
too heavy now, but it will be all right until tomorrow. Hubert
Wilkins arrived wearing big white rubber boots. He has been wearing them since Boston, because he wants to prove that they are cool
and comfortable in warm weather and comfortably warm in the
cold. He is head of army equipment in the Arctic regions. It is
marvellous to be with these Arctic people again. I have been away
from them too long, and I am now reliving it all, and am pleased
to hear about their progress. Wilkins is full of stories and wisdom.
I will take notes, and already have some material for an article.
But much is changed up here. He says that the Eskimo women of
Point Barrow fly down to Fairbanks to have their hair perma-
nented. The flight costs only 36 dollars, and that they can afford.

There are altogether 800 Eskimos at Barrow, and they are almost
all employed by the government to work on the oil pipes or as
truckdrivers, etc. He says they work better and are more reliable
than the American workers they get up here.

We have told Gilbert about whaling; he wants to do a whaling film in the Antarctic Ocean. But he doesn't know anything about it. I have warned him that people may find it cruel and blood-thirsty and there is a chance that it will be prohibited by the societies for prevention of cruelty to animals. . . .

. . . Well it's 5 P.M. now and we have been for a long walk up in Rainier Park, the most beautiful spot within my memory—5557 feet up there are forests with enormous trees. Nature has not been touched there. There are good roads and wonderful abysses and glaciers and much more. We were, of course, photographed inside out, but altogether it was splendid. They are great fellows, full of stories and tales of expeditions and people. I am writings things down in my notebook and have much I can use for articles later on.

We are flying to Alaska tomorrow. It will hardly be as hot as here, and it is where our adventure really begins. We are all four of us very pleased with everything. The object is to show each of us as someone who helped build the Arctic countries. And there-fore each of us is going to show his "specialty." I mostly as walrus hunter. It will be real fun to do that again.

Well, we just had a good lunch. MacMillan and I ordered sal-mon, the others roast lamb and we all had apple pie and coffee. Lots of storytelling and we had a hilarious time.

Goodbye for today and stay well. Keep all mail, so there will be something to read when I return.

Dear little Dagmar

your

Peter

Lowell Thomas has gone out to play golf.